CW00832889

I HAVE NO REGRETS

THE GERMAN LIST

I HAVE NO REGRETS

Diaries, 1955–1963

BRIGITTE REIMANN

Edited by Angela Drescher

TRANSLATED BY LUCY JONES

LONDON NEW YORK CALCUTTA

This publication has been supported by a grant from the Goethe-Institut India

Seagull Books, 2019

Originally published as Brigitte Reimann, *Ich bedaure nichts: Tagebücher 1955–1963*
© Aufbau Verlag GmbH, Berlin, 1997

First published in English translation by Seagull Books, 2019
English translation © Lucy Jones, 2019

ISBN 978 0 8574 2 668 0

British Library Cataloguing-in-Publication Data
A catalogue record for this book is available from the British Library.

Typeset by Seagull Books, Calcutta, India
Printed and bound by Hyam Enterprises, Calcutta, India

CONTENTS

Chronology of Brigitte Reimann   *vii*

List of Abbreviations Used in the Footnotes   *ix*

Editorial Note   *x*

Translator's Acknowledgements   *x*

Diaries, 1955–1963   **1**

1955   **3**

1956   **39**

1957   **79**

1958   **95**

1959   **128**

1960   **149**

1961   **177**

1962   **257**

1963   **309**

CHRONOLOGY OF BRIGITTE REIMANN

1933	Brigitte Reimann was born on 21 July in Burg bei Magdeburg, the eldest of four siblings and the daughter of a bank clerk and a housewife.
1947	Contracted polio.
1951	Completed school, then worked as a teacher.
1953	Married Günter Domnik. Admitted to the working group of young authors of the German Writers' Union in Magdeburg.
1954	Premature birth. Suicide attempt.
1955	Publication: *Der Tod der schönen Helena* [The Death of Beautiful Helena], Verlag des Ministeriums des Innern (Publishing House of the Ministry of the Interior).
1956	Publications: *Die Frau am Pranger* [The Woman in the Pillory], Neues Leben, Berlin. *Kinder von Hellas* [Children of Hellas], Verlag des Ministeriums für Nationale Verteidigung (Publisher of the Ministry of National Defence). Admitted to the German Writers' Union.
1958	Divorce from Domnik.
1959	Married Siegfried Pitschmann.
1960	Moved to Hoyerswerda. Publications: *Das Geständnis* [The Confession], Aufbau Verlag, Berlin. Radio plays, written together with Siegfried Pitschmann: *Ein Mann steht vor der Tür* [A Man at the Door]; *Sieben Scheffel Salz* [Seven Bushels of Salt].
1961	Publication: *Ankunft im Alltag* [Arriving in Everyday Life], Neues Leben, Berlin. Awarded the Literature Prize of the Free German Trade Union Association (FDGB, Freier Deutscher Gewerkschaftsbund) together with Siegfried Pitschmann for the radio plays *A Man at the Door* and *Seven Bushels of Salt*.

1962   *The Woman in the Pillory* broadcast as a television drama.

Awarded the Literature Prize of the Free German Trade Union Confederation for *Arriving in Everyday Life*.

1963   Publication: *Die Geschwister* [Brothers and Sisters], Aufbau Verlag, Berlin.

Began work on *Franziska Linkerhand*.

Election to the Board of the German Writers' Union.

1964   Siberia trip as a delegation member of the Central Council of the Freie Deutsche Jugend (Free German Youth).

Divorce from Pitschmann.

Married 'Jon' (Hans Kerschek).

1965   Publication: *Das grüne Licht der Steppen. Tagebuch einer Sibirienreise* [The Green Light of the Steppes. Diary of a Siberian Trip], Neues Leben, Berlin.

Awarded the Heinrich Mann Prize of the German Academy of Arts for *Brothers and Sisters*.

Carl Blechen Prize of the Council of the District of Cottbus for Art, Literature and Artistic Achievement.

1968   Cancer and surgery.

Moved to Neubrandenburg.

1970   Divorce from Kerschek.

1971   Married Dr Rudolf Burgatz.

1973   Brigitte Reimann died on 20 February in Berlin.

1974   Posthumous publication: *Franziska Linkerhand* (unfinished novel), Neues Leben, Berlin.

LIST OF ABBREVIATIONS USED IN THE FOOTNOTES

AVA	Staatsbibliothek zu Berlin, Preußischer Kulturbesitz, Dep. 38 (Aufbau Verlag) (Berlin State Library—Prussian Cultural Heritage, Dep. 38)
B.R.	Brigitte Reimann
BRS	Brigitte Reimann Sammlung (Brigitte Reimann Archive in the Literaturzentrum Neubrandenburg)
ND	*Neues Deutschland. Zentralorgan der Sozialistische Einheitspartei Deutschland*, leading newspaper of the Socialist Unity Party (SED) of Germany
NDL/ndl	*Neue Deutsche Literatur* (Berlin), literary magazine in the GDR (1952–2004)
PMA	Stiftung Archiv der Parteien und Massenorganisationen der DDR im Bundesarchiv / SAPMO (Archive of the Parties and Mass Organizations of the GDR in the Federal Archives)
S.P.	Siegfried Pitschmann
SVA	Stiftung Archiv der Akademie der Künste, Archiv des Schriftstellerverbandes (Foundation of the Archive of the Academy of Arts, Archive of the Writers' Association)

EDITORIAL NOTE

Brigitte Reimann recorded her manic lifestyle in the diaries that she began to write as a teenager. Because she destroyed her earlier journals, these diaries start in the year 1955 when her marriage to her first husband was falling apart, when she met the writer Siegfried Pitschmann and experienced her first success as a writer. The reader is drawn into the fascinating story of a woman, as gifted and uncompromising as she was hungry for life; a woman who emancipates herself from prevailing moral concepts, dogmatic expectations and political disillusionment.

The square brackets and ellipses in this volume indicate deletions in the original German version by the editor Angela Drescher, either due to repetitions or to protect the privacy of people mentioned.

TRANSLATOR'S ACKNOWLEDGEMENTS

I am indebted to John Green, Steph Morris and Karen Margolis for their helpful editing and comments.

DIARIES

1955–1963

1955

—

I'm back home, a week of bliss behind me, and I just wish I could do it all over again. But we're only given these kinds of gifts once, of course [...].

Many things have happened, difficult things. I've broken up with Günter.[1] That's why I have a new diary. Günter has my other one and won't give it back. He wants to use it against me in the divorce. [...]

After a very nasty scene—it must have been three weeks ago now—Günter left me but came back the next day, our wedding day,[2] with a lavish bunch of gladioli. We were both feeling down and on edge [...]. Then Günter kissed me quite unexpectedly and asked me to swear I'd be faithful, then everything would be fine again. I swore and right then, I had every intention of keeping my promise [...]. A week of happiness between us followed; we are living separately,[3] but Günter still climbed through my window every night and we made love like Romeo and Juliet. [...]

1 Günter Domnik (1933–95) was B.R.'s first husband. She published under her maiden name.

2 B.R. and Domnik married on 17 October 1953 but celebrated their anniversary every month.

3 Since it took a very long time for young couples to get a flat, both still lived with their parents. B.R.'s small room was on the ground floor of her parents' house.

4

And then it came: the letter from Georg Piltz[4] I'd secretly feared and longed for, inviting me to Rheinsberg to discuss my book.[5] After quarrelling for a long time, Günter finally let me travel to R. for three days. And I want to be honest: despite promising I'd be faithful for those three days, I was expecting the usual flirtation [. . .].

I won't deny it. Piltz had made an impression on me, and after a difficult journey of over ten hours, I arrived in Rheinsberg, my heart pounding. There the world is boarded up with planks and nails: the railway track ends, the town is tiny and lacks culture, and there's none of the bustle you find in other places.

Piltz was waiting for me at the station and took me to the HO[6] Ratskeller Hotel—the only hotel in R.—where he was also staying. At first, I was very self-conscious, and at dinner, he managed to embarrass me dreadfully because he wouldn't let me pay for myself: I was to be his guest. That went against my self-esteem but he just laughed at me [. . .]. I'm very touchy about these things and want to avoid acting like a kept woman.

But he insisted. I was his guest there the whole time and we lived it up. I ate more whipped cream than I'd done all year. The more I insisted I shouldn't eat so much to watch my figure, the greater his pleasure in ordering—but I didn't gain weight. Probably thanks to our long walks and the rowing trips, which did me good in all respects—even my cough has disappeared. Partly because I wasn't allowed to smoke much: Georg advocates a balanced life, and frowns on alcohol as well as cigarettes.

4 Georg Piltz (1925–2011) was an art historian, writer and editor who moved to the communist German Democratic Republic [GDR] in 1948. In 1953, he joined Aufbau Verlag publishing house as editor of the cultural-political weekly, the *Sonntag*.

5 The manuscript of B.R.'s novella *Die Frau am Pranger* [Woman in the Pillory] was sent to the *Sonntag* where it was printed as a serial.

6 HO (Handelsorganisation): Trade Organization, a state-owned commercial company for the nationalized retail and restaurant/hotel sector of GDR; founded in 1948.

But I'm racing ahead. The first evening, we only talked briefly about my book—Piltz said that he'd liked it very much, I was talented, but that there were all kinds of flaws that needed smoothing out.

Before dusk we took a short walk from our hotel to the castle—it's an early Knöbelsdorff, and so Georg told me a great deal about him. We only looked at it from the outside [. . .]. Then we wandered through the park, which Piltz explained in great detail. He's very clever, formidably knowledgeable, and so shockingly sarcastic and brilliantly ironic that I couldn't always follow him but just listened in silence, filled with admiration [. . .].

The obelisk stands on a little mound [. . .]. From it, you can look across the lake to the palace, with the park stretching out on both sides. We sat on a bench; it grew dark, the lamps were lit in the palace, crickets chirped and the wind rustled in the trees.

We spoke about all kinds of personal things [. . .] and slipped into a very intimate conversation that gave Piltz the opportunity to laugh at my naive views more than once, without failing to put a friendly arm around my shoulders, which I deliberately ignored. (Püschel[7] had drummed it into me that Piltz is a womanizer. I told him this quite candidly later on, and he was amused but a little insulted, and soon persuaded me that Püschel said things like these out of egotism.)

When we finally set off to go back, a very different, intimate tone had crept into our conversation, even though I was holding back very much. Meanwhile it was pitch black, and when Piltz began talking of ghostly dogs on the shadowy boulevard, I trembled with fear. I was glad when we left the park at last because there was a threat of something more than a ghostly dog along those eerie pathways. We were supposed to go back to the hotel but Piltz soon

---

7 Walter Püschel (1927–2005): editor at Neues Leben publishing house.

talked me into going down to the lake with him. [. . .] There we lay in the grass listening to the crickets, and the silence grew so terrible I desperately wished he would say something trivial to free me from the agony of waiting [. . .].

I don't know how he drew me into his arms—but you never remember afterwards. We kissed, and from that first evening, we realized we were fond of each other, very fond—but back then we didn't know what entanglements it would lead to.

The first *Du* we said to each other was so strange that it touched me very deeply, and I was afraid and longed for the next one at the same time. We hardly spoke on the way home. The following morning, we set off early on a rowing trip. Georg hired a boat and rowed across Grienericksee; I sat at the rudder. The lake is quite green, very clear and huge. I sat opposite Georg and looked at him, his broad face—'Kashubian' he calls it, and he really does have something Russian about him—his wild, straight hair that's always falling across his forehead, his blue eyes and full mouth [. . .]; when he laughs he looks like a boy, and you forget the grey hair around his temples. But it's his grey hair I love especially [. . .].

We rowed to Remus Island and sat in the boat on the shore talking about my book. Georg has rigorously cut passages, but he's right about everything; he's strict and I even cried. He laughed at me and kissed away the tears on my face and told me exactly why I couldn't write this or that in such a tight novella. He said I could be a second Seghers if I find my way. But if I lose it, he thinks I could end up being outright mediocre. He doesn't want me to be dragged along by the dominant trend in contemporary GDR literature [. . .]; he doesn't want me to 'toe the Party line'—I should follow my own path, not heed Party rules, create real characters, and write books that are not only relevant today but that will endure. He has very headstrong views, which he's sometimes hated for, but I think he's right [. . .].

We swam in Lake Rheinsberg and, still wet, lay in the hot sun; we kissed and tussled—I was truly ashamed, even cried when he touched my breast and insisted that I should leave my bedroom door unlocked that night. I'd sworn I would never commit adultery [...]! But as we drove home that evening, I already sensed that it was inevitable.

That night, he came to my room [...]. We slept together on my narrow bed and it was dawn by the time he left. I embraced him wildly and passionately and I'm not ashamed. Surely lovers have a natural right—and I'm in love, Jesus Christ, I'm in love. At the same time, I'm still not over my shyness and Georg smilingly called me his 'coy young lover' but he's convinced that I'm very sensual and could even be an artist of love [...].

Once I went over to his room, it was around dawn when a terrible storm was raging over Rheinsberg. I'd woken up from the thunderclaps, scared, and a sudden burning desire to be safe in Georg's arms drove me to him. [...] I woke him with kisses and he was moved to see me standing there like that, asking nervously if I could stay there. [...] It was the morning before I left to go back to my room—not caring about the other guests. On the last day, Georg said he would never forget that scene his whole life long: the way I stood there in his room, shocked by my own courage and still listening fearfully for the storm. He thinks I'm a child, and compared with him, I really still am.

I stayed longer than I meant to. It didn't matter any more [...] and I enjoyed those blissful days in Rheinsberg [...].

Georg has complete faith in me [...]. I will always consult him in the future—he should read my work and be ruthless in his criticism, and that way it will get better.

[...]

On the last day, we walked to the lighthouse. We sat there on stone steps and looked out across the expanse of countryside, the dense forests, the yellow fields—at that moment, I had a premonition that this could never happen again because it was so surreal and beautiful. True, we agreed to meet again in Rheinsberg next year—but who knows what will happen next year? If he loved me— [. . .] I'd be content to be his lover, we'll never be able to sanction our relationship because Georg is married . . . I don't want to think about it, I want to enjoy things rather than dwell on them. If I can . . .

The morning I left was awful, and I felt like crying all the time. We kissed each other, and I sensed he was affected too. We'll see each other in the next few weeks—an eternity! [. . .]

At the station, he put his arms around me, thanked me for the beautiful time we'd had, which had ended without a sour moment, and I kissed him again and again—I didn't care that people were around us. I'd go to any lengths of stupidity for him . . .

I wanted to be brave but when he walked alongside the departing train, holding my hand, the tears came after all. I had to leave him behind, he waved, his large, powerful frame grew smaller; Rheinsberg slowly disappeared, a week of intense happiness disappeared, Georg disappeared—and I cried in the end.

[. . .]

Burg, 1.[9].55

Günter came in the usual way that night—through my window. I woke up in his arms, and he claimed that I'd murmured Georg's name while he was kissing me awake. So, he already knew everything. I didn't hide my new love; I spoke very calmly and said he could file for divorce. I only got upset when he let it drop about using my diaries to ensure a 'guilty' verdict. Even though I'd already agreed to take all the blame. Even though he's not entirely blameless in the way things have gone. I only stipulated that Georg's name must never come up in the whole proceedings [. . .].

I was almost pleased to have a reason for being upset by Günter's pettiness—I'm still very attached to him and the separation won't be easy. [. . .] Two years of your life can't be erased just like that . . .

When I asked him to take the wedding ring off my finger, he refused; he wanted to kiss me one last time as a married woman. And *how* he kissed! I had to fight back the tears. And then I gave in to an unforgiveable weakness—I slept with him one more time. [. . .]

Günter says he still loves me [. . .]. I feel deeply sorry for him—but what should I do about the terrible mess we're in? If only I could leave Burg and be with other people who could help me learn to forget!

Incidentally, I visited the publishing house on the way home: they have finished the cover design for my novella *The Woman in the Pillory*. The book is going to be very attractive and discreet: clothbound, olive-coloured, with fine golden lettering and a vignette of a woman's head. The cover shows a woman's face, not too pretty, marked by suffering, with sad, beautiful eyes, that have something touching about them, a simultaneous hopelessness and courage. [. . .]

Junge Welt[8] is serializing my story [The] 'Death of Beautiful Helena'. It's about time—I desperately need money, I'm penniless right now. It doesn't bother me too much but it's not very pleasant either—soon I'll have more debts than hairs on my head.

Günter still comes, and I can't always refuse him—despite the fact that he's already been to court to find out the technical details of a divorce [. . .].

---

8 *Junge Welt* was the official daily newspaper of the Central Council (Zentralrat) of the state-run Free German Youth (Freie Deutsche Jugend, FDJ) movement (see note 36). Today's left-wing daily *Jungle World*, which is an offshoot of *Junge Welt*, was founded during an editors' strike in 1997.

Now he's prepared to give me free rein as long as I stay with him: I'd be allowed to go to Berlin, kiss other men, run riot—only sleeping with them would be off limits. With all the rationality of a mature person, this boy—I've always felt slightly superior to him—is now telling me I'm too young for a committed relationship [. . .]. He wants to give me time because he's convinced I'll have calmed down in a couple of years and will be content to live happily with him.

[. . .] Is it possible to love two men at the same time? I think so—there are supposedly famous examples.

I'm off to Berlin the day after tomorrow, and when I think of seeing Georg again, it makes me tremble. [. . .]

I know I should [. . .] go to Berlin, give in to this new love, and begin a new life. Oh, [. . .] this damned apathy! I'm such a coward—but it's so comfortable being cowardly [. . .].

Burg, 11.9.55

So, I went to Berlin and it was all almost exactly as I'd pictured. I worked hard at the publishers: little Lewerenz[9] agreed to all my cuts. He believes in my book and likes the effort I'm putting into improving it. Of course, though, I had to swear solemnly not to make any more cuts in the galleys.

We get on very well, and as far as new literature goes, we share the same opinion: it's bad, cowardly, banal, unscrupulous—you name it . . . little Lewerenz made a subtle hint that I ought to appreciate his saintly patience in carrying out endless changes to my book. I've been with this publisher long enough to understand. I think he'll set aside an evening for me the next time I'm in Berlin. We both went red as we talked about it—it's an enormous effort for Walter to play the Casanova. Depravity doesn't come naturally to him; he has to try really hard. That's what I like so much about him.

---

9 Walter Lewerenz (b. 1933): from 1954, editor at Neues Leben (see note 19).

[...]

And then—Georg! We met on the first evening at the Niquet-Keller restaurant.[10] [...] His nerves are frayed again [...]. His position is being undermined; they're trying to provoke him and force him to step down. He's just too honest; he's open in expressing his outrage about all the sordid intrigues that go on in our 'cultural politics', and some people just can't take it. I'm flattered he confides in me.

After a huge meal—he's determined to teach me the art of eating—he took me to the station. I was starved of his kisses but Berlin's too bright and loud, there's no space for lovers—how blissful Rheinsberg is!

The next day we drove to Potsdam and lay for hours in the woods by Templiner See. [...]

On the way back through Potsdam, he pointed out all the historic buildings; I'm always amazed at how knowledgeable he is, and I feel very small in comparison. Not that he ever talks down to me, and I'm happy and willing to learn from him. In an antiquarian bookshop, we found an old edition of Goethe's letters, which I bought for him, even though he refused at first [...]. Oh and he'd brought his own books to give me [...].

And anyway, he anticipates my every wish [...]. Once in passing I told him I like fruit, and he bought me a whole pile of bananas and delicious peaches [...].

On the last day, we only had a few hours together and he brought me to Ostbahnhof. I had a pain in my appendix—at least I thought it was my appendix—and he was very concerned, led me along and treated me in a gentle way that was really touching. He curbed all his biting jokes—he can be so cynical it shocks me—and

---

10 A historical cellar restaurant, built in 1839, formerly at Jägerstraße 41, and a popular meeting point for intellectuals; demolished in the 1960s.

*

perhaps the fact that I'm shocked spurs him on to make some really nasty remarks about others.

Our parting hurt but there was a small comfort: on the 21st, he plans to come to Burg, as the millennium celebration of Magdeburg Cathedral is on the 22nd [. . .]. We kissed a lot on the train: I couldn't care less what people think of me. [. . .]

The Frog[11] comes by every day: we row and make up non-stop. He torments me with his suspicion and jealousy, and I find it hard to play offended all the time—he's right, though, this affair is making him suffer but I can't change things [. . .]. If only I had my freedom, then I'd definitely make his life nice too. Ah, freedom!

Burg, 29.9.55

So much has happened but I couldn't write it down any sooner because, with downright criminal shrewdness, Günter ferreted out this diary from my bookshelf and took it with him.

Georg really did come on the 21st. [. . .] I'd had a few drinks to calm my nerves and stood there like an idiot when he came through the barrier dressed in a formal suit, not his usual style. [. . .]

Only after he'd changed back at the hotel did I thaw a little; he was much more familiar in his light gabardine suit that I like so much. He'd brought two items of news from Berlin: a sad one—the *Sonntag* can't take the *Woman* now for political reasons; and a happy one—the Ministry of Culture has shortlisted the *Woman* for its contemporary writing competition. If I won it, all my troubles would be over, and not just my financial ones: my whole standing would be confirmed within an important circle, and my name would become known. [. . .]

The next day we drove to Magdeburg but, unfortunately, we couldn't take part in the cathedral celebrations. Instead, Georg told me about the cathedral, the history of how it was built. How often

11 Frog (in German 'Frosch') was Domnik's nickname.

I've walked past without noticing it [. . .]. I suddenly realized that buildings are like music, or dramas: built according to very strict laws. You just have to find the key—the subject, more or less—and then everything becomes clear and manageable, and the architecture —its beauty, clarity and laws—is unlocked.

[. . .]

That evening I gave myself to him again. I can't write about it: it hurts so much to remember how tender and good Georg was, his terms of endearment, how transformed he was—he who usually makes fun of everything . . .

We were still lying together when the doorbell rang. I immediately knew it was Günter. He was already at the door, shook the handle, and yelled that we should open up. [. . .] It was straight out of a novel: I've often read scenes like this—tragic ones or, as in Boccaccio, amusing ones. I don't think I thought anything; I was just afraid for Georg. I fled onto the veranda and Georg followed me. Right then, there was a crash: in his anger and desperation, Günter had broken the door down. I clung on to Georg, trying to protect him and wanting to be protected at the same time.

Günter found us. The terrible thing I was expecting didn't happen: he seemed almost calm. We went into the room and the two of them sat down, with me in the middle. The next scene was appalling even though we barely raised our voices or became abusive. Günter made accusations, of course—the situation was quite clear. Georg mediated and asked for a clear-headed discussion.

So they got it all out in the open. I can hardly put into words how I felt: on one side, the man I've lived with for two years and whom I trust more than anyone else; on the other, the man I'm passionately in love with [. . .]. And yet I still enjoyed the situation, as perverse as that may sound.

Günter said that despite everything, he wouldn't let me go, that Georg was not going to have me even if he had to weld me to his side. Georg claimed [. . .] he was prepared to get a divorce and marry me. That bowled me over. He's never said anything like that to my face [. . .]. He always claims he's just not the Romeo type, and can't go into rhapsodies [. . .]—unlike me, apparently, I'm the Juliet kind [. . .]. Could I imagine anything better than living side by side with such an intellectual man, beneficial to me in every way?

Günter stubbornly stuck to his position, even when Georg tried to make it clear I'd be a renowned personality in a few years. That's something he's never said personally to me either—that he thinks I'm such a significant talent, the first great talent he's met among all the young writers.

Perhaps all this intoxicated me: in any case, when asked point blank, I decided in favour of Georg . . . But how ashamed I was when Günter reproached me for sleeping with him only two days ago, when I swore I loved him. Yes, I did, and I even meant it at the time. [. . .]

The next morning, I met Georg again. He assailed me with the idea of moving to Berlin: he'd make sure I could study, as he's a friend of Prof. Kantorowicz, who is bound to help. As he was talking about it, picturing our future, it didn't seem that difficult. I thought: I could stop being a coward and start a new life . . .

The whole day long we walked around the churches and climbed spires—I still feel a trace of muscle ache today—and strolled through the town, visiting its meagre sights. It's easy to make fun of this staid little town when I'm with Georg! But I still can't leave it behind . . .

Towards evening, we went to his room at the Roland again. In reply to my insistent questioning, he said that he couldn't imagine anything more beautiful than being with me forever [. . .]. But his children! I sense again and again how fond he is of them [. . .]. Can you build your own happiness on the unhappiness and disappointment of others [. . .]?

At home, I discovered my diary was missing. Günter must have broken in during the afternoon.

On Sunday morning, I had to go my writers' group.[12] But beforehand, I dropped in at Günter's workplace to reclaim my diary. He was quite transformed: pale, stern, stiff—he said he'd drafted the divorce papers and was determined to drag Georg into it. And that's exactly what I had been afraid of. [. . .]

First, I begged. That just bounced off him. Then I cursed. He was unmoved. Then I crossed the street to the station where Georg was already waiting. I cried bitterly—at first, I didn't want to tell Georg anything because *I* was the idiot after all—why do I keep a diary! But Georg just sensibly went through how I could get out of this dilemma. I was so helpless and desperate—I could have killed Günter.

[. . .]

I went, with all my pain, to the writers' group. At the beginning, I was totally useless; I welled up with tears whenever anyone so much as talked to me. It was evening before I came to life—I was attacked (with the best provocative intentions, as I later learnt) and accused of snobbery. At that point I exploded. I railed and held an impromptu lecture; I was so worn out I spoke my mind regardless of the others, accused them of writing functional literature, said they'd never become real writers, and claimed that I, at any rate, would keep well away from any kind of commissions, said I didn't want to turn into an opportunist, and so on. All these things that have been eating away at me for so long, I simply hurled at them—and they liked it! They were ecstatic that I was showing my former fiery self for once—didn't they notice all my accusations were aimed at them?

---

12 AG (Arbeitsgemeinschaft): working group, here of the young authors of the GDR Writers' Union (Deutsche Schriftstellerverband, DSV). The Magdeburg AG had been founded in early 1953 and B.R. became a member on 14 March 1953.

I think Georg is right: they always think you're referring to the person next to them.

All the same, this outbreak limbered me up so much I was ready to get into some scrapes that night. Horst [B.] and Helmut Sakowski were up for it too, as always . . . We recruited one more companion, packed everyone into Horst's car and cruised from one pleasure dome to the next. Except that one was closed, the next had a works party and the third was overcrowded . . . so we ended up in a dingy bar, drank some Dutch courage, cast off our nightcaps and stormed the Dalmatia bar with the last remaining adventurers. It turned out to be quite entertaining and I managed to drown my sorrows for a few hours.

On Sunday, of course, it all came back. I wanted to go home and whom should I bump into at the barrier in Magdeburg station? Günter. Dressed up to the nines—he was off to the press party. [. . .][13]

At home, I discovered he'd taken all his photographs while I'd been away and had even torn up a photo album. That was the last straw. I threw myself on the couch and screamed. [. . .]

It wasn't crying, just screaming, loud and wild. I had to vent my feelings, otherwise I'd have shattered to pieces from all the vileness that was choking me.

That night, Günter came. There was a nasty scene at first, we were very harsh and ugly to each other—I don't even want to remember it—until I couldn't take it any more and had another screaming fit. Of course, the whole house woke up. I threw Dad out, yelled at everyone—and banged my head against the wall; I felt like shattering my skull just to have some peace at last.

It was Günter who took me in his arms and tried to calm me down in the end. [. . .] And in total desperation, I was tender to

---

13 Annual party held by the local newspapers in GDR district capitals (see also note 37).

him again. He stayed the whole night—and that wasn't wise in the light of a certain clause: if a married couple sleep together after the divorce papers have been filed, it means forgiveness and the lawsuit becomes invalid. In God's name, I hadn't thought of using his weakness, but that evil thought came to me the next day when Günter insisted on pronouncing me the guilty party and wanted to name Georg as co-respondent in court. [. . .]

Now [. . .] he's withdrawn the divorce suit. He's signed up for three years with the KVP[14] and wants to serve with the river police. That actually upset me [. . .] and I have to cry every time I think of the long separation.

[. . .] It's just absurd but I can't break up with Günter: instead, I cast my future prospects [. . .] to the wind. It's absolutely crazy! But it's not just out of pity [. . .]. He's such a good man, so caring, and I feel glad whenever he turns up looking well dressed and freshly shaven—he knows that's the way I like him [. . .]

Burg, 17.10.55

Today's our wedding anniversary, the second . . . I never thought we'd make it, but the way things stand, we'll be cheerfully celebrating the next few wedding anniversaries too.

The Frog was turned down by the KVP—on account of his bad teeth. At first, I wasn't sure whether to be happy or down. But now I'm happy it's turned out this way. [. . .] Cleverness, good looks, money and other men's positions pale in comparison to his love. [. . .]

Now things are like they used to be—superficially, at least. Günter is living with me again properly, we go out together and I'm playing the housewife, but deep down, not everything is running

---

14 KVP (Kasernierte Volkspolizei): Barracked People's Police—the name of GDR armed forces from July 1952 until January 1956; in January 1956, renamed Nationale Volksarmee, NVA; or simply Volksarmee (i.e. National People's Army).

along the same old lines. Some things have got better, and I hope it stays that way: Günter is more attentive, makes more effort, pays more attention to his appearance than he used to, and he's doing a course to improve his education. Yes, he's been reading a great deal, nearly every evening. [. . .] I admit he still tortures me with his jealousy. If I look like I'm daydreaming, he suspects I'm thinking of Georg—he talks more of him than I do and unwittingly churns up my memories all the time.

I've changed too—admittedly, not for the better. I analyse myself [. . .] and I recognize my mistakes quite clearly, even though I don't admit them to others. I'm moodier than usual and hector Günter—mostly in jest but very often in earnest [. . .]. I'm a step ahead of him: he's fighting for my love . . .

Having said that, I really love him again [. . .]. Sometimes though, my thoughts wander to Georg but it doesn't hurt very much. I would like us to be friends—but that's a stupid phrase [. . .].

I just received a letter from him and my heart began to thump again. Folly! I have to get over this. Should I be allowed a second— dubious—love if it means all these sacrifices: the Frog unhappy, Georg's children fatherless, his wife no longer provided for [. . .]! And could I wish for a better, tenderer husband than Günter? He'd die for me—that's what I call love!

Herbert H[. . .] also wrote to me. He's madly in love with me [. . .]. I'll certainly show Günter the letter; he should see how others covet me! (Yet another evil thought!)

[. . .]

Isn't it funny—there you are, married and sworn to absolute fidelity, and then several men do all they can to seize your husband's position, deploying their—sometimes considerable—charm, and you're supposed to remain stubborn and as cold as ice. But they make me pity them, and I always find it hard to say no . . .

[. . .]

Burg, 21.10.55

I was in Berlin again and—of course—at Georg's. The Ministry of Culture organized a conference for adventure-story writers, which I was invited to.

The conference was very interesting: the four-hour lecture by Frau Dr. Ludwig was excellent, but the discussion about Karl May[15] wasn't to my liking—he was rejected almost unanimously. It's unfair—they're probably scared of the competition.

In the evening, I went out with a colleague; it was quite dull. As long as he talked about literature, he was bearable, but once he started fawning over me and wanting affection, I ditched him. It's actually fun to cold-shoulder someone—this whole kissing business leaves a bad taste in your mouth when people expect it of you. Perhaps I'm becoming cooler and more composed.

The next morning, I went to the Ministry of the Interior publishing house[16] which informed me by telegram that my manuscript of 'Death of Beautiful Helena' has been accepted. Jürgen Gruner[17] and Eberhard Panitz[18] welcomed me like good old friends; they

15 Karl Friedrich May (1842–1912): German writer best known for his adventure novels set in the American Old West. Karl May's works were initially not allowed to appear in the GDR since they were not only regarded as unrealistic and unchallenging from an artistic point of view, but their heroes were also seen as the embodiment of the German Übermensch in fascist ideology. The first editions were published from 1983 with an afterword by the former first secretary of the Writers' Union, Gerhard Henniger, who tried to refute such generalized opinions.

16 Verlag des Ministeriums des Innern (Publishing House of the Ministry of the Interior): After 18 January 1956, when the KVP was renamed the Volksarmee, the publishing house was renamed the Verlag des Ministeriums für Nationale Verteidigung (Publisher of the Ministry of National Defence). Later still, it became the Militärverlag der Deutschen Demokratischen Republik (Military Publisher of the GDR).

17 Jürgen Gruner (b. 1930) was senior editor at Neues Leben (1954–55), editor and editorial manager at Verlag des Ministeriums für Nationale Verteidigung (1955–60) and chief editor at Kongreß Verlag, Berlin (1960–62).

18 Eberhard Panitz (b. 1932): German writer, screenwriter and editor, a committed leftist and social realist, who has published numerous books since 1955. He won the Youth Book Prize of the GDR in 1956.

were very enthusiastic about my story and presented me with a contract straight away—I'm even going to get a higher rate than other writers because my story is of such high quality. The publishing house wants to win me over, they offered flattering proposals and tried to talk me out of staying with Neues Leben.[19] [. . .] Yes, I'm slowly becoming an acclaimed personality . . .

Then I sent the Frog a telegram saying: 'I love you and will be back tonight.' I simply had to—I want him to look forward to me and thought longingly of him in that far-off town.

And then I went to visit Georg in the offices of *Sonntag*. [. . .] The moment I saw him, I knew that I still loved him with the same passion as before—regardless of my love for Günter. It's difficult to understand, and I avoid thinking about it: it would be easy to lose my mind.

[. . .]

A smug cheer was in the air when I turned up at the publishing house. That terrible cynic Berger[20] now works for my publisher too.

[. . .]

They were outraged when I told them about the M[inistry] o[f the] I[nterior] [. . .]. They seem to set great store by my writing for NL in the future because they've offered me a contract for my new book, even though it's not even halfway written yet. [. . .] Well, I'll think it over.

19 Neues Leben was a publishing house for new writers, founded in 1946 by four partners: Edith Baumann, Erich Honecker, Paul Verner and Friedrich Wolf, all of whom were politically active in the KPD (Kommunistische Partei Deutschlands, KPD; later Socialist Unity Party of Germany, i.e. Sozialistische Einheitspartei Deutschlands, SED). It published books and novel series, as well as the magazine *Mosaik*, among others, and most of B.R.'s works. B.R. often refers to Neues Leben as NL.

20 Karl Heinz Berger (1928–94): editor at Neues Leben from 1952 until 1957, when he was removed from the position for 'anti-Soviet tendencies' owing to his efforts to publish the sequel of Boris Djacenko's novel *Herz und Asche* (Heart and Ashes, 1954) in which the writer broached the taboo of Red Army soldiers raping German women in the last days of the Second World War. Berger lived in the GDR as a freelance writer.

They fetched a bottle of cognac and all tried to drink me under the table. [...]

I was quite tipsy by the time I ended up in the Niquet-Keller, and Georg, who'd been waiting quite some time, was astounded by how temperamental I became when we began a discussion about cultural politics that went on for so long that we had to sprint to catch my train.

The alcohol gave me courage—I told him the truth straight out about how cowardly his editorial office is—but what good does it do? Georg agrees with me anyway, and I can't get at the others. I'm up against a brick wall and can't change anything.

The final moments were ours alone. [...] I wanted to cry but he can't stand that. [...]

Burg, 24.10.55

I was at the writers' group again yesterday, and got rubbed up the wrong way, of course—but that belongs in my other diary, devoted to work.

On Sunday, we were in a HO cafe; we were in a wonderfully playful mood again and joked and laughed so much everyone around took notice of us. I was the centre of attention. I always like that and when I feel it happening, my entire personality changes; I even become witty, soaking up laughter and praise and compliments with pleasure. That evening, many suitors were lined up as per usual, wanting to take me home. However, someone else had caught my eye. Two young students were sitting at a table, and they got talking to us. And soon one of them was making eyes at me. And I at him. And as it sometimes goes, the smaller student (who happened to be taller than Günter) [...] played the Casanova so well that I even fell for it. He insisted on taking me home. I sent away my other admirers—all I wanted to do was to tease the boy, teach him a lesson, because his daredevil posturing was getting on my nerves. [. . .]

No sooner were we alone than his self-confidence evaporated, and a few mocking words reduced him in no time to a helpless little boy. I can't recall our conversation, but it was psychologically very interesting [. . .]—he'd never even slept with a woman; he couldn't understand that my fond gazes meant absolutely nothing. [. . .]

I was really moved—his tender-and-ever-so-vulnerable heart lay open before me and with a few cynical remarks, I could have quite simply torn him apart. I felt thrown back to my own youth, which I spent utterly helpless in the face of the world's evils, shaken by the experience of love and my shattered ideals. [. . .]

Perhaps all this [. . .] overwhelmed me so much because, for a long time now, I've only had men around who act purposefully, try to seduce me at all costs and who know, like me, that we're only flirting. [. . .]

Burg, 24.10.55[21]

This diary is not dedicated to my adulterous escapades; it's not about love and liaisons—I want to record whatever happens to me on my journey to becoming a writer. Yes, I write—some already refer to me as a writer—but inside I feel I'm a dead loss, a literary nobody. I want to write good things, to work, to dedicate my whole life to this one aim; to help people through literature, and fulfil my duties, the duties we share towards the rest of humanity.

For a while, I was so depressed, so pessimistic, felt that this life was meaningless, that it wasn't worth the huge effort of crawling towards a goal I'd never reach. Of course, these moods will often overcome me but I do believe that I've found my mission even if, admittedly, I haven't yet found a real meaning in human existence. The primary reason for our existence escapes me, but I probably

---

21 This entry and the next were underlined in the original.

shouldn't dwell on it unless I want to end up hanging from a rope in a madhouse. I just mean—and this is a primitive philosophy, I admit, but I don't have a better one yet—that once we're born on Earth, for reasons we don't know, we should try and make the best of it, not only for ourselves, but also for others—and it comes back to us in the end: the satisfaction when you've behaved like a positive hero.[22] The guidelines our society represent are unequivocal. I believe you could follow them with a clear conscience; there is nothing vague about them, no burbling on about paradise on Earth. It's something much more tangible—look, this is the way you should all act; believe this and fight that—then nothing can go wrong. We have to be careful not to let the bureaucrats water down our ideas or let the fanatics—basically anarchists—incite us to mass murder[23] (I also mean intellectual and spiritual mass murder); we have to be careful that 'our idea' remains pure and that people keep their basic rights, freedom in every respect, [. . .] intellectual freedom and in everyday life, as long as they don't preach war and murder in any form. That's obvious, and in this respect, I agree with our laws that are sometimes not at all to my taste—perhaps because theory and practice don't always tally. But we'll see—it's not the writer's job to think about it, after all. 'Humanitarianism' is our grand slogan.[24] 'Humanitarianism' is my agenda; for all its limitlessness, that's its limit. [. . .] That's what I stand for, and I'm prepared to suffer for it.

22 Positive hero: a concept of Marxist–Leninist aesthetics. 'He characterizes a type of literary-artistic hero whose actions coincide with objective historical necessities and requirements and is driven by high subjective moral or political motives. [. . .] A characteristic is his ability to act in order to shape history and his ability not to be an object but a subject of social struggles and processes' (Harald Buehl [ed.], *Kulturpolitisches Wörterbuch* [Cultural–Political Dictionary]. Berlin: Dietz Verlag, 1970, pp. 207f.).

23 Allusion to the victims of Stalinism.

24 'Humanitarianism: principle of thinking and acting, which is directed towards the freedom and dignity of man. [. . .] True h. is only possible on the soil of socialist society; here, the sources of man's oppression and lack of freedom are removed, alienation overcome, the cause of war eliminated' (ibid., p. 220).

I have a good—the best—tutor and guide: Georg Piltz. I want to learn from him. I trust him, perhaps too much [. . .]. Well, that remains to be seen; I want—in as far as my uneducated mind allows—to test and weigh up and stand up for what I have decided is right. I might change my mind once in a while—in fact, I'm sure I will. We are all subject to mistakes; even the greatest person of all is not infallible—what counts is to follow your conscience and not become a hypocrite. If I'm wrong, I want to own up to my mistakes and do better in the future—but no one will be able to force me to say something if I'm not convinced. Money and glory are not likely to be plentiful in my life if I follow my good intentions to the end; I already sometimes find myself opposed to the prevailing view on this or that issue. But in the end, reason has to be victorious; truth and humanity have to triumph. This is the only way it can be; if we were to doubt this, our last resort would be to escape into nirvana, renounce the world and its affairs as our final salvation.

[. . .]

Burg, 30.10.55

I have drawn up a contract with the Ministry of the Interior publishing house for an adventure story, 'The Death of Beautiful Helena'. [. . .]

When I told them about this at Neues Leben, they were shocked because they want to keep me. As if I could leave them—my publisher! They've been understanding. They've really helped me; above all, little Lewerenz, 'my' editor, puts a frankly touching effort into promoting me and my work. NL wants to draw up a contract for a new book straight away (working title: *Girl from Chronos*)[25] even though they haven't read it yet. I didn't respond at first—what if it

---

25 This story was not published under this title but later appeared as *Kinder von Hellas* [Children of Hellas], 1956.

doesn't turn out well in the end? A contract in good faith would be tantamount to deceit on the part of the author. [. . .]

What rankles me too is that I won't be included in the pro-gramme for 1956[26]—what nonsense to leave a finished manuscript lying around for a whole year. On one hand, they're crying out for good new literature, but on the other, they're stubbornly sticking to their plan . . . I want to put a bit of pressure on them. [. . .]

The serialization in the *Sonntag* seems to have fallen through. Damned cowardice on the part of the editors again! Georg is in favour of it and the entire editorial staff thinks the book is good—but no, they daren't publish it because they're afraid they could get themselves into hot water. Wilhelm Pieck[27] has called an amnesty for war criminals—so now you can't say anything against these criminals. [. . .] The main thing is making sure no one bad-mouths the chief editor. Just keep trotting obediently along the dotted line, don't step out on your own—your precious existence might be endangered! I argued bitterly with Piltz, quite unnecessarily because he agrees with me. [. . .] I can't even denounce this whole dirty mess in public because I'd drag Georg into it too. [. . .] Because he wasn't supposed to reveal the real reasons for its rejec-tion. Just phoned the publisher: they like the story very much but can't publish it—it's an integral whole, they can't chop it up into episodes.

The whole of 'German fiction' scoffed at this lame excuse . . .

Now, once again, I'm working passionately on *Girl from Chronos*, which is based on the story of Helen of Troy. Admittedly,

26 In the publishing industry of the GDR, it was customary to stipulate titles and circulation levels in a programme in the previous year so that the state-assigned quota of paper and printing capacity could be allocated.

27 On the 31 September 1955, President Wilhelm Pieck sent a letter to the Soviet leadership in which he asked for the release and return of all German 'war convicts' (not war criminals, as B.R. writes), a term used in the GDR and the Soviet Union to refer to German political prisoners held in Soviet forced-labour camps.

Piltz gave me a good tip for how to resolve the conflict, which I'll use in the new version: Helena won't spit in Costa's face after his betrayal as originally planned but, because she loves him so deeply, she'll become a traitor too and join him—that means the conflict will be fully resolved. And the tragic moment: when she's deserted, Helena will gradually comprehend the crime she's committed—she kills Costas and returns of her own free will to the People's Army where she's executed by partisans.

'A struggle between duty and affection'—as little Lewerenz calls it. [. . .]

A few days ago, I corrected the galleys of *Woman in the Pillory*. The story still felt so touching I could have wept at the lovers' unhappy ending. If only it moves my readers in the same way! [. . .] I can still remember how bitterly I cried back then after I wrote the scene in the barn. It tormented me, and I wanted so much to let the lovers live!

Burg, 1.11.55

It was Günter's birthday yesterday, his 22nd. The evening before, we'd gone to the Roland again after a long break, for a small party that started with bubbly and cognac, and ended up in a fine state of tipsiness. We'd both got dressed up; I felt slightly ridiculous, in a sweet way—like a young couple that goes out 'on the town' every few months and then acts as if they drink bubbly for breakfast.

Well, in any case, we had a ball.

In any case, I kissed the Frog into a frenzy for the first time in ages—I'd cooled right off. Georg is not far off the mark with his 'Frigitte' label, even though, all sensuality aside, I don't really understand this shocking coldness of mine.

But then Günter ruined it all again yesterday: I'd made everything nice, prettied myself up for him—and he swayed in an hour late, drunk, with considerable debts. Still, I shouldn't have let myself go like that: I'm generous to myself—why not to him too?

This morning, all hangdog, he asked me to forgive him, but I was just as ashamed, even though I didn't show it (my willpower doesn't stretch that far yet!)

Burg, 9.11.55 [28]

I'm feeling dissatisfied again with *Woman in the Pillory*; [I'd] like to withdraw it from my publisher. They won't return it, of course; and it's an extremely bad idea to keep making changes to your work [. . .].

I was in Berlin for three days and worked through the galleys with Berger. He's a dreadful man, an absolute cynic, and he maddens me all the more because I'm no match for his witty taunts—I can't ward him off when he starts cheerfully laying into me. He has quite a few criticisms of my book; I was quite depressed but it serves me right. I was too conceited about it, delighted by all the praise, and presumptuous enough to consider myself a writer on the basis of this little book. Damned vanity!

Little Lewerenz made me anxious: Peterson went mad because of the adventure story and the publishing house not getting it. I visited him—and he was quite amiable, [. . .] and we talked about the new book, *Girl from Chronos* (working title). Peterson warned me: it's a complex subject because opinions differ on the Greek fight for freedom and we don't know how our relationship with Greece will develop, etc. That irked me—as if literature depended on day-to-day political issues . . .

The partisans' fight was good and just during its time, and anyway, what concerns me is the fate of my lovers—the human conflict.

---

28 This entry was underlined in the original.

At the Ministry of the Interior, where I corrected the galleys of the *Beautiful Helena* with Panitz, we spoke about this problem. Gruner, who joined us, offered me a contract for the book but I refused—I don't want to leave NL just like that. Having said that, the contract would be very handy; Gruner promised to publish the book as early as April.

That's my main concern: the book ought to be published before I go to the Institute for Literature.[29] Gruner phoned Peterson to ask if he'd would consider giving the manuscript to the MoI. And you know what? The good man promptly changed sides and said he wanted to keep it. Panitz sneered: NL would pull itself together and include me in its programme for next year. [...]

Now I'm not sure what to do: [...] I'm pleased about how unbureaucratic this young publishing house is . . . On the other hand, NL is destined to be my home in publishing. [...]

Burg, 10.11.55

I spent three days 'on business' in Berlin.

On the first day, I met Georg at the Niquet-Keller; unfortunately, he couldn't spend the entire evening with me [...] and I went to bed very grumpy, and very early.

Each meeting with Georg is torture—despite all the pleasure. He says I'm leading a double life and have to decide once and for all. If only I could! [...]

Georg and I rarely speak about our love; we mostly quarrel about literature. He laughs at my idealism, perhaps rightly so. [...]

The next day I went to the MoI and worked through the galleys with Eberhard Panitz. When I said goodbye, I asked him if he had

---

29 The Institute for Literature (Institut für Literatur) opened on 18 September 1955 in Leipzig. The first director was Alfred Kurella. In 1959, it was renamed Literaturinstitut Johannes R. Becher (after the eponymous German politician, writer and poet) after his death. B.R. did not attend classes there.

time to toast the book. I've noticed Eberhard is always happy when he sees me.

We [...] went to a dance bar. We were in an excellent mood. [...] E. told me about his new book, we had a lively discussion about literature—in short, we got on famously. We danced, and I was already a little tipsy when, all of a sudden, E. [...] drew me gently towards him.

[...] By around midnight I knew he was in love with me—and me with him. Yes, really, [...] I like Eberhard very much; he's still very young, barely a year older than me, and a good-looking, tall, clever lad.

We were so happy, the pair of us. I don't know how it happened —but we suddenly kissed on the dance floor—just very softly, but I was trembling. [...] He didn't get pushy, which I appreciate very much. I didn't get home until five o'clock and it was terribly hard for me to leave him. We'll see each other on the 18th again—[...]. I feel quite ecstatic but it bothers me deeply that I can't remember his features. I close my eyes and try to imagine his face but it never forms a whole—I can only picture his mouth, his forehead or his eyes.

Perhaps I will publish my new book with the MoI so I can work with Eberhard.

[...]

Günter is tormenting me to death with jealousy and distrust.

Burg, 15.11.55

Three days ago, I received a letter from Eberhard. Needless to say, I was very happy. And there was a spark on those two pages that revealed perhaps more than the writer intended. And the postscript, which took a long time to figure out—Eberhard's handwriting is almost as bad as mine—was quite something. [...]

Georg also wrote to me but with distressing news. He's very ill, laid up in bed, and won't be allowed out for a while. So, our educational trip around Berlin's underworld has been cancelled for the time being [. . .].

Georg wrote that he was delighted by the sarcastic, sassy tone of my last letter; if I developed my writing along these lines, he could see a rosier future in store for me. I didn't even have to force my 'sassy' tone—perhaps it's the reason I can adapt to others in a flash: I'm sentimental with the sentimental, cynical (though it's not my strength) with a cynic. With Georg it took a little longer—I was too madly in love from the start—but I'm slowly getting to his essence [. . .]. And strangely, my sarcasm when I'm with Georg is just as genuine as my sentimentality when I'm with Günter . . .

[. . .]

Oh, Georg! I think I'd have found perfect happiness by his side . . . to this day, I can't fathom what he sees in me, or why he, a thousand times superior, has grown fond of me. [. . .]

Berlin (Johannishof), 19.11.55

I've just spoken to Georg—albeit on the telephone. He's still quite ill, you can hear it in his voice. He sounded so different that I suddenly felt afraid it wasn't him and I was saying my tender words to a stranger. But when he called my contract with the MoI 'folly', I was certain.

It hurts to be in a big city, among strangers, in a hotel room— and not be allowed to see him. My heart pounded up in my throat just now on the phone, I was so happy and sad at the same time. Well, God knows, the phone is not a poetic invention and ill-suited to lovers' words—but at least I had a little of Georg.

This time my visit to Berlin has been a disappointment—on the personal side, I mean. In business, everything worked out: I drew up a preliminary contract with Gruner, went to Neues Leben and was given a surprisingly friendly reception—they weren't too angry with me and are thinking over my next books.

The MoI put me up in the Johannishof, which I liked simply because my beloved Gérard Philipe[30] stayed here. But that aside, it's the best hotel I've stayed in so far: warm, cosy, almost sophisticated, with a cute porter and a very homely room. You can get lost in the corridors—a wonderful thing. And it's teeming with foreigners. Some Chinese are staying next to me; I've met them several times but I don't dare stare at them as much as I'd like to, as fascinated by everything exotic as I am.

But on the personal side, as I said, it's a disappointment. Yesterday [. . .] I spent a very lonely evening in my hotel; I went to bed with *Martin Eden*,[31] and because the preface was by Piltz, it was some comfort.

Today I was supposed to meet Eberhard, but this morning, the porter brought a letter in which he wrote that his mother had turned up unannounced in Berlin. I went to see him and I'm afraid I lost my rag. I was sad and angry and had to fight back tears. [. . .] But it serves me right that this date fell through as well; I lied to Günter [. . .] to come here—it was more about my new flame than about the contract.

Sometimes I believe in something like the dear Lord who looks down on little girls and raps them fiercely on the knuckles when they're naughty . . .

Generally, I'm feeling very despondent again. Even despite my recent, cheery declaration that I'm [an] eternal optimist! But somehow, I enjoy my depressions because I imagine, sometimes subconsciously, they are helping me. How can anyone not familiar with desperation become a writer? I'm not talking about cancelled

---

30 Gérard Philipe (1922–59): prominent French actor and a heartthrob who appeared in many films between 1944 and 1959, including in the GDR.

31 A novel by Jack London, published by Macmillan in 1909.

meetings or unhappy love affairs—the former is rare and there's no such thing as the latter, except for my poor, bittersweet love for Georg—but how many hours have I already brooded over my work? Will I ever achieve anything? And what exactly do I want to achieve? To make people happy? Yes. Help them move forwards? Certainly. Take them to task? Absolutely! Isn't one eye always on fame, on recognition? Doesn't this thought at the back of my mind tarnish the purity of my aims? In the end, don't I write out of egotism—because I want to be admired and superior to the petty folk from my hometown, or because writing gives me a selfish plea- sure? That's what it's about too—pleasure: for me, writing is rarely the torture others describe it as being. Perhaps they just want to sound important with their creative birth pains . . . But there are hours when I'd rather die. What's actually holding me back [. . .]?

The ancient Greeks were right: when all the evils escaped from Pandora's box, only hope was left behind. Lovely, damned hope! We invariably expect things to change and become good and wonderful again, [. . .] but we don't even know what it is we long for so keenly.

[. . .] In fact, it's foolish to get upset over every little thing. What does it matter in the bigger picture? [. . .]

Burg, 22.11.55

I've come back, changed in a strange way: I love the Frog again. Or should I say: I love him again more than I have recently. [. . .] The effort he makes to please me! When he comes home at night, he changes—and he really is a handsome young fellow in my opinion. He also shaves regularly. It might sound ridiculous but paying atten- tion to his appearance like this raises his status in my eyes [. . .].

That evening I did go dancing with Panitz after all. Unfor- tunately, the only place we could find a seat was a dive bar, represen- tative of the Berlin underworld—in moderate form: hard guys with easy girls, but not even real ones. We headed home early.

On Sunday, next day, I visited Eberhard in his flat even though I knew how risky it was. We drank a bottle of bubbly, felt tipsy and in love, and lay on his bed, kissing as usual. [. . .] I stayed until the evening and only managed to catch the last train. Strangely, in those few hours, it all changed between us, [. . .] and he didn't arouse my passion again. I went into raptures about Piltz and that seems to have shocked him—after my ardour just a few hours earlier.

[. . .]

A peculiar person! Yet something about him fascinates me. He looks like Genghis Khan (not that I've ever seen a picture of him). He has Mongolian features and narrow, dark eyes, without being handsome in any conventional sense.

He says he's falling in love with me—forever. The reason—and that astonished me—is my work. A real writer! That's how I like it. A man who loves a woman who can write. [. . .] Unfortunately, he's misjudged me—my passion is quickly quenched. Once I've had a man I find attractive, kissed him and listened to his confessions, I go off him in no time—perverse!

[. . .] We agreed we're both very fond of one another—and in the end, I shocked him by laughing and asking in a friendly way whether he really believes everything I tell him. He was playing the ladies' man, so I couldn't resist being mean—and he promptly keeled over.

[. . .]

Eberhard is not my Prince Charming—and nor is Georg (as much as I love him). It's Günter, after all.

Burg, 8.12.55

I wanted to visit Georg yesterday, but he had to go to Dresden, to visit his publisher. [. . .] Luckily, I still have Georg's letters, which mean a lot to me. He's very strict with me and my work, and his letters hurt because they speak the truth. But the best part, despite all the sarcasm and irony, which is often quite bitter, is a line that always stands out from the others, revealing his love for me.

Burg, 9.12.55[32]

[. . .] There are many problems plaguing me and as I haven't seen Georg for weeks—through a chain of unhappy circumstances— there's no one except myself to whom I can talk about them.

I've read [Anatole] France. [. . .] *The Opinions of Jérôme Coignard*[33] has confused me terribly. I'm now familiar with the lessons of the epicures. Georg often talked about them, quite pessimistically, which, I admit, doesn't seem to be the nature of the epicures, but P.'s sentiments held some truth—and how wonderfully eloquent, forceful and convincing they are in France!

I have to admit that I don't entirely understand why this book is published in our country because it's likely to cause the greatest confusion in the heads of young readers, quite unlike any other. On the other hand, the publication seems to be an encouraging sign that greater freedom in our thinking is being allowed—in thinking, and in forming our own opinions. Admittedly, I. I. Asimov very cleverly tries to disprove Coignard's point of view in his after- word—and I agree with him to a great extent—but what can he do against the compelling influence of this book?

Perhaps I've grown so fond so quickly of the good abbot Jérôme because I keep hearing Georg's voice through his. Oh, and while I was reading, I had a fierce disagreement with Coignard-Piltz, but many of my illusions and my firm views were turned on their heads. Please! How can I call them firm views? [. . .]

---

32 This entry was underlined in the original.

33 Anatole France (1844–1924) : author of *Les Opinions de Jérôme Coignard* (1898), sequel to the better-known *La Rôtisserie de la reine Pédauque* (1893).

If I were given Hegel's books, I'd be a staunch Hegelian; if I were given Marx's books, I'd be an enthusiastic Marxist. [...]

But there's something to it: this well-meaning misanthropy, this almost tender irony, this amicable, superior contemplation that understands how pointless all earthly endeavours are and holds suffering or happiness in such low esteem—I almost envy those who can manage that!

And yet: Are people truly 'evil and stupid' as the abbot contends? I've believed so firmly in people, in their goodness, and have been let down, but if I had such a low opinion of people wouldn't I be condemning myself too, and in addition deny all progress, stifling every effort to achieve progress?

It's very good not to have too high an opinion of your own ability. [...] But to damn all humanity in the process and consider it worthy of downfall—it goes against all the things I've been taught over the past few years; everything I believe in, hope for and work towards.

[...] Georg reproaches me for having a philosophy that's primitive and Rousseauian—'no wonder when you live in the wilds', he adds. And perhaps Rousseau's sensitivity is finer and stronger than his logic—but wouldn't more sensitivity be good for all of us? My rose-tinted idealism won't be cured so easily, it seems, but there are some things in France's book that I should adopt.

[...]

Apart from this, I'm working on *Helena* with equal diligence and reluctance, thoroughly put off by G.'s sarcasm. [...] My accomplishment as a writer is not enough to overcome it—and to make matters worse, I'm also reading Goethe's novels: I shudder when I realize my mistakes, without being able to correct them for the moment.

[...] But I feel comfortable, I let people praise me and I believe them, and I curse Georg when he tells me bitter truths. Why is it that we object so vehemently to what's good and right, even when we've already recognized it as such? I know I should put my book aside—perhaps forever, perhaps just for a while [. . .].

It's true I've grown fond of Helena and Costas;[34] but I can't weep for them as I could for Alexej and Kathrin,[35] and this seems like a bad omen to me. Or is it good and sensible to have some distance from your characters and not let them bully you too much?

My cardinal sin is my ambition!

[. . .] I almost hope that Gruner dislikes the new version. I'd feel relieved if our contract were cancelled.

But if I finish this book, I will write love stories—tight, careful ones, following the best rules of the masters. I only need to see my writing through Georg's eyes to know if it's good or bad. But I don't dare show him Helena—that would be a death sentence!

[. . .]

Burg, 16.12.55

Now I'm stuck in my everyday routine again, and to top it all, it's spiced up by a delightful cold that I caught on a freezing express train.

The two days in Berlin were wonderful, despite having to rearrange all my plans. [. . .]

At five o'clock I was supposed to meet Georg in the Niquet-Keller. I arrived a good half hour early and got talking to two men at the next table. One [. . .] tried hard to drink me under the table but failed miserably. When Piltz arrived—shocked to find me in male company yet again—he got into a heated debate with Neuhaus about literary criticism; I wasn't able to follow it all, so instead, I

---

34 The two protagonists in *The Death of Beautiful Helena* (1955).

35 The two protagonists in *The Woman in the Pillory* (1956).

dived into the eyes of the man across from me, an FDJ[36] journalist who published *Helena* a while back and who knew an awful lot about me.

[…]

We visited the Gemäldegalerie.[37] I shouldn't get started on the paintings, otherwise I'll lapse into raptures over them—I must have stood in front of the *Sistine Madonna* for a quarter of an hour and it was like praying. You could be converted back to godliness by such a work of art.

We didn't 'do' much of it. Georg explained the pictures to me, spoke about the masters, the artistic periods—in short, we only managed a few rooms. Sadly, I missed Giorgione's *Venus*, as the gallery closed at 8 p.m.

I was very taken by a Gauguin—South Sea girls in barbaric colours—superb!

[…]

Yesterday, Piltz and I spent the whole day at a district[38] conference for Berlin writers—Georg, out of duty, and me, out of interest. He'd managed to get me a ticket. Although the discussion seemed futile because the central problem was avoided, it was still very interesting, and I was introduced to some well-known men.

---

36 FDJ (Freie Deutsche Jugend): Free German Youth, the only officially sanctioned youth organization, established in the Soviet Occupation Zone in 1946; members were identified by their blue shirts. Membership was voluntary; however, young people who did not join faced discrimination in the GDR. The purpose of the FDJ was to raise a generation in the Marxist–Leninist spirit. In 1989–90, as a consequence of the fall of communism and German reunification, the organization became insignificant.

37 Literally, 'Picture Gallery'. On 27 November 1955, an exhibition from the Dresden Old Master's Gallery (Dresdner Gemäldegalerie) opened in East Berlin's National Art Gallery (Nationalgalerie), featuring paintings that had been taken to the Soviet Union as spoils of war and had been returned to the GDR on the 1 April 1955.

38 In 1952 in the GDR, the traditional five *Länder* (counties) were replaced with 15 smaller *Bezirke* (administrative units) including East Berlin. The process was reversed in 1990. It is translated in this manuscript alternately as 'district' and 'regional'.

My gourmand then took me for an excellent three-course meal, and afterwards to the station, where I almost got sentimental again.

[...]

Luckily, I had a fierce row with a narrow-minded policeman[39] who insisted on rummaging through my briefcase. I became very feisty, and so did he. He came within a hair's breadth of arresting me. The little adventure pepped me up.

Back home, the Frog was waiting for me at the station. That was the end of Berlin, and I kissed him, and I was happy. And anyway, you shouldn't take things too seriously.

---

39 A member of the VoPo (Volkspolizei): the 'People's Police', the GDR police force.

1956

Burg, 14.1.56

Over Christmas and New Year, I stopped writing my diary and letters to Georg. I'm always hopelessly melancholy and talk utter drivel at the end of the year.

[. . .]

New Year's Eve was modest. I was ill and ended up completely drunk after three glasses of wine. Günter had to bring me home, and then he went out on his own. Didn't bother me.

After New Year, I slaved away. Which succeeded in making me even more ill; had dizzy spells and terrorized everyone. But I finished the book.[40]

Georg wanted to get me a ticket to the Writers' Union Congress.[41] I wanted to go on Wednesday but on Tuesday I had to give up the idea: I was bleeding terribly and [Doctor] Grüning threatened me with childbed fever and other pleasantries. I cried and cursed but it didn't help [. . .].

Yesterday I got up again, today I worked, but [. . .] I feel nauseous as soon as I start and have constant headaches.

---

40 Refers to *Children of Hellas*, which was published in 1956.

41 Fourth Congress of the GDR Writers' Union, which took place from 9 to 14 January 1956.

Burg, 14.1.56[42]

[...]

After Christmas, I worked every day for at least twelve hours on my story 'Children of Hellas'. [...] I know how it should be written—but can't do it. A complete eunuch!

[...] Today I worked again, wrote the report for the writers' group—I was honest and so I was slated. But I'm still finding work difficult; I have constant, terrible headaches. Despite this, I'm going to start my love stories on Monday. 'It's a damned hard job, that's for sure. But there's no other career I'd die for,' as Michael Vierkant[43] said.

Helena has been published. It was just a booklet but I still expected to feel more joy and pride as a young author. Strange that wishes rarely come true—fulfilment doesn't exist [...].

Burg, 31.1.56

I'm working and getting a lot done. I've written two novellas in less than two weeks and I think they're better than anything I've done before.

Our writers' group conference was the highlight of the past weeks [...]. We had to give reports and mine caused a stir—no kidding! [...]

My report was unexpectedly successful too: oh and I won over Rainer Kunze[44] (he basically says the same as me in his report—we're the only real disciples, enthusiasts who believe in our vocation with wonderful delusions of grandeur).

Rainer—my sworn enemy! [...]

42 This entry was underlined in the original.

43 The protagonist in Leonhard Frank's autobiographical novel *Links, wo das Herz ist* [Heart on the Left], 1959.

44 Reiner Kunze (b. 1933); mostly spelt by B.R. as 'Rainer'. Writer and GDR dissident, Kunze left SED following the invasion of Czechoslovakia in 1968 and was eventually expatriated by the GDR regime to West Germany in 1977. While in the GDR, he published his work under various pseudonyms.

Burg, 5.2.56

[...]

Back to that memorable evening of reconciliation with Rainer!

[...] He told me [?] some unpleasant truths about my gullibility, which really got to me—because he's absolutely right. He made me promise that I'd turn to him if I had any kind of private problems because people think of him as my enemy, as he put it, but he's the person in the group who understands me best.

And then—I can't remember for the life of me how—we began to flirt. [...] He separated me from other admirers, and took me home, to the hotel. [...] We walked for an hour or so through the night. And then we kissed. Rarely has a kiss stirred me as deeply as Rainer's.

I always thought he was a communist, and a knight of fidelity and chastity, but now I wonder what made him open up to me like that. [...]

The following morning, I was demonstrably cool towards Rainer, kept him at arm's length, and thought I'd been mistaken. Then we talked for a long time about communism and morality and about the position of the artist in society. I'm very proud that Rainer confided in me that he feels very distant from the collective. He's an individualist and not the dogmatist I took him for. [...] because the whole thing moved me quite deeply, I think this experience will find its way into a story.

When we voted for the new working-group leadership, Rainer nominated me. So now I'm part of the collective's leadership with the approval of all my friends, and that makes me proud and happy.

[...]

Burg, 15.2.56

Georg sent me a postcard from Düsseldorf. He's on a trip through West Germany—hopefully he'll come back!

I celebrated Rosenmontag[45] and had a great time. As Günter was out getting sloshed again, I went off on my own in my Chinese costume, which caused a real stir. [. . .] It's amazing how many attractive men there are out there! [. . .] But I was really happy when my Frog showed up at around one o'clock. His presence always makes me feel protected—he's so strong and good. [. . .]

At five in the morning, Günter started a fight—he thought I'd been insulted—and sprained his thumb. [. . .]

27.2.56[46]

I've finished two novellas, *Corn Flowers* and *The Lamppost*. The third novella, *Girl on the Border*, won't come together, so I've put it aside for now. Instead, I've started on a new story: 'Giorgiu Wears the Mask'.[47]

Work is a slog again. I work in a quarterly rhythm anyway. Sometimes I fiddle about for weeks on niggly things and can't finish, then I get a rush and write reams in a frenzy in a few days.

Yesterday I heard back from NL at long last, and it was good news: the *Berliner Zeitung* has accepted my *Woman in the Pillory* and is going to publish it in instalments. The publicity department asked for my permission. It obviously wasn't necessary. That same day it was advertised (as a 'novel'!) and it starts today. I'm proud—the *BZ* with all its readers! And they were the ones who deflowered me in the literary sense: about eight years ago they published my first short story, which nowadays I'd call a rough draft at best.

I sometimes wonder if I'd already guessed or known at that time that I'd write a novel. I'll have to look through my old diaries

45 Rosenmontag (Rose Monday), which falls before Shrove Tuesday, is the highlight of German Karneval (carnival).

46 This entry and the next were underlined in the original.

47 'Kornblumen', 'Der Laternenpfahl', 'Mädchen an der Grenze' and 'Die Maske trägt Giorgiu': unpublished works. In the BRS, only the story 'Die Maske trägt Giorgiu' has been preserved.

to find out. It can't all be about my daily changing loves, great and small. Or didn't I take writing seriously back then? Perhaps I saw it as a casual pursuit? That's possible—I was dying to be a director[48] . . . Talking of which: I don't take care of my own interests enough. I still haven't got in touch with the Defa.[49] I am supposed to write a screenplay! I wouldn't want the chance of fulfilling my old childhood dream to slip away and—even if it's only for a few weeks—to direct, i.e. hang about as an assistant. Because a real director—no, I don't even dare dream about it any more . . . What's the point? I have a wonderful job—the most wonderful job in the world!

Burg, 8.3.56

[. . .]

I almost forgot the most important thing: my book's arrived! I saw it for the first time at Leipzig Book Fair, and it was strange to see it on public display. In fact, it was a sobering moment and I was disappointed because I didn't feel anything I'd dreamt of—that overwhelming joy.

That only came when my publisher sent me my copies and I was alone with my book. It's quite fantastic after all, and I'm very proud and happy. I even read it again—it seemed new, almost foreign and I was really on edge about how the plot would develop— even though I was so sick of it, and thought I couldn't touch it any more because I almost knew it off by heart.

My family is really proud, of course, especially Lutz and Günter, who are doing a wonderful PR job. I think the Frog is really happy about my book—because I dedicated my first work to him . . .

48 'Originally, I wanted to study theatre studies and become a director. I passed the qualifying examination at the Theaterhochschule Weimar [Weimar Theatre Academy], but had to quit my studies at the beginning of the semester because of an accident that made acting impossible' (B.R. in a resumé from 7 April 1954, in SVA, B.R. dossier).

49 Refers to the DEFA (which B.R. always wrote as 'Defa'): Deutsche Film-Aktiengesellschaft (German Film Company), a film-production company founded in 1946 in the Soviet Occupation Zone; from 1952, a state-owned enterprise.

Burg, 15.3.56

Yesterday evening I came back from Berlin where I'd been revising 'Children of Hellas' with the Verlag der KVP.[50] I sat with Gruner all afternoon in the Adlon—he's not easy [to] work with because he's easily distracted [. . .]! But on the other hand, he cuts me a lot of slack, and I can run riot with my style; he's easily persuaded too, which is a risk because I need a tight rein, and he [. . .] lets me get away with things Lewerenz, for example, would cut.

I got to know a new editor at the publishers, Lieutenant Colonel Strahl:[51] a fresh, temperamental young man, just a year older than me. Everything that followed was down to the fact that, coincidentally, it was Panitz's household leave day.[52] When Strahl asked me why I wanted to speak to P., I said as a joke: 'Actually I'm just looking for someone to go out with tonight.' He laughed, and offered to accompany me. I inspected him and liked the look of him, and as I didn't want to spend a Berlin evening in bed, I took up his offer.

He arrived punctually in the hotel foyer at 7 p.m., and we drove to the Press Club,[53] which you can only enter with an ID (St. is a member of the Writers' Union as well as the Press Club). We were served a splendid wine—a white Bordeaux, the best I've ever tasted.

[. . .] We were slightly blotto by the time we arrived at the Hafen Bar, a dance bar with intimate lighting and garish decor, a wild band, and 'atmosphere' [. . .]. Rudi is a fine companion [. . .] and it was morning by the time he brought me back to my hotel.

50 In the meantime, it had been renamed Verlag des Ministeriums für Nationale Verteidigung (see note 16).

51 Rudi Strahl (1931–2001): German playwright, novelist and poet. He was one of the most widely performed playwrights of the GDR. He was member of the Volkspolizei from 1950 to 1959, during which he worked at the Verlag des Ministeriums für Nationale Verteidigung.

52 Every person who ran a household had one day a month off work to attend to domestic chores.

53 The club of the Union of Journalists (Verband der Journalisten, VDJ), GDR Writers' Union, in the Admiralspalast, Friedrichstraße 101, Berlin.

[. . .] But the incredible thing is I don't have a guilty conscience. [. . .] I'm young, I'm sensual and my passion is quickly kindled, and I have an awful fear of ageing. So why shouldn't I enjoy life? In ten or twenty years, it'll all be over anyway—if I don't die first.

Perhaps it's mean, at least towards Günter, who loves me so fiercely. He tortures me with his jealous questions, and I've become so evil and arrogant. It's a real mess, and sometimes I think I'm a bad person. Yes, my conscience pricks me. [. . .] I feel regret, and yet I don't. I feel a strange mixture of revulsion and joy, good memories and guilty feelings. [. . .] I'm just a really superficial person. [. . .] I need attention and affirmation because I have terrible inferiority complexes.

[. . .]

Burg, 24.3.1956

In essence, everything that's written in a diary is a lie—or it's all just a half-truth, and half-truths are lies too.

I've been plagued more than I care to admit by something you'd probably call a 'conscience': over the past few days, I've reflected a lot and it's awful that I can't even write it down. Perhaps I will put all this into one of my characters, perhaps into Martina from the Jewish book that was inspired by Rheinsberg. [. . .] And I just have to get that period out of my system. [. . .]

I can't seem to get any further with my writing; with every line, a whole new book flits through my mind, driving me quite crazy. [. . .] I want to settle a score with myself, get some insight, and, with it, clarity.

It just occurs to me that I should hang that splendid Heine saying over my bed:

'Beat the drum and do not fear / Kiss the market woman'[54]

54 Heinrich Heine, quoted in Hannah Arendt, *Reflections on Literature and Culture* (Stanford, CA: Stanford University Press, 2007), p. 286.

Burg, 24.3.56[55]

[...]

Since then I have been congratulated many times, drunk to my debut[56] a dozen times and received the first reviews. A second edition is already coming out, the *Hamburger Volkszeitung* is going to publish it in instalments—and now I'm painfully unhappy, and want to write it all over again from the beginning. That is, I wouldn't want to because my love stories have consumed me, but I just don't like the *Woman* any more. It's a cross to bear! I ask myself what others see in it; it's badly written, and only works because of the plot (to which, incidentally, a lot of petty bourgeois have taken umbrage).

Most of all, I'm plagued by a new book, *A Star Falls in a Human Heart*.[57] I can see Martina, she's me ... it will be a confessional book [...]. And Stefan Rad is Georg; I've known that for a long time, and I'm not pretending otherwise. [...]

I think I'm unhappy and perhaps that's why I've been throwing myself into new adventures but can't find peace [...]. Sometimes I could cry out in pain, but I'm not even sure what is torturing me so much. I'm often so afraid of the unknown I'm worried I might take poison again one day [58]—but this time, I won't let Günter intervene so quickly!

Perhaps spring is just making me crazy, and Georg would probably make some cynical remark about the biological causes of my

---

55 This entry was underlined in the original.

56 *Woman in the Pillory* was B.R.'s first published hardback.

57 *Ein Stern fällt in ein Menschenherz* (untraceable).

58 'After a terrible marriage dispute, I took poison [...]. I have always said that I was happy in my marriage—in truth it almost killed me' (letter from 7 April 1954, in *Brigitte Reimann in ihren Briefen und Tagebüchern. Eine Auswahl* [Brigitte Reimann in Her Letters and Diaries: A Selection], Elisabeth Elten-Krause and Walter Lewerenz [eds]. Berlin: Neues Leben, 1983).

desperate mood. And that's what I have to pass on to Martina—
perhaps it'll help. It's like a confession [. . .].

Burg, 28.3.56

Georg's silence is eating at my heart. [. . .] I dream about him more
and more often—and they're such awful dreams! I see his face perfectly clearly, hear his voice; it says such terrible things [. . .] and
then he shuts a door behind me, and I sit outside on a rock and cry.
It hurts so much that I still feel the pain when I wake up, and for
hours I'm at the mercy of my memories of Georg.

[. . .]

Life has not been kind to me for a long time—it's been ghastly.
I have everything I could wish for on the one hand, but none of the
things I want. On the outside, everything's going as well as it possibly could. I have a good husband, have a book published, have
contracts for new books, have money, have a comfy room, and I
have the looks (and can dress) to attract men aplenty—for a day or
a week or longer, whatever takes my fancy. But in truth? My ambition is unstoppable, I want to write good books, have fame—will I
ever have it? I'm mortally afraid of getting old; I've dedicated myself
entirely to love and cannot imagine life without men's admiring
glances, kisses and flattery. And the one man who will always be
the fairy-tale prince of my dreams will never be mine, not in all
eternity. I'm deeply unhappy.

Burg, 30.4.56

I shouldn't take such long breaks. Now I don't know where to start.

[. . .]

It took a long time for me to deal with Georg—emotionally. I
think I've found myself. Today a letter from him arrived, and
his book *Erfurt*, which I corrected in Rheinsberg. His letter is very

official. And rightly so. Yet he still says that we have quite a few things left to discuss. Fine, I'll visit him on Wednesday. I hope I can stay matter-of-fact.

[. . .]

I'm almost ashamed to write down what I got up to two weeks ago in Magdeburg. If I had written it down then it would have been a very long, very romantic, very infatuated story . . .

[Werner] Havemann and Lewerenz from my publisher's came to our writers' conference. In the evening, we went to a ball together—far out of town. First, we drank wine, then the others slowly slipped off. Walter and I stayed.

And then it started; it had been long overdue. We danced, drank, flirted. But it wasn't just the usual flirt; it was pure torture. We like each other, and have done for a long time, and perhaps that evening we fell in love. [. . .]

Past midnight we went into the back room and had a long talk. Except that we didn't talk about anything, just chatted about trivial stuff to avoid having to talk about the real stuff, and when our eyes met, we jumped. To be honest, I didn't know I was mostly just play-acting; I'm never honest, and basically everything's a lie anyway.

Finally, Walter asked me straight out why we were kidding ourselves, playing such stupid games. [. . .] It was all [. . .] so unfathomable, so unclear. I could've laughed and cried at the same time . . .

In the morning we drove back into town. It wasn't worth going to bed any more. We sat down in the club and carried on talking. [. . .] And all of a sudden, we flung ourselves around each other's necks and kissed, and kissed. Until the others turned up . . . It's all very difficult to understand.

[. . .] But I'm not so smitten with him we won't be able work together in professionally. [. . .]

Burg, 7.5.56

[. . .] I went to Berlin for three days and have come home a few centimetres slimmer. Sorrow and alcohol have taken their toll on me.

[. . .]

I got on with the people from the Defa—that is, everything was fine as long as Renner,[59] the nice, shy, enthusiastic dramaturge, sat next to me—and I was willing to write the detective screenplay they wanted. But since then, I've had some serious misgivings and I'd much rather cancel the whole thing. Having said that, a screenplay would sort me out financially . . .

The Defa definitely wants to make a film with me, in any case; I'm not sure why they've hit on me—Renner thanked me with gushing enthusiasm when I agreed.

[. . .]

On the first evening, I went to the Hafen Bar with Lewerenz. We drank a bottle of bubbly and danced, and at the beginning everything was just as unclear and awkward as it was in Magdeburg. [. . .] I used all my skills of seduction and there's probably some truth in what Walter says, that I just want to get my kicks out of him. I wanted to see a fallen angel . . .

[. . .]

He was supposed to go home at 2 a.m. but missed the train, and we stood there like two teenagers in a doorway and kissed for hours with increasing passion, although we had long since sobered up, [. . .] and Walter showed a spirit I didn't think he possessed.

He must like me an awful lot, otherwise—strict and duty-bound as he is—he would have gone home the following evening instead of coming by again. We had been working on the book at

---

59 Wenzel Renner (b. 1924): dramaturge at the DEFA between 1955 and 1960.

the publisher's that afternoon to give it the finishing touches before the next edition.

While doing this, I freely admit I started to cry because Walter heaped insults on me and described my book as total rubbish—kitsch that no revisions could improve. Unfortunately, I lost control a little—I threw the book into a corner, and screamed, running riot until I'd calmed down again, demanding that the next edition be cancelled. Walter kept some semblance of calm and waited for me to wind down.

Then we went to the Johannishof where I was staying in a comfortable room, and we carried on working there. But soon it was Walter's turn—as I was leaning on his shoulder, pretending to be matter-of-fact, he threw the book aside. He was angry: the bloody thing wasn't going to get any better, why on earth was he wasting his time on such a thing—and I was an idiot and just wanted to drive him crazy, and tomorrow I would fall in love with someone else. Then he took me in his arms [. . .].

The situation tipped into something precarious after a while—but at nine, Georg phoned and said he was waiting downstairs in the hotel foyer, [. . .] and I threw on my cocktail dress, and Walter left.

I spent the evening with Georg at the bar in the Johannishof. We spent the last three hours glued to our bar stools slurping cocktails I'd never even heard of before. Georg got all worked up at the sight of my plunging décolleté, and we had a lot of fun. He asked me whether I wouldn't get a divorce—but strangely, especially in the company of other men, I feel more tenderly in love with the Frog than usual.

[. . .]

On the third day, I met Georg in the Niquet-Keller. I had been a little afraid of seeing him again, but with Georg you just can't be sentimental. [. . .] So, I acted as if I didn't care, I was even cold-hearted, and that fiend had his fun with me. To tell the truth, I sometimes took a sidelong glance at him and tried to find the emotion I once felt. It's buried, or has completely disappeared, I don't really know.

I bragged terribly, saying I'd slept with other men. Perhaps it just proves that I'm not completely indifferent to him.

We had a fierce row about literature and avoided private matters. We were friends in the way we should've been from the start, and we hardly spoke a word about the past. It was both terrible and good. It's too early for me to write about it yet [. . .]. By my behaviour, I wanted to convince Georg that I didn't love him any more, and I think I succeeded. Except that when he implied he'd like to sleep with me one more time, I got upset. Not with Georg! With anyone else—but not with him, because I loved him so passionately.

As we were saying goodbye, we shook hands and said, 'Take care.' And with that, the dreaded 'heart-to-heart' was over. I only felt sad once I was walking down the street alone—that a love like that had to end this way. [. . .]

Burg, 3.7.56

I haven't felt like dealing with my diary for a long time—it's all a sham. The whole world is a web of lies; I should just hang myself. But I don't have the courage, so things just drift along and sometimes I pretend I'm happy.

We went to Ahrenshoop for a fortnight. It was rotten: the weather was terrible, there was no toilet, no culture—I was bored to death by myself. The Frog, who is so refreshingly naive or stupid or healthy that he doesn't brood on things, deserves a different wife.

I haven't seen Walter again, or Georg [. . .]—basically I don't care about either of them. And I'm certain that they don't care about me either. How could it be otherwise? We aren't that different from animals and plants, which only exist for their own sake. This whole earth deserves to perish.

What pains me the most is that none of my ideas find their way into my books—my characters are optimistic, heroic and untrue, like nearly all the characters in novels I know: I find them convincing while I'm reading their story, but later I sense how all writing is hollow.

I sometimes wonder if other people feel the way I do, or whether I'm ill—whether it's not the world that's sentenced to death but me. Yet I can't talk to anyone about it: either they lie or they're stupid, and so we prattle nonsense about the success of books, and new acquisitions, and money, and politics, and love . . .

And yet I'm attached to this numb existence, and I'm hoping for some kind of miracle; and I do feel good when something happens that might be filed under 'happiness'.

I've fallen in love again. In fact, I've been in love with this man for four years, but up until now it's been platonic. Wolfgang Schreyer[60] has often written to me, sometimes visited, and we've often spent time together—always behaving ourselves, always just as friends [. . .].

Last week he visited me again and we drove out to his house in the country. Near Möser [?], we discovered a pretty spot in the woods [. . .]. First, we talked quite sensibly, although I was quite self-conscious lying in the middle of nowhere next to a young, attractive man. Then the usual flirtation began: we tickled each other with stalks of grass, played the 'good comrade' towards each other, and yet both of us knew exactly where we were heading [. . .].

The afternoon went as expected: kissing, caressing, stroking, sun, love, etc. Wolfgang has the soft skin of a girl, and his green eyes with their long, curling lashes are very beautiful. [. . .] I'm

---

60 Wolfgang Schreyer (1927–2017): German writer of fiction, historical adventures and science fiction for television and film.

looking forward to our next trip. The way this will all end is clear to us both, but I'm still too weak to act. Vile!

Berlin, Johannishof, 30.8.56

This is my third day in Berlin, and for the first time in months I feel that life is worth living again—at least for some hours at a time. The past two months have been horrible—no work, no alcohol, no cigarettes. I was pregnant[61] and suffered a lot, as much from constant nausea as from—above all—the idleness that consumed me. [. . .]

I found a doctor in West Berlin to operate on me. I haven't quite recovered, probably because instead of lying in bed, I started work again immediately, and at an intensive pace because I wanted to fulfil my contract (for a film treatment) with the Defa on time. I actually managed to write the treatment in three days, earning 1,250 DM a day, which is no mean feat; no doubt about it, it's a substantial fee, and it makes my income from 'serious literary work' pale in comparison. But I will still start on my book as soon as the film is finished because the subordinate role of the screenwriter in film production doesn't satisfy my ambition at all. (Incidentally, my second story, *Children of Hellas*, has been published. Some say it's better than the *Woman* but only its language is; I find the concept very awkward. Rainer, who I gave it to, likes it very much.) [. . .]

On Tuesday, I went to little Lewerenz at the publishing house as I had a summons to go to the Defa the following day. [. . .]

We went to a very old wine bar, the Münze on Spittelmarkt, where Berger was waiting for us while drinking with Panitz and Djacenko[62] on the pretence of carrying out business negotiations.

---

61 B.R. had a premature birth back in January 1954.

62 Boris Djacenko (1917–75): German writer of Latvian origin. In 1957, Berger's efforts to publish the sequel of Djacenko's 1954 novel *Heart and Ashes* was stopped owing to novel's 'anti-Soviet tendencies', following which he wrote detective stories under the pseudonym Peter Addams.

Berger had asked me to accompany Lewerenz, and he would have been only too happy to get me together with Berger; Berger, with whom he would have had pleasure in pairing me off, as he said. My arch enemy, of all people! Only two days ago I'd been adamant that Berger, the most obnoxious man I know, couldn't stand me at all; I was so convinced I didn't even waste a flirtatious glance on him. Even that would have been too much effort for someone who claims no woman can tempt him [. . .].

Boris Djacenko is a pleasant person; very lively, and eloquent. He makes mistakes in German, and his Slavic accent makes his funny expressions even odder. He often has to ask what the word for this or that is in German. He was looking for a word—'What is name of cupboard where you put sausage in before it rots?'—and beamed when he found it: 'refrigerator'. His smile stretched across his Eastern, very masculine boy's face. I think he knows how attractive he is and flirts a little with his lack of vocabulary.

He and Panitz left early. We were already heavy with wine and stayed, all three of us, although I had arranged a rendezvous with George.[63] (I've just remembered: If Püschel comes back and tries to get close to me because his rival has left the field clear, things'll get a little tricky; [. . .] manoeuvring my way around a publishing house making each man feel he's the chosen one [. . .]—I might have to change publishers.) Berger persuaded us to go back to his place—he's divorced and now lives alone—to listen to his Brecht tapes.

We went to Pankow, already quite sloshed. I don't know how it happened that my attention slowly turned to Berger. Perhaps due to a remark he made, and seemed to mean: he felt like Joseph in my presence and that's why he was so spiky [. . .]. In short, we listened to Brecht songs from the *Threepenny Opera*, then to a couple of excellent jazz recordings, then to Kate Kühl's horrifying lullabies,

63 Georg-Hans Steinbring: a classmate of B.R. at school and member of her amateur drama group in Burg.

and then we were feeling down and needed a couple of sugary tear-jerkers to get our morale back on an even keel.

We danced. When Berger went to make some tea, I danced with Walter. When will the boy finally understand the feelings that move the woman in his arms, and draw his own conclusions! [...]

In the end, Walter left and I was alone, slightly against my will, with Herr Berger. At midnight, he really was still Herr Berger to me, and I'd only stolen the odd glance at him until then, because he fascinated me, much against my better judgement. He looks like Mephisto—the way I imagine Mephisto, in any case, with large, beautiful eyes (slanting Mongolian ones like mine) his slightly bent nose, his impossible mouth, his little Van Dyke beard. ... And his detestable laughter—penetratingly harsh, bleating, cynical and painfully clever.

At first, I was terribly self-conscious despite my skinful of wine; it's an odd feeling to sit well past midnight alone in a room with a man that you don't trust, or who isn't even familiar. But he knows how to put people at ease. [...]

I stayed the night with him. We slept together on his couch, where there was easily enough space for three or four people, and I was very happy. I didn't let him seduce me, which astonished both of us. When he first told me that he likes me very much, I laughed at him and believed it. [...] It's good to feel power over a man who fights back stubbornly against this power—first not acknowledging it, then succumbing to it. It's a shame [...] I can't take anything seriously, or have to pretend not to take anything seriously—I think something has died in me since my thing with Piltz. 'Sensuality and naivety' is what Piltz said, and which Lewerenz thought he could read from my expression. Only the sensuality remains. My precious naivety, which I think back on wistfully like a childhood memory, has vanished [...]. I'm sometimes so cold-hearted it even feels frighteningly strange to me. [...]

Yesterday afternoon I went to the Defa. Renner thinks my treatment is excellent. It's good to be able to work with Renner, a gift—he's a very good person, I think. [. . .] I'd like to know what kinds of depths of despair someone like Renner feels; are there skeletons in his closet too? [. . .] He doesn't look at me the way most men look at women. When I'm with him, I feel as though I'm in a cool, warm, still, gently stirring forest. [. . .]

Berlin, Niquet-Keller, 30.8.56

I have to finish my story. At the moment, I'm sitting waiting for my interview with the chief dramaturge, Böhm[64] (R. claims he likes me so much, I'm the only person he has time for—because of *The Woman in the Pillory*.) [. . .]

Yesterday evening was wonderful. The men acted like cockerels around a hen. Lewerenz didn't clear the field; Ernst[65] and I went back to saying *Sie* to each other, hurled nasty accusations and then, when we were both slightly drunk, exchanged compliments, outdoing each other in niceties. [. . .] How stupid all this is! [. . .] In the end, the three of us slouched on our barstools [. . .] trying to be cynical, not that it suits any of us, and yet it was close to the truth. Even Walter, who sneered as he expressed his contempt for the world, looked terribly sweet. They wanted to persuade me to go with them to Pankow, but I'm not a pervert after all. So, I behaved myself and slipped under the covers of my hotel bed, put Günter's picture on the side table and there was no need to feel ashamed.

Those days in Berlin are like dark-red roses in the simple posy of my provincial existence—but they have such a strong scent that I can barely take more than three; otherwise I'd overdose.

64 Rudolf Böhm (1917–97): chief dramaturge at DEFA; dismissed without notice in 1958.

65 Karl Heinz Berger, whom B.R. refers to here and over the next few pages as 'Ernst' (see note 20).

Berlin Pankow, 31.8.56

I'm still at Ernst's flat; he already left for the publisher's offices. [...] I cried like a teenager—how could I lose myself to this unpleasant man? Am I just lying or do I really love him? I can't tell the difference any more between truth and lies.

I made love with Ernst last night. I think I could spend a lifetime together with him.

Burg, 6.9.56

The day before yesterday, Ernst was at my flat. I wasn't expecting him until the afternoon. When I came into the room after getting back from town and saw him, I was ecstatic [...].

He'd come on the pretence of having a down-to-earth talk with me, the married woman, and appealing to my conscience—but for the first few moments when we saw each other again, he forgot his fine intentions and was just foolish and infatuated [...]. I don't know what fascinates him so much: doesn't he see my wickedness, my falseness? I don't know whether I'm just play-acting for both of us. [...]

He had wanted to travel back to Berlin in the afternoon, but when I asked him, he stayed until the evening—only too gladly, I flatter myself.

No, I can't write. I'm so mixed up. [...] Sometimes I'm afraid of going mad or committing suicide. Does it take so much courage to go [?] from here to there?

Burg, 29.9.56

I spent four sweet, blessed, wonderful days in Berlin—now it's back to Burg and everyday life and work and the Frog.

I left on Sunday—to see Ernst, of course. [...]

I can hardly remember what I did in Berlin; it was a whirlwind, a mad rush, a blur—much lovemaking. The best part was the publisher's party. Lots of people gave lots of speeches at the official celebrations in the Press Club [. . .]; it was very ceremonious but a bit boring. Afterwards we drove to the Zenner in Treptow where there was a huge set meal and wine and bubbly and cocktails and sexy music. I could hardly move for men, many of whom asked me to dance before the music started, and—soon tipsy—I was passed from one pair of arms to the next. What a pity that Ernst isn't the jealous type! [. . .]

The most ardent suitor was a young Czech, the director of the Prague Youth Publishing House. He already showed up at the first dance and wouldn't let me go. His name's Chemir [. . .] and he has beautiful, dark eyes—red-hot! [. . .]

People said that we were dancing very close and making bedroom eyes. But that's slander. Still I was deeply impressed, then flirted with a dozen gentlemen, and Ernst besides [. . .].

At the bar, I fell into the clutches of a children's publishing director, Rodrian—a pretty, aggressive man. He proved himself extremely—and I mean *extremely*—charming towards me. At one point, I toasted to friendship with Walter Lewerenz—just an excuse for us to kiss [. . .].

When it was over—much too early, just as I was getting into the mood—Rodrian walked me to the bus [. . .]. And there, the son of a gun managed to kiss me, as if by accident. I was completely baffled [. . .].

There are a few disadvantages to living with your lover. You can't do exactly as you please. [. . .]

The next morning we overslept, of course. I think the whole publishing house is smirking at us. I feel very at home with Ernst. When I'm with him, it's as if we were married—but it's much nicer because we aren't. I answer the phone with my own name, quite unabashed. I almost don't care what others think.

The negotiations with Defa went well. It's a pleasure to work with Renner—maybe precisely because I don't flirt with him. When men throw lewd glances, it sometimes makes me sick, but Ernst says it's my own fault because I look like some kind of sex bomb, and there's something a bit coarse about me, and that's what turns them all on.

I met Piltz again, just for an hour. There's just a trace of the old magic left in him. He gets more and more caustic when he talks about *our literature*, and I end up being thoroughly annoyed with him, but I still admire him and would sometimes like to kiss him.

[...]

On the last day, I went to the publishing house. The whole editorial department had read the first chapter of the *The Informer*[66] and were full of praise. [...]

Ernst took me to the Press Club, where I'd arranged to meet Chemir. Unfortunately, I left him waiting an hour and a half—not unintentionally—and then my stupidity and cowardice bothered me after all. [...]

I sat in the Press Club to wait for the night train and worked on my book, accompanied by French brandy. I was restless—somehow the atmosphere was charged [...]—and anyway I felt a little insane. We miss out on too many beautiful things for stupid moral reasons. Who knows how long I have left to live!

66 The story takes place at the high school of a small town. Eva, a fervent FDJ member, accuses a teacher of indoctrinating students with reactionary thought. Because the teacher is very popular, no one believes her. He is only exposed when he talks disrespectfully about the antifascist struggle, and then flees to West Germany. B.R. had been working on the manuscript of *The Informer* since 1952. On 15 October 1952 she gave the first two chapters to Aufbau Verlag with the request to forward it to Anna Seghers. In May 1953 she sent the novel to Mitteldeutscher Verlag, Halle. Because the decision-making process at the Mitteldeutscher Verlag took a long time, she gave the manuscript in February 1955 to Neues Leben , who wanted to publish it. Meanwhile she had written the first part of *Die Frau am Pranger* [The Woman in the Pillory], which the publisher preferred. In mid-1955 B.R. was no longer convinced of the version of *The Informer* that existed at the time. She revised it several times.

[...]

My conscience didn't prick me until I was standing in the Frog's room and saw he had filled all the vases with flowers, tidied up and made everything nice for my return.

[...] He didn't give me the third degree but repeated that he would definitely leave me if I cheated on him.

But I think I know only too well that he won't leave me, and his speeches annoy me. To test him, I started—half seriously, half tongue-in-cheek—to make a confession. And what do you know? He bent over me and said, very fast and afraid: 'Be quiet, don't tell me anything ever again. I don't want to know.' [...]

Potsdam–Sacrow, 19.10.56

This is my fifth day at the Lieselotte Hermann House for the Defa writers' seminar and I already feel quite settled—in fact, I'd rather not go home at all this evening.

On Saturday and Sunday, I was at Ernst's. He came back from Leipzig in the evening—and there I was, already lying comfortably on his couch, teddy in my arms, and I think he was happy to see me. We read Ringelnatz all night long, argued about modern painting, and I let him play me 'Mack the Knife' of course.

[...]

On Sunday morning, we read from the Bible for hours—the Book of Ruth and the Song of Solomon. At moments like these, we're very close. I'm glad to have him—and perhaps we'll become good friends. Although he sometimes treats me as like I'm a child, he actually thinks I'm mature and wise beyond my years. And he appreciates my work, and teaches me good, clever things.

[...] In the evening, my usual despair set in because Ernst made some cynical remark (even though I know his cynicism isn't real), and I cried bitterly. First, he laughed at me, but then he suddenly kissed my hands and said very seriously, 'Child, when you're that sad, I want to say: Move in with me, let's get married'.

But I wouldn't want to marry him—even if the Frog weren't there. We still row all the time, and after a week we'd get on each other's nerves terribly. We're clashing opposites and can't put up with each other for more than three days in a row. What's more, he's the archetypal lone wolf and doesn't like to have people around [. . .]. And God help me, I must be the most difficult, troublesome woman he could find. [. . .]

On Monday morning, I left for Potsdam after a tender parting from Ernst. I missed the ferry and Böhm had me taken by car to Sacrow. All the writers and dramaturges were already gathered there. Wenzel Renner, Jürgen Lenz—very masculine, an almost handsome man—Annemarie Reinhard, a handful of lesser-known writers, then Hans Buchmayer, a good-looking, funny young man, and Herbert Otto, also young and small, the author of the successful novel, *The Lie*.[67]

[. . .] In short, we were divided into groups each led by a dramaturge, and we will work on the films we've already started [. . .]. We won't be tortured by too much theory—mostly two hours set aside for lectures in the mornings, held by some or other name in the film business. Rodenberg was there, Slatan Dudov, Werzlau, Gerd Klein, and others will be coming. There'll be screenings for us in the studio in Babelsberg; yesterday *Murderers among Us* and *Marriage in the Shadows*—I cried bitterly. We've already visited the film studios too.

I haven't written a single word so far—like almost everyone else. It's like being on holiday. It's absolutely gorgeous here. A huge, heavy solitude. The beautiful house lies in the middle of a gigantic park, which itself is surrounded by woods and lakes.

Sometimes you hear a steamship's horn blowing in the distance, ravens cawing or wild geese crying—otherwise the silence is like a

---

67 *Die Lüge.*

wall. Day after day, a mild autumn sun shines, and the trees shimmer like gold; in the gardens, the last flowers are in bloom. I've landed myself a single room in the attic; it's warm and cosy, with a soft down duvet and a desk and armchairs. The windows face east and in the morning the sun comes in.

The food is excellent—to the detriment of my slim figure. We stroll around in the park during the day, in the evening we mostly sit in the library and tell jokes—it's incredible how much time is spent messing about here. We're invariably in a fun mood, and during mealtimes there's much laughter and the occasional good conversation.

On the very first day I made friends with Herbert Otto. [. . .] We've been roaming through the park and chatting—but our views are dissimilar on many things [. . .].

In the evening, we were sitting over a bottle of cognac in my room. Otto was telling me about himself: he studied in Moscow after he'd been a prisoner of war [. . .]. I was a bit tipsy and took a liking to him. I thought I might take him as my sweetheart for six weeks.

And the next day, I got to know the dramaturge Wolfgang Ebeling. [. . .]

He's young—twenty-eight—tall, handsome, with a girl's mouth and beautiful blue eyes.

After lunch, we went for a walk through the park [. . .] and kept a polite distance. He should have been working with his mentees but every time we approached the house during our rounds, we found ourselves immersed in a discussion of an important problem and had to turn around again. He made the greatest conceivable effort to explain dialectics to me, and I pretended to be more stupid than I already am, and tormented him with questions. He wanted to see the naive little girl in me, like most men who approach me, so I played up to that role—so perfectly that the next day, when I proved to him that I wasn't, he was completely floored. [...]

Then the following day Wolf came to my room to say goodbye as he had to go back into town.

[...] I was in very high spirits and let him have a taste of yet another Brigitte, so that in the end he just didn't know what was real and pretence. A dramaturge looked in at one point with a terribly discreet expression on his face [...]. All at once, Wolf said he was sad to have to leave. I automatically said 'Me too,' turning it into a stupid joke. He laughed and drew me onto the armchair, and all at once we were kissing and knew that we'd been waiting for this kiss all the time. [...] Wolf says that he is a bit sentimental. I like that. I am too although I don't dare show it any more. But I'm allowed to with Wolf. I can say all the sweet silly things I have to hide when I'm around Ernst. [...]

That night he came to me. We lay on my bed. At last I was allowed to be myself—I didn't have to put on a show of cold-heartedness, scorn, cleverness, maturity and all that nonsense. Wolf loves me as I am; it's the very reason he loves me. He says that I'm delightfully natural and should keep my naturalness. He knows so many affected, unnatural, coiffed-up women whom he's sick of, and only wants to be with me.

[...] I'm grateful he's not too pushy. [...]

After dinner.

Now things are getting complicated. Werner Reinowski has discovered he has a soft spot for me. [...]

Sacrow, 23.10.56

From Saturday to Sunday, I went home. Frog and I went to the Oktoberfest—in great style, with wine and bubbly. I was quite drunk and totally in love with the Frog, flirting with him as I did back in May the last time. Parting again was difficult. [...]

Now I am quite at home here, and Burg is far away. And so [. . .] is Günter [. . .].

Sacrow, 29.10.56

On Friday I stayed the night at Ernst's. He has a sweet, tiny cat with whom he speaks and plays tenderly as if it were a beloved child. But he doesn't like people, the peculiar fellow! Due to my new relationship with Wolf, I was able to assume an air of coolness and maturity. Ernst likes that. He would be less keen if he found out why, I suppose [. . .].

On Sunday, I met up with Wolfgang. We wanted to take a trip to Rheinsberg but the weather was so rotten—it was pouring with rain—that even the most beautiful town would have seemed bleak under that grey autumn sky.

We drank a bottle of bubbly to cheer ourselves up then travelled back to Sacrow—a completely rash undertaking, no doubt, as our dear colleagues exchanged looks and suspected something. We didn't rise to the bait.

We spent the afternoon in my room. [. . .] He admires me for my directness and freshness, and my naivety, so he says. [. . .] I have never met a man several years older than me who didn't think I was an innocent, simple little girl, and treated me accordingly. No one wants to believe that I have hidden depths (ooh!) . . .

[. . .]

I went to bed early that evening while Wolfgang—to keep up appearances—stayed chatting to the others in the lounge. Later he came to me. I didn't want to make it easy for him, really [. . .] We made love [. . .]. And how sweet and tender he was afterwards, when he turned the light back on so that he could see my face . . .

[. . .]

Wolf was sleeping next door in Schulz's room. I don't think I've talked about Schulz[68] yet, even though his role is not small in my Sacrow life; he not only knows about mine and Wolf's love and helps us in any way he can, he is also one of the most likeable, trustworthy people I have ever met. He is worthy of love, in the best sense. At first, I never even noticed him; there's a gentle cheerfulness about him, which isn't attention-seeking. [. . .]

He noticed I had fallen for Wolfgang straight away, and he warned me. I put flowers in his room, and he came over, very moved. [. . .] Now he's our confidante, covering up our escapades, and we can be open with him (he's one of those people who has to be everyone's confessor). [. . .]

I think he sees us as children (even though he's only a few years older) and shakes his head over our affair, half-amused, half-worried.

[. . .]

Sacrow, 30.10.56

Just last night I was in such good spirits [. . .]. And now I'm lurking in my room, a bottle of brandy in front of me, playing the world-weary woman. And [. . .] I have to get drunk to block out my thoughts.

[. . .]

Hans-Dieter visited me this afternoon with a press photographer; he wants a portrait for his newspaper. I was in a very good mood—until he left. Just before leaving, he told me [. . .] that he's heard rumours Günter has taken up with a girl. It nearly knocked me out.

I went straight to Schulz and told him—he knows how to listen and comfort. [. . .] I am deeply shaken. But why? Doesn't this

---

68 Max Walter Schulz (1921–91): writer and, in 1962–63, the secretary of the Writers' Union.

suggest a solution, or even salvation, come to that? How often have I toyed with the idea of leaving Günter but was afraid of all the pain I'd cause? [...] It would certainly be better if he lived with a simple, good, uncomplicated woman instead of me—we're just not the same intellectual level. We talk at cross purposes and don't under-stand each other in the slightest. But now [...] I could weep at the thought of separating.

Perhaps most of it is wounded pride [...]. Perhaps it's good he's found someone else, someone better, and we part. The route to Wolf would be clear. But Wolf? Would he [...] get a divorce [...]? And even if this enormous hurdle was cleared, do I love him so much I could build a new, more beautiful life with him? [...] I am a deep pessimist and don't believe in the kind of happiness I sometimes imagine. I'm condemned to being alone. Perhaps it's the best thing for my work. [...]

Sacrow, 1.11.56

Schulz came to me in the night, and we drank the rest of the bottle. I was sloshed and unhappy; we toasted to calling each other *Du* and gave each other a kiss. I don't know how it could have happened; well-behaved Joe [i.e. Schulz], comforter of souls and missionary, as he mockingly refers to himself, has fallen in love with Maja, the girl on the lotus flower ... And either knowingly or unknowingly—who's to decide?—I have pushed him further into his confusion, although in everything we talked about or did, Wolfgang was between us. [...]

Because of all my worries, I'd have probably slept with Joe. But he is the most loyal friend and didn't want to exploit my vulnerable state. He said he will leave his room every time Wolfgang is with me—he can't bear to know we're embracing and kissing in the next room. [...]

I don't know whether I'll tell Wolf about last night. Then he'd finally see some of the abject depths inside me. [...]

Sacrow, 9.11.56

It's midnight and I've been working the whole time. I've botched things with Joe because I squabbled with him—over a trifle; I just had to shake up our cosy togetherness a little bit. [. . .]

I spent Sunday back home. Hans-Dieter lied to me; Günter— how often have I said this already—is as true as gold [. . .]. We gleefully tormented each other, and in the end, I confessed my fondness for Wolf to him. He was very unhappy and madly jealous. And when I was at home, I understood again that I can't leave him— he is one of those rare people who could die from love. [. . .] Parting was painful. So painful that once I reached Sacrow that afternoon, I phoned Wolf and told him that I wouldn't be coming to Berlin as we'd planned.

Instead, I spent the evening with Joe—the fickleness of women. That's when it began. [. . .] At first, I was just pretending, as usual, deliberately making him lose his head, and in the end, I was stirred too. Joe is more mature than Wolf and in some ways reminds me of Günter. [. . .] I feel safe and a gentle, warm tenderness for him.

Joe puts me on a pedestal. He tries to understand me in vain, he sees both the angel and devil in me, naive child and cunning woman; he thinks I'm clever, talented, kind and at the same time capable of cruelty. I play out my countless roles in front of him, and he never knows which is true and which false. Oh and I don't know myself. [. . .] I don't let anyone get to my deepest core; no one should own me. Joe knows this, and it hurts him. He doesn't 'have' me, even in our most beautiful, intimate moments—somewhere inside me, an untouchable, untouched spot remains. He gets desperate when I make fun of him. He says I'm not capable of true love. Perhaps he's right. Perhaps I've never met a person I could give myself to entirely. I don't want to either. I want to hold onto myself. I don't want to give anything, but in doing so, I take whatever I need for my work from the people around me. I'm an egotist par excellence, and not even ashamed of it. [. . .]

I'm becoming more and more of a man-hater. That might sound like a paradox given all my romances but it's still true. I hate men's desire to possess, their hunting instinct, and wherever I can, I hurt them to keep and prove my independence.

A few days ago, things got serious between Joe and me. He came to me at night and we wanted to sleep next to each other, and it almost turned out that way too. But the time had obviously come. I made it difficult for him. He once said that a man likes to humiliate a woman, to floor her, before taking her. I couldn't forget he'd said that, and when he was blissfully happy holding me in his arms, I told him coldly that he shouldn't imagine he had me. He was sad; he thinks I'm as far away from him as I ever was. [...]

We're now sleeping together every night [...]. Yesterday Joe wept for joy. [...] Why do the good men lose themselves to me, of all people!

Wolf has been here in the meantime, thankfully for just a few hours, so that the necessary talk didn't take place. Incidentally, no matter what relations are like with Joe, I still have a soft spot for Wolf. When he played the piano in the evening, and looked at me adoringly with his beautiful lynx's eyes, I couldn't stop myself from throwing him a few fiery looks in return. When Joe approached me, jealous despite saying he wasn't, I steeled myself once more with *froideur*, and Wolf was more than a little confused.

[...]

Oh, and I've managed to inspire Joe to write a delightful comedy, *Venus in Corinthia*. At least I've generated something useful for once, even if indirectly. If Joe's material is a success with the Defa, the film's going to be a hit. [...]

Sacrow, 15.11.56

The pleasant—or rather delightful—news first. Yesterday we had a nice evening—informal, not forced in any way. I'd worked until eleven o'clock, because my deadline runs out today, and the treatment isn't even halfway finished. I went down to the lounge—the arc of the staircase! Going down it is an aesthetic pleasure—just to unwind for a moment.

Downstairs, I encountered a merry, already slightly tipsy group, who enthusiastically welcomed a female member and wouldn't let me leave. It was fine by me: I was already sick to death of my film treatment. We drank really heavily, there were a few kisses to 'everlasting friendship', and I let the men adore me. Most of them have taken a liking to me. Understandably, as I'm the only woman who is young and pretty.

[. . .]

Once the bottle was empty, and the high spirits were ebbing, the others retired, grinning because Conny [Schmidt] and I stayed to play a round of table tennis. We did play in fact, because tennis is my passion, and I always annoy men with my terrible dilettantism.

Afterwards we sat [. . .] on the stairs for another hour. [. . .] I was glad of the idolization, but then I was so damned sober I turned to serious things. Most men only become bearable when they talk about their area of expertise—then they stop thinking about all the rubbish in their heads for a moment. Over the past few years, I've had to listen to so many compliments and assurances, tender words and sweet lies, it makes me puke. [. . .]

[. . .] It was very nice and funny on the stairs—but unfortunately, most men don't understand when you're sick of it and want to be alone.

I crept over to Joe. Like every night, we were sweet and tender with each other, but this morning he confessed that he's not really happy. He has a really well-tuned instinct [. . .] and sensed I'd come to him 'through the wrong entrance'.

Sacrow, 18.11.56

Last Saturday and Sunday, Günter came here. I should have gone home—how could I have exposed to him to an encounter with my lover! [. . .]

In the evening, we sat together in the lounge. After the first glass of wine, Joe retired for the night. Perhaps I wasn't able to hide my disappointment entirely—from that moment on, Günter knew what I'm up to.

That night and the next day a chain of cruelties followed: accusations and defence, suspicion and fighting back, and scandalous lying.

Only when I read Günter the first chapter of my new book did things improve a little; he listened attentively, and with visible appreciation, and we were closer to each other than usual. [. . .]

As the evening drew on, it got worse. An hour before he left, Günter suddenly said, out of the blue, a sentence—a word-for-word quote from my diary. My heart stood still. He'd read my diary and knew everything [. . .]. He wasn't angry or mean; he was endlessly sad, and he forgave me—I've lost count of the times.

[. . .] If he'd made a scene, called me names, taken revenge, I'd have run away sooner rather than later. I'm chained to him by his kindness [. . .].

Günter wants to wait. He thinks I'll find my way back to him one day—when I'm sick of all the others. But I know that more will always come. Because the fundamental flaw lies in our marriage: we're not intellectually suited. Year after year, it'll go on like this. Pain will be heaped on pain, disappointment on disappointment—until one of us cracks from this hellish existence, or until we both crack. And the most destructive part is that neither of us has the strength to separate. [. . .]

He cried when we said goodbye, and ran off as if being chased. I cried too when I came back to the house. And at midnight I lay in Joe's arms and we were sad and happy, and knew that we were sinning. But we couldn't do otherwise. [...] I'm proud of him and me, because suddenly, the floodgates have opened up in him; thoughts have developed that could change his life and turn him into an artist. And he claims over and over again [...] that I'm the one who has woken this new feeling in him. If we lived together, perhaps we could mutually inspire and help each other, create something worthwhile.

No, we won't stay together, we have duties and we'll have to separate even though it'll be bitterly painful. Separation lies like a shadow over the present. [...]

Sacrow, 19.11.56

I should do some work but I can't. The primitiveness of film disgusts me. I have to write a book; I've promised to, and perhaps it will liberate me—or entangle me more deeply . . .

'I'm going to spend tonight alone, Jerry.'[69]

Jerry's here. He's been here for five days—five years or five centuries—and he's as alien and familiar as a person can be.

I met him five days ago. No, I don't know him, [...] I have understood that two people can never be one [...]. Sometimes there are moments when we're very close together, and it's so intense that it's more than two lonely creatures even dare hope for. Five days ago, he sat down at the table with Conny and Herbert Otto and me. We drank. [...] We lit candles. [...]

It was the atmosphere in this Sacrow madhouse. We toasted everlasting friendship, without even knowing one another's names. But he knew me, he'd read my book—and had felt an affinity. When he kissed me, his long, soft, light-blonde hair fell for the first time over my face. [...]

---

69 Jerry (Herbert Nachbar, 1930–80): novelist and screenwriter, editor at Aufbau Verlag between 1953 and 1957; received the Heinrich Mann Prize as an essayist in 1957.

Then I learnt his name: Herbert Nachbar. It hit me. I knew straight away. A year ago, I read a fantastic story in *Sonntag*, the best I think I've read in the past ten years. I'm sure I asked Piltz in a letter back then who this Nachbar was, [...] but Piltz didn't reply. And then this man was sitting in front of me, a young person, 26 years old, tall and broad-shouldered, handsome [...] and very distant. [...]

Later we happened to be standing together by the piano. We had been talking about politics, about the events of the past ten years, all the atrocities that had taken place in the name of socialism and humanity. Suddenly he said, with shocking certainty, that he knew he only had a few more years, that he would be destroyed by the conflicts of our times.

I think I began to love him at that very moment. It was the first 'greeting from one lonely soul to another' that we exchanged.

We stayed in the lounge when the others left. I was lying on the couch, Herbert—no, Jerry—was sitting next to me, we talked and fell silent. It was as if we'd known each other for years, because we expressed things people normally only admit to themselves—and sometimes not even that. [...]

He suddenly asked me whether I would give [...] him a kiss. I kissed him. He held my hand, I switched off the light. The darkness was good because it was inside us too.

When I went up to Joe's room later, [...] I found him awake. He had written me a letter that brought tears to my eyes. He [...] was almost insane with jealousy [...]. I slept with him. I'll never forget his face—when he suddenly pressed me to him and whispering, cried out: 'Brix, my agonizing love!' He called me Brix, the way I called him Joe—because it had to be that way, because that name suited him, and no other.

The next day, Jerry read me a passage from his new novel. A story of such deep anguish, pessimism and multiple layers that it cuts deeply [...].

The heroine of the book is called Maria. That evening, Jerry called me Maria for the first time. The name has stuck, we don't care if the others gawk at us and talk in whispers when he uses it. [...]

Sacrow, 20.11.56

Now everything has fallen apart, the game is over—this frivolous, naive but terrible game that the three of us have been playing. I can't even say how it all came about—this entire messy affair, this strange connection between two men and one woman. The men didn't have what it takes to hold out until it ended naturally, when everyone returned to their circle, enriched by a memory both good and bad that might deeply affect their literary work.

Do I have what it takes? I think I love them both and perhaps deep down I'm indifferent to them. Jerry claims that I'm possessed by a hunger for life—*Maria Vulcanita*. [...] They call me the Sphinx and don't know how to figure out what I'm thinking when I smile. And when I suddenly burst out laughing—quite without reason, according to them—they are completely confused and exchange helpless looks, and then I sense the distance between men and us women.

How we tortured each other, we three! 'I will spend the night alone.' I will spend all my nights alone, Jerry. I'll be alone all my life. Sometimes the thought causes me terrible pain, sometimes it leaves me cold. I don't need anyone. But yes, I need a person, people, and that old restlessness will keep me on the run.

Three hours later

This Sacrow madhouse! Now everything's changed again, and I'm even more confused than before. I'm giving up thinking and dwelling on things; I'll try and spare my diary the events in Sacrow too [...].

Sacrow, 24.11.56

Joe has left. My dear, good, clever Joe. We both cried when he came to me last night for the last time. The letter he left me is so like him—a reflection on the First Letter to the Corinthians—that tears come to my eyes when I read it—over and over again. What have I lost! [. . .]

These days with Joe may have been the best of my life. He has to come back! Today I wrote him a letter I won't post. [. . .]

I've moved into his room, and now I'm sitting at his desk, and a little of him is still here. [. . .]

Jerry has moved from the house next door to the neighbouring room. We have agreed to a 'loving comradeship' and sometimes we're like brother and sister.

Last night, agitated by Joe's departure, we both went to bed together like brother and sister and didn't make love. Perhaps we'll never do it. We're both cold by nature. [. . .]

Sacrow, 28.11.56

[. . .] I have to leave on Saturday; supposedly because the house is full, but the truth is probably that the housekeeper caught the whiff of a scandal.

When I heard that 'no' yesterday, [. . .] I thought: it's all over now. [. . .] I pushed my glass away. What I felt precisely was the desire to die. It was a strange transformation: tears, bitter-sweet desperation, raging anger, the pleasant thought of making peace with yourself—and then the image: a bottle of pills, cutting your arteries over the sink, seeing yourself flowing away, emptying out and fading . . . I have never come so close to this unknown realm. And suddenly, calm, happiness: the door standing open over there—just one step and you're out. [. . .] And then I was quite cheerful and relaxed and kissed Jerry. I will work. I will always be alone. I destroy people who love me, and I emerge stronger from my own destruction.

Jerry is at his tether's end. [. . .] I even managed to thaw his iciness [. . .]. We made love. We will never forget each other. Perhaps it's good we've not been granted these ten days—we'd never be able to separate. [. . .]

Jerry and I have no gift for being happy—or making others happy. [. . .] One more of these terrible scenes and we'll leave this life together. No, I'll not leave. I'm hungry for life. I'll drain my cup to the dregs.

[. . .] They say I'm beautiful. They're blind—or they mean a different, higher form of beauty. I'm not even clever, I just have a vivid imagination and am sometimes bad, sometimes good. Why do they say that I have everything—good and evil, and a profound innocence?

Jerry says I'm a thousand years old. We have met, many times: in the Asian steppes and at the court of a French bishop. [. . .]

Jerry has given me his pen. I'll write a book with it, our book— Joe's and Jerry's and Maria's book. I'll not sneak away; I want to go to hell in grand style.

[. . .] He is handsome, as handsome as a man can be. [. . .] When his long, blonde hair falls across his face, I want to kill him.

[. . .]

Now I'm all alone; the house is empty. Buchmayer just left for the ferry.

An hour ago, I took Jerry down. I'm always having to say goodbye to people. A passing woman said my husband was waiting on the opposite shore; he hadn't made it to the ferry. So, I was allowed to kiss Jerry goodbye.

[. . .]

Burg, 10.12.56

Now I'm back home again—as if I had such a thing as home. [. . .]
I'm bogged down in everyday things, struggling not to let them get
me down. Actually, I have found peace, as far as there can be peace
in my situation. [. . .]

But I've written a story, the very story I promised Joe and Jerry:
'I will be alone tonight.' I've literally worked on it day and night.
I had to go to Gera for an author's reading, and I wrote in the train
and in the waiting rooms, and among all those noisy people, I was
alone with myself and my characters, who are both real and made
up at the same time. That night I wrote the last line, made love with
Günter—for the first time in a long time. He was so happy! [. . .]
I was almost happy too. [. . .]

The farewell party for the seminar in Sacrow was awful. Ernst
was in Sacrow and, instead of helping me, he hurt me with his
insensitivity. He happened to be in the right. [. . .] But still, I was
fed up to the back teeth with him and recoiled from his advances
later. He was drunk in any case. Everyone was drunk, and Jerry was
the craziest. He wanted to numb himself with alcohol, and we
argued all evening. [. . .]

All in all, the party was loathsome. A few women from the Defa
were there, and a chaotic tangle of people were sleeping together.
Men and women kept disappearing—those who had made malicious remarks about mine and Jerry's sincere, tender love . . . In the
end, only Jerry and Ernst were left drinking. I went up to my room
at four o'clock. Walter was asleep in my bed. I went into Jerry's room
and lay down to sleep. He came later; I don't think he even noticed
that I was lying next to him. [. . .]

Jerry and I spent the last days all alone in the deserted house.
We still managed to get a lot done, [. . .] and I finished my
treatment. [. . .]

On the last night, we heard on the radio that Dr Harich[70] had been arrested. I thought that the entire literary group[71] which he belonged to had been caught. Ernst is one of them, and Walter and Piltz. We were terrified and angry. That night I phoned Ernst, although Jerry advised me not to, because he was worried that someone else might have been sitting at the other end of the phone if Ernst had been arrested. He hasn't been arrested—not yet. The group is now illegal. Intellect is illegal in our country—my God, what a world!

My fears for Ernst made me I realize that I still like him. And in any case, I have to keep him on the boil now he's been appointed editor of the literary journal for us young writers . . .[72]

[. . .]

Burg, 31.12.56

As it's the last day of the year I have to write a few words. Not a review—no way! In total it wouldn't be very cheering. Or perhaps it might—I don't want to be unfair. Two books have been published, I have a film contract [. . .] and I'm back with Günter, after some

70 Wolfgang Harich (1923–95), at that time chief editor of the magazine *Deutsche Zeitschrift für Philosophie* and a professor of philosophy at Humboldt University, was arrested in 1956 and sentenced to 10 years' imprisonment for the 'establishment of a conspiratorial counterrevolutionary group'.

71 The 'Thursday Circle' (*Donnerstagskreis*), referred to by the GDR's State Security Service (see note 78) as the 'Deutscher Petöfi-Club', included Wolfgang Harich, Fritz J. Raddatz, Heinz Kahlau, Manfred Bieler, Jens Gerlach, Günter Kunert, Erich Arendt, Karl Heinz Berger, Walter Püschel, Georg Piltz, Paul Wiens, Günter Caspar and Heinz Nahke.

72 For young artists who wanted to create discussion forums in 1956, there were several possibilities: besides the Klub junger Künstler (Young Artists' Club) (see note 91) and the Thursday Circle, Heinz Kahlau, Jens Gerlach and Manfred Bieler planned to found an independent journal for young writers. Karl Heinz Berger, editor at Neues Leben at the time, was asked to be editor-in-chief, but he rejected the offer. Instead, the magazine *Junge Kunst* (see note 90) was set up, which was published from November 1957 by the FDJ Central Council.

twists and turns, and not just for show, [...] which is perhaps the best thing I can say at the end of this year.

I've committed adultery a few times, I've loved, was happy and unhappy—all very mixed. I haven't quite recovered from the weeks in Sacrow, but I don't want to think about that any more.

I've joined the Writers' Union, and that's only right.

For the New Year, I wish the Frog and me much luck, much love and success in writing—and peace on earth!

1957

Burg, 25.4.57

I haven't touched my diary for four months—why not? Perhaps Sacrow got to me after all . . . I haven't seen either of them again, and perhaps it's for the best. I'm not writing a book about these experiences—my writing style is brash, ironic, detached, and only sometimes does my cruelty get me down, dragging these two people into my cynicism, making fun of genuine feelings.

I have worked hard in the meantime and—I can hardly believe it myself—barely fallen in love at all. I spent weeks in Berlin and worked on the script for *Garden of Desperation*[73] with my director Horst Reinecke. We managed to draw quite a bit out of the dry material. [. . .]

In March, Günter took off for West Germany—that was his payback for Sacrow. [. . .] Then he wrote to me—and I rushed off to Swabia and fetched him back. The happiness of our reunion!

I spent some wonderful days in Berlin. I drank the nights away—in the Adria-Bar or the Esterhazy Keller, washed in freezing cold water in the mornings and went off to work with Reinecke. It's good working with him. [. . .]

Burg, 25.9.57

Several times I've resolved to devote myself to my diary but I can't relate to it any more; it all seems a bit juvenile.

---

73 *Garten der Verzweiflung*, probably a new film project.

I never write down the things that really move and excite me anyway—perhaps they're more difficult to put into words; perhaps because I know that it's not worth putting most of this immature stuff into words; perhaps because I'm simply too lazy to deal with a vast number of problems—most of them quite political—by writing them down. [. . .]

My love affairs only interest me for the first three days and are quite absurd all in all. I've given up having a guilty conscience; regret is one of the most pointless feelings, probably *the* most pointless.

I flicked through this diary earlier on. Dear God, what prattle! How real is all the drivel about loneliness? [. . .] No, I shouldn't laugh at it. 'He jests at scars that never felt a wound'.[74]

[. . .]

I've become colder and wicked—'wicked' in the original sense of the word; I sometimes still cry but very rarely! And my rare tears aren't caused by real emotion but by jumpy nerves and overwork.

Where are the feelings—the overwhelming emotions—the ideals and fine intentions of my youth? I've peeled them off the way a snake sloughs its old skin, and it damned well hurt. But now I have my skin, and it's more colourful and tougher than the old one.

Sometimes I mourn these youthful ideals, and I was certainly a 'better person' back then. But the world doesn't need good people any more [. . .]. It won't be long before I can step back from this drama and look at it with indulgent irony (because there's no belief in it).

My indifference hasn't yet penetrated deep, I don't think, otherwise the consequence would be suicide. No, my whole life long, I've never been taken consequences, and perhaps it's worse to live with indifference than to die.

Oh and I notice how stupid it is to confide more than a few facts in a diary. I haven't got the patience to pick over my soul. The

74 William Shakespeare, *Romeo and Juliet* 2.2.1.

fact that I've changed, and the way I've changed, will show itself in my books—if I write any more.

I've moved on from my first two books. I've cast them out like children who have turned out badly.

Two more have been rejected: *The Informer* was counter-revolutionary[75] (I was half a year too late. That swine Ulbricht[76] had already begun to take a new, much harder line.) And it allegedly supported—I demanded it in writing—'those citizens who wish to re-establish a capitalist order in our country'. [. . .]

The second, *Joe and the Girl on the Lotus Flower*,[77] was also returned, covered with remarks like 'decadent, morbid, bizarre, etc.' In a book disguised as a love story, I couldn't refrain from smuggling in insolent political and philosophical ideas.

It was a damned hard blow, and it took me a long time to recover. [. . .]

Burg, 28.9.57

On Thursday, I was interrupted: the Stasi[78] came to visit me. I'd actually been expecting them: my conscience isn't clear, I can't hold

75 Neues Leben sent B.R. a rejection for *Wenn die Stunde ist, zu sprechen* [When It Is Time to Speak Out] (the title of the new version of *The Informer*), but it does not contain the term 'counter-revolutionary': 'The section about the life of secondary-school students and about a certain developmental stage of our antifascist democratic order (1949–50) [. . .] gives a distorted image [. . .]. There have been intolerant functionaries and anti-human practices in the penal system. [. . .] But the exclusive representation of these phenomena conceals the positive aspects [. . .] and would also benefit those forces who have recently been looking to destroy these positive things' (BRS, publishing correspondence, sheet 98).

76 Walter Ulbricht (1893–1973): first secretary of the Central Committee of the SED from 1950 to 1971. From President Wilhelm Pieck's death in 1960, he was also the head of state of the GDR until his own death in 1973, although he was effectively removed from power by Erich Honecker in May 1971. Following student unrest in several Warsaw Pact countries in 1956, the Ulbricht regime tightened its hold on students and intellectuals through the following years.

77 *Joe und das Mädchen auf der Lotusblume.*

78 The GDR's State Security Service (SSD, Staatssicherheitsdienst) also known as the Ministry for State Security (MfS, Ministerium für Staatsicherheit) was referred to in

my tongue and refrain from saying things in public that are not meant for everyone's ears. I pleaded for Harich—his case upset and shocked me terribly—and I stood up for Janka in every way I could.[79] When Kantorowicz defected to the West, I wrote him a letter, which was one long violation of Article 6,[80] and I reproduced the explanation[81] he gave to the SFB[82] and distributed it among my friends. In short, I have a few things on my record and, like I said, was counting on a visit from the Stasi. [...] I was sure I wouldn't be afraid and would get through the whole thing with composure.

How little I know myself. When Herr Kettner stood at my door and showed me his ID, my heart jumped—not exactly into my throat, but thereabouts. I showed him into the room, and when I lit a cigarette, I noticed that my hands were trembling. At least I still mustered the insolence to let him know in a conversational tone that he shouldn't imagine I was trembling with fear; I was just tired and overworked. Perhaps he even believed me ...

We talked for four hours. I was—probably out of stubbornness and resistance—completely candid. I'm not the kind to shroud

popular slang as the Stasi. Historically it is considered one of the most effective and repressive intelligence and secret police agencies that has ever existed.

79 Walter Janka, manager of Aufbau-Verlag from 1952, was arrested on 6 December 1956 on charges of counter-revolutionary conspiracies and sentenced to five years' imprisonment after a show trial (23–26 July 1957).

80 Article 6 of the GDR Constitution of 7 October 1949 stated: 'Incitement to boycott against democratic institutions and organizations [...] are crimes within the meaning of the Criminal Code' (Horst Hildebrandt [ed.], *Die deutschen Verfassungen des 19. und 20. Jahrhunderts* [The German Constitutions of the 19th and 20th Centuries]. Paderborn: Schoningh, 1992, p. 199f).

81 Alfred Kantorowicz (1899–1979): professor of modern German literature at the Humboldt University, Berlin, from 1950. Expecting persecution from the SSD, he defected to West Germany in 1957. Here, B.R. refers to Kantorowicz's radio address via Sender Freies Berlin on 22 August 1957: 'Why I Broke with the Ulbricht Regime'. Until her death, B.R. kept a typewritten copy of the speech from *Der Tagesspiegel* newspaper dated 23 August 1957.

82 SFB (Sender Freies Berlin): Radio Free Berlin, the public radio and television service for West Berlin from 1954 until 1990 and for Berlin as a whole from German reunification until 30 April 2003.

myself in mystery anyway. Well, Kettner is a sensible man, with whom you can discuss things, and he hadn't come to arrest me for my minor lapses but to carry out a kind of opinion survey. Why he chose me from the 14 writers in our district is a mystery to me—he claims he finds it easier to make contact to a woman than a man. I hope he's not expecting me to take this explanation seriously; or to believe I have a good standing with the Stasi.

Whatever the case: the Stasi has a task in mind for me. No, I don't want to call it informing. Kettner explained to me that the Stasi is not only concerned with exposing enemies; it also wants to inform, and to investigate views—of writers, in this case—and clear up mistakes and grievances that lead to disgruntlement.

Admittedly, Kettner is a good psychologist, and he did a wonderful job taking me in; he almost convinced me of the ideological purpose of his institution. Apart from this, the adventure appeals to me; I have to laugh at these games of cowboys and Indians—code names, hideouts and suchlike. Thirdly, I think I could contribute a little—despairing and wavering and filled with reluctant loathing and disillusion as I am (I made no secret of it)—if that's what it's about, liberating the clean cause of socialism from all the filth that has stuck to it. I had to sign a declaration swearing to strictest secrecy (a clause that I'm already violating by writing this diary entry) to accept the code name 'Caterine' and declare that I'm willing to pass on legitimate complaints about errors and inadequacies to the Stasi so that they can take remedial action. I rejected an ambiguous clause about 'enemies'. I won't name names, and in any case, mine and the Stasi's opinion about 'enemies' differ widely. Our discussion about Harich, for example, ended in stalemate.

I won't personally benefit from the whole thing, and I would never demand anything either. At best, I could write a book about working with the Stasi later—Kettner's suggestion—and they would supply me with material.

If I think hard—and I've been brooding over it non-stop for two days—about why I let myself get involved in this affair, and if I rule out an artistic thirst for adventure, what's left in the end is a rose-tinted ideal, no matter how fiercely I resist it. I've renounced all my ideals—and then along comes someone and persuades me that my modest help could serve socialism (someone whose moral qualification I'm not even sure of!) And I fall for it, damn it! And there are hours when I even believe that I'd be doing something good and useful.

The future will teach us whether this system is good and just. I've been studying Koestler's *Darkness at Noon* but I'm still none the wiser. Koestler is a wonderful writer and exceptionally intelligent—but he gets tangled up in the convolutions of his own mind and stumbles over his own intellect. He's a Jesuit who ran away from Jesuit school; he has an answer for every question, as he was taught to have, and leaves the reader deeply dissatisfied, because he has strong arguments for both sides.

The only sure thing is that when compared with capitalism, socialism, in its original form, represents a higher development, a progression of mankind.

[...]

I have to think of Piltz and the others sometimes. I'm not sure that they would still shake my hand if they knew what I'm about to do. And yet in their own way they're also working for our cause. Or are they just dictated by their salaries?

Well, I won't have to think it over for long. I can still refuse the Stasi; it won't cost me my head.

As far as my rich love life is concerned, I think I already mentioned that the magic of Sacrow has faded. Understandably, the ecstatic love—at least between us young ones, Hendrik—sorry! Herbert—and me, turned into violent aversion. We corresponded for a while then drifted away from each other in our letters. We never met. Hendrik asked me not to phone or visit him as—in the light of the Harich affair—he thought he was under surveillance. So what! In real life and work, Hendrik is a completely different person when he's on his own, a proper egotist *comme il faut*, concerned only for his own safety and keeping a clean slate. That's what I wrote to him, very harshly. When I was in Berlin a short time later, he paid me back on the telephone, not showing the best of manners either. In the evening, he came to the Niquet-Keller where I was drinking with Berger and Loest and Püschel, and asked for forgiveness. Unfortunately, I was already quite drunk, otherwise we would probably have got intimate again that evening.

Well, since then he's won the Heinrich Mann Prize. I congratulated him, I was really happy his work had been honoured. He thanked me—but our ties have broken off since then. [. . .]

I exchanged a few letters with Joe, but there was no way forwards whichever way I looked at it. [. . .]

Perhaps he's the kind of man you only meet once in a lifetime. [. . .] But you can't marry your ideals. [. . .] An ideal in slippers, with sexual intercourse regulated through matrimony, would soon lose its lustre.

Berger and I still have a good, honest friendship. We like each other, and at times he treats me with genuine affection. In the meantime, he's also learnt to appreciate me as a writer. [. . .] I recently wrote a short story—hopefully the last examination of the Joe experience—and showed it to Ernst, because I've lost every shred of self-confidence and don't dare publish anything. Ernst found the story delightful [. . .]. He made some corrections, and I was unusually compliant in following his suggestions. And the story—'Waiting All This Time'[83]—was improved by his edits. [. . .]

I've started a new novel [. . .]. My publisher wanted me to sign a contract. I've decided that won't be necessary for the time being, as I'm already deep in financial debt with them.

---

83 'Warten, all die Zeit' (not traceable).

But the first chapters are really good. My style has changed noticeably. I'm writing more coolly, factually, with detachment and without sentimentality. At the same time, it's like I'm sitting in the box at the theatre and watching the drama. True, I'm not passionately interested in my characters any more—I let them die cruelly [. . .] and say things that I would never even have dared think, let alone write, in the past. I think it'll be a mean, hard book. I have no illusions about myself any more and try to liberate the readers too. I think I can predict that the novel *Whatever You Do*[84] won't find as many readers as the first, more lyrical book.

I recently visited Ernst in Leipzig. He's studying [. . .] at the Institute for Literature there.[85] Buchmayer and Joe are there too. The rest are lame ducks. Kurella[86] hasn't resigned yet unfortunately, contrary to all the rumours.

I met Joe again. We talked a bit about the things that old lovers talk about when they meet again. I'm sure no one noticed how terribly nervous I was!

But I can't have looked that carefree after all, because Ernst kicked me and said: 'Laugh!' So, I laughed, but it was pretty bad [. . .]. I hope we can draw a line under this romance, and that's that.

[. . .]

I met long-lost Georg Piltz last month quite by accident on Friedrichstraße; he was in the city for the first time in months. He resigned from the *Sonntag* after Janka,[87] Just and Zöger were

84 *Wie man nur tut* (working title).

85 See note 29.

86 Alfred Kurella (1895–1975): director of the German Institute for Literature (Deutsches Literaturinstitut Leipzig) in Leipzig. He held leading positions in the Academy of Arts, the Writers' Union and the Cultural Association of the GDR.

87 After the arrest of the deputy editor-in-chief Gustav Just and the editor-in-chief Heinz Zöger from the witness stand at the Harich trial, further members of the *Sonntag* editorial staff were reprimanded internally and ideological guidelines were tightened. While Johannes R. Becher and Horst Sindermann strove to transform the *Sonntag* into a liberal newspaper for the intelligentsia from autumn 1955, Walter Ulbricht and Alfred

arrested, and his resignation was clearly a protest. Now he's turned to private matters, is writing experimental stories and has become terribly bitter [. . .] and a whole lot more intellectual than two years ago. Perhaps I know how to appreciate his intelligence for the first time; he does witty riffs, a pleasure to listen to [. . .].

I stood up Panitz to see him; we had a discussion—in other words, he talked—until my train was due to leave and he was remarkably sweet to me, insofar as Piltz is capable of being 'sweet'. [. . .] Two weeks later we went to the Interbau[88] show together. I was really looking forward to it—I still can't meet that fiend Piltz without my heart hammering. He's a fascinating man, precisely because I find so many things about him repellent: his cynicism, his boundless arrogance, his absolute opposition to all the things you might call human values.

Unfortunately, I'd been boozing all night and was as drunk as a lord that morning, so I wasn't able to follow Piltz's illuminating lecture on architecture properly. [. . .]

In the end, he almost got angry with me because I couldn't enthuse about western architecture and mathematical furniture as passionately as him, and behaved pretty badly in general. Clearly taking a cable car or sitting in a crane basket with a litre of alcohol in your stomach is not the most pleasurable experience. In the end, we bought a few banned books and crept gleefully past the border checkpoint.[89]

I'd spent the night before with Werner K[. . .], a very odd young man, who is two-thirds insane at a conservative guess. I can't

Kurella undertook the task of restructuring the newspaper (see Gustav Just, *Zeuge in eigener Sache. Die fünfziger Jahre in der DDR* [Personal Witnesses: The Fifties in the GDR]. Frankfurt am Main: Morgenbuch Verlag, 1990, p. 24ff.).

88 International Building Exhibition held in 1957 in the Hansaviertel District of West Berlin.

89 At the checkpoints between East and West Berlin, there were security checks to prevent smuggling and import of illegal products, including certain publications.

deny that his advanced schizophrenia attracts me. What attracts him to me, I can't tell; perhaps he senses a kindred spirit, and it's true that I was at least one-third insane in those days, and so wasted that a bullet out of the blue would have been my salvation.

We first met at the editorial offices of *Junge Kunst*,[90] who wanted me to give them a story; so actually, we've known each other for 10 years. [. . .]

Then we went to the Young Artists' Club,[91] which I didn't like at all—because of the young artists, or whatever these cocky young-sters call themselves, and we drank martinis and gin fizz. [. . .] Well, and then we ended up at his flat. Flat is a grand word for it: an empty, enormous, dirty studio, behind which is an indescribably squalid, messy room where I felt more comfortable than I ever had before.

This K[. . .] is a real bohemian, an anachronism living in Berlin's ex-red-light district [. . .]. He's writing a fantastic novel—very modernist and original [. . .].

We played really old records on a really old gramophone, and then we kissed [. . .]. Well, the usual. And yet it wasn't the usual: the whole thing was marked by something psychopathic [. . .]. That night we talked about things that you normally tell yourself on sleepless nights but never someone else. I've seldom felt such a strong contradiction between a lust for life and suicide.

We decided to die. We wanted to turn on the gas tap. And I can write this down now without a blush or a mocking smile, because the desire to kill ourselves was real. We weren't afraid. Why didn't we do it in fact? I suppose it was indifference [. . .].

90 *Junge Kunst* (Young Art): a monthly magazine for literature, criticism, fine art, music and theatre, which was published from November 1957 to September 1962.

91 Klub junger Künstler: a club where young artists met and held discussions from the end of the 1950s, had various locations in Berlin, most recently in Klosterstraße in what became the Haus der jungen Talente (House of Young Talents).

The next evening I went over to his place again. I stayed the night and we made out. We didn't even try to pretend we were doing it for love. We did it out of tedium and loneliness and with the aim of offending and hurting each other. We hurt each other and suffered; it was grotesque and sad and vile.

We decided to take leave of each other very coolly in the morning but, strangely, our parting was almost tender after all the wild insults and self-inflicted torture; it had a smack of regret as if at the last minute we had to compensate for all the nastiness.

Burg, 29.9.57

Last night Günter interrupted me, even though I was already very angry with him after he'd come home drunk again, two evenings in a row. Recently, he's been brutal and mean when he's drunk whereas before he always behaved in a merry and pleasant way. It takes all my patience to compose myself, but it takes just one word and he threatens to hit me.

Well, the night before last, he really did hit me, quite hard [...]. Of course I screamed and cried, less from pain than outrage, and of course the whole house woke up, and Lutz wanted to beat Günter to a pulp. I didn't expect anything less from my brother, but then I felt sorry for Günter again. I slept upstairs in the children's bedroom.

This damned boozing will tear us apart in the end [...].

We said we would break up—for the hundredth time—but this morning, we made up again, although it was Günter who made the first step, as usual. [...] When I see his pretty, fresh, bearded face, I can't understand how he can transform into a scowling wild animal [...].

If the Frog was a little steadier [...], he'd be a perfect husband [...]. But if he ever catches me *in flagranti* there'll be bodies,

I'm sure, and I'm scared stiff about it. I don't feel completely safe anywhere, and I'm always expecting him to track me down [...]. He's developed an incredible shrewdness when it comes to me, and I'm afraid he's going to take me by surprise and kill me.

But at the moment, my latest love probably won't lead to sex or such terrible lapses; it's an almost infantile love, which amuses and touches me. The lucky man is Rolf, [...] my—or more accurately Lutz's—former school friend. [...]

We've known each other for seven years, and we've always been good friends [...] without it ever occurring to us to fall in love. Why we never did, I don't know [...].

In any case, I have something to look forward to again, and the whole affair is so pure and innocent that I'm almost in a good mood—what more could I wish for?

Werner K[...] and his gas tap don't make life more worth living; perhaps we should all take things far more lightly.

Burg, 8.10.57

I left out an important man in my little black book—he reminded me with a letter: Dr Walter Schmitt, leading dramaturge at the Defa.

He says he already fell in love with me in Sacrow. (I had to give him the distressing news that I hadn't even noticed him back then) [...]. An old man, in his mid-50s, with grey hair and a goatee beard to match, daring as a teenager, waxing lyrical because he's going through his second adolescence—I find it foolish.

Using the excuse that he wanted to work with me on a film, he enticed me onto his motorboat one day, and took me out on the Berlin lakes. The boat is wonderful, with a cabin and a deck bar and a gas cooker, and a thousand other conveniences. We were quite drunk, and after much dithering, I let Walter kiss me, but otherwise my conscience is clear, thank God! I take no credit for withstanding his advances so valiantly: it's just seemed perverse to sleep with a 50-year-old man. [...]

He taught me how to drive a motorboat: it's wonderful to steer a small boat—thankfully not a great deal can happen at 20 kilometres an hour, but this intoxicating feeling of having an engine in your hands ... If I had a car, I think I'd probably kill myself in a short space of time.

[...] I know I could get my foot in Defa's door through Dr Schmitt, and achieve more than by the straightforward route. Still, the thought of sleeping with him to benefit myself didn't enter my head for a second. And I told Schmitt this in a roundabout way [...].

He presumed to swear that he would give up his position as leading dramaturge so that I couldn't accuse myself of sleeping my way to the top. I thought this was idle talk of course—what man would sacrifice a high position, just because of a woman?

[...] The day before yesterday, he wrote to me saying that he had indeed resigned and will only work as a screenwriter from now on. Well, [...] that won't bring him any closer to me.

[...]

Burg, 17.10.57

Writing this entry on my fourth wedding anniversary, of all things, is tasteless. Well, so be it, I have some time today and am back on my feet (I had the Asian flu) and managed to survive all the Book Week readings. I just reread what I wrote about Rolf. [...] Now I'm seriously wondering whether I truly thought it would stop at kisses and innocent affection. [...]

At the beginning of last week, we were behaving ourselves again [...].

Three days later, I went up to visit him in his room. I had come back sick from Thale, where I collapsed at the forum, and what's more, I'd just stomached a talk with the Stasi.[92] To nurse me back to health, Kettner force-fed me a bottle of schnapps. I arrive at Rolf's in a dire state, shivering from fever, half-drunk and bathed in sweat. He put me to bed, and I didn't put up much resistance when he undressed me and covered me up.

His landlord and landlady had gone out. So he came to me and, in a nutshell, we made love.

[. . .]

Burg, 25.12.57

Christmas Eve is—thank God!—over. I spent it alone. Three weeks ago Günter was arrested for resisting state authority. While I was in Schönebeck on a seminar of young authors, he beat up a policeman. That was on a Saturday evening. On Tuesday, I still didn't know Günter's whereabouts.

I don't want to describe everything I did after finding out that he was being held in custody. I went through a terrible time, and what completely shattered me was a letter from Günter, full of desperation and self-recrimination and pleas for help. God, if only I could save him! I would willingly serve half his time.

---

92 At this first meeting with the Stasi after signing her declaration, B.R. was already uncooperative: 'At the beginning of the meeting with the GI [*Geheimer Informator*, secret informer, a precursor of the term IM, *Inoffizielle Mitarbeiter*, informal collaborator, which came into usage in 1968], [. . .] she initially expressed concerns about working together with us and regretted her commitment. [. . .] At this meeting it was again stated that the GI is very politically ambiguous, that she tends to be very politically unstable and that the main reason for the meeting was to work on her political education. She kept asking questions about problems in our politics [. . .]. In this context, it was also made clear to the GI that the Ministry of State Security [MfS] was by no means a reconnaissance centre of the National Front of the GDR, and its task is not merely to inform people but also to receive information. The GI then stated that she would not provide the MfS with appropriate information until she was convinced of everything' (Withold Bonner, 'Brigitte Reimann in den Akten des Ministeriums für Staatssicherheit' [Brigitte Reimann in the files of the Ministry of State Security] in *Wer schrieb Franziska Linkerhand?* [Who Wrote Franziska Linkerhand?]. Berlin: Steffen Verlag, 1998, pp. 87ff).

There were a bunch of minor, political, petty intrigues; I cheated and fought my way through them and managed to obtain favours not given to ordinary mortals. This legal machinery is unimaginably cruel, with a springy resilience that you just bounce off.

I called on the MdS[93] for help and made inroads; they're making me pay a high price for it, but so what if I torture myself and rage in turmoil—they have the power, and whatever I do, I do for Günter.

[. . .] My publisher has proved generous: I have an advance contract for my new novel and a grant of 1,000 Marks: no, I'm not worried about money. What's worse is my conscience, which is wearing me down. I've been drunk every night for two weeks; now I don't want to drink ever again. [. . .]

Yesterday I received a special permit to talk to him—for a quarter of an hour . . . God, it was almost worse than being alone. I embraced him, even though it's forbidden—I wasn't allowed to kiss him. Then we sat at the table, a guard between us, and I cried without wanting to. [. . .]

Oh, my sweet darling—and I know I won't be faithful to him. [. . .] Sometimes men make me sick. Jochen has been taking care of me as if I'm insane, and I feel like slapping him for every tender, indulgent word. I was invited to Schreyer's—and he tried to seduce me. I remained chaste, it goes without saying.

No, it doesn't go without saying. [. . .]

Burg, 31.12.57

It's getting on for midnight. I'm alone. When you actually need other people, they are never there. Well, I don't care any more.

---

93 B.R. means MfS, or Stasi.

I've decided to write the last chapter of the prologue to my novel on the last day of the old year, after not managing to work for weeks on end. I'll finish my bottle of vodka at the same time.

When the bells ring, I'll drink a toast to myself and think of the Frog.

1958

It's two minutes after midnight, and the bells are ringing in the New Year, and fireworks are exploding on the street, and people are shouting 'Cheers!' and I'm sitting and crying and doing the only thing a writer can do to comfort herself: write. [...]

I don't have any New Year's resolutions. Or only this one: Be good to others!

The fact that I haven't written in here for so long is a good sign: since that lonely New Year's night, I've begun work again and achieved quite a bit. Although I'm not at all happy with the speed at which I work. How many hours do I waste thinking about things I can't change?

I must stop working with the Stasi;[94] I have no choice. They're trying to blackmail me [...]: They promise to give Günter probation and let me see him more often than normal (officially you're only allowed to talk every quarter of a year), and that they'll secretly deliver my letters. [...] God, they're pigs! They're playing on my feelings [...]. In return, I'm supposed to deliver reports on our writers.

---

94 At this point B.R. tried to stop the cooperation with the SSD by cancelling or postponing appointments. She did not appear at meetings either or provide reports.

[. . .] Excellent material for a novel! This terrible decision: to help my loved one and work as an informer in return, or to bail out and leave Günter to his fate. At first, I was determined to throw my moral misgivings overboard and I gave him hope. But I can't stand it. There are certain things a person with the vestige of a conscience can't do. I don't even know for sure what Günter would think about the whole thing. [. . .]

And afterwards we can't even leave for the West. Recently K. came to see me. He claimed to have heard I'd fled to the West. He openly threatened me: I would be immediately arrested over there—the Stasi has my written declaration and can blow my cover any time.

If only Günter could be more calm and collected about his imprisonment! But he's completely broken and I hardly recognize him. I visited him on Friday. We were lucky because the guard on duty was young and understanding. We were allowed to kiss [. . .]. He slipped two letters to me, and when we were hugging, I slipped him cigarettes [. . .].

To get back to the ominous matter: I went to Wolfgang Schreyer and told him everything. He's not taking it too badly but seriously enough to discuss it with me often. We have to put a stop to it—but how? One way or the other, I'm going to come a cropper, and I can count myself lucky if they don't arrest me. Wolfgang says that the union[95] shouldn't put up with these constant accusations—I'm not the only one they wanted to enlist, it seems. Well, we'll see. I admit I'm still struggling with whether to cooperate with them or not [. . .].

What's the right thing to do? I'm not skilful enough to lie to both sides at the same time. Good that I've got Wolfgang at least! Our friendship has become even firmer and more honest [. . .]. I'm so grateful he still trusts me despite my confession.

[. . .]

95 The GDR Writers' Union.

Burg, 20.2.58

Günter's hearing was a good while back. The hearing was abominable, and I cried a few times. But Günter bore up wonderfully; he was calm and presented his defence skilfully. It was impossible to say who had actually hit whom first (one of the witnesses had mental problems, as was proven when he appeared before the judge, and the policeman wasn't blessed with much intellect either), and so the reason Günter was sentenced to six months' imprisonment—despite the good impression he made in the courtroom—was mostly because the judge said he portrayed his crime as insignificant, i.e. he said that the police are often themselves to blame for being attacked because they don't know how to treat people.

Günter asked for probation when they read out his sentence, and he spoke so well that everyone thought they'd comply. [. . .]

We were allowed to talk in the break, and because we have a nice guard, it was like being alone. [. . .] I told Günter about the Stasi's offer. He was outraged and prohibited me to work with these people on his behalf; he'd prefer to serve the six months. He's an honourable man.

As he was led away, we were allowed to kiss in a corner, and for the first time in months, he hugged me and I felt his hands on my chest and hips.

I really ache for him. The nights are the worst. [. . .]

I won't cheat on him. I can bear being without a man. What's more, I've made a surprising discovery: I have a conscience, a very delicate conscience. It's strange. Before I was able to cheat on him almost unscrupulously. But now . . . It's probably to do with the fact that I love fair play. And it's definitely unfair to cheat on a prisoner, who can't fight back.

Burg, 4.3.58

[...]

For the first time in months, I've fallen in love again. [...]

On Saturday, I went to the work conference in Halberstadt with Schreyer. I had been planning to go back to Burg that evening because I wasn't expecting much from the company in H [...].

When we arrived, the young authors had already gathered, and in the foyer, we heard that Günter Deicke,[96] editor of the *NDL* and a respected poet, was also present. I remember I made a mocking remark—I don't like these *NDL* people, and I'd always imagined Deicke to be the kind of optimistic, youthful hero I can't stand.

[...] In the break he came over to me. Youthful hero—well, not quite! [...] Deicke is averagely tall and gentle, not exactly young any more, has a narrow, pale, exotic face (Mongolian eyes a bit like Ho Chi Minh) and a dark beard. As soon as he spoke and looked at me, I knew what [...] would happen; I knew with such certainty that I didn't bother playing hard to get. I immediately sense when a man will be mine, and then it makes no difference what he looks like [...].

We had lunch together and spent that evening in the hotel, as if it was meant to be. It felt as if we'd known each other for a long time; using *Sie* would have felt ridiculous and pointless. Then we went to a bar together [...].

Late that night we headed back and Günter came up to my room. We smoked a cigarette together and then we kissed. It wasn't even that exciting—we were driven to each other, and there was no point in fighting it [...].

He asked me at one point if he could stay the night, and I said no, and we talked a little about it, and he didn't pressurize me [...].

---

96 Günther Deicke (1922–2006) is the proper spelling of his name; a German poet, translator and journalist, he was the editor of *NDL* between 1952 and 1958, the leading literary journal in the GDR, founded in 1952 by the GDR Writers' Union.

[...] We spent the entire Sunday together, and he drove me to Burg. He asked for the manuscript of my novel, and if he's not thrown out of the *NDL* in the near future (the editorial staff is being ideologically purged now too) he wants to publish the prologue. He advised me to submit my book to Aufbau. He thinks it's very good. I discovered and enjoyed Günter's poems for myself. We were very happy and a little bit sad, and the best part was that we didn't sleep together. The respect Günter showed me made me even fonder of him.

Once, when I was making coffee, I gave him my story about the blue sailing boat that I haven't showed anyone so far because it's really decadent, and he liked it very much. He wants to give it to Peter Huchel; perhaps he can publish it in *Sinn und Form*.[97] [...]

Towards the morning, our kisses became hotter and more frenzied. Günter wrote a little poem for me, and I keep reading the last line:

'Your trace and mine
—perhaps—
are a beginning.'

[...] At around six in the morning, I accompanied him part of the way to the station [...]. Only after our last kiss did I sense what these two days and nights mean to me, and will mean for the time to come.

[...]

Burg, 13.3.58

[...] I'm only working at night at the moment, with alcohol. I have to get rid of this ghastly boozing habit once and for all. Not that it affects me physically. I'm still sober after half a bottle of vodka and

---

97 *Sinn und Form. Beiträge zur Literatur:* a literary journal, published in East Berlin by the Akademie der Künste, since 1949. Peter Huchel (1903–81) was its chief editor from 1949 to 1962.

never have a hangover. Everyone destroys themselves in their own way. Rubbish!

[...]

I've achieved a lot in the past few days. Deicke put in a word for me. The prologue to my novel will be published in the May issue of the *NDL* and Aufbau is not averse to taking the novel. Well, it'll all turn out right in the end. Now Neues Leben also wants to have the manuscript. But I'm pessimistic, and refuse to pin my hopes on anything (although deep down, I still do). [...]

Friedrich Wolf (Writers' Home), Petzow, 21.3.58[98]

I was supposed to be sitting here with Deicke. As if! [...] He wrote me some wonderful poems and, despite being the Antichrist to poetry that I am, I wrote a poem too, and he thought it was wonderful, and still likes it—despite everything—because he wants to include it in his cycle and collection. He was deeply affected by our encounter and produced a lot of work, and couldn't thank me enough for it. [...] Then he reorganized his life and I'm sure it would have been wonderful but, unfortunately, his wife had a nervous breakdown when he revealed that he wanted a divorce. A divorce, for Christ's sake! These poets are really way too over the top. I don't know if he was seriously hoping I would leave Günter for him. [...] Obviously, he hasn't understood [...] that I wasn't even ready to commit adultery.

Why, in the devil's name, was I born a woman? I'm damned never to find friendship because of my gender; men are incapable of separating body from soul. Not one of them understands that I want to be loved for my intelligence, my talent or, to use that word again, my soul. Because everyone expects me to trade sex for good

---

98 Heim Friedrich Wolf: a writers' retreat in the former villa of Marika Rökk, a Hungarian dancer, singer and actress who gained prominence in German films in the 1930s and '40s.

conversation, or the affection of an intellectual man. It's enough to make you sick! Why do men make it so difficult for a woman to remain decent? [...]

Now there are only six guests here, including the celebrities [Willi] Meinck and Kupsch—and Eberhard Panitz. He's a ray of hope. [...]

I'm not here for adventure. I want to work; hopefully I'll finish the first part of my novel, because (and now comes the best part) there's a possibility that my darling will be released at Easter. [...]

Petzow, 29.3.58

Everything's gone mad, of course: no work, and all my plans are ruined, including my good resolve. [...] Meinck has fallen madly in love with me, and I like him very much too. Perhaps I was in love with him yesterday, but it's all changed again. Wherever I am, I cause disturbance, mayhem and trouble. [...] Kubsch isn't entirely wrong when he says that 'this woman' is seducing the whole house into foolishness (the woman in me laughed at that). Fox[99] [...] often takes me out for spins; he has a red Wartburg, and because of me, he lost his driver's licence on Saturday. We were in a pub in Werder, and afterwards he drove back drunk. We were caught, and had to spend that night at the police station and in hospital, and were only allowed to go home with a police escort the next morning.

Yesterday he drove me to Burg. I wanted to take Günter some clothes but the prison was empty. Three prisoners brutally murdered a guard and now the others have been transferred to Magdeburg, and perhaps Günter's reprieve is also up the spout. I have to make a terrible confession: I secretly wish that my poor, dear comrade won't come home just yet. [...] ([...] I've met someone who unsettled me from the very first day, because I saw

99 Fox: 'Fuchs', refers to Willi Meink.

our affinity in his eyes) and I'm certain of his gift for madness—he's one of these people who'll end up committing suicide or going insane, I'm sure. And what a mighty talent! Siegfried Pitschmann;[100] Siegfried—he's anything but made of horn:[101] a young, handsome person with wonderful eyes, and thin, nervous hands. We avoided each other, barely exchanged a word, not while the normal, healthy Fox was here.

Last night, Siegfried came to visit me. I asked him to read me a passage from his book. Wonderful language, and the characters are all psychopaths like him. [. . .] I never had such a strong sense of being with someone who suits me so completely. [. . .] It's as if he were a piece of me, a more wicked, sadder part of my sick soul. [. . .] There was no lust, not a hint of physical desire, that's the worst part. We're siblings—but not quite, we're more than siblings. Oh, my fateful, lost brother! [. . .] I kept him with me; it was so natural [. . .]. We lay next to each other, arm in arm, and we sometimes kissed and stroked each other but there was no arousal, and when he said: 'My sister', it touched me to the core. [. . .] I love him. [. . .] Fighting it is pointless. But he's more talented than I am, and I have a greater chance of getting off lightly than he has. He has a scar on his wrist from a suicide attempt. If I kept him, we would destroy each other, be terribly unhappy and destroy each other . . .

Petzow, 30.3.58

[. . .] I think Siegfried loves me. Even though he doesn't normally like being around people, he comes to me—he can find peace with me. [. . .]

---

100 Siegfried Pitschmann [henceforth S.P.] (1930–2002): a writer and B.R.'s second husband from 1959 to 1964.

101 This undoubtedly refers to Siegfried's horn call in the second act of Richard Wagner's opera *Siegfried*.

Burg, 6.4.58

[. . .] Six days ago, I wrote that I thought Siegfried loved me. Now I know he's completely lost himself to me. [. . .] He listed everything he loves about me, and it moved me to the core when he said he loved my way of walking,[102] which was sweet and exciting. No one has ever said that to me. [. . .] What will sight be like after such blindness?

[. . .] We sat together for nights on end and pictured how it would be if we divorced and married each other, and were able to live together, and how we would write books, criticize and complement each other, and write films and become famous. Our wonderful dreams—and underneath, the terrible fear that nothing, none of it, will come true. What will become of Günter? [. . .]

Burg, 15.4.58

I still can't fathom how I could have fallen so insanely in love—the moment I imagined my affection for Comrade Günter to be safe. [. . .] These two loves don't overlap in any way, and can't co-exist [. . .]. I don't have a clue what to do. Well, I do have a clue—but will my two men be able to stand it? I wish we could live together, the three of us, and I am sure it would be a wonderful, fulfilling life.

The night before last, Siegfried drove to Petzow, and I'll join him the day after tomorrow. We'll have three weeks together [. . .].

When we came back from Petzow before Easter, he stayed with me for two days in Burg, and when he drove back to the writers' retreat, for another two days. At Easter, he wrote me a letter—the most beautiful, ecstatic love letter I have ever received—and ecstasy envelops our entire relationship. [. . .] Where is my coolness, my sobriety, which made me so self-assured?

102 B.R. contracted polio in 1947 and had limped since then.

I have given him his second name, Daniel. God, that awful young hero's name Siegfried doesn't suit this sensitive, tender, almost fragile Daniel at all. I can't comprehend how anyone can love me so endlessly, with an abandonment and tenderness that's like female submission and has room for my lesbian tendencies, my masculine nature, in many ways; we complement each other wonderfully. I'm prepared for anything with Dan, and there's nothing that repels or surprises me. [. . .]

I don't want to write any more. It's late at night and now the bleak thoughts are coming, which if I let them, will drive me insane. [. . .]

Petzow, 15.4.

[. . .]

I don't know why everything in me balks at writing down that I slept with Dan, but I have some idea at least: deep down, I feel that our relationship has been destroyed. It was beautiful, of course, and Dan is wonderfully tender, in an almost feminine way. He's like my female, not my male, lover. I wish I could live differently with him; perhaps like a child I love above all else.

[. . .]

Petzow, 16.4.

This afternoon, Günter Rücker was in Potsdam; he drove me to the post office so that I could post my proofs to the *NDL*. That was just a pretext, of course—certainly for him, and partly for me too. When we were here the first time (at least a hundred years ago), we slunk past each other and played Hero and Leander; but Hero didn't put her light in the window.

[. . .] Rücker can't be described or even categorized. He doesn't fit into any kind of category. He's outrageously intellectual, educated and a very good writer, but that doesn't capture his essence, and I don't know any attribute that does. As always, I have a strange affinity for him, mixed with awe, which takes away all my self-confidence when he's around. At lunchtime, I had to ask him not to look at me all the time (we were sitting at the same table), because I was so self-conscious I couldn't eat.

[. . .] Nevertheless we're due to meet this evening; he went shopping—vodka, food. He wanted to buy me flowers and was disappointed there weren't any in the shop. He can't concentrate any more on his work (he says). In the morning he kissed me, very tenderly, lightly, more a breath than a kiss. I'm completely defensive and aloof—but I don't know if my defensiveness and aloofness are genuine. They're not.

[. . .]

Petzow, 17.4

Last night we got drunk; I was at Rücker's until midnight, and we had sex without touching each other: just in our fantasies—tender, cruel, obscene fantasies. Günter is an expert at whipping a woman into a frenzy with words—and this sweet feeling somewhere between shame and lust . . . how unhealthy it all is! I veer between lust for this new man's debauchery—and longing for the tender body and soul of my wonderfully healthy comrade.

P., 18.4

Dan interrupted me yesterday. Well, with him here, I wouldn't have been able to describe what happened that night with Rücker. [. . .] I was determined not to fall in love. And I didn't. [. . .] There's a little affection, but it stems from my genuine admiration for his considerable talent, and my appreciation of a man who is simply charming. I don't believe his declaration of love.

After midnight, I fetched Dan and things got bad. Both men were in pyjamas and I was lying next to Rücker, and was tired, [...] and the men began arguing, first about politics, then about me. [...] One of my hands was on Rücker's chest, the other holding Dan's hand. In the morning, my arms were covered in bite marks, and I don't even know who gave them to me. Now and again I drifted off to sleep, catching snatches of their quarrel that got fiercer and more cynical.

But I didn't care—I found both of them obnoxious. When I woke up the next morning, I was lying in Rücker's arms; he was sober and just as crazy about me as in the hours just passed. Dan had gone and I left too.

And the hangover! [...] I was sick of this whole story, sick of my work, and them pulling me in all directions.

Petzow, 20.4.58

Rücker left yesterday, and everything is OK. I was a bit sad that night—I must have fallen in love with him after all; one of my many three-day loves. [...] Daniel is happy and is working, and I'm happy that he's happy and working.

[...] Meanwhile, the others have noticed what's going on between us and accept our relationship [...].

My chapter is finally going somewhere. [...] I manage to do more at home, but I wouldn't want to miss out on the atmosphere of the writers' retreat—our talks and the people, some of whom I really like.

[...]

Petzow, 1.5.58

I just wrote this sentence in the chapter that I've been chewing over for weeks: 'I'm in a damned predicament,' and it reminded me of my own predicament, which is cursed three ways.

I'm sitting at the window in the lounge, looking out onto the lake, which is scandalously beautiful, and the hazy sky, with sailing boats in the distance and the blue shores in the fading light of dusk. It's hard to imagine I'll soon be sitting in Neuendorfer Straße, looking out at the front garden where the roses will be in blossom, and Günter will be there, and Dan so far away [. . .].

If it wasn't for Günter, I wouldn't have the slightest reservation about running off and living with Daniel somewhere, somehow [. . .]; the only important thing would be our togetherness, our work and—although it's the second priority—our tenderness and ecstasies. Ecstasies—this word has only been part of my vocabulary for a short time; Dan taught me it and I understood it.

[. . .] Having said that, we hadn't even slept together—until the night before last, but it was completely different than with Günter, and now I think there is something much more beautiful and tender than instant sex.

Petzow, 3.5.58

[. . .] Now we're treated like we're man and wife, and I'm always surprised at the way people take a liking to our relationship. Perhaps because they appreciate us as writers; at our reading event, it was proven that Dan and I were the most talented by far [. . .]—although I think Dan's better than me.

True, he works very slowly, and he's always having crises, and he's not healthy in body or mind—but he's going to write a couple of really good books, real literature, of that I'm sure. And he's recovering under my influence; he works more than he used to—and he puts it all down to me, and I am the only one who's allowed to chase him, to drive him on, precisely because I'm also a writer and am able to write. Jesus, yes, I'm proud of it and I think of his work as being mine, and sometimes I think it's more important to me than anything else to force a few good books out of him. But of course, I have to write too and be successful, that's an unalterable condition for me, otherwise in my own eyes, I'll lose the right to be Dan's partner.

[. . .] Maria liked us from the very first day [. . .]. She said that I had a strikingly masculine intellect and a strikingly feminine body—and that's why I was the ideal partner for Dan, who needs someone else's strength so much.

Thinking back, I now realize how much has happened, all of it in the open for all to see but only important to us [. . .].

To be sure, lots of less personal things have happened too: [. . .] my fortunate meeting with the critic couple, Zak and Annemarie Auer [. . .]; a visit from Kaspar,[103] the head of Aufbau Verlag—he arrived yesterday; he's working with Daniel, and if I'm lucky, he'll be working with me too. The publisher wants to take on my book. K. seemed very taken, even though he gives neither praise nor criticism. He doesn't improve or delete either—he just makes suggestions and leaves it to the author. He loves Hemingway, and this love has already created a link between us. Dan said he'd remarked that Reimann was a very interesting woman—and that means a lot coming from K. Most people call him a snob. I don't believe it; he's shown us nothing but warmth and compassion, and I think it stems from his respect for a certain skill, which he wants to develop and cultivate. [. . .]

Petzow, 6.5.58

[. . .]

Yesterday, Annemarie Auer drew me into a conversation about mine and Daniel's relationship—and she spoke with so much tact and warmth that I'm slightly proud, because it shows me that our love for each other is being taken seriously and, more, that we're

---

103 Günter Caspar (1924–99): chief editor at Aufbau Verlag from 1956 till 1964. He took the place of Max Schroder from August 1956 after Schroeder fell ill. B.R. spells his name alternately with a K and a C.

being taken seriously as writers. Annemarie also advised me—as Maria did—to stay with Günter for the time being, until he's got the atmosphere of prison out of his system and then to talk to him calmly and reasonably. [...]

With Daniel, I can work together wonderfully. He comes to me with each new page, we converse for hours about it and I'm a strict, even harsh critic. In fact, I set the bar higher than for myself, and I don't let him get away with anything—especially because I have so much faith in his talent.

He knows that he's sliding into greater dependence on me all the time, but it's a willing, happy dependency that binds me to him too. I'm blossoming under his influence! There's mutual give and take, although I'm the stronger one; Dan is passive by nature, and subordinates himself to me in a wanton kind of way, both in the intellectual and sexual sense, without losing himself in the least. And he mustn't either; and although I'm working off my masculine desires on him, at the same time I wish I didn't have to be the dominant one all the time. He's certainly the more gifted of us both [...], and I never make this a secret—even if a little literary jealousy has crept in.

Mühlhausen, 14.5.58

I arrived here last night with Daniel. The two-day stopover in Burg was terrible. On the first afternoon, I couldn't stop crying. I saw the room again where I'd lived with another person, the bed I'd slept in with him, and the furniture we'd bought together—a vision of the future that's already the past. Is it really so—irreversible? [...]

Daniel is the one I was looking for and found, I'm sure. But still, it makes me feel sick to imagine Günter going out the door all alone, down the street all alone, the street we've walked down together a thousand times, then disappearing in the distance, alone and unhappy. Jesus Christ!

Mühlhausen, 15.5.58

I've more or less settled in. It's always difficult for me to connect with new surroundings, new people, even if they treat me with utter kindness. And Frau Pitschmann has treated me with great kindness, and has done everything to make me forget the awkwardness or strangeness of the situation. Well, it's true that there's no bond between Dan and her any more, [. . .] mostly because of their differences in attitude and personality, and she has her lover, and a refreshingly unconventional outlook—at least as far as marriage is concerned.

[. . .]

It's wonderful to be loved by Dan [. . .]. And from an intellectual harmony, a beautiful physical one has grown. He's roused a wild passion in me that at times shocks me—but it's a sweet shock, and I have discovered I'm imaginative in this area too, and I enjoy things that disgusted me before; it gives me pleasure to make Dan happy [. . .] Sexually, I was very screwed up, very stupid and inexperienced and twisted—and it's only in the past few weeks that I've learnt all the good people can do each other. [. . .] In the past, I thought you had to separate the physical from the intellectual—now I know these things are inseparable.

[. . .] And yet I still fear that I'll capitulate under the storm of complications threatening us: Günter, Dan's son [. . .], two divorces, our economic situation. There's no end to it. How often do we picture ourselves setting up our two desks and how we'll live together—and then suddenly, it's as if we're two children fantasizing and none of our dreams will be fulfilled. [. . .]

But how am I supposed to go back to my old life? [. . .] I'd never shake off the thought, the certainty [. . .] that a once-in-a-lifetime chance for happiness had passed me by. If Günter were dead—dear God, forgive my sin; it's terrible and I loathe myself for it—but I could bear Günter's death more easily than seeing him suffer. If only I knew or could guess what he will say or do! But with Günter, anything's possible—he might kill me, pack his bag in silence, or do himself harm.

Mühlhausen, 20.5.58

Tomorrow is our anniversary: on 21st March we fell in love with each other when Daniel read aloud from his boarding-school book. [. . .] Two months . . . It seems like just as many years.

[. . .]

Dan has finished his chapter, and I've finished mine, the same chapter that we spent weeks playing with in Petzow without success. Sometimes you have these phases. We need phases like these; we have to get a lot done because we have no money left and don't know how we can keep going. [. . .]

Mühlhausen, 29.5.58

Today's my last day in M. We made love again. [. . .] Dan drives me insane, I cry out in desire and pain, and can't tell the difference between the two any more. I lose my mind when he caresses me. I made a terrible mess of him today again, scratches and bites all over him. Every bite stirs a sadistic mania in me, an insane yearning to kill, see blood—I'm beside myself when Dan puts his arms around me.

We've barely worked this week. Günter's homecoming looms over us [. . .].

I can't work any more without Dan, and he can't work without me. We have to stay together; there's no other way. True, Dan isn't as handsome as Günter [. . .]—but what's beauty to me, or a magnificent body? And still, I'm afraid of succumbing to G.'s charm [. . .].

[...] We haven't got a penny left. What will happen? Perhaps we'll have to go hungry, but that wouldn't be the worst; people can live for a while on dry bread. I'll certainly be able to bear it, but I'm worried about Dan: he's already so skinny and needs to eat well. And cigarettes? And alcohol? What the hell, it's going to be a horrible time. When we talk about it, we're always depressed for five minutes, then we laugh. If we're together, we can stand anything. Neither of us is much good when it comes to money, we're both hopeless with finances—and apart from that, we're optimists. God won't desert a hard-working writer.

Burg, 2.6.58

On Friday night, I came back from Mühlhausen.

My whole life here is unreal. [...]

I have to have him again, as soon as possible. I can't work, can't breathe without him.

Burg, 7.6.58

Günter came back—a day earlier than I expected. In the morning, a car drove up. I sensed who it was, froze, hid Dan's letter and pictures in a great hurry, and my diary, and then Günter came into the room.

What an indescribable moment! I was shaking like an aspen leaf. He was very pale, had become thin, and was wearing his black camping shirt, in his hand a bundle of clothes, his hair trimmed very short. I began to cry.

The week that had passed since I had said goodbye to Dan was horrible. I pictured terrible scenes, I suffered—God, I've already paid for my wrongdoing, I'm still paying, and I'll have to pay in the future. [...]

Five minutes after Günter had sat down, he knew almost everything. He bore it with remarkable composure. He'd already seen it coming for the past two months. He'd been reading between the lines of my letters and had [. . .] guessed the truth.

No threats, no accusations—he shamed me with his magnanimity. He was sad, so sad [. . .]. How could I have done this to him! In that hour, I realized how much I'm still attached to him. How five years have created a bond between us—and perhaps there were moments when I was prepared to betray Daniel. But it's too late for me [. . .].

And then sitting next to Günter; hearing him say that he'll never love another woman as he does me; seeing the tremendous willpower it cost him to accept this enormous disappointment: watching his face that I've kissed a thousand times (the images of his drunken homecoming pale in comparison, as do the lonely nights where I lay, sleepless, waiting for him) [. . .] True, he doesn't understand my conflict, but he understands—or at least he pretends to understand—that Daniel suits me better [. . .].

In the afternoon, we were in the garden, and Günter was full of wonder and new discoveries. Sun and fresh air and trees and flowers and freedom—to go wherever, and do, or not do, whatever he wants. He must have suffered terribly in prison. I want to spare myself the details of the GDR's penal system—what's certain is that prisoners are deeply humiliated and their humanity systematically taken away. And Günter is so proud, so self-confident, so thirsty for freedom!

I slept with him again—double adultery. And as I did [. . .] I felt desire, and gave desire, and the whole time I thought of Daniel and at the same time of Günter, and both of them merged into one . . .

[. . .] On the street today, I suddenly burst into tears. [. . .]

What's bad is that Günter can't leave to do construction work elsewhere for the time being; [. . .] perhaps we'll bump into each other on the street now and again [. . .]. I'll have to know what happens to him in the future, how he is, what he's doing, what he's up to. And I want him to come and visit me every week. I don't have a firm promise from him yet, but I want to force one out of him. It'll be torture every time, perhaps even pure masochism, but he's still my husband after all [. . .]. If only I could live with both of them! But that's utopian; I've grasped that. Günter doesn't even want to see Daniel.

I'll probably let Daniel come on Monday. Until then, I'll stay with Günter; then he'll move out. [. . .]

Burg, 18.6.58

Yesterday was our wedding anniversary, and Günter visited me at night with flowers and chocolates and liqueur, and we sat and lay together until one o'clock; I was very gentle to him. Dan went to the cinema so that he didn't bump into Günter.

So now I have two men and two weddings to celebrate every month: on the 17th and on the 9th, because Daniel came on the 9th of June and from that day on, we've been husband and wife [. . .].

On the 9th—it was a Monday—I said goodbye to Günter. We had spent four days together, with tears and kisses, and on the last day we packed his case together. We had a great deal to sort out and were very busy, and tried to gloss over our sadness with all the organizational stuff, but some of the time I just sat on the couch, hands in my lap, and cried [. . .].

But I'd already sent the telegram to Dan, and it was no longer reversible—and anyway, life with G. would have been self-deception; sooner or later we would have slipped back into the old world that's not my world any more, with people whose language isn't mine, a lifestyle that doesn't suit mine, or never did, and this horrible loneliness [. . .].

Then the bags were packed, two enormous cases, and all of a sudden, the room seemed empty to me, even though its appearance had barely changed.

At quarter past nine, Dan's train arrived and before I went to the train station, I said goodbye to Günter. He was wearing his dinner jacket and looked more handsome than ever, and I kissed his hands in tears [. . .].

He said we would never see each other again and he would never take me back, even if I wanted to come back. Then I went to the train station, and Dan came through the barrier with his case, and he was a complete stranger to me—he had cut his hair shorter than usual—and on the way home, we talked about trivial things.

The rest of the family were incredibly affected by Günter leaving; Puppa[104] was downright rude to Dan (now she's niggling him the whole time and annoying him in her teenage way); Dad retired so he didn't have to say hello to Dan, and only Mum welcomed him—in a reserved but not unfriendly way. On the first night he stayed in my room, and since then in a hotel.

It wasn't easy for me to get used to Daniel again, and he thought I'd changed too. These lonely, anxious weeks, and then four days reprieve with Günter have done me in; I've become more serious, and sometimes have attacks of melancholy, which spoils the fun for both of us. Having said that, our lives are difficult enough [. . .].

We live quite pitifully, surviving on tea and soup cubes and dry bread to go with it, and if we both weren't so indifferent to money matters, we'd certainly pity ourselves. We get through the occasional worries by dreaming up crazy ideas about the future, about great books and fame and riches [. . .].

We've rearranged the room; it looks odd but I've got used to it. In the centre stands a bookshelf and to the left and right in front of the window are our desks, a kidney-shaped table, and armchair. We

104 B.R.'s sister Dorothea Reimann (b. 1943).

can't see each other when we're working, and if one of us has something to say to the other, we knock on the cupboard. In the centre of the room is an armchair and a cocktail cabinet, and we're using the couch as a dining table. It's not very comfortable or cultivated, but I only realized from Mum's shocked expression how funny and touching our paltry meals on the couch seem. [. . .]

External factors aren't making us melancholy—it's work [. . .]. Neither of us can make any progress. Sometimes Daniel gets very depressed [. . .].

He's written to Caspar in the meantime, asking for an extension, and C., who seems to welcome Dan's new alliance, promised him understanding and leniency. He also admonished me, and forced me to finish the first part of my novel by the end of next week.

If only I wasn't distracted the whole time by thoughts of Günter! [. . .] Although he swore he'd never visit me, a few days later he turned up under the pretext of fetching his drawing board. [. . .]

He didn't come into my room; he still doesn't want to see Dan, let alone shake his hand. He brought money for me, but then he talked about Dan offensively—because he's not in a position to feed a woman—and I gave him back the money [. . .], and in the end, he apologized and forced me to take it again. He feels duty-bound to keep looking after me and keeps piling on accusations about our Bohemian lifestyle, prophesying illness and early death for us.

[. . .]

On Sunday, we went to the press party in Magdeburg, and D. got to know the other writers. He finds it hard to make contact with others, but he liked Wolfgang Schreyer; Horst B[. . .] revolted him so much that he felt nauseous. B[. . .] is probably a Stasi man and what's more, he's trying to push me out of the union because he thinks I'm decadent and my new book is harmful. Well, these are all very unpleasant things [. . .]; we went less because of the press party and more to have a discussion with Wolfgang, whose advice we need.

The Stasi won't leave me alone. They're determined to pressure me into snooping on my colleagues and submitting reports, and although I've said no a hundred times, they keep coming back and can't be shaken off, first making threats, then promises. It's repulsive and depressing, and Dan is frightened to death I'm going to be arrested when I am finally blunt with them—and I'll have to be blunt to ward off these blowflies. To add to this, I'm being systematically spied on, so it seems, and I have information that not only the Stasi but even the Party are watching me. They're interested in my personal life—much more interested than is necessary or tasteful. True, I've exposed myself and said things in public that others only think. They've already got something on me, and the Stasi could frame me for defamation if they really wanted to. Me, damn it, me—even though I love socialism, our cause, in a way not many other people do, even though I'm prepared to work for this idea in an honest, decent way [. . .]. When a car drives up at night, I flinch and prick up my ears, expecting them to come for me. And in my current desolate state, I'm so emotionally overwrought I'd go to pieces and do something irrevocably stupid, perhaps even give in—hatred isn't enough to prop me up. Hatred—against single injustices, mistakes, failures and dirty tricks—isn't enough to bolster someone.

The Stasi will be back this week. I'm not going to go along with them, no matter what happens after that. I don't want any part of their filth, not at any price. I want a clean conscience as far as my friends and colleagues are concerned—let people like B[. . .] turn into informants. He does it out of conviction: 'A recognition of necessity',[105] as he probably calls it, or 'revolutionary vigilance'. Sorry, but I can't stand that kind of vigilance. If worst comes to

---

105 Originally by Hegel—'Freiheit ist Einsicht in die Notwendigkeit'—and adopted by Friedrich Engels in his book *Anti-Dühring* (1878).

worst, Wolfgang will bring the union to my aid. I'm not sure he can actually do anything as several of our colleagues are stuck in jail and no one gives a damn about them. In the end, everyone stands alone, and dies alone[106]—bitter, but that's the way it is. We just have to get used to the idea.

On Sunday evening when we came back from Magdeburg, I heard Günter whistling 'Kleiner Bär von Berlin' as we were passing the cinema. We carried on and Günter started whistling again, and then I had to stop. I said goodbye to Daniel—partly worried that there was going to be a scene—and walked on alone. G. followed me, even though he called himself a doormat for doing it [. . .].

He took me home and stayed until half past two in the morning. [. . .] We talked quite sensibly and in an almost friendly way. [. . .] That evening, I actually believed we might find a decent solution to our disagreements.

Dan was in a terrible state, however, when he came back to my house the following day. He thought I'd slept with Günter. But I really hadn't [. . .].

Burg, 19.6.58

I had to stop writing when Dan came back yesterday. He'd been over at my family's flat for one of their musical evenings [. . .]. From now on, we want to do the same every Tuesday evening. I know it does Dan good to play the piano now and again. Mum was very taken with his playing; she likes Dan in every way [. . .], and this morning she said with a laugh—but she meant it seriously—*he's a real catch*. Well, the more she enthuses, the sooner we can push for Dan to move in with me. We're already living like husband and wife.

---

106 A reference to the title of the Hans Fallada novel *Jeder stirbt für sich allein* (1947), published in English (Michael Hofmann trans.) in 2009 as *Every Man Dies Alone* (New York: Melville House) and *Alone in Berlin* (London: Penguin).

Of course, if Günter finds out, he'll never come again. I lied to him and he thinks that I haven't slept with Dan yet. Why am I lying to him about it? [. . .]

I daren't imagine our last goodbye, and still haven't seriously considered divorce. But one day, it'll happen [. . .] and Dan is doing everything he can to make me forget my lawful husband.

[. . .] I've lost count of the times I believed things couldn't get any more intense [. . .]. A few days ago, Dan wrote me a letter that put me in a frenzy, and later, when we were lying in bed together, I read it aloud to him with all its insane tenderness and perverse fantasies . . . that night there was a moment where I went over the edge, beyond the limits of human experience, I was thrown into a delirium of madness, lying there, quivering and appalled, ragged with an unbearable desire [. . .].

Burg, 29.6.58

A few minutes to write:

I've shaken off the Stasi, at least for the moment.

Seehausen, 12.7.58

I had to interrupt writing the last entry, God knows why. Now I'm in Seehausen; we're at a Writers' Union seminar and Dan has gone with the others to cut hay.

I'm rid of the Stasi[107]—hopefully for good. I gave my 'supervisor' a long lecture in which I stated my reasons, both moral and political. He left with a bleeding heart [. . .]. When I wrote down all the things that have happened, I felt sick, and I cried when I

---

107 After B.R. was unsuccessful in avoiding further communication with the Stasi, and after being pressed hard by another Stasi officer, a Lieutenant Niepel, she broke the silence that had been imposed on her. At the end of June, she presented her case for further discussion in the circle of her colleagues.

remembered all the obnoxious things they've done to me—blackmail, using my love for Günter as a bargaining chip . . .

[. . .]

Burg, 21.7.58

I wanted to begin my new quarter of a century in a laudable way by working, but I've still got too much on my mind to concentrate on Lady Jo.[108] In front of me on my desk are twenty-five dark-red roses from Daniel. On my left hand, I'm wearing a golden ring with a very pretty, milky lapis. Daniel gave it to me last night at midnight as a kind of engagement ring: it has the date when he moved in with me engraved on it: 9.6.58.

We went to the Roland with Lutz and enjoyed ourselves in a cultured manner. We drank white Bordeaux, and even Daniel joined in and was charmingly tipsy by the end. Lutz and I were pretty drunk. We didn't dance much; we talked instead—Lutz and Daniel like each other and I'm happy they get on so well.

In the early evening there was an incident that's still on my mind: Günter came. He stood in the door for a while and I saw him straight away but pretended I hadn't. He was wearing his black dinner jacket. He came over to our table and shook my hand, and Daniel's. He stayed for a few minutes by our table. I didn't look up. He exchanged a few words with Lutz and then shook hands with us again and left. At the door, he turned again. When I reached for a cigarette, I noticed that my hands were shaking.

In hindsight, we should have asked him to sit down with us. [. . .] It must have been terrible for him to stand next to us, next to the woman who is still his wife, drinking wine with her lover. This has been haunting me and I have been close to tears a few times.

---

108 Reference to Johanna, the heroine of B.R.'s novel *Zehn Jahre nach einem Tod* [Ten Years after a Death]; the manuscript remains missing.

Afterwards at the bar—the Roland now has a new, completely modern bar—Daniel raised his glass and said we should drink to Günter. And we did. [...]

Günter's changed horribly. Last week he came by; he didn't know that Daniel is living with me now (we've been sleeping together for a few days now: Mum has been unexpectedly tolerant). He came at midnight. I was half-undressed and lying next to Daniel when I heard someone jump over the fence and walk through the front garden. We hadn't quite closed the shutters and Günter climbed onto the windowsill and looked at us through the gap. He banged his fist on the shutters and shouted that I should at least get dressed.

I went out to him. He was tight again; he has reason enough. He asked to be allowed to speak to me alone and came into the house. Daniel was standing in the hallway. It was the first time that the two had seen each other. Then Daniel went upstairs and I sat down next to Günter in our room. It was a ghastly, nerve-wracking night. [...]

Later, Günter flew into a rage and I thought he was going to smash the room to pieces. He threatened to kill Daniel. His anger was terrifying, the way he hunkered there, his enormous, rough hands on his knees with his small, drunken eyes, glittering. It made me tremble with fear. For the first time ever, I was terrified of him, paralysed with fear, and I didn't know how to calm him down. I couldn't bring myself to touch him.

He begged me to sleep with him one last time but I said no and no again until he locked the door and threw himself on me and tried to rape me. I screamed and he let me go. Then he attacked me again, this time with his hand over my mouth. I saw the cruel, desperate pleasure he had in torturing me, and perhaps he hoped Daniel would hear everything and come down to find the door locked and would have to listen to what he was doing. I have no idea how I got free in the end. I was completely broken with fear and terror, and at the same time, I felt pity. God, yes, I pitied him and I still do. I know he was never capable of cruelty before and it's my fault that he is now.

Towards morning was the worst part. He started begging again, and when I told him no, he ripped the chain from my neck and gripped my throat and choked me. It happened so suddenly I could only let out a single scream, and then he squeezed my breath away, and for a few seconds, I thought it was all over. I didn't defend myself any more either. Suddenly he let go of me—I'd just looked at him. His voice was very soft and quiet in pity and mockery as he said I'd looked at him like a small animal, terrified to death. Then he was shocked at what he'd done, and made me swear not to tell anyone.

Finally he left, in the morning. At the door, he held on to me one last time and whispered into my ear: 'I love you.' [. . .]

Burg, 20.8.58

[. . .] Now we're getting down to business with our divorces. D's papers have been submitted. I'm afraid there will be some filth; gentlemanly divorces are passé[109]—nowadays, there have to be allegations and counter-allegations. I don't know what I'm supposed to do. In the end, seeing as I was one who left Günter, I can't divorce him . . . And Günter is hardly going to make the first move: he still doesn't believe that we've permanently separated.

[. . .] Last week we met at the bar in the Roland—not in very good taste, admittedly—to discuss the details of our case (at the time we didn't know about this complicated business of guilty

---

109 With the abolition of the Allied Control Council laws in the GDR on the 20 September 1955, the previous regulations for divorce became null and void. From November 1955, a new divorce law was passed, which abolished the principle of debt burden and was founded on the principle of irrevocable differences.

parties). We drank cognac and a few times we were on the brink of sliding back into bitter recriminations. [...]

We've been quarrelling very often, almost too often. I think it's just down to our nervousness. Or rather: my nervousness, because Daniel is admirably composed even during my uncontrolled outbursts. Sometimes we have bitter rows (if I remember rightly, our quarrels are usually down to jealousy or some triviality we're surprised at later) and Daniel goes off and walks around town for an hour [...], and when he returns he always brings me a box of chocolates. But after this hour of being alone, I'm so softened up anyway that I run towards him as soon as I hear him, and throw myself into his arms [...].

Before I forget: we've given up smoking, for three weeks, and forever. A test of will power—passed!

Burg, 22.11.58

[...] Last week we had our first divorce appointment. Günter and I had agreed beforehand; he was on his best behaviour and the whole procedure [...] took less than an hour; the judge even seemed very divorce-friendly. He didn't torture us with questions about our intimate lives [...].

Honestly, I'd imagined a divorce to be much more interesting, more dramatic and tearful [...], but I found the whole thing completely trite and boring.

Burg, 29.11.58

[...]

Today Daniel went to his first appointment in Mühlhausen [...].

I got divorced yesterday. The hearing was unspectacular; we made our statements as fairly as possible, neither accused the other of anything, and in the end, it was put down to unsatisfactory intellectual communication between us. Neither Günter's boozing nor my adultery were mentioned in detail. The judge was tactful and pleasant.

We weren't in court for the actual verdict. An unnecessary trial of nerves, which we were spared because the court didn't think it was critical for us to be there. If we had, perhaps I would have had a fit of sentimentality.

We went to the courthouse pub afterwards, drank a schnapps and talked for a while. I was never so aware of how much I've drifted apart from Günter. [...] What did we talk about in the past, for God's sake?

He's a young worker with narrow-minded views I find downright appalling. [...] He'd have ruined me in the long term. [...] Where did I find the energy to try and break away, or the courage to write books?

I feel like that horseman after his ride across Lake Constance[110]

...

We parted like good acquaintances who had met by accident on the street. When I see Günter again, perhaps I'll still get a shock, and my heart might hammer for a few seconds—but I won't feel regret, not a hint of longing to be back together—of that I'm certain, for once and for all. The tension between Daniel and him is over. After the first appointment two weeks ago, we sat down together in a pub and the pair of them, after inching forward very carefully and diplomatically, had a nice conversation together. [...]

---

110 Refers to *Der Reiter und der Bodensee* [A Horseman and Lake Constance], a ballad written by Gustav Schwab in 1826. The poem describes how a horseman crosses a frozen Lake Constance in the dead of winter, thinking it to be an icy field; when people come to greet and congratulate him on the other shore, he realizes the danger he had been in, falls off his horse and dies.

Silence now, not another word about days gone by, peace at last . . . and freedom at last, at last! My God, I am free for Daniel, for Daniel, for Daniel!

[. . .]

Burg 20.12.58

Daniel is in Mühlhausen for his—hopefully—final appointment.

This afternoon, a decision will be reached.

At the union yesterday we had a criticism session with the Stasi. It was terrible. I was prepared for all kinds of unpleasantries—but what actually happened surpassed my worst nightmares. The head of the Stasi, Colonel Knobbe, fired a tirade of insults at me: he called me an agent, said that I was working for the West, and that I'd deliberately stirred up this scandal to bring the Stasi into disrepute— and he'd have long since arrested me and put me on trial if it wasn't for the fact he'd have to call other writers as witnesses.

I'm normally cold as stone when dealing with the authorities (including the time I was interrogated for five hours; only afterwards did I collapse at home); but this time, I lost my cool. For starters, I wasn't prepared for such a massive onslaught, and then I was staggered to realize I have no legal rights in front of this loud, coarse, brutal, bellowing peasant. Distrust as a principle . . . What am I working for, if all my work, all my efforts, and my struggle for clarity, are worth nothing?

And all the insults culminated in the demand that the union chairman throw me out so that I can be arrested without a fuss. That was when Wolfgang Schreyer banged his fist on the table and shouted: 'If Brigitte's thrown out, I'm leaving too!' For the first time since I've known him, I saw Wolfgang pale and shaking with anger. Using very sharp words, he prohibited the Colonel to talk to me in that tone. I started crying. The other writers gradually shrank in fear.

I don't want to go into detail of what followed. It was a nightmare. The Colonel hadn't even got the right information about what happened exactly: he screamed insults and false accusations. When Wolfgang said that I might well have defected to the West, given the pressure I was facing, the guy was stupid enough to say that I couldn't have gone back before my mission was accomplished. And I couldn't even punch his face, I was desperate and wept and shouted at him that his accusation was scandalous and untrue—but what use was it against this elephant? A man without warmth or feelings, 'rationality' in fleshly form . . .

Then they turned on Wolfgang. He put up a brave show for me, then for himself, and he didn't buckle despite the pressure they put on him. What a vile, terrifying scene! I was filled with doubts again—and I wasn't alone. Brennecke, normally cautious, dared say to the Colonel that his behaviour made him lose trust. His condemnation by the writers and their defence of me subdued him a good deal.

But what now? I've deliberately only sketched out the details. I'm completely crushed. It wasn't so much the threat of arrest that destroyed me but the appalling humiliation: I had to stand by and be insulted without being able to defend or justify myself. [. . .]

Burg, 31.12.58

I've been expecting my arrest every day now: every car makes me nervous. Well, perhaps it'll all turn out all right. Despite everything, I had the most wonderful Christmas ever—and I'm sure Daniel did too.

He's divorced now, after a four-hour hearing. On Christmas Eve we got engaged. I'm happier than ever before, and wish for nothing more than to make Daniel as happy as I am. I've forgotten the other men—even Günter. For the first time, the thought of having to spend my whole life with the same man (no, being allowed to!) doesn't make me anxious. Who could be more hand-some, clever, good-natured, softer and stronger than Daniel? [. . .] I've forgotten the embraces of all those strangers. [. . .] No, there's no one besides him: I am his and his only in a way that I wasn't ready for in the past. The thought that a tragic accident might take him away from me is terrifying.

I haven't even made any New Year's resolutions for the coming year. With Daniel, everything is bound to turn out well and won-derfully, whatever happens.

[. . .]

I'll end this year now—which was my worst and best—and all the good things came from Daniel. I have found what I was looking for; what more could I wish for?

At the close of trading I'm massively in credit.

1959

Petzow, 5.2.59

We drove to Petzow, to marry at last—after a thousand problems (mostly bureaucratic) that kept delaying our date. [. . .]

On the second day, the paralysing atmosphere of a writers' residence was noticeable; we were impotent as writers yesterday, and for the first time in a long while I got—moderately—drunk.

[. . .]

We work a lot; it's tough and painful. Our rows, which are sometimes bitter, come from work: when Daniel rebels against all my goading, [. . .] or, in one of my fits of pathological emancipation, I accuse him of wanting to oppress or intimidate me—figments of my imagination that sometimes take over my rationality.

Instead of a diary, I now use a small booklet from Aufbau Verlag (with whom I've now signed a contract) in which I'll make comments about my work's progress or obstacles.

There are quite a few people in Petzow we don't think much of: Koplowitz, Petersen and others. There's an elderly lady who's interesting, a Pole, Marchlevski's daughter; she does isolate herself though.

But I have made [. . .] one of the most valuable and moving friendships in years: Bodo Uhse. A fascinating man, quiet, cultivated and full of melancholic irony. Daniel, who was considered Uhse's protégé ages ago, often enthused about him to me. Now I understand! Uhse is an outsider (aren't we too now?) and perhaps that's the source of this odd magnetism between us. We sat together for three days over several hours, not talking much. [. . .] Uhse himself barely writes any more: I think he drinks a lot—he looks terrible. He talks softly, sometimes without context, as if he were translating passing (yet profound) thoughts into language.

[. . .] I think I understand why he—a former fighter in the Spanish International Brigade and emigrant—has become a pariah and outsider these days (whom we admire and revere) [. . .].

Daniel gave him a chapter of my novel to read, and this morning [. . .] we spoke about it. Uhse said there's nothing to object to: I write with an incredible power and self-confidence. The subject matter is so difficult that he wouldn't touch it, but he's sure I'll manage it. We lingered on the subject—the age-old question of guilt— for a long time, as fruitlessly as all those before us who didn't have an answer to the question. In the end, unlike Caspar and Daniel, he tended towards my view—that I can't water down Hendrik's[111] guilt with happenstance, 'simply following orders', etc.

When his car came, he gave me his address: he wants to see us again, hear about our work, and he'll be waiting for letters from us. Shortly before he left, he said (and this is the key to his melancholy): 'Meeting you both was very painful for me. You have the strength to achieve everything I lack the strength to do.'

Burg, 22.2.59

We've long since returned home, and are so exhausted by work I wasn't even able to tell the story of our somewhat curious wedding.

The ceremony at the registry office in Werder was the simplest possible, without a sentimental sermon. Daniel gave me a wonderful pink bouquet of carnations and two luxury volumes of the *Decameron* and I gave him Heine's complete works. We were given an old edition of Kleist's complete works from the guests at the

---

111 Hendrik is the soldier in *Ten Years after a Death*.

writers' residence, and from Caspar, who arrived late in the afternoon, Hoffmann's works and two bottles of bubbly. Frau Ihlenfeld prepared a wonderful meal for us—everyone was terribly nice to us all round, just because we were getting married. Unfortunately, they all felt obliged to tell us about marriages that had gone wrong (everyone in the home has been divorced at least once), and the evening before, Frau Marchlevska—a splendid, cultivated woman whom we've befriended—discussed free love and 'marriage as a lie' with us.

But Caspar crowned it all—true, only after he was drunk. In the afternoon, we drove to Sanssouci and walked for a few hours through the wintry park; we were only slightly tiddly. After we returned, a real drinking bout ensued; Daniel was the only one who held back. First Caspar drank a pledge of eternal friendship to me; he insisted on calling me 'Lisa'. Then he tried to drink me under the table (we'd hatched the same plan from the very outset) [. . .]. The result was that while I was tipsy, he was completely drunk and could neither walk nor stand.

He prophesied that our marriage would soon collapse—I would ruin Daniel, and he regretted ever sending Daniel to Petzow a year back, as he had noted then that I gobble up men for breakfast. When he finally claimed that Daniel would cheat on me in five years at the latest, I said I would slit his throat if he did—and that's still my firm intention. It was highly entertaining to see Caspar beside himself with rage; he swore I wasn't allowed to kill such a talented person, and bemoaned Daniel's fate—fixated on that terrible vision. For hours, we wrangled over Daniel's poor throat [. . .], and Caspar wouldn't let himself be escorted to his car before I swore I'd let Daniel live. It was hilarious and a little macabre [. . .].

Today we still can't grasp that we're finally properly married after such a long period of living in sin [. . .].

For the first time today, I thought about giving up my name and taking Daniel's. I want to make a sacrifice for him—and it's a sacrifice that I would never have expected to make, as keeping my name seemed like a symbol of independence. But now I'm about to give it up—at least formally. Inconceivable thought. Daniel is so happy and I'm a little vexed by my own decision, and happy at the same time. But am I not a new person since I met him? Why shouldn't I start afresh under a new name, seeing as I have long since outgrown my first books? I just have to mull it over again. It's actually very difficult for me.

[. . .]

Burg, 22.6.59

I don't know whether I wanted to give up my diary after the wedding, or whether the drudgery of writing it got in the way. We've certainly been grafting away for the past four months, wildly and with determination, but in vain, we fear.

We're in the direst, most difficult situation. Not only no money (I can get used to living in constant poverty); but as we recently realized, our books aren't going well.[112] [. . .] We wonder what the point is of our work at a time when no one wants to know about literature any more (or what we think of as literature). We can only hope for a new, more liberal policy [. . .].

A really dreadful spring! There's been a terrible drought for weeks; the fields are dying of thirst and the dusty, dry earth is

112 In late 1958, the publishing house had already criticized both the overall concept as well as the characters, conflict resolution and language at the beginning of *Ten Years after a Death* but agreed to wait and see how the manuscript would develop. On 12 May 1959, Günter Caspar and Joachim Schreck talked with B.R. about the second part of the novel, and these initial objections were apparently confirmed. 'My wife suffered a nervous breakdown today [. . .]. Brigitte is completely at the end of her tether and she seriously intends to throw away her book after two years of working on it for nothing.' S.P. wrote the following day to Caspar (AVA, p. 1235). She did not understand nor could accept the criticism: 'The way some people would like to see the heroes in books [. . .] is nowhere to be found, no matter how hard you try to exaggerate, abstract or anticipate them' (ibid.). S.P.'s manuscript *Erziehung eines Heldes* [Education of a Hero] was accused of being 'too gloomy, unoptimistic or just not positive enough' (letter from S.P. to Günter Caspar, 5 June 1959, in ibid.).

cracking. Our beautiful flower garden, which we've put so much work into, is drying up.

The Geneva Conference,[113] which we'd pinned our hopes on, was aborted without an agreement. We were made fools of for weeks on end! An appalling farce! East and West are badmouthing each other in the dirtiest way, most of all the Germans. We're marching again on the brink of war, deliberately kept in uncertainty and fear.

[...]

Five weeks ago, I visited Caspar in Berlin. To sum it up, my book is at risk, [...] and I'd really like to switch to a different publisher. [...] When I came back from B., I had a nervous breakdown. I wanted to give up on my book.

Three days later—out of anger, desperation and spite—I sat down and within a month wrote an 80-page short story; Daniel likes it. I'm not so sure what to make of it. [...]

 D. has been dealt a heavy blow. At a public discussion about 'hard writing style'[114] (Strittmatter's obsession), his book was cited and denigrated as a cautionary example. We have reason to assume we're victims of an intrigue, of which many are spun among our socialist writers. Neither of us can work. Protest is probably pointless. We've turned to C. for help.

Sometimes I think that it would be best to quickly and quietly creep away from this country, this life.

---

113 A conference comprising several meetings of foreign ministers from the US, USSR, UK and France with representatives of both East (GDR) and West (FRG) Germany was held in Geneva between 11 May and 20 June 1959 to discuss problems of the German peace settlement and European security. It did not yield any concrete result.

114 On 11 June 1959, Erwin Strittmatter, secretary of the union, used S.P.'s novel *Education of a Hero* as an example of 'undesirable' (i.e. not socialist) 'hard-boiled' writing, such as is found in American writers like Ernest Hemingway or Norman Mailer. At the First Bitterfeld Cultural Conference on 24 April 1959, Strittmatter had also publicly vilified S.P.'s manuscript. The manuscript was missing until 2015 when it was published posthumously.

Burg, 4.7.59

Last week, we spoke to Strittmatter; he took Daniel's manuscript, and perhaps, finally, this unfortunate situation will be cleared up. He must see that Daniel has a great gift and Baumert's slander is absurd.

After endless days of being worried to death, we managed to get hold of Caspar on the phone and discovered that he's on our side, at least. [. . .]

We're in a terrible state. We are penniless, and, for the moment, we don't even know how we're going to afford the journey to Berlin. [. . .] If it wasn't for Dad, who sometimes lends us money, we would have starved long ago.

Today, I took my book in hand again. I think it's good, despite everything, and I'm going to finish writing it, no matter when and how. And it'll be published, even if I have to hawk it from one publisher to the next. I need success too. Earlier it occurred to me that I'm going to be 26 this month. [. . .]

Wernigerode, 12.8.59

We are taking a literary tour through the Harz mountains—a really tough undertaking, which the clean woodland air isn't making any more pleasant [. . .].

Daniel was released from hospital a week ago, where he'd been bedridden for a week. Perhaps it's good I didn't have the wherewithal or time to write about what's been happening to us (Mum is also in hospital, and I had to take care of the household). Today I feel able to write more calmly [. . .].

Daniel tried to poison himself. He was in Magdeburg on Sunday [. . .] and came back that night at half past one, staggering, slurring his speech, his eyes half-closed. In his pocket was an empty packet of Kalypnon;[115] he'd taken twice the fatal dose at the railway station.

Dad drove straight to a doctor and called an ambulance [. . .], and D.'s stomach was pumped. By early morning, his life was out of danger.

I was only allowed to see him again at midday. He could barely talk or see, and he was desperate to have been brought back to life. The next day, he couldn't remember anything about my first visit, and for two days I was worried he'd done himself some permanent mental damage. I wrote to Strittmatter who—not without reason— I held partially responsible for Daniel's breakdown, and asked him to come and talk to him.

That meeting in Berlin basically went as badly as it could go. It was sheer murder; Daniel's book was torn to pieces in the crudest, unfairest way imaginable. Above all, it was that little blockhead Baumert, and Klein, who made ill-founded attacks on the protagonist, whom they characterized as 'petty bourgeois'; on his inner conflicts, which they called 'the little twinges of an intellectual'; they condemned the book as 'un-socialist', and of course they knew far better than the former concrete worker P. what conditions were like in the Schwarze Pumpe.[116] [. . .] Strittmatter, who is not a theorist, spoke little; but at least he verified Daniel's great talent and praised his rural depictions.

And in all this, these people believed with unshakeable certainty that they'd steered comrade P. onto the right path, and had 'helped' him. Oh, these backslapping gestures of help, this indulgent superiority of narrow-minded critics who, of course, know much

115 A barbiturate available on prescription in the GDR but banned after the fall of the Wall.

116 VEB Schwarze Pumpe Kombinat was an approximately 25-square-kilometre lignite and gas refinery near Spremberg, GDR, from 1955 to 1990, referred to from here on as 'the plant' or 'the works'. It was the biggest lignite refinery in Europe at the time. S.P. worked as a machinist in this plant from 1958 to 59 and *Education of a Hero* deals with that experience.

better! They know the theory, but they haven't a clue about the practice; and where practice doesn't fit into their ideas, it has to be reshaped into lies and tugged into line.

For Daniel, who was already worn down by our continued hardship, this criticism was the last straw. Caspar couldn't help him either. [. . .] But C. is another chapter that I don't want to write about here: I don't think he'll last much longer—he's drinking himself slowly to death, and his political stance is mistrusted. [. . .]

Daniel thinks he's a failure, [. . .] who will never be capable of finishing a book. I can completely understand that he was desperate and unhappy; I can even understand his decision—but never the fact that he took it without me, that he wanted to abandon me, even thinking that I'd find my way more quickly without him. I was very unhappy, and very hurt that the person closest, most beloved to me would make this final decision alone. [. . .]

So I wrote to Str. although I was slightly worried that he wouldn't understand what Daniel had done, or even find it ridiculous or despicable. Nothing of the sort. Two days later, St. came to see me, we discussed things and then drove together to the hospital. [. . .] St. behaved impeccably; he [. . .] did everything to cheer up Daniel and encourage him to continue working on his book. And I think we have achieved something: Daniel has taken heart again, and even though he has put his book aside for the time being, he's determined to begin work again.

St. also helped us out financially. He left me some money and promised us a grant that would help us over the worst hardship. The union will pay for our move to Hoyerswerda[117] (where we will

117 The First Bitterfeld Conference of 24 April 1959 demanded that artists establish contact with socialist companies, the motto being 'Grab your pen, comrade; the German socialist national culture needs you!' However, it was only possible with support from the Writers' Union for B.R. and S.P. to go and work at the Schwarze Pumpe plant, which was about 20 kilometres from Hoyerswerda, a new town built in 1957 to house those who worked at the plant.

introduce ourselves next week). Our most pressing concerns are over. I think that St. has high hopes for Daniel and me, otherwise he wouldn't have sacrificed an entire day of his precious time. We have a very good impression of him: he's sensitive and not at all dogmatic, and he looks after his fellow members—we're among the youngest—in an honest, compassionate way.

Burg, 22.9.59

Daniel is a wonderful companion. Quite aside from the fact that he spoils me, as far as our modest means allow (and in fact beyond them). [. . .] Mum is in hospital and we have been taking care of the household together. Daniel doesn't balk at any kind of 'women's work'.

A few days ago, we began writing a radio play together, a quite trivial, undramatic story that takes place one night at the Schwarze Pumpe. We enjoy working together and we like the story—but we've become very sceptical and have already earmarked it as a flop.

Burg, 12.9.59

Last week we went to Hoyerswerda: we went spontaneously, hoping to put an end to the silly, pointless exchange of letters. H. is overwhelming and the refinery is so wonderful that I walked around all day as if drunk. I don't want to go into descriptions here—H. and the refinery will appear often enough in stories or even a novel, if I can manage such a thing in literary form.

We were given a very friendly reception, stayed in an entire suite in the Glück auf Hotel and were given help by the personnel department and trade union without a lot of red tape. [. . .] We won't be given artist-in-residence positions; together we've been allocated a job-share on the shop floor as laboratory workers. Hourly wage: 1.56. On top, the trade union will give us 200 DM a month, and for that, we'll do book reviews, etc. So we can earn a really good living. Admittedly, though, there won't be much time to write. [. . .]

Our laboratory boss is refreshingly honest in a gruff way: I think he doesn't expect two crackpot writers to be very productive. And it didn't suit him—and he's right too—that we only want to work during the day. So we said we were prepared (with huge reservations, I have to admit) to do night shifts too.

I'm afraid, miserably afraid, of failing. And having to endure the derision or even pity of others if I am physically too weak. I find it so difficult to stand up or walk around for hours. Of course no one will reproach me for this weakness, but the thought fills me with terror. [. . .]

Lehmann drove us around the new town all morning; I was captivated by the colourful blocks of flats and thrilled at this tremendous architectural undertaking. A beautiful, modern town is sprouting up here and you can watch as it grows. An optimistic landscape—perhaps I can achieve spiritual health here. The opposite doesn't bear thinking about.

In the evening, we visited our colleague Siegrist and he read a passage from his novel set in the Pumpe,[118] which he'd thrown together in a few months. Dreadful! It was torture having to listen to him and even worse not to be able to criticize him. S., terribly self-confident, is one of those people who will become your mortal enemy if you criticize him. [. . .] We have to keep our distance from him; a real dead loss who makes grand Leninist gestures and boasts about his working-class roots, which I find really repugnant.

---

118 Heinrich Ernst Siegrist: author of the 1960 novel *Stürmische Jahren* [Stormy Years]. Siegrist had worked at the Schwarze Pumpe for a long time and was responsible for writing a company chronicle. As he was considered an experienced author, the Writers' Union suggested that he mentor S.P. in Hoyerswerda, who needed 'solid ground under his feet' after his suicide attempt (SVA, portfolio 105, sheet 5).

The flats, incidentally, are absolutely beautiful; we [. . .] have already furnished ours in our minds, each day differently. But nice furniture is really difficult to come by: we trawled for hours through various furniture shops in Magdeburg and Burg but didn't find anything that matched our taste in the slightest. True, we can't afford to buy anything for now anyway. We don't have a penny to our name. [. . .] I still don't know how things will turn out—I have a pile of outstanding debts but it's difficult to squeeze even a few marks out of the publishers. I'm not in Aufbau's good books at the moment because I turned down their contract for my short story. They throw thousands of marks at other writers, but in our case, they're insultingly petty.

Neues Leben want to publish *Woman in the Pillory* as a paperback edition but can't pay my fee till next year. It's so humiliating to have to fight for money on all fronts. [. . .]

I'm very sad when I think about saying goodbye to Burg and Mum and Dad. [. . .] Sure, we're headed towards a lovely, exciting and productive adventure and I won't let anyone know how I feel deep down, and that I'm a coward and above all, terribly, terribly afraid. Daniel is happy. Is that not something?

Burg, 4.10.59

Our chronic financial worries have been solved—for how long? Last week we were in Berlin. Caspar put himself at my service (as he has done so often!) and managed to procure me a new, very decent contract for the short story. The first instalment was paid immediately in cash—good God, the feeling of having a couple of hundred-mark notes in my pocket, to be able to pay off debts and not have to creep past shop windows like a tiny nobody. Daniel showered me with presents; he didn't want anything for himself and I had to spend a long time persuading him to buy a pair of shoes at least.

I felt like severing my book contract and going to Günter Deicke, but Günter Kaspar doesn't want to let me go just yet. When we were talking about my novel, I took the opportunity of raising a few unpleasant aspects of his behaviour—his way of treating young authors, ignoring the readers, etc. Daniel stood by me and Caspar had to hear all kinds of things. At times, he looked angry and frustrated. [...] For the first time, he attested to my talent—albeit a workaday kind of talent, as he called it. He thinks I'm lazy and expect everything to fall into my lap on its own. There is a jot of truth in this but what does Caspar know about my inner torture, the evenings spent brooding and hours of depression ...

In the past, he decisively rejected editing our texts (not without reason, as he's inundated with work); but this time, he seemed more open to the suggestion of going through our work systematically, page by page, for a few days. He needs two more years, he says, and then he will have squeezed some real literature out of me. [...] But I know very well that I can't manage the volume of work he expects from me yet. In this regard, I'm good at assessing myself and my artistic limits.

(Oh and Deicke[119] has picked up my manuscript and wants to read it; he wants to acquire it for his publishing house. I'd probably have fewer difficulties there. Reason tells me to listen to Caspar and push myself—but I want some success and be freed of this damned novel at last.)

Burg, 11.11.59

Just burnt my diaries from 1947 to 1953—all twenty of them—and now my heart aches as if I've destroyed a living thing, some part of myself. The many hundreds of pages, covered with my childish, spidery scrawl, and later, a pretentious, energetic hand ... Thousands of hours of my sufferings as a schoolgirl, the tiny and momentous

---

119 In the meantime, Deicke had become the director of Verlag der Nation, Berlin.

events, day in, day out, meticulously recorded . . . I could cry the tears all over again that I cried over those diaries. Why does it hurt so hellishly? Three books on my first true love (Klaus, my God! Did he really exist? That handsome blonde boy who has a paunch these days, the beginnings of a bald patch and a child?), the [. . .] fiery dreams I had (didn't I want to become an African missionary?), my gushing, enthusiastic confessions—well, now I'm crying. I've burnt my childhood, my youth, and all the memories I don't want to recall any more.

If only my diaries had been a little more factual and objective (when will I *finally* become objective?), then at least they'd have some documentary value. If I'd reported on political events in detail, on our ideological conflicts at school, my work as an FDJ officer,[120] my time as a teacher and my dear little pupils (who are today young women, some extremely beautiful), our cultural groups, and so on. But everything's all mixed up with my endless love stories and when I read them today, I feel ashamed about my hundreds of liaisons; friends I don't see any more, a fiancé I can barely remember [. . .]. There's such an unpleasant precociousness in those early diaries, and a restless, impatient temperament in the later ones.

[. . .]

I think I regret having thrown all of them into the stove. Of course it's also a burden and in the end, it was because of Daniel that I had to clean up these leftovers from the past. [. . .]

I've only kept the last ones from '53 on, at least for now. Even though they contain the dirtiest and unhappiest chapters: my doubt and desperation about our cause, my first steps as a writer, my marriage to Günter, objections to his drinking, my adultery and sickening, deceptive manoeuvrings, decadence and tedium, misplaced illusions, nights spent agonizing over books never published, weeks

120 See note 36.

and months spent in perpetual drunkenness, waking up in strangers' beds—quandaries, wrong turns, mistakes, cheap ways of getting high . . . And at the end of the last book, meeting Daniel. Where would I be today if he hadn't appeared? I enjoyed success too early, married the wrong man, and hung out with the wrong people; too many men have liked me, and I've liked too many men.

[. . .]

I've just decided to throw away the books from '53–'54 after all. Love stories from an overstretched imagination, away with it all!

[. . .]

Burg, 12.11.59

When I took the ashes out of the stove early this morning—fine, snow-white, delicate flakes of ash—I was foolish enough to be astonished. As if I hadn't reckoned on the evidence from the past ten years turning to ash in a few minutes. Early this morning, I carried on with my annihilation: letters—hundreds of letters (where are all the Georgs and other men who wrote me love letters and poems?)—newspaper clippings, pictures and old manuscripts. I held on to a few old relics.

I am so confused, my emotions are hallucinatory, surreal. I shouldn't have read all that old garbage again (which I'm emotionally attached to), only the last pages of my 1958 diary: a young, beautiful person with wonderful eyes, thin nervous hands, an encounter like no other before [. . .].

His name is Siegfried. Today he's called Daniel [. . .] and when I wake up in the night, my head is lying on his shoulder. Daniel is really—my God, whom do I have to thank for him? [. . .]

DECEMBER 1959

Burg, 7.12.59

Last week we were supposed to move to Hoyerswerda. Our plan has been wrecked yet again. The flats won't be ready on time. The construction teams have done sloppy work [. . .]. At least two weeks' work, valuable time and a lot of money down the drain. Who would buy a badly written book from us? They should ensure that the workers are made to feel responsible for botching it.

I finished my radio drama in a fortnight, a brutally short time, but I worked until I was fit to drop. I hope the radio people will take it on. We've already written one radio play together and have submitted it to a competition. [. . .] At first, working together was damned difficult and we only managed to communicate after some bitter, unproductive quarrelling. In the end, we found the whole play stupid and primitive, and we were astonished when Caspar, after reading it, wrote to us that he thought it was a good, well-rounded piece of work, and he was happy we'd dropped our affected style. Are we really such unreliable judges of our own work?

Financially, things have improved. I received an advance for *Woman in the Pillory* and the fee for my short story 'The Confession'.[121] Aufbau Verlag will publish it next year. I based it on a report by public prosecutor Kluth built on my research of a legal issue in my novel. Caspar was annoyed: he cited 'The Confession' as evidence of my 'workaday talent'—meaning that I can write a decent short story in four weeks—and my defiance. He said I only wanted to prove that I can make a worker the central character of a book. He's not entirely wrong, but why did he then accuse me of only being able to write about artists and intellectuals?

[. . .]

121 'Das Geständnis' (1960).

Burg, 9.12.59

I stayed in bed all day yesterday with terrible nervous pains, but this morning I couldn't stand it any longer and got up even though I knew I wouldn't achieve much. I am in a terrible mood—no, it's not just a bad mood; it's a depression that has gone on for several days now, making me snappy, spiteful and sad. [. . .] Every time I glance at the newspaper, or even in the *NDL*, I'm frustrated. Our literature is going to the dogs. They babble on about masterpieces that will be published in the near future, but in truth, with very few exceptions, no good book has been published for years. Opportunists and numbskulls everywhere. The only subject worth discussing in a novel, it seems, is the need to increase work productivity; whitewash and dogmatism have replaced honest, critical debate. Human problems are not in vogue and I'm expecting the idiotic phrase 'bleeding-heart humanitarianism'[122] to turn up at any moment.

Recently—without any conviction—I was crossing out things in my latest novel [. . .] and it's this helpless, cowardly kowtowing to an unjust censorship that's the most oppressive thing, more oppressive than the censorship itself. An author always having to make concessions in order to buy the right to be published. When will they finally grasp that literature shouldn't be a slave to propaganda or extol the ruling order? I recently heard a radio interview with a Spanish author, de Castillo[123] (a young man who went through the Nazi camps) who said that if you've written a book and haven't come a step nearer to loving humanity or understanding a

122 'bleeding-heart humanitarianism' (*Humanitätdüselei*): a frequent criticism during political discussions when matters were not judged from the point of view of the class system but from a 'general human perspective'.

123 Michel de Castillo (b. 1933): actually a French author born in Madrid, who was interned in a Nazi concentration camp in Mende, southern France, during the Second World War. He is well known for his novels *The Child of Our Time* (1957) and *The Disinherited* (1959).

certain situation by the end of it, your book is worthless and has been completely in vain […]

If it was the working process that was the problem, we could just disband the Writers' Union and content ourselves with being 'correspondents of the people'. Oh, I don't know, I don't want to write another word.

[…]

Burg, 11.12

For the last three or four days, I've been sitting here, dejected, in front of a blank sheet of paper, trying to reconnect the threads of plot in my novel, which snapped more than three months ago. I'm definitely in the thick of the tricky part—Hendrik's story of his crime in the Soviet Union […] I have to get to know my characters again like friends I haven't seen for a long time. I've decided, after endless arguments with Caspar and nerve-wracking discussions with myself, to write the first part of my *Johanna* book from scratch. This colourful, sad and slightly insane woman will be a bit duller, but at least I'll be able to develop her and I hope that this new concept will make people believe in her more readily than they do now.

[…]

Burg, 13.12.59

This morning, the 3rd Sunday of Advent, an urgent letter arrived from the works: the flats are ready, we can move in. After being all set half a dozen times, but having to postpone because the block hadn't been ready, we now have to up sticks just before Christmas. It's damned hard; for the first time, I'll have to celebrate Christmas without my parents, brothers and sister. Celebrate, my God. We'll be up to our ears in work and horribly homesick. I would never have taken a step like this if it weren't for Daniel, that's for sure. Of course I can't concentrate on my novel any more, a thousand things are going round in my head [...]. I don't know how I'm supposed to manage without my wonderful, ever loyal, ever helpful mum.

B., 18.12.

We are not moving until 6 January; we can't get a removal van any sooner. [...]

Yesterday I tidied up my correspondence folder from the past six years [...].

I went through all my feuds with the writer's group again, our bitter, fierce clashes: I left the group a few times, despairing of my talent or loudly protesting against the 'reservoir of mediocrity'. [...] Oh and it seems I must take most of the blame for the disputes. I was, it seems, a rather difficult character; I couldn't fit into the collective—and I still can't today. Sometimes my solitariness troubles or frightens me; a few days ago, at the union's Christmas party, I fled, although the others clearly disapproved; the sight of colleagues discussing their cars and their groomed wives (none of whom has a career) and their well-brought-up Stefans and Matthiases set off a panic in me. I was paralysed, incapable of a friendly word—I would have suffocated in that staid, middle-class atmosphere. [...]

Burg, 27.12.59

For two days there's been a vile mood between us. Outside the window, a wild blue, early spring day is glittering brightly, and Daniel is creeping around, downcast and at the same time dangerously on edge, and says he's disgusted with himself. He was recently X-rayed and examined [...]: Daniel has a serious heart defect, and if he doesn't give up smoking once and for all, the doctor says he's only got another two years. This revelation has badly shaken him, as he's already prone to hypochondria [. . .]. Besides, he doesn't talk about it, I have to rely on assumptions, and his pale, suffering expression irritates me almost to the point of anger. Till now, we always contemplated death with equanimity or even a hint of cynicism . . . [. . .]

Lutz says I'm brutal. He's probably right. I am hard-hearted enough to keep pushing Daniel, to chivvy him into working even if he doesn't feel well, and to reproach him if he can't brush aside physical weakness. But I force myself too! I often feel really sick, and I have almost constant severe headaches, which not even tablets cure—but I still work. Daniel says I'm a workhorse. And it's true. If I don't manage to write for two or three days—because of silly, time-wasting household chores—I get sick and hysterical. I need my work like—really, like an addict; it means happiness to me, self-gratification, both a selfish and altruistic pleasure . . . Apart from those writers who do it for the money or to pass on information and facts, I have yet to meet a serious and credible writer who dared say he wrote with the reader in mind (such claims, cloaked in clichés are still reserved for cultural functionaries); for every writer, work is a self-examination, and it seems that precisely therein lies the art: to make this self-examination universally interesting and accessible to the widest possible readership.

[. . .]

Burg, 31.12.59

Daniel gave me white lilac and a bottle of bubbly. We're celebrating at home (celebrating is too sophisticated a word), and now we're listening to the Ninth Symphony—as we do on the last day of every year—and I don't think I'm listening to it with quite the same standard enthusiasm as before; I've developed a new relationship to music through Daniel, or, rather, I have a modest relationship to it for the first time. [. . .]

Daniel is better, although not physically; he has the flu again. Perhaps the holidays, a time for peace and family, have depressed him; he can't contact his parents, who fled the Republic in May. His siblings are also all over there. Christmas Eve was very nice. Daniel showered me with gifts; with amazing skill, he even made something for me: a bookmark sawn from a sheet of silver, depicting the outline of our Schwarze Pumpe with its three chimneys and cooling towers. But no matter how hard we try to recapture some of the sweet excitement of childhood, we never quite manage it. There are brief moments of that sunken bliss but the golden glow has gone and can't be rekindled. Perhaps we will rediscover a hint of it when we have a child . . .

[. . .]

It just occurred to me that I normally take stock of the year on New Year's Eve and in my diaries at least, make a whole host of noble resolutions. That's pretty silly, and this time I don't want to.

The radio people sent me back my play; they 'liked it exceptionally', the adaptation was given friendly praise, but they regretted . . . That political 'but' . . . How many of my works have already been annihilated by risk-avoiders and narrow-minded dogmatists! Well, I don't want to become bitter and vindictive; what makes me that way in the end is not a rejection decided after a plenary meeting of dramaturges, but the point Daniel made—that there's no longer a demand for the subject. Of course they don't openly admit it; not even Caspar openly admits it. But no matter where I read from my novel, I feel the German discomfort of wanting to forget the terrible past as quickly as possible. Enough! My blood is seething. Sometimes I hate the whole German pack, this nation of sycophants and lemmings, little people who only do what those above them order . . .

[. . .]

The final chorus from the Ninth . . . Good God, a few more lines to this ethereal music and I'll start making noble plans for the future after all. I'm convinced that next year will be difficult, hard work and often as depressing and unsuccessful as ever. Our adventure at the Schwarze Pumpe is fast approaching, and I fear we won't be up to it.

Next week on Wednesday, we move.

1960

Hoyerswerda, 21.1.60

[. . .] Over the last few weeks, we have been inundated with an abundance of experiences, new faces, new people and bewildering impressions that overwhelmed us. [. . .]

The first few days were bad; I was so homesick it made me ill and I cried for hours [. . .]. I cried for Mum like a stubborn child (I'm twenty-six, for heaven's sake!) [. . .]. She's already written to me [. . .] full of tender exhortations and advice for the kitchen, trying to comfort me and giving funny little reports from home.

To begin with I loathed this building, which feels like a giant honeycomb, crammed with menacing, alien people and constantly noisy. I had feelings of hatred towards people which I can only justify given the idyllic tranquillity of our house on the edge of town, where we were surrounded by people I knew and loved. The whole overpowering newness of Hoyerswerda didn't appeal to me (although I know all too well how much the beautiful, comfortable, sunny flats mean to our young town and its residents, who for the most part have left cramped, stifling conditions); but it has no tradition, no atmosphere, it's just modern. It does have a certain romanticism—but it's one thing to wander the rutted streets stacked with wooden planks and building rubble for a day, gazing around in enthusiasm, and another to live in this town as one of thousands.

The condition of our flat has, of course, added to our depression; it was dirty and dusty, and we couldn't move for crates and books and boxes and furniture. [. . .] but today we've already made it spotless, beautiful and colourful. True, Daniel's room isn't finished yet; we have no money until my fee arrives from the *Wochenpost* which has been serializing my 'Confession' as a pre-print since the beginning of January. But the editorial office has remained politely silent on the subject of money. Our modest reserve is dwindling alarmingly [. . .].

We were in the plant last week to introduce ourselves. [. . .] We start in the lab on the 1st of March. We need to catch up with at least part of what we missed due to all our literary projects over the past few weeks.

We were warmly welcomed by Krupper, the man responsible for cultural work.[124] He fetched the librarian [. . .]. She kept reassuring me how eagerly she'd been awaiting the 'Pitschmann couple' and about how keenly they anticipated our contribution to their cultural work; and I thought with horror, as I listened with a polite expression, about my novel and all my literary plans, my precious time. [. . .] However, when we demurred modestly, they seemed to understand our wish not [. . .] to be promoted from writers to full-time cultural officials. I think we'll have to muster some energy and be a bit selfish so that they don't just ride roughshod over us. [. . .]

Hoywoy, 8.2.60

Yesterday I discovered the first white hair on Daniel's head and pulled it out; I was so shocked—solemnly shocked—that I had to raise a glass of vodka.

[. . .] I've started writing a girls' book, which Lewerenz is already salivating over. But the publishing house has treated me so shabbily that it'll cost them: I'll squeeze concessions out of them that won't suit the accountant. I'm livid at those little penny-pinchers.

---

124 Factory plants and large state-owned companies in the GDR employed full-time cultural officials and ran cultural centres for the staff and people in the community.

The fee for the pre-print in the *Wochenpost* was very low (900 DM—before taxes are deducted) [. . .]. I was banking on that money to furnish Daniel's room [. . .].

Last week we signed the contract with the plant.[125] They prepared the big event in a dignified manner, with good wine and sandwiches (they seem to think that writers are always hungry), and were quite cross when we raised objections to the contract and pointed out that our union also has a say.

We almost got into an argument and I had to explain sharply that we are not here as private individuals, that we have a strong trade union behind us, just like the one behind the plant stewards.

We also found a better solution for the practical work: each of us will take on a socialist brigade[126]—we need the contact, it'll save us time (because we will only work one day a week in our brigade); the work in the lab wouldn't have been useful, either for us or the plant.

We spent the last few days biting our nails: Mum wrote that Gretchen had been taken to hospital (on the same evening that Lutz finally came back from Rostock after passing his exam [. . .]) and that she needed a Caesarean section. We [. . .] were happy yesterday

---

125 'Friendship Treaty' dated 3 February 1960. The Central Club Committee and the Schwarze Pumpe union pledged to grant B.R. and S.P. insight into all parts of the operating units; to involve them in important consultations, exchanges of experience with socialist brigades, cultural leaders, etc. who dealt with cultural problems; to provide the opportunity to express their opinions on company radio and company newspapers; to provide them with support amounting to 200 Deutschmarks from the cultural fund. The authors undertook to organize readings of different writers' works and literary events, and to provide support for the workers' theatre that they would establish on the plant's grounds and to run a circle called 'worker writers'.

126 Artists and writers in factory works would invariably be allocated a specific brigade or work team which they would lead and in which they would play an integral role. The Nikolai Mamai brigade from the Bitterfeld Electrochemical Plant established a competition under the slogan 'Work, learn and live in a socialist manner' (3 January 1959). As a result, the brigades set up cultural and educational plans that had to be pursued to earn the title of 'Socialist Brigade'.

when Lutz's telegram came: an eight-pound, dark-eyed little tot was born. [...]

Good heavens, I so long for a baby ...

Hoy., 12.2.

I am in an absolutely foul mood: found out that the winners of the 'Promotion of Contemporary Literature' competition were announced yesterday. First prize for short stories went to Morgner,[127] the wife of the terror (terrorizing editor at Aufbau) for a story at least three levels below my 'Confession'. Not even an acknowledgement for me [...]. I've also heard that my chief enemy is on the jury: the she-Wolf, who already messed up the pre-print in the *NDL*[128] (which Deicke guaranteed me at the time) by dirty scheming. I curse this bloody literature business three times over! [...]

Last night I had a vivid dream about Georg Pilz. We were at Nellessens, I felt terrible among those middle-class people; Georg came, we left together, regretted that we'd ever separated. He showed me a dreadful tome of a thriller: the only type of literature that people could still enjoy. He wasn't in good sorts, was terribly dressed, with clumsy, torn shoes. I kept having to look at his shoes; the sight gripped my heart. I think we love each other very much. Then we were kettled by a convoy of brand-new cars, all sparkling with chrome, that sped towards us, sirens screaming. We were frozen to the spot, with men in uniforms shooting at us. Georg pulled out a gun—we wanted to die of our own free will, not knowing the way

127 A reference to Irmtraud Morgner (1933–90), best known for her experimental work *The Life and Adventures of Trobadora Beatrice as Chronicled by Her Minstrel Laura* (1974). Her first husband was Joachim Schreck, an editor at Aufbau Verlag.

128 The *NDL* editors had been waiting for a new version of the manuscript. Günter Caspar wrote to B.R. on 5 March 1959: 'Christa Wolf assured me that the printing of the play had only been postponed, not cancelled. We have arranged to speak to the *NDL* editorial staff again when we have read the second part more closely' (AVA, p. 1030).

forward or back. When he put the gun to his temple, I woke up and had a sudden sharp longing for Georg.

Been restless all day; I want to write to him, ask how he's doing— but perhaps he is no longer in the Republic. His name is never heard any more; ever since he left the *Sonntag* editorial board out of protest, he's been banned, become a non-person. [. . .] now I recognize the wisdom and validity of his teachings [. . .].—I have terrible nightmares every night—a treasure trove for a psychoanalyst.

Hoy., 14 2.

Again—or still—upset, nervous, angry at everyone and everything. Cursing this backwater and the idea to come here—and knowing that I'll be enthusing about it again tomorrow or next week as a result of some minor experience, some encounter with a person I like.

All the damned work is to blame. [. . .] I'm not happy with myself, beginning to grasp that I will never write what I want [. . .]; my girls' book is just hard slog to earn money. We have to get out of this mess, out of the depressing hand-to-mouth living and I can't rely on Daniel as the breadwinner for the time being (my daydreams of a baby, God, don't think about them; a child in our precarious life would be irresponsible) [. . .].

Our motto is lying on our desk: 'Three difficulties when writing the truth: True is whatever the editors believe is true. Beautiful is whatever the editors believe is beautiful. Typical is whatever the editors believe is typical.'[129]

Last week, the worker writers' circle[130] was set up. Of the twenty invited, only four turned up; none with any potential, I imagine.

129 A reference to Bertolt Brecht's essay 'Five Difficulties in Writing the Truth', written in 1934 as a response to National Socialism about the role of the writer under fascism. See *Brecht on Art and Politics* (Steve Giles and Tom Kuhn eds) (London: Oxford University Press, 2015), pp. 141–57.

130 In the worker writers' circle, set up following the First Bitterfeld Conference, working people from different author-led circles had a chance to introduce and discuss their writing efforts.

Only little Volker Braun,[131] who got his school-leaving certificate and then worked on the factory floor for four years, seems to be gifted. He reminds me of my Ulli-brother—in every respect a late developer.

The plant is starting to squeeze their money's worth out of our intellects, all for a ridiculous 160 DM (which just about covers the bus fare). We've been reading manuscripts, giving receptions for writer-workers, having hour-long discussions; now we're style-editing a brochure. This is not what I'm here for, God damn it, this is editor's work. On the 24th, I'll meet 'my' brigade; I'm curious and slightly sceptical.

Hoy., 15.2.

Horrible headaches all day [. . .]. Tablets don't help any more; these attacks are killing me. And then the nightmares: every night, murder and homicide and the great white ghost horse, which laughs with bared teeth. In the mornings, I wake up soaked in sweat.

[. . .]

I'm now reading—with jealousy, indignation, envy, and empathy—the insane diary of Countess zu Reventlow. My God, she really lived it up! And how dishonest she is, how wild, vicious and gifted—a full-blooded woman (that's a stupid and hideous expression, but it describes the Countess very well). I can identify with her somewhat; if Daniel hadn't turned up . . . who knows where and with whom I'd be gallivanting. I admit it: bohemian Munich—and the Berlin Press Club . . . [. . .]

---

131 Volker Braun had completed a practical year in a printing company in Dresden after leaving school in 1957, because he wanted to become a journalist. Dismissed for making unpopular political statements, he then found work in the Schwarze Pumpe, first in the engineering department as a pipe layer, and later in open-cast mining, where he acquired a skilled craftsman's diploma. He was not a member of B.R. and S.P.'s writing circle, but already belonged to the Working Group of Young Authors (AJA, Arbeitsgemeinschaft Junger Autoren) in Cottbus.

At night. [. . .] My pale-skinned boy lies on our bed and says that diaries are a form of masturbation—not even an intellectual one, but (in a tone of deepest revulsion) simply masturbation per se.

[. . .]

Hoy., 16.2.

At night, more dreams of nuclear explosions, mushroom clouds and scorched landscapes. I have experienced Hiroshima a dozen times in my dreams.

Ulbricht's letter to Adenauer (a masterpiece in the art of diplomacy: 'You're no longer a novice . . . ');[132] the GDR wants to ask its allies for missile bases. Nuclear armament—after we angrily, pathetically judged the West Germans for years for living under the direct threat of rockets. Who is the GDR? Which of our workers wants their factory surrounded by missiles?

The letter produced outrage. In Café Klein, two comrades excitedly shouted that we would at last 'infest', beat up and smother West Germany in its cradle. They want to march again. Deep surprise at my objection that it would be a war of aggression, and that we would be morally in the wrong. 'But they don't have a hinterland'. We have one, that's clear. Which is a great consolation if the 'sun of Satan' rises over our cities.

[. . .]

132 GDR premier Walter Ulbricht's letter to West German chancellor Konrad Adenauer: 'If the government of the West German Federal Republic does not stop nuclear armaments in the shortest time [. . .], the government of the German Democratic Republic will be forced to take appropriate defensive measures and ask all of its allies to provide missile weapons. [. . .] I do not think you are so ill-informed that your opinion about the GDR could be explained with ignorance, nor so inexperienced that you do not give an account of the terrible end such a policy would bring about. After all, you are not a novice in politics. Therefore, we can only conclude that by spreading falsehoods about the GDR [. . .] you are deliberately sowing hatred to make the population of West Germany ready for a war of fratricide and revenge in Germany' ('Walter Ulbricht's letter to Konrad Adenauer' in *Wochenpost*, Berlin, No. 5, 1960, p.1ff.).

Hoy., 27.3.

[. . .] Three weeks ago, first '10th Anniversary' brigade book reading:[133] 35 pipe-layers and welders; then a big booze-up at the Schwarze Pumpe bar. The young people feted me, my book has been well received—a book for young adults, set in my brigade. They are proud, hoping to find themselves in it (but I have to generalize; explaining this is difficult). Perhaps I really do know how to get on with others—especially so-called ordinary people. I was warmly welcomed, they were able to empathize with my heroes; we discussed it for a long time and laughed a lot.

On the subject of schematism: they want Curt, the plant manager's son, to perish. They don't like all these stories with happy endings or about collectives because they disprove themselves: their effort towards outsiders, their conflicts with individual colleagues— no, their lives, or life itself, disproves their views and mine on schematism.

Hanke, the foreman. A wonderful man, smart, good, astute, and an inventor who has a number of important suggestions for improvements up his sleeve. (Recycling of waste oil. The Leuna works charge 2,000 DM per metric ton. Hanke has developed a system that would enable the plant to recycle its own oil. 300 DM per metric ton. [. . .] Trials with GDR electrodes. So far only Western electrodes for high-alloy steels. [. . .])

H. is 36. I guessed he was 50; he's very overweight and almost bald. A man with infinite humour. He's the positive hero par excellence. Last week he walked for hours with me through the factory buildings, explained everything and patiently answered my questions (I'm just an idiot when it comes to technology). [. . .] The day after tomorrow will be my first shift. I'm really scared, but Hanke will calm me down. The brigade is looking forward to

133 The '10th Anniversary' brigade was so named by B.R. to refer to the founding of the GDR in 1949.

seeing me with overalls and dirty hands—they want to arrange for a photographer. [. . .]

Neues Leben is very pleased with my first chapter. The other day Lewerenz was here; he [. . .] played it cool, sceptical, astonishingly enthusiastic. We became closer again (weren't we friends for years, in love with each other? My God, we met a long time ago; I was 20 and the publisher's great hope. Too bad I didn't meet expectations, am practically forgotten these days and have to make my comeback). After a bottle of vodka, we warmed up a bit. Daniel watched us benevolently and said that all my editors were shamelessly in love with me.

This week, three days in Berlin, and then in Prieros at the NL's Authors' Conference. The first afternoon with Caspar. [. . .] Waffled on about my novel, about Harich, Kantorowicz [. . .]. Nachbar has supposedly written a wonderful novel: slightly envious. C. said that authors no longer wrote, no more new publications at the book fair (why?). Authors live off advances—we, too, are thousands of marks in debt to Aufbau Verlag, but C. isn't pressurizing us, at least not too much. Gave me half a year's holiday for the young adult book. After that, a novel. [. . .]

Bus ride to Prieros. The president's comfortable summer residence in the past. Swimming pool in the park, huge estate, pines and birches. On the first evening, a long game of skat. Publishing director Peterson teased me. The next morning everyone knew I had 'greatly impressed him'. P. is sixty, for Christ's sake!

Interesting conference, lively discussion, bold views. A new political course seems to be emerging. Refreshingly young writers.

Not too much beating about the bush. I feel encouraged. Later loud and fiery one-on-one conversations at the dinner table [. . .].

Wonderful evening. Sat with Lewerenz, Jakobs and some other writers at the table. We drank vodka and later French white wine [. . .]. Wild debates on jazz and literature. [. . .] An hour before midnight, Peterson took advantage of Lewerenz's brief absence to sit down next to me. [...] At midnight I couldn't stand it. Told Walter we should get some fresh air and left the publishing director sitting there. [...]

We felt like schoolchildren who had slipped away from a strict teacher. Strolled (no, staggered) through the park and gradually sobered up. Barbed wire, a twinkling river, pines, white birches (ah, cowboy and Indians, letters on birch bark ...). Cool, windy March night, the air wonderfully pure, a few lights between the trees, we were heady with spring [...]. Walter said I looked like a teenager and behaved like a seventeen-year-old. Even at sixty I won't be any older than I am now. [...] It's only with Walter that I can walk through a park like this, feeling so young, playing the romantic, like a virgin [...].

The next morning, Peterson sat down at my table. [...] And also took the bus seat next to me [...]. P. told great stories about his time in emigration. Later, in the publishing house, everyone smiled because old P. [...] had become so lively. He asked to see my manuscript (Sellin claims that he hasn't read a manuscript for ages) [...].

Hoy., 2.4.60

Damned little time to write. [...] Cultural conference, FDJ meeting with big plans: I spurred on the young people in my brigade to give our two maladjusted members moral support and help at work. First indifference, even callousness, then a sudden enthusiasm for the job. I'm very proud. I'm sympathetic to everyone who has suffered setbacks in life—but now it's an active sympathy.

On Wednesday my first day on the shop floor: grinding valves, not too badly. Managed quite nicely. (The next day, slightly sore muscles.) The brigade is very kind to me. Volunteers always stand next to my vice trying to talk to me. Writers seem to be a kind of confessor for others.

APRIL 1960

[. . .] Felt wonderfully strong in overalls and with dirty hands—a new feeling, slightly exuberant . . .

[. . .]

Hoy., 10 4.

Our wedding day:[134] showered with beautiful gifts from Daniel, including an Indian-red handbag, which he is even more proud of than me (up to now I've been running around with very shabby handbags—should start trying to be more elegant; not my strong point unfortunately). [. . .]

Serious argument with Siegrist yesterday: I told him the truth at last, more gently than he deserved. He was—or seemed—shattered. [. . .] We tried to suggest that he revise his book again. He won't do it. [. . .] Hopefully the criticism will knock him out! [. . .]

Production day. Walked around the briquette factory for an hour with Hanke and came back as black as a negro. What a man! [. . .] I thought he was a comrade, but now I hear that he's in the NDPD.[135] Weird, gratifying change of consciousness in me: because a man is good and smart and patient, I consider him a comrade [. . .]. Learnt that he had been disciplined some time ago because of some business with a woman, and I was somewhat relieved: at last, a blemish on his shining image [. . .]. He often reminds me of Erwin Garbe, whose strong personality shaped my ideas of what a good communist is.[136]

134 On the 10th of each month B.R. and S.P. celebrated the day they got married.

135 NDPD (National-Demokratische Partei Deutschlands): National Democratic Party of Germany, whose programme demanded, among other things, the promotion of the middle class. It was part of the ruling National Front, an alliance of political parties and mass organizations that was led by the SED.

136 Erwin Garbe was the Reimann family's neighbour in Burg. As a German soldier in the Second World War, he had changed sides in Yugoslavia to join the Yugoslav Partisans, and had fought under Tito's leadership. His descriptions of his experiences deeply impressed B.R. and, among others, inspired her to write *The Death of Beautiful Helena* and *Children of Hellas*.

Berlin, 29.4.60

Sitting in the press cafe, waiting for Daniel [...]. Yesterday, Neues Leben; in the evening, a discussion in the youth club about my new book. Success. Lewerenz read from it; I was amazed myself how well the first chapter is written (I listened with detachment, as if it had been written by some other author). Up till midnight with Lewerenz in Café Budapest, drinking wine, discussing Thomas Mann, and Büchner's *Danton's Death*. A harmonious evening, and chaste . . . Lewerenz is the best editor I've ever met: clever, warmhearted and upstanding.

Much rejoicing: We won the award for best radio play in the national round of the International Radio Playwriting Competition. Our first collective work. When the news arrived by telegram, we raced around like crazy, laughing and crying. Payment, finally! A future, after such a long time of doubt and discouragement and sacrifice. 4,000 DM. Now we can set up Daniel's room, and a little car is no longer just a dream. (Next week I'll get my contract from NL.) Urgently need a car because of the huge distances we have to cover at the plant.[137] We also have to drive home more often—especially now.

Lutz has left for the West with Gretchen and the little one. At this very moment he's perhaps only two or three kilometres away, but unreachable all the same, in the Marienfelde transit camp.[138] For the first time, painfully aware—not just intellectually—of the tragedy of our two Germanys. Families torn apart, conflicts between brothers and sisters—what a literary subject! Why doesn't anyone tackle it, why doesn't anyone write a topical book? Fear? Inability? I don't know. Lutz is a muddle-head. He wasn't prepared to kowtow to the Party—now he'll have to do it for his capitalists. He says he'll always advocate the expropriation of big business; he

137 Journeys of up to 40 kilometres had to be made across the plant premises.

138 This was the central reception centre in West Berlin for refugees from the GDR, especially between 1950 and 1961.

believes in the victory of socialism—yet he leaves. He has his justifications, he's certainly been badly treated politically; he's been unfavourably and, I believe, unfairly appraised by the party group, given a position that didn't add up to his abilities and doesn't have the faintest perspective of getting a flat, and yet [. . .]. In principle, I condemn his actions—but Lutz is my brother, I love him, we have got on well for many years. [. . .] I am very sad. I cried when I heard Mum's voice at the door, her heart-rending 'Goodbye'. But gradually I have to get used to the idea that families fall apart, children leave their parents' homes, brothers and sisters move away, find new circles, new people.

[. . .]

Hoywoy, 2.5.60

I'm collecting men again, feeling young again, radiant, letting them adore me and knowing that my home is with Daniel. The others—Christ, a bit of a thrill, the excitement of tempting and retreating, affirmation at last, and something to soothe my abnormal inferiority complexes. But it's all just a trip to a foreign country I'll never inhabit again: drinking, dancing, flirting, men begging me—none of this is part of my life any more. Daniel and my work, a consuming ambition to write good books, and the plant: that's my role, my real purpose in life. Only now and then, a burning lust for life blows me away (isn't that petty bourgeois and ridiculous in essence?) perhaps it's a fear of the end. Forgotten the next morning. [. . .]

This is more serious. I really like Hanke—this stout, almost bald man, always in good spirits, humorous, calm, the brigade's anchor. A wonderful man! He loves me. His declaration of love—oh, too beautiful, too moving for me to make an ironic comment or repeat here. [. . .] With him I can't play the old, clichéd game. [. . .]

Hanke, who had been watching how I suffered when I was sanding the valves, has constructed a machine to make it easier for me. That is also characteristic of him—actively compassionate and attentively helpful.

Hoywoy, 11.5.

I am in love, sixteen years old and in love with an equally young Hanke, who's like a swooning schoolboy. Went to his place in the housing compound. He picked me up from the bus, immediately took my arm, we went through the compound to his blockhouse, his narrow room, which he shares with the 'half-rooster'; Günter, who grew up in an asylum and is illiterate, was saved from intellectual and financial poverty by Hanke, whom he worships unconditionally. I like Günter, a poor man, seriously ill, trampled and humiliated by life, only now awakening, good-natured, always helpful, always the first to sign up for voluntary work and overtime. Heard earlier on that Hanke gave him 800 DM for a cupboard unit—probably some stupid pompous thing, but immensely meaningful to Günter as the first sign of prosperity, a symbol of his new, better life.

Drank wine from beer glasses with Erwin. He explained to me his ideas for improvement, his plans [. . .]. It's difficult for him, because he's no longer a Party member (I really should make his adventurous life story into a book some time); fought with the Party bureaucracy. Showed me his many awards. Perhaps he'll receive the 'Banner of Labour' this year. He would be the first in the plant to receive this great distinction. [. . .]

Later . . . We kissed, exchanged sweet nothings [. . .]. And a relapse into my Christian upbringing: Is this already a sin? Not adultery, that's certain (and there will be no stepping across that threshold!), but sin all the same, affection for another man— and a childish fear of a punitive God, who can see into the tiniest blockhouse room and awaits the opportunity to deal me a blow. The cool (cool-acting) sensible lady, atheist, Marxist, convinced by Feuerbach when still a schoolgirl, who left the Church at eighteen—but fears divine punishment for a few forbidden kisses. (Caspar says, 'Lady Reimann is an eternal teenager.')

I also have to hide my diary again, hide it from my dearest Daniel-husband, who would only smile ironically—maybe—if he knew of my infatuation. How I hate this sneakiness, how I detest myself for not saying anything! No matter how I look at it, I'm in the wrong. And otherwise, aggressively honest [. . .]. Like recently in my disagreement with the plant's Party secretary: precisely because I knew he could damage me, I attacked him—I would have suffocated. I don't want to be a coward. I'd rather risk a thousand difficulties—anything but keep quiet, anything but be a silent onlooker at something that's wrong, thereby tacitly approving it.

But I am lying to Daniel? Oh, enough of this navel-gazing!

Berlin last week, reception at the radio station. Professor Ley. Critical discussion in a small circle. Many problems raised, none solved. Same old story.

At Aufbau in the evening. Publishing party. I felt paralysed. The earnest editors let their hair down. [. . .] Damned scum! During the day, they put on moral corsetry, throttling literature with their dogmatic quibbles, and in the evening, among themselves, they lose all self-control. I left [. . .].

Tonight, we're going to the Kastanienhof bar with Hanke. We even have the same taste in people! Daniel loves [. . .] Lewerenz and Hanke [. . .], even mocks his own fondness for his wife's admirers.

Hoy, 20.5.

[. . .] Hearing thousands of stories from Erwin; if I ever get on top of my book, I'll have a great deal to thank him for. Trying to learn from him.

Recent visit from the publishing house; publishing director, chief editor and my little Lewerenz. Erwin dragged them through all the dirtiest, hottest sections of the plant (and I, of course, had to keep up). Our guests were completely exhausted; the power station, oppressive machines. Beginning to find my way around the briquette factory. Guests thrilled with the Pumpe—and with Erwin. He really is a positive hero; I don't even need to add anything to him for my book. Was very proud of him. [. . .] He looks like he could be my father. Comforting, terrible thought.

Hoywoy, 22.5.60

Daniel read my diary but said nothing until the day before yesterday, even though he knew about my whole romance with Erwin (and he takes it more seriously than I do). A viciously unjust comment from me provoked a terrible explosion of rage in him—I thought Daniel was going to strangle me. A gruelling scene, tears, curses, great declarations of sacrifice. I'm innocent, like anyone driven by their instincts—alternatives are nonsensical: him or me . . . but why? I'm [. . .] not taking anything away from him if I fall in love with another man.

[. . .] Always these tasteless love triangles! [. . .]

In the evening, the dam burst at last; I can write again. [. . .] Desperately looking for faults in Erwin; can't make fun of his paunch or bald head—but discovering a certain ridiculousness in the object of my desire is the surest means to cool it off. Bad traits— if they come from strong feelings or strive for a respectable goal— don't put me off. My hero can be evil but not petty; immoral if his immorality has merit. (Lewerenz, who likes to analyse me, says that I am the aesthete par excellence—aestheticism is profoundly immoral. My favourites, Julien Sorel and Raskolnikov . . . [139]

[. . .]

139 Julien Sorel: the hero of Stendhal's novel *The Red and the Black* (1830). Rodion Raskolnikov: the hero of Fyodor Dostoevsky's novel *Crime and Punishment* (1866).

MAY 1960

Hoy., 27 5.

Production day. Exciting work: damaged furnace slide from the power station, urgent repair work. The wedge had become jammed; first tried to warm up the casing with the welding torch (acetylene + oxygen) and at the same time freeze it, to make the wedge contract. Two people whacked it with a sledgehammer; Lehmann broke the shaft, and the hammer (25 pounds) clattered down beside him. Hanke almost froze his hand in the process.

The trick didn't work, we had to cut it. No one wanted to do it, and finally Hanke took the blowtorch himself, stood alert and still in the shower of sparks that sprayed off the casing (and I thought they were cold, because he didn't wince). I only understood when his colleagues congratulated him on what he had done: smooth cut without damaging the sealing ring. [. . .]

Later with H. in the pressing basement.[140] They've started rebuilding it and it should be finished by 3rd of June. We're working in three shifts now to make the deadline. The pressing room in the basement is oppressive. Dark, stinking catacombs and coal dust, water seeping down the walls. H. carried me over muddy coal puddles. The Taiga bear . . .

[. . .]

Hoy 29.5.

Brigade trip to Oybin yesterday.

[. . .]

We set off early, 31 people, some had brought their wives with them. [. . .]

Erwin brought me bananas; he already knows my soft spots. Passed through the charming Lusatia landscape: rolling meadows, apple trees in blossom, slate-roofed houses with tiny windows,

---

140 Pressing basement: where the coal was pressed.

gardens, gardens, overgrown with trees. Began to long for a few weeks of rest and seclusion [...].

At Oybin around eleven o'clock. We hiked up Töpferberg, terrible paths over rocks and naturally formed steps; our lungs, damaged by cheap cigarettes, gasped. I feared for our poor Günter with his heart problem. [...]

In the afternoon, went up Mount Oybin through the ice-cold Knights' Gorge. Museums, ruins, very picturesque, too many people, everything geared to tourism. Later a bus to Johnsdorf. [...] Evening at a village near Bautzen, nice dance bar, pretty girls, hot music. We pushed a few tables together and were soon quite lively. The band played a dance especially for the Pumpe crowd—and I was proud to be one of them.

Danced the whole night with Erwin; he learnt to dance for my sake. We rocked around to provoke the others. It was reckless, but we were slightly drunk, so we didn't care. [...] Home at three o'clock. On the doorstep, had a discussion about the next trip; I insist on Dresden, the art gallery—not always these aimless excursions. But I can understand that my colleagues want to get away and relax once in a while, and not admire art—the work is hard enough and doesn't let you to think about anything else.

Hoy, 15.6.60

Just came from a terrible meeting with the club committee and Siegrist. Scarcely able to write a few lines, close to a nervous breakdown. S. has spread the foulest rumours about me and us. Slander—no, it's impossible to put on paper. He tried escaping the noose today by defaming us politically. At least we were able to bombard him with so much evidence that he didn't utter a word when I called him a pig in front of the others. No, I can't write any more, I am totally exhausted. When will that old bastard finally sling his hook?

Hoy., 18.6.

The club committee seems outraged over S.'s smear tactics. I am interested—not very—in seeing how this unpleasant affair develops. In the meantime, S. has come up with new effrontery: wrote an article for the *Sonntag* about 'his two worker writers' circles'. 'My method, my circle . . . ' Nice. He turned up at the circle once (which, in the meantime, we have turned into a 'platform' against him to undermine his work).

[. . .]

On Tuesday, visit from Potemkin, publishing director of Komsomol publishing house in Moscow, and Gurnov, correspondent for the *Komsomolskaya Pravda*. H. guided our guests through the plant, he looked exhausted for the first time, with deep wrinkles like a fifty-year-old: he hadn't slept for two or three nights; nonstop incidents.

In the afternoon they came to visit us; lively discussion despite language difficulties. Potemkin is interested in the 'The Secondary-School Graduates'[141] and wants to secure translation rights and reprint in good time. Charming companions, very Russian (as I have always imagined Russians after reading their books): loud, lively, very warm-hearted and insanely polite, vodka-drinking, undogmatic (the discussion about Nilin and Kuznetsov—my God, we're such oafs!). Anecdotes and proverbs instead of abstract theories. We were very entertained by Gurnov, who had permission to take photos and whose passion for journalism was unstoppable: despite our horrified warnings, he lay on the rail tracks to take a snap of an approaching electric train, climbed on top of pillars and hopped around in the forest—the last bit on the plant site.

When they left [. . .] and best wishes for my book . . . 'If God wills, and you don't fall ill . . . ' [. . .]

141 'Die Abiturienten'.

Hoy, 14.7.60

A month of silence. Terrible trouble with S., meeting in Berlin; the magnificent, incorruptible Strittmatter ('You use your Party badge as a shield for your machinations'). The obligatory sackcloth and ashes—and a pasha in the plant. Discussion about his book, all-round rejection. Now he's pretty done-in. Well, enough of that, I'm just angry because that pig stole so much of my precious work time. And because of the Party's unsuccessful debates on the unity of form and content [...]. Ten years of futile speeches at congresses and cultural conferences ... Deepest parochialism, dogmatism and intellectual narrow-mindedness—alongside one of our amazing industrial giants. Inadequate 'work with the people'. Argued again with the cultural secretary yesterday, even though both Siegfrieds were kicking my shins blue under the table. I just can't keep my mouth shut when I hear so many platitudes and stupidities uttered with claims of infallibility.

[...] Yesterday was the premiere of our radio play *A Man at the Door*[142] in the plant studio. [...] No one in my brigade was able to come: all working in the pressing basement, 12-hour shift. [...]

Heart hammering insanely: my words coming from a stranger's mouth. Some scenes disturbingly unfamiliar, because of a mismatch between our ideas and the director's interpretation. After quarter of an hour, (clutching Daniel's hand) I was able to listen halfway objectively. Came across a whole bunch of mistakes, and was unhappy, as always, with my—our—work.

The radio people were represented by departmental manager Dr Rödel, who loves our play, chief producer Popp, who directed it, and the completely loveable, youthful, clever chief dramaturge Rentzsch (we're developing our new play with him; we're the only authors with whom he works personally, perhaps he has a soft spot

---

142 *Ein Mann steht vor der Tür.*

for us. He has a wonderful imagination). The others—loved it. Women sobbing. We were partly embarrassed, partly delighted about the deluge of praise.

Little premiere party in Glück auf. Group completely drunk. Daniel, sober as a judge as always, sat there and watched. K[. . .] overstepped the moral boundaries. I was sozzled to the gills but managed to behave until we got home.

The radio pirates from the plant had taped the broadcast: they're going to play it for the other brigades too.

Hoy, 18.7.60

A few sentences from my Lutz-brother's latest letter: 'I've had a job since Monday at the Deutsche Werft. It's right next to the transit camp and what's more, we'll probably get a flat through my employer. But it's not all good. The pay is lousy (650 marks gross) and I don't particularly like the workplace. Here, even as a qualified engineer, I'm downgraded to a technical draughtsman. Even worse than on the other side. We have to keep the furnaces alight and we have to work. They don't make long-drawn-out calculations here— they just go by trial and error. That's the only way they can keep up such a pace and turn out the ships so fast at such low prices. The organization isn't half as comprehensive and complicated as in the East. Perhaps it's as a result of never having been short of materials? [. . .] It's not that easy. The worst thing is being weighed down by a kind of homesickness I've never felt before. Perhaps because of all the freedom we're given here? Freedom isn't good for everyone. And I have some traitor complexes, as I'll call them. Others used to feel the same, more or less. They all got over it in the end, and so will I. If it hasn't got better in two years, then we'll come back. Perhaps we'll be one nation again by then. In desperate times people believe in fairy tales . . . [. . .]'

Sayda, 17.8.

The plant's holiday resort, Ore Mountains. Pretty area (too charming for my taste—I'm not so into hilly districts nor the non-committal, 'nice' people). A cold August, rain; sunshine for the first time again today. Wrote the obligatory 200 postcards—a task that was only fun when we started playing around with the captions.

Today the beginning of our co-production, *The Young Expert*[143] [. . .]. Commissioned by the radio, and a lot depends on it. If they like our play, we'll be given a contract for next year which would ensure us a very generous monthly income—by our standards (broadcasting fees are paid on top). In return, we would have to deliver two radio plays. Fair conditions all in all, and I think we can sign up for it without fearing eternal damnation.

Chief dramaturge Rentzsch has visited us several times; we get on very well. A charming lad, talented, witty, with verve; has a pirate's profile. Same views on art and cultural politics as us. Talks with R. are a relief from provincial stuffiness. This wonderful plant—and the narrow-mindedness, dark dogmatism on the other hand . . . a decade of contradictions.

[. . .]

18.8

Suddenly in a terrible mood, don't feel like working on the radio play; just carrying out the job, no inner conviction. Thought I could replace feeling with discipline. A miscalculation . . .

[. . .]

Sayda, 24.8.

Rough outline and first scene written. Do feel like working after all. This time—unlike with the first play—deep peace between Daniel

---

143 *Der junge Meister.*

and me; we have adjusted to each other. [...] Next to me, on the chair, is his shirt; it smells of sweat, the scent of Schwarze Samt and his skin. Wonderful! [...]

Yesterday we went to Olbernhau in the sun and heat, walked around like a pair of young lovers, window-shopping and eating cake with lashings of cream. Thought up great plans for the future. Unless something happens to one of us I think we'll achieve a great deal. Incredible fits of love sometimes.

[...]

21.9

Feel pumped dry and incapable of another thought. Working on the radio play and—in stolen hours—on my book. Yesterday, worker writers' circle; our group is growing, we have lots of people with talent; perhaps we'll be ready to publish a little anthology next year [...]. Heard the most despicable stories about our circle leader; at some point, I'll report it to the district—a disciplinary commission should be sent. Recently, a comrade accurately described the mood in the plant as a 'go-fuck-yourself atmosphere'. No one dares criticize any more, because they are afraid they'll be stabbed in the back—schooled by bad experiences. [...]

Hoy, 17.10

Completely wiped out and exhausted. Wrote a lot, sat at my desk for the past few days for 12 or more hours. Publisher has forced an impossible deadline on me. Radio play finished at last. Rentzsch thinks 'it hangs together well'. And: 'We need more of this kind of thing.'

TV and Defa visited. *Woman in the Pillory* is apparently going to be adapted for TV. Very happy. Might be a great thing.

Was on my own for five days. Daniel was in Burg, coming back tonight. Heart racing and terrible homesickness. It was awful without him. I left the light on every night, my horrible dreams . . . shouldn't have read E. T. A. Hoffmann at such a young age.

In an hour I'm leaving for the station. If Daniel ever left me for good—I would kill myself after three days at most.

Hoy, 27.10

Survived a few crazy days: Sunday, telegram from Marchlevska, who's staying at the guest house of the Central Committee in Berlin; invitation to see the film *Julian M.* Towards evening Daniel hired a ridiculously expensive car, drove to Berlin. Sonia in the Volksbühne, finally managed to get hold of her in Karl Liebknecht Haus, great joy and warm embraces. Evening conversations; back in Hoy at four in the morning.

Sunday, finished writing Chapter 6; Lewerenz urgently demanded the manuscript. Monday, not having slept enough, went to Berlin. Ate in the K.-L.-Haus, with Sonia of course and H. Heine, former International Brigades man.[144] Sonia all young and charming and pretty with her snow-white hair. Volksbühne, *People from Budapest.*[145] We were thoroughly upset; the play throws up thousands of bitter questions, but doesn't answer them, or only inadequately. Sonia, the old communist, nodded, got excited, nudging us. Once, I had tears in my eyes (the intellectual when his old comrade is arrested: 'He *must* be a criminal—otherwise everything we have believed till now is a lie.')

[. . .]

Afterwards with Sonia and Lotte Löbinger (the woman can laugh—wonderful!) at the studio of a completely insane sculptor,

---

144 International Brigades: paramilitary units set up by the Communist International to help the leftist Popular Front government of Spain during the Spanish Civil War (1936–39).

145 Experimental play *Pesti emberek* (1958) by Hungarian dramatist and writer Lajos Mesterhazí.

very talented, but a drunken sot. Lives with a small, nice nurse, whom he tyrannizes brutally. [. . .] A few awful Berlin types were visiting—Isa with a fur boa and a coarse whore's voice, a remnant of Döblin's *Alexanderplatz* era. Red wine and heated discussions. [. . .]

Authors' conference at Aufbau on Tuesday. None of the grand old men were present. Clever but not very original talk by Caspar. Chatty Petersen. Herbert Nachbar, nauseously arrogant. His question about what I am working on was asked in such a tone that I couldn't help turning my back on him. A shame. Was furious for Daniel, who is at least as talented as Nachbar. He just has to publish something, soon! We walk through the literary world as 'great hopes' and still lack the published (if not written) evidence.

Happy reunion with Günter Deicke. In the evening with Caspar and Deicke in the cafe, later back to Deicke's flat. [. . .] I slept on the couch, Daniel and Deicke talked quietly. Now and then I woke up and listened to them, my eyes closed. But it wasn't meant for my ears. They spoke a lot about me. Daniel was wonderful . . . at some point, Deicke said I was more moral than all the people that accuse me, or had accused me, of immorality. I was strangely moved to hear the way they talked about their marriages calmly and often only by allusion, opening up their hearts. When Daniel left the room for a moment, Deicke sat down next to me (he thought I was asleep) and looked at me in a way that made me feel something like pain, then kissed me on the cheek. At six o'clock, they went to bed. It was strange to wake up in a stranger's flat (as in the past) yet not at all like in the past, next to my darling, one-and-only Daniel. I was quite at home lying in his arms, on his shoulder. [. . .]

Journey home at midday in a works car in the pouring rain. In the evening, the literary ball, at first utterly exhausted, then livened up and slightly drunk—I danced with my worker writers until three in the morning.

Hoy, 4.11

Terrible weeks: work, work, so much I'll soon go under, and hundreds of distractions that make me downright bitter because of the deadline for Neues Leben.

At last a meeting with the district committee of the SED Party about the unpleasant Siegrist affair; in the presence of a representative of the regional committee. Burgmann tried to cover up mistakes ('let's talk about perspectives instead'). We insisted on clarification. B. got loud, I got louder, B. apologized in the end after I said that he shouldn't talk to us like political greenhorns. S. has taken a terrible knock, he'll (allegedly) have to report to the office. [...] How small these dictators become as soon as a superior gets involved! Really, you can't let yourself be shoved into a corner or lose your direction because of these bigwigs.—Peace, joy and happiness at last; I even shook hands with the completely devastated Siegrist (a superfluous gesture of pity . . .).

My dear Erwin has started writing short stories; we're infecting each other. [...] Finally, he's noticed how difficult it is to write; stands in awe in front of bookshops. On Sunday a visit from our lovely, adorable Sonia Marchlevska, bringing wonderful presents from Poland, and books, and a terrifying portfolio of prints (*The Stones Shriek*, Bronislaw Linke; the images found their way into my dreams), a Central Committee Sachsenring[146], and a driver who looks like Paul Wegener, and who has as much heart, humour and lip as only a Berliner can have. He told us shocking stories—also belly-achingly funny ones—of open or hidden battles between the Party and state security apparatus, between Central Committee chauffeurs and 'shadows'.

[...] A lovely, harmonious Sunday . . . We read from our new works. Daniel read his May story, and I was touched again, agitated—and a little depressed. His language—wonderful! [...] But will he ever come into his own?

146 A big limousine, often used by Party bosses.

Hoy, 22.11

I'm not interested in projects any more, I'm not interested in anything any more. Not good music, theatre, nothing, not even books. There is no tyrant more terrible than art, in my opinion, although my sort of literature has little to do with art. More frequent attacks of melancholy, despair even. I doubt myself and everything around me. An awful condition! If only this hellish work were finally over! I waste time, hardly get out of the house, sometimes drink, not much, but that's still to come, it's inevitable. Ah, shit!

Hoy, 4.12

Battered and exhausted, without actually being tired. The first winter storms are raging, the bad weather is also making Daniel, who's normally calm, restless, almost afraid. I'm sick of my book—just a hard slog, that's all. I've long lost the desire to do it, probably because of the pressure of the deadline.

Horrific heart pains yesterday. I got frightened all of a sudden.

Strange discrepancy between my 'private life' and the impression I make . . . H. calls me 'lively' and this is surely the impression others have of me.

A few nice, happy, encouraging events; our new radio play *Seven Bushels of Salt*[147] was broadcast in the works, our brigade was there, the Party leadership, Rentzsch; the kind, clever Böttcher from the regional committee, the theatre director Popp, and actor Erich Franz. Great success—our workers are a splendid audience. [. . .]

ND slated us; praise in the other papers.

Yesterday: evaluation of the Second Cultural Conference, meeting of the district committee. Our friend-enemy Burgmann (secretary for agit-prop) sang hymns of praise to us, our competence, our success, our radio plays etc. First production of *Man at the Door* by the Workers' Theatre.

147 *Sieben Scheffel Salz.*

From the plant's director Kühn we received the badge of honour in gold as 'Builders of the Schwarze Pumpe'. [...] I was so proud, perhaps more about the warm-heartedness of the others (including Jakob, the district secretary) than about the medal. A huge step forward—now we really belong; the plant has acknowledged us.

Böttcher said we will be getting our car within the next quarter. I am looking forward to it, inasmuch as I can look forward to anything. If only my damned book was finished!

1961

Christmas at home; a few days of rest. Happy to see my parents and little sister again, who gets prettier all the time, and my Ulli-brother with his wonderfully carefree outlook and gift of the gab. I missed Lutz very much. New Year's Eve at the Klub der Intelligenz. A doctor turned off the radio in the middle of the 4th movement of the Ninth and put on a record by the 4 Brummers.[148] It was indicative of the tone of the whole evening. I was pretty drunk by then, and Daniel says that I danced as if my grandparents had been cannibals in the jungle.

On 5 January, *7 Bushels of Salt* was broadcast at the Cottbus club. Rentzsch was there. Discussion till midnight; was happy that Dr Scurla (Humboldt specialist and Rahel Levin's biographer) vigorously defended our play. We're been heftily criticized by the official reviews. There's no more thankless a task than writing contemporary drama. On the other hand, the radio people are firmly behind us. We were praised by the chairman, Prof. Ley, and received a bonus of 2,000 marks.

Stayed until 3 o'clock in the Kammerbrettel, a pretty rough bar. R. and I drank bubbly. [. . .] No sooner had we reached the dance floor than R said: 'I like you very much.' I've been aware of his feelings towards me for a long time and can't pretend I don't feel the same. [. . .] At home we drank another bottle of fabulous Muscovite

---

148 A popular easy-listening band from Dresden.

vodka without getting in the least bit drunk. Around dawn, Daniel lay down to sleep. R. and I chatted quietly, a few times we kissed. [. . .] When I moved back the curtains at about ten, the sun streamed into the smoky, sweltering room reeking of alcohol. I still felt quite fresh. An hour later R. left.

Daniel had woken up towards the end and had been secretly listening to us—with jealousy but also with admiration, he confessed, relishing the erotic atmosphere, and, he said, he would not understand if R. hadn't fallen in love with me. A strange reaction from a husband. Afterwards he embraced me wildly, almost with hatred.

[. . .] At times I have a real fear of dying, especially when I feel a sharp physical pain in my heart. I am quite wrecked for 27 years of age. I'm working like a dog. My book has to be finished by the end of next week.

[. . .]

Hoy, 28.1.61

Daniel has gone to Burg (it was Mum's birthday yesterday). I'm sitting alone at work on the last chapter, which has to be completed by the day after tomorrow, and these last few pages in particular are really difficult. And then? I've longed to finish this book—thousands of plans: to go on holiday, read a lot, go to the writers' retreat . . . nothing of the sort. We can't go to Petzow because the writers' circle needs us now (final editing for our first publication), and we won't go on holiday because I have to write a television play straight away. What's the point of rushing around all the time?

I'm quite exhausted, distracted, overwrought [. . .]. My alcohol consumption has risen alarmingly over the last few weeks. I've also started some more love affairs . . . and imagine I'm getting old and have to enjoy life—and other such nonsense, which I already wore down to the heel years ago. But this silliness vanishes into thin air when my head is clear. And I have to reduce my alcohol intake because my heart is rattling miserably.

The day before yesterday, our 'Working Group of Socialist Artists at the Schwarze Pumpe Construction Site' was set up. [. . .] Our fraternization with the officials is reaping rewards; oh and it's all above board—at least on our part—[. . .] and the opposition seems to be genuinely fond of us too [. . .] of course, I'm glad that we've managed to overcome our differences and peace has been restored. I like arguing with Burgmann; although I don't accept all his views, I try to understand and respect them and I learn something at the same time.

Daniel has been elected the leader of our working group and stuttered in the most charming way during his inaugural speech. At moments like these, my love for him takes on a maternal hue [. . .]. No, speakers we are not. Doesn't matter. At least it makes Daniel a better writer [. . .] He has terrific material for a new story, and my terrible atomic bombs are to blame; perhaps his story will help reduce my complexes.

Well, tomorrow I'll write about K. [. . .]. I only had two hours' sleep [. . .].

Hoy., 1.2.61

Tired, exhausted, no desire to work (and I have to rewrite the last chapter again!). Came back late from Berlin yesterday. In the morning, at the publisher's for hours, friendly dispute with Lewerenz, the ideal editor. In the afternoon I met Rentzsch in the press cafe. Far too many people around. It was a replay of that other sleepless night. We hardly said twenty sentences in an hour and a half. Occasionally we looked at each other. I tore my matchbox apart. ('Love scenes are very different from the way we write them,' said R.) [. . .]

The last few days, while Daniel has been in Burg (he's coming back tonight), I've been constantly drunk. This morning I took away an arsenal of empty vodka bottles. This evening at nine, my tragi-comic, slutty bachelor's life will be over. [. . .]

So, here goes: Jon K[149] [. . .] (30), a philosophy student who dropped out before the final exam, twice kicked out of the Party, works at the Machine and Tractor Station [. . .] still not any smarter or calmer, a bulldozer driver with the construction and assembly plant. An enfant terrible. [. . .] K. is ugly (he looks so much like my U-brother that I call him my 'incestuous love'), bright, sharp-witted and has a devilish logic: he can prove anything, and then give convincing evidence against what he has just proved. A person who can never really be happy because he analyses and dissects everything—every thought, every feeling—and derives principles from them. We had taken him on in the writers' circle as a critic. At the time, he vowed never to write a line—he knows he is a good bulldozer driver and preferred to stay one instead of becoming a bad writer.—Meanwhile he's written [. . .] a really good story and is full of plans . . .

A terrible person. We immediately 'tuned in' to each other. We quarrelled bitterly: emotion versus reason. [. . .]

At first, it was [. . .] all just a game. The usual story. A flirtation (less than flirtation), serious and exhausting, the way these things usually are in these German parts. The occasional brush of skin might still have been accidental [. . .]. Once, when Jon was sitting next to me on the couch [. . .], things got serious for a few minutes: I looked at his face—his Negro lips, the narrow eyes behind his glasses, his small, disfigured hands—he was wearing a grey pullover, unbuttoned at the neck. I felt like biting him on the shoulder. I wanted him to touch my hair, although half a dozen people were sitting around. Of course he didn't. He's very similar to me: we never do exactly the thing the other longs for. [. . .]

149 Hans Kerschek (1932–95): a member of the writers' circle of the Schwarze Pumpe.

At the Circle of Active Artists,[150] we sat next to each other—as we always do when we're out together somewhere. Suddenly, without us having said a word, it was all clear. He came the next evening. Daniel had left that morning.

We drank a lot of vodka until midnight without getting so much as tipsy. All else aside, Jon is a pleasant boozing buddy.

The next day we went for a ride on his motorbike [...] K. lent me a windbreaker that was much too big (I'm as thin as a starved cat), and he wore an identical jacket, and we look a little like brother and sister anyway. [...]

Afterwards we drove to Bautzen through little Sorb villages and a small town where there were crucifixes on the walls, and, further on, images of the Virgin Mary in the fields; through forests—we didn't know exactly where we were—with birches and withered heather and past old ditches, and it was cold and windy, and I leaned tightly into Jon's back. Once we stopped to kiss on a forest path, and now it seems as if we sealed something [...].

We were completely stiff and frozen when we arrived back at the blockhouse. [...] We were alone in his flat. We made coffee and slowly thawed, and wanted, I think, to be sensible. But then [...] we lay on his bed, the radio was playing silly pop music, but we weren't aware of it any more, and I only remember us stroking and tormenting each other, and Jon twisting my hair in his hand and saying: 'You're a stroke of fortune' (and he wasn't even ashamed of it, God, how divine), and I screamed and sobbed, and Jon kissed my hips and ribcage [...]. Did we not make love simply because we wanted to save it for later?

Eventually, after a very long time, we sat back down at the table and there was no feeling of *tristesse* between us. Jon said, 'I love you like a fine work of art—with the advantage that you happen to be

150 Künstleraktiv: groups of artists in the GDR, including painters and writers, who organized cultural activities in factory works and other state-run businesses.

alive.' He kissed my fingers. 'Every single finger deserves the highest seal of quality.' [. . .]

As we were driving along the F97 on our windy journey, Jon had turned his head to me and shouted, 'You are a great adventure, a flight into anarchy!' Yes, yes, we are immoral and mean, and we are cheating on our partners, and nevertheless—it is divinely beautiful. [. . .]

We analysed our relationship very coldly and rationally, and laid down the rules of the game—we already knew that something was growing between us that was going to drown all reason. [. . .]

This game has turned into a raging, destructive passion—how long? Those three days we had? Or three weeks, three months? Jon believes in years. My God! I know what we're like. In a quarter of a year at most, we will begin to say brutal things to each other—

[. . .]

Hoy, 2.2.[61]

A few more words in the chronicle of poor lovers:[151] K. came back on Sunday. I had switched off the doorbell, he left, and returned a few hours later, during which time I'd switched the doorbell back on again. He confessed he'd panicked. He was angry with himself, because he felt he was losing his independence. How similar he is to me! I already feel the need to take revenge on him for every minute I've wasted with my heart hammering.

Once he said, 'Turn around. Now for something banal.' Then he read me the beginning of a story [. . .]. I was deeply moved, not least because it was a beautiful, fervent declaration of love—K. can write, and as I was listening and trembling, I didn't forget my profession or sense of judgment. [. . .]

---

151 Allusion to the title of the novel *Cronache di poveri amanti* [English title: *Family Chronicle* (1947)] by Vasco Pratolini and the film with the same title (1954, directed by Carlo Lizzani).

Last night I went to the station to pick up Daniel. He didn't come. I stood in the icy waiting room under the cold light, quite desperate. I thought horrible things, I thought he'd sensed something was up. [...]

Daniel arrived in the night. I was ashamed, and my shame made me defiant; I started a bitter row with him. It wasn't until this morning that I pulled him to me and kissed him and tried to make him forget my vicious accusations ('You write too little, you have no energy, you don't achieve anything'). Daniel said he doesn't have my brutal egotism. When I work, I don't give a damn about the world. I don't even think that's it; I give a damn about everything, but maybe work just slightly more—and is that egotism? Maybe. Because I don't write to make others happy. No good at bringing light into other people's lives. I write to make myself happy.

Tonight we want to watch the *Irkutsk Story*[152] on TV. [...] Great love and poetry and pathos and lively people ... Soviet drama marches on. Whereas we award Hedda Zinner the Lessing Prize for her dreadful *What If—?*[153] [...]

But Sakowski is suspected of Party hostility and tactlessness towards the oh-so-sensitive farmers in the ND for *Stones in the Way*[154] (I too stole potatoes once and was chased from the field). S. got a shock. Who cares?

Hoy., 9.2.

I threw away the last chapter and wrote it again. It's driving me mad ... [...]

152 A 1959 play by Soviet dramatist Aleksei Arbuzov.

153 The novel *Was wäre, wenn—?* (1960) by German writer, actress and comedienne Hedda Zinner (1907–94).

154 *Steine im Weg*: a TV drama critical of agricultural collectivization by Helmut Sakowski. After it was broadcast for the first time, the authorities demanded that the entire play be filmed again with a different ending in which the main character, Alfred, stays in the GDR rather than fleeing to West Germany.

Hoy., 12.2.

Our writers' circle party was on the 10th, and all the Pumpe bigwigs took up our invitation [. . .], even the new plant manager Lissinsky, a good-looking, young—astonishingly young—man. He must be phenomenally hardworking; he's also in the Central Committee, I think. He looks quite gentle, but that's misleading; he has that wise toughness about him necessary to his position.

But I'd rather wait until tomorrow to talk about that evening; I'm completely exhausted, although I slept in. I cleaned and did laundry till the afternoon; the flat was in a mess. Now comes the backlash: as long as I was working on the book, I could, or had to, downplay my exhaustion, but now that's over.

Caspar visited us last week [. . .]. He browsed through my book, and couldn't help giving me some surly praise. He's angry that I've finished another piece of work while his protégé Sigi still hasn't written a single book. At some point he sent me outside to tell Daniel I was outrageously gifted [. . .].

Hoy., 13.2.

So, the writers' circle evening . . . From midnight on, I was so insanely drunk that I can't say for sure what happened. I dimly remember dancing wildly to rock 'n' roll with a FDJ secretary—a blonde guy as tall as a tree who isn't part of our crowd at all—and doing something resembling a dance with Jon, a long hug, and a kiss in the middle of our improvised little dance floor. Crazy. Even the forbidden lovers' instinct for secrecy had gone. (I'm still so soaked in vodka that if I cut my finger, high-proof blood would flow out. Enough, enough of this debauched lifestyle!)

Luckily, the others were just as smashed. [. . .]

But first, everything was beautiful and worthy and ceremonial with a cultural programme of sorts: poets on poetry and Chopin and Ravel (the incomparable *Bolero*) and Gershwin (*Rhapsody in*

Blue), and then there were addresses and acceptance speeches, and the writers' circle gave us books and a giant vase of flowers, and we were quite moved. The flowers were for our wedding anniversary . . . [. . .]

Earlier at the door, Jon (who had turned up in a morning suit and lent the whole thing the tone of a state reception) said: 'In case I have no opportunity later, I will tell you now that I am madly in love with you.' But he did find occasions to repeat it afterwards . . .

Daniel and I sat for a long time with the new plant manager, who had obviously been told a lot of nice things about us, and the devil must have been sitting on my shoulder for me to argue with him. The other officials boasted a great deal about their cultural plans—but my brigade doesn't even have a breakfast room, and they have to eat with dirty hands at their workplace instead. First you have to create the right economic conditions before you can start rolling out the book trollies.[155] And then the damned Doctors' Ball—the social event of the year.

ND completely over the top, *Constanze* style![156] 'What were people wearing?—Black velvet down to the golden tips of their shoes, swathes of white tulle . . . ' etc. Dreadful. Piltz already complained five years ago: 'They've turned the revolution into a garden party.' I always imagine a Red Workers' battalion with machine guns marching through the drapes of white silk into the dance hall—to mix with these society fat cats whose arses we have to lick so that they are gracious enough not to run off to the West, and treat our ill workers instead—on their umpteen-thousand-mark salaries.

But then: 'You radical leftist!' 'You anarchist!' Oh and they're not even wrong; I probably tend towards anarchy precisely because

155 The factory librarians came with book carts to brigades to bring literature to the workers.

156 A reference to a West German women's magazine, *Constanze*, that was published in Hamburg between 1948 and 1969 before it merged with the magazine *Brigitte*.

I'm from the middle class.[157] I've already had a hundred fights with K. about this; he has leftist tendencies and refers to himself as the 'last Stalinist'.

Lissinsky has this devilish habit of turning his head towards you in conversation, then looking at you and talking very calmly—he never gives in. He's not pushy, but you notice that he always or almost always wants to be proven right and has an iron will. But when he was dancing, he seemed so young and full of verve. His kind is totally alien to me and a bit creepy, maybe the communist of tomorrow. I'd like to get to know him better just to write about him some time; maybe it would make me stronger, more stable. (My heroes are just as unstable as I am—which proves that I am not a writer after all.)

[. . .]

In the evening (on the 11th) it was carnival at the FDGB,[158] but after an hour or so I was so pissed off at all that German conviviality, with its singing in rounds and smutty jokes and shrieking women, that I got a lift home. It was a fit of misanthropy that I regretted bitterly later when I found out how worried everyone was, asking after my health because Daniel had said I was ill.

[. . .]

Hoy., 15 2.

Rentzsch came on Monday. [. . .] Big discussion in the afternoon about our new radio-play project—a marriage story, two characters

---

157 B.R.'s grandfather from the Rhineland was a small manufacturer while her father, a trained bank clerk, worked as a journalist; the publisher August Hopfer in Burg published his illustrated books such as *Deutsche Bauten* [German Buildings] and *Heimbücher der Kunst* [The Fireside Book of Art].

158 FDGB (Freier Deutscher Gewerkschaftsbund): Free German Trade Union Association, established in 1948. Because farmlands and machinery were owned by workers and labourers according to official propaganda, the FDGB did not function in GDR factories as a representative of the workers vis-a-vis the employers or the state; rather, the union was a tool to control workers. When mass demonstrations against sudden rises in prices and production quota broke out in June 1953, the protest was organized outside of the framework of the FDGB. The FDGB dissolved in May 1990.

at night in a hotel room, without the obligatory love triangle for once; the conflicts arise from the work of our two heroes (she is a painter; he is a power-plant engineer). Debate: morality and relationships in civil and socialist society. R. (less cheerful than usual) lectured us on love. A funny slip, when, turning to me, he said: 'I love you.' In fact, he had meant the heroine. [...]

I am just listening to a mean, dirty, brutal pop song, cynically tragic, from a Western broadcaster: 'We weren't nice to little Joe, we were mean to little Joe ... Where might he be, little Joe? He'll be in heaven, little Joe ... '. Systematic desensitization. As far as I know, this 'hit' is forbidden in the Federal Republic; but it's played in West Berlin. A sudden feeling of fear and outrage at the same time, and to top it all, I have to think of my Lutz-brother, who is about to become a good Federal German citizen, and maybe someday we'll be enemies. Wouldn't we be already if he wasn't my brother? [...]

Yes, and then the Chamber of Technology[159] ball. [...] Daniel danced with me the whole evening; he even enjoyed it. We have to put a red cross in the calendar [...].

Finally, we relocated to the bar where there was a fantastic trio with a saxophonist who played himself into a frenzy—a superb musician. He went down on his knees and spiralled up again and squawked and made the dancers spin madly. The Party leaders, the intellectuals—everyone—rocked and rolled around the room, and our well-behaved, deadly-boring Lipsi dance[160] didn't stand a chance. It's always a bit strange for me to see comrades peel off their masks and become weak. (I have this nice childhood belief in how the power of ideas can change people, right to their innermost core. But no, not a trace.) [...]

159 KdT (Kammer der Technik): Chamber of Technology, a socialist organization of scientific, technical and economic engineers and innovators, founded in 1946.

160 A type of ballroom dance invented by the GDR in an attempt to counter the popularity of the Western rock 'n' roll, taken from the Latin 'Lipsia', meaning Leipzig.

In the last few days, I've been busy with the young plant manager (who, so we've heard, likes us very much). He has mixed feelings towards me: my temperament is not typically mid-European, he thinks, so Daniel is handling me the wrong way. Once, wanting to annoy me or hurt my feelings, I don't know why, he pondered over things with Daniel for a long time, before finally saying: 'We can't provoke your wife, we're not intellectual enough.'

On the dance floor [...] he said: 'I like your husband—such a quiet, nice, fine man. But you're a scamp!' A scamp, OK—but he's only met me when I'm half—or totally—drunk, dancing wildly and arguing wildly. I want him to see my other, better side. I am a serious, diligent worker—I really am, and he should know that. [...]

Hoy, 17.2.

Yesterday work began on the final editing of the writers' circle publication. K. was there all day. He brought his love story with him [...].

Daniel has finally started on his own work again and is compiling a series of short stories for Caspar. Last night he read a passage from the boarding-school book he wrote when he was 23 and never finished. A wonderful piece of literature! The hay scene, which was why I fell in love with him ... and yesterday, the magic was back again, and I felt crushed and confused because I can't write like that, and because Daniel himself doesn't write like that any more (who in this country would even publish this ecstasy of words?) [...], and at the same time I loved him passionately (the way to my heart is always through my mind).

Hoy, 22.2.

The wonderful, difficult days are over; yesterday, we took the finished volume to the printers in Dresden. For the last three days, we slaved away until dawn, and Jon went straight to work from here, and we slept three or four hours a night at most. Last night K. was so exhausted he fell asleep in the armchair.

I think the book has turned out well, and the Party and the trade union are tremendously proud. There are a couple of really outstanding pieces of writing [...].

We became very close to K. during this time, and Daniel's sympathies for him are sincere and heartfelt—even though he knows only too well what K. feels for me.

[...]

We rewrote some stories, and edited down and improved others so that the authors themselves, happy and amazed, did not recognize them. I am [...] really disappointed with the poetry: imitation Mayakovsky that makes my hair stand on end: bad prose, chopped into short lines, rhythmic gimmickry with no rhythm—and all this as a pretence at sophistication. It's time Rainer Kunze visited us (we send each other sporadic but beautiful, warm-hearted letters. R. is a wonderful person).

One night—I think it was on Monday, but it doesn't matter—we took a half-hour break, while Daniel typed up a manuscript in his room. I was lying face down on the couch and Jon was sitting in the armchair with his eyes closed, and his fingers stroked my hand, then walked across my face. I kept my eyes shut and lay still and felt them. Strange, we had never been as close as that before, although we didn't say a word and didn't move ... After a very long time Jon straightened up and said, shocked and happy, 'It was an adventure.'

Hoy, 26.2.

Ill, terrible back pains (and terrified that I might end up like Siggi B [...], who is already walking with a stick and knows he'll be a cripple in eight to ten years) and a breakdown at home, of our marriage. The day before yesterday, when I came back from a trip with K., Daniel confronted me; his anger was sparked because I addressed K. formally with *Sie*; he doesn't believe that when we're alone, we hold back from using our first names, and he's infuriated by this farce. He called me a 'whore' and I took it, and I came close to humiliating myself because I love him, and I really am cheating on him—[. . .] it is cheating, yes, because we have thought about sleeping with each other a hundred times already, and sins of the mind are at least as bad as sins of the flesh. [. . .]

Just now he insulted me so terribly—and with such a calm, cold expression!—that I walked out on him and have locked myself in my room and don't feel a trace of humiliation and guilt any more. I am angry—and all the angrier because, insulted or not, it's me who's in the wrong . . .

Yesterday he took away his photograph that used to stand on my desk, and now I have to stare at the empty, dusty glass in the frame. He also wanted his letters back, but I won't give them to him.

I'm looking for a clean, decent solution. Oh, our discussion of socialist morality! There's no solution without pain, and what we're going through is probably called an 'irreconcilable conflict' in literature—because simple decency is not the way out, or, at best, it is merely a compromise.

But it is so sweet and wonderful to be with Jon! We are now past the stage of intellectual infatuation, and when we say, 'I love you, I'm crazy about you,' we no longer apologize for these banalities with a mocking smile.

On Thursday, we—Erwin, J. and I—were in the Kastanienhof bar. Daniel stayed at home to work on his book. [. . .] I still enjoy dancing with Erwin as much as I used to [. . .]. But dancing with Jon . . . Actually, it was just a pretext so we could hold each other [. . .], and he said, 'You'll break me—and it will be a pleasure to fall apart because of you.'

Why do men say such gloomy things to me? [. . .] It's nonsense, of course. A man who loves his work doesn't go to pieces because of his feelings. Sometimes I convince myself I'm a nice, cheerful girl—but what if Daniel is right when he calls me 'a brutal intellectual animal'? However: if I write two or three good books, my personal life isn't worth a scrap. Work is the only thing that counts. The woman I see in the mirror, and her passions and wickedness don't count. [. . .]

2 hours later.

I have begun my story 'Seven Bushels of Salt'. [. . .] I missed working so much! All that time-wasting recently wiped me out completely. [. . .] Now I feel something like happiness; I'm curious about the people in my story. I can even ignore my diabolical pains with good grace.

Hoy, 2nd March

I have—no, we have—just spent a few hellish days, the three of us, unhappily chained together. At last I've seen K. suffer, and I'm pleased that he's suffering—why should my dear, one and only Daniel suffer? I always drag so much hatred into relationships! I revolt myself, I'm fed up with me and my miserable character, my drive for self-destruction. This morning I thought I might be mentally ill (a convenient excuse). [. . .]

Hoy, 6.3.

K. has been here almost every day, and almost every day we had huge discussions, either between the two or the three of us, and of course it didn't take us a step further. Love triangles are always faintly ludicrous, perhaps because they are so overworked in literature. I came close to hating K. because Daniel morally outstripped him and, even worse, suffered so deeply. Jon and I have a heap of confusion where other people keep their morals. We are very similar.

The next evening, I sent him away. He acted all reasonable and suggested [. . .] we set ourselves a kind of time limit. But I've recently taken a disliking to time pressure and said we might as well end things straight away, that very minute. I can remember it was exactly 5 minutes past 10. Daniel came into the room at that moment, and I informed him with as much indifference as I could muster. (Later, he said that in that moment he'd seen the pleasure of destruction in my face.) I saw K. to the door; he was completely distraught. [. . .] Daniel ran after us, down the stairs, and implored us to think about it—he felt sorry for K.! Then K. left quickly, and I felt sorry for him.

Bitter row with Daniel, who all of a sudden started beating me, senselessly, shouting 'Murderer, murderer!' If I had just destroyed him, it would have been bad enough; but now I've ruined K. too [. . .] This man is a treasure; he's too good for this world.

Then: alternating outbreaks of insane hatred (do other married couples say such purposely malicious things? The more intellectual the partners are, the better they know how to hurt the other) and declarations of love. [. . .] It was hell.

[. . .]

On Friday, Dorschan from TV was here. We worked like Trojans for twelve hours flat and managed to finish the treatment for *Woman in the Pillory* down to the last detail. I was totally exhausted. D. is a superb dramaturge, an odd fellow with good ideas, which he presents as if they were the author's.

On Saturday—Jon came over, as he does every day—Daniel left, allegedly to drive into town. He didn't come home that night. During the afternoon things were still calm; I wrote letters, Jon edited D's story, he lectured me on *Das Kapital*, conformism and Volkswagen shares, we ate a simple supper together at the kitchen counter, [. . .] later, we were very affectionate to each other; no less and no more, and the moon shone through the window, but more of a Soho moon, not the romantic companion it was on the night with Daniel.

At three o'clock in the morning, I awoke with a start and dimly made out Daniel sitting in the dark on an armchair. I swear I even heard the cushion rustling. He sat for a long time, not moving, and then came towards me in the darkness and asked if I'd slept with K., and, horrified, I said: 'No, no.' The next day I learnt that Daniel had been out all that time, dead tired at the wheel, on the motorway, about to swerve off the road from exhaustion at times. But he was perched there in the armchair, Jesus Christ! [. . .]

He had taken Siggi's car, driven to Burg to talk to my parents, [. . .] and set off again in the middle of the night to be back in the morning. He looks terrible: all thin and wasted. At first I was angry, because he has also dragged my poor mum into this, but maybe it helped him a bit. When Jon came over in the afternoon—Daniel was asleep next door—I told him we should at least try not to kiss any more. [. . .]

Just this: we separated our bank accounts this morning. Not a nice move. I have my own account, good God, and I am no good with money, and will soon be bankrupt. [. . .]

Hoy, 9.3.61

I've just finished my treatment. A hideous job—not because I couldn't cope with the material, but because of my physical pain all the time, sometimes so agonizing that I want to scream. But I bear it like a punishment from dear God, in whom I still believe, perhaps with some particle of my brain that I can't control. [. . .] I'm not kissing K. any more. I didn't think I could muster this much self-discipline [. . .]. But I'm talking nonsense, I'm sick, I feel very nauseous and my hands are trembling. [. . .] K. has been here almost every day, but we don't talk about us any more. I guess we have made our decision. The day before yesterday he told me: 'I will love you until my last but one breath. When I take my last, then I will think of myself.' [. . .]

Hoy, 25.3.61

Dear Brigitte R.,

You have the best husband in the world and it's incomprehensible why you—even if only for a few weeks—would fall into the arms of another. You are an idiotic scrap of a woman.

Yours sincerely, Brigitte R.

Evening

Alone. Daniel is in Rheinsberg, where the plant has sent him, almost by force, to recuperate. Recuperate . . . what a fantasy. D. has to write the last story for his collection. Today, a reminder came from Caspar but I haven't forwarded it to him so he doesn't worry.

I've had an exciting few weeks and haven't been able to get down to any work. Five days at home in Burg, enjoying my U-brother's delightful big mouth, his sunny mood, having discussions with my lovely, wonderful, understanding parents, dying to see Daniel. I'd barely got off the train when yet another car turned up at the front door: I had to go to Berlin to look at the—gorgeous—book cover for *Arriving in Everyday Life*.[161] An hour with Rentzsch who's writing a film script and looks very run down. The following day, a Writers' Union meeting in Cottbus. D.'s extremely nice sister came to visit from Hameln. I was only able to spend the last two days with her. A pity. She's such a lovely person. I find it difficult to make contact with people I don't know, especially women. I feel a schoolgirl shyness, a hidden fondness and respect towards them. I even flirted with her a little. And she has a sixth sense. When K. visited, she cried in the night and Daniel had to comfort her. Without anyone saying a word, she's guessed everything.

161 *Ankunft im Alltag.*

Hoy, 26.3.

Today, Sunday: spent the whole morning mopping and waxing the floor. Had a good, long sleep—such as I haven't had for weeks—and felt very young and full of get-up-and-go. Letter to my dearest Daniel in R., feeling as if I married him only three weeks ago—when in fact, our marriage is now beginning for the first time, or starting again ...

If only I knew what the stages were! I'm interested (the cool, psychological interest of a writer) in working out why I went back to him and why Jon lost. [...]

I just realized that I still have 400 marks in my account. (The other money has been paid into the car savings account.) I had wanted to go with Jon to Dresden and buy a summer party dress. But I will pay a small, banal penitence and buy a typewriter for Daniel instead. Not a very original way of showing remorse and love [...].

A day before E. left, Daniel made love to me again. E. was out shopping, and D. and I were arguing, in self-defence, as it were, and suddenly I abandoned all the defiance and all the nastiness, and suddenly, it was the way it used to be when we were cohabiting in chaos [...]

Three days later, D. went to Rheinsberg. I had to go to the Neues Leben authors' conference in Prieros. Caroused throughout the night: vodka, a bunch of brilliant young men who talked too much, my little Lewerenz, in love with me as ever; after midnight we played blackjack, and I gambled away house and home. [...]

Hoy, 29.3.

Yesterday evening, returning from Berlin, I found a wonderful, painful, unsettling love letter from Daniel, which he wrote in Rheinsberg on Saturday. At night, in bed, I read it over and over again. [...]

Horrific dreams: atomic bombs being dropped, people wrapped in damp sheets, pushed to the ground, the wave of heat surging over us (oh God, and I really felt it), then the end: desert, no houses, no trees, no grass, white ash a foot high; my face was covered with burns.

For the record: on Saturday I met Jon in the club committee room, where I was preparing the course for our writers' circle. We went together into town; I bought a typewriter for Daniel. We ate at Café Klein. We recognized, without sentimentality, the fatal outcome of our relationship—a first-class state burial. [. . .]

Yesterday: Berlin. Eagle-Eye drove us—a likeable young roughneck. Jon came along, also on writers' circle business. First stop, the Writers' Union. Of course the secretaries were in a meeting; E. Klein came out for five minutes. The others stared at me as if I had committed a sacrilege because I wanted to speak to a secretary who was in a *meeting*. [. . .]

The writers' circle course has again done a 180-degree turn. Almost reproached because our workers write good stories, because we're publishing their work and are writing a play for the workers' theatre—the worker writers are supposed to scribble articles for the bulletin board, point out maladministration at work, and so on. Why aren't these geriatrics from the Writers' Union happy that fresh blood is being pumped into their calcified arteries! [. . .] The Party, trade union or even the State Security services are responsible for dealing with serious grievances and can be much more effective than some little article. Ugh! I was absolutely furious and didn't budge an inch from my point of view. In the end, though, I managed to get hold of the speakers, after some wearying waffle about organization. Damned bureaucrats and smart arses!

From some window in the street, I can hear the interlude from *La Traviata* . . .

Went for lunch in the Bukarest: spicy Romanian food and a lot of *mastică*. Then to Caspar [. . .]. C. was gentle and amiable, we didn't quarrel [. . .]. We drank a few cognacs and talked about Daniel, and I was able to broker a deal for him for a better deadline and a half-promise that his stories will be published in a proper, stand-alone volume. [. . .]

On one occasion C. rebuked me when I referred to Neues Leben as my publisher: my publisher was Aufbau, he said, NL had only borrowed me. By September he'd like me to have written a volume of stories. How, in God's name, am I supposed to manage that?

[. . .] Then I went to NL because C. wants to have my *Arriving in Everyday Life* for the bb paperback series.[162] Lewerenz was angry, and we haggled and argued for an hour before he agreed at least to provide C. with a manuscript.

[. . .]

Hoy, 30.3.

Last night Jon and Erwin came over, the latter already tipsy and as happy as a sandboy, although he'd just been through an annoying couple of weeks; he'd been searching for a certain type of steel that we have to buy from West Germany. Jon stayed an hour longer, I lay around on the couch, leant against his shoulder, and told him foolish little tales that happened to come into my head [. . .], and Jon made one of his peculiar declarations of love: 'You look like a schoolgirl who hasn't done her homework this afternoon.'

In bed, I read the old-fashioned *La Dame aux Camélias* and it made me cry. It really did. In the morning, staring at the grey sky, I thought for a few minutes that I'd be lying if I wrote here that I wasn't in love with Jon any more. [. . .] I have to work. Daniel is coming tomorrow.

Terrible pain in my hip.

162 The bb paperback series was published by Aufbau in Berlin and stood for 'billige Bücher' or 'cheap books'. They first appeared in 1958 and were discontinued in 1991 after German reunification.

Evening.

Wildly disappointed: D. sent a telegraph; he won't be back until Saturday. My heart hurts all of a sudden. No matter how much there is to do, I'm very lonely without him. And then I read his letter again [. . .]. Damn, I can't wait to see him [. . .].

Hoy, 31.3.

Good Friday. Very lonely. [. . .]

Yesterday I did the washing until midnight, then fell into bed, dead tired. Fell asleep with a novel in my hand—for the first time in ages without feeling terror and a childish fear of ghosts. Would like to read the chapter about the crucifixion of Christ again today. If I remember rightly, the most poignant description is in the incomparable Gospel of John.

Evening

Terribly uneasy. I really believed that Daniel would still come . . . instead of working, I stood at the window and stared out at a road where there's nothing to see. [. . .]

Hoy, 3.4.61

Between this entry and the last, there should actually be a big gap, an empty line, a caesura—because I feel like a new life has begun. These three days with Daniel [. . .]—no, not a honeymoon, it was pure gold.

I'm tired and run down; typed for D. yesterday the whole day long [. . .]. My arms and wrists hurt, but even that is good and precious because I know I helped D. a bit. We have to get the manuscripts finished by tomorrow. He is still sitting next door in his room, typing on his new machine.

[. . .]

APRIL 1961

Hoy, 5.4.

Early this morning, D. went back to Rheinsberg, and I feel empty and numb. Actually, he had planned to leave yesterday morning, but we kept postponing it from one bus to the next, and in the end, it was too late [. . .].

Now I am sitting at my desk wanting to start the story which I have been dreaming about for days: *Brothers and Sisters*,[163] the story of my Lutz-brother (the way things should have gone but didn't). I was electrified and enthusiastic, and now that I have time to write, I've forgotten everything. Always the same . . . Before, it was all in my head, word for word, pages long, and now everything sounds wooden and dead.

Hoy, 7.4.

D. came on Friday night. He had been all alone in his ancient mansion and in the evening, as the storm howled and the rafters creaked, he couldn't stand it and fled—straight to me. We talked until dawn, and kissed, and our slight alienation faded away.

And then we had a wonderful Easter, from morning to night: work, work, work. We wrote and edited his old stories together—and at night we slept with each other: we got married again.

[. . .] A thousand organizational meetings for our writers' circle course. The club committee got a few things mixed up: yesterday the whole course was hanging in the balance, because suddenly they said there were no beds in the mansion house. Today everything is OK, touch wood.

I wrote to Daniel every day. I suddenly wanted to have his child, a boy who I'd name Jonas and who would be as gentle as his father . . .

163 *Die Geschwister.*

Jon was here. I read my story to him. We went for a walk like a pair of old ravens. A spring breeze, soft and warm after a few weeks of this cold snap, and we strode through the streets and discussed people who defect to the West and the like. Jon spoke most of the time. He gave long, clever political lectures, and I couldn't get a word in edgeways. Which was good, because I learnt a great deal. Afterwards he dragged me off to Glück auf to eat. And the whole time: discussion about lessons learnt, class consciousness, Uli (that's my hero) and his relationship to the Party. Afterwards I felt dead and shattered, but now I see the thread running through it: the story has a proper political framework, and if I can write it decently ... let's see. In any case, I'm actually looking forward to it now.

Hoy, 10.4.

On Sunday Daniel came home at lunchtime [...].

I was so happy to have him back; he looks a bit better than before. I no longer pined for my bachelor life. There is nothing more beautiful than falling asleep on his shoulder again in the evening—[...] I've been sleeping well since he's back; before, I'd often lain awake for hours, sweating profusely, terrified.

Yesterday was our wedding anniversary—and we didn't even have the money to give each other anything. There was solyanka and pineapple, and we ate with great ceremony. Now I am sitting idle and restless, waiting for the journalists who had announced they were coming this morning. [...]

Hoy, 12.4.

The *Neue Berliner Illustrierte*[164] is going to publish photo stories about our new work: with accompanying articles. New work from the publisher: articles, biography, essay on my own book. Radio

---

164 A magazine, later referred to as the *NBI*.

play synopsis has to be finished by the 19th. Various tasks for the writers' circle, course, tomorrow *NBI*, then Friday, Circle of Active Artists—Sunday, Rheinsberg. Daniel is running around town, making calls, organizing—things that are the club committee's responsibility. I wrote letters half the day. We are just secretaries, cultural officials, not writers. Invitations to dozens of readings; I have to cancel all of them. We are both run down. Yesterday: another half-dozen visitors. [. . .] If I didn't check the calendar, I wouldn't know that it's spring. [. . .] On Sunday I saw a flowering tree from the window of K.'s flat. It moved me to my core.

Afternoon

The start of a new era: the first manned space flight. Major Gagarin can orbit the earth in his sputnik in 108 minutes. This deserves an entry in red pen.

Hoy, 17.4.

I think I'm pregnant. I'm quite desperate. I keep crying. I want to work, not play at maternal bliss. Daniel is sad because I don't want to keep the child—but I probably have no other option. That's why I don't dare hate or curse this thing, because if it's born, I would bitterly regret hating it in the past. I'm superstitious.

The three days of the course in Rheinsberg were soured, despite sunshine on the first day, the blossoming trees and shrubs, and despite Daniel's love and the successes of our writers' circle. I can no longer write, no longer concentrate. [. . .] And Daniel [. . .] is bursting with pride and already envisions how wonderful it will be and how sweet I will look with a big belly. But I don't find it sweet; I find it rather disgusting [. . .].

Hoy, 29.4.

[. . .] I'm not pregnant after all. Just as well. All the same, I was a bit sad when I remembered the trip to Rheinsberg and I began to feel happy, and Daniel was so tender and proud, and kept asking: 'How do you both feel?'

Not written a line of *Brothers and Sisters* for days. Course in R. instead (great success, visits from top Party people, wonderful discussion); private meeting with Herbert Warnke[165] to whom we presented our writers' circle publication and gave him a second copy for Walter Ulbricht, who has sent us a letter of thanks in the meantime; a hundred meetings, discussions, book reviews etc., read through the page proofs of my book, which is to be published in July; interview for the *NBI*, with hours of photo snapping; reception at the Party on the GDR's 15th anniversary; compared notes with the Wismut circle in Aue where we did a huge presentation [. . .]; literary ball, reading; visit to the TV station—I have ditched the treatment and don't want to resume it for the time being [. . .]; in Cottbus [. . .] with K at the Young Authors' working group, who cannot match the standards of our circle; brigade party . . . Yes, yes, yes, it's all important and good and useful, but I want to write again. I'm going crazy. If I accepted all the invitations piling up around me, I could quit my profession and become a professional literary traveller.

Hoy., 3.5.

My God, it's starting all over again. This morning I sat in the bathroom and cried, because Daniel flew into such a terrible, jealous temper—just because I wanted to go over to Jon's this afternoon and work with him on his bulldozer-driver story.

[. . .]

---

165 Herbert Warnke (1902–75): German trade unionist and politician; chairman of the FDGB.

MAY 1961

Hoy., 6.5.

Yesterday—yet another conference in Berlin: problems of worker writers. [. . .] We were very prominent at the conference: K. made a splendid contribution to the discussion—once he'd got going, he performed like an actor, a total diva. [. . .]

All the time I've been wanting to write about him—to gain clarity for myself and because I'm keen to pin down this highly interesting character (somewhere in a recess of my brain, a story is beginning to form whose significant, pitiful hero is my dear K.) [. . .].

Something binds me to him, and this makes me feel it could last for decades and become deeper—it is certainly the first stage of a friendship of the kind I have only experienced once or twice, most intimately, and in the end most painfully, with my Lutz-brother, who has moved so very far away from me in terms of his outlook. In Jon I love Lutz (as I would have wished him to be) and my loud Ulli-brother . . . There is some sense of responsibility (repressed maternal instinct, I suppose)—Daniel needs me less in a way, because he's not as screwed up. Daniel has what I would call integrity. Jon is instability personified, and if he has any kind of anchor point, then it's Marxist philosophy. Everything else [. . .] changes constantly—he is playful, infantile for all his cleverness [. . .]; he is the man that has been missing in my life, and our contact hits all the wrong notes in me, and precisely because of this (healthy, intense opposition . . .) he has a very beneficial effect on me. He is my means of coming to an understanding of myself [. . .].

He lets me say things to him that no one else would dare utter. People are afraid of him, his sharp tongue, his—sometimes hurtful —irony, and I know a lot of people in the plant who avoid discussions with him in the first place, because they know that he will just talk them into the ground. He's unpopular. Ignorant people hate him. He has never hurt me; sometimes he ridicules me with the patient tenderness of a big brother.

He's incredibly conceited and arrogant, and I like it. He's ugly, and I like it, I like [. . .] his sweet, strange ugliness that makes him so similar to Ulli (but Ulli has beautiful eyes with long, girlish eyelashes) [. . .]. It would be an absolute disaster if we were married or bound in any other way; we would kill each other or let ourselves go completely and live in squalor. But this kind of friendship is a happy kind. I hold on to a hundred little episodes, pictures, scraps of memory, maybe they're silly: we're driving through a terrible rainstorm on a motorbike trip and Jon hangs his coat around my shoulders and gets soaking wet himself. We walk through C. and eat slices of salami from a bag and ice cream along the way and K. watches so that I don't cover myself in grease stains and blobs of ice cream (Daniel told him how I ate chocolate in the theatre and somehow smeared it on my cleavage, and then walked through the foyer with splotches of chocolate on my neck and chest). We went to the Distel cabaret yesterday after the conference (I was enchanted by Ellen Tiedtke—my God, she could turn me into a lesbian!), and Jon lost his poise and screamed with laughter and dug me in the ribs. [. . .] On the train, he sewed new hooks onto the belt of my blouse that was too tight. He wraps his scarf around my neck when we ride his motorbike home from the Pumpe. [. . .] He's stopped drinking (and his pledge is for a quarter of a year), because I cursed him as a stupid drunkard . . . I'm probably writing all these things down because I will use them later, shamelessly, as all writers do.

Oh, I wish we really were siblings so that Daniel wouldn't worry any more. No, it's not [. . .] all wild like it was earlier, and that's for the better. [. . .] But it would be horrible and unimaginable if anything were to tear Jon out of my life.

Hoy., 7.5.

A quarrel with Daniel this morning. I'm both sad and outraged. He did precious little last week, and now he's trying to put the blame on me: in some mysterious way I have held him back . . . That's so unfair! I took on all his work; he had the time and the peace to write. I don't want to imply that he wasted his time—it's probably down to his terrible pedantry, his damned obsession with writing every sentence twenty-five times over. He doesn't tell stories, he tinkers around. But books are there to be read and to reach people; the author's aspiration to write everlasting works are not important, especially if the writer needs a decade to write such 'everlasting works'. We need the book now, not in ten years. This bloody 'being held back' theory—Caspar's hobby horse, which he rides as soon as he sees us together: 'Get a divorce, B. is a successful woman, she's holding you back, she's destroying you.'

Daniel threw the name K[. . .] into the quarrel again. It seems to me that he's trying to mask his failure with emotional complications, which I don't believe in, because this week was beautiful and happy, [. . .] we are having sex—K. is not disturbing our marriage. [. . .] And it's ridiculous for D. to claim he can't work here—anyone who has something to say, and wants to and can write, can do it in any old place in the world. I hate this wastefulness. And I want to bemoan and pity *myself* for a moment: I [. . .] rush from one conference to another, I keep the flat in impeccable order, I wash and iron and scrub: our household runs like clockwork. And my *Brothers and Sisters*? No one asks when and under what conditions I write. And it's not important. The story has to be good, the writer is of no interest. [. . .] My books are not literary treasures by any means (and nor will be my future books), but they have moved tens of thousands of people and have influenced a few. What else is there? [. . .] In two years, Dieter Noll writes 1,000 pages that cause turmoil across half the Republic, and there isn't a perfectly formed sentence on a single page. So what? His *Werner Holt* gripped and stirred me a hundred times more than, say, Thomas Mann, with his accomplished works of art. But D. finds it primitive: for him, Mann is the be-all and end-all of literature, even if no one reads him. [...]

Sometimes, I fear for our future together. [...]

Hoy., 8.5.

Yesterday, I was pretty nasty and unfair again. When I'm angry, I say a lot of things in the heat of the moment, without thinking. Early this morning we quarrelled again because of Thomas Mann, and Daniel called me primitive and a left-wing extremist, because I advocate useful literature. But I simply love the fighters and rebels, the ones who change things: I love Gladkov[166] and Libenski (my big discovery: *One Week*),[167] and now I know why I can't warm to Mann: he analyses things but doesn't help change them. Swansongs instead of 'The Internationale' . . .

But we'll eventually find a common viewpoint, Daniel and I. I'm not going to start *The Magic Mountain* again, I swear! But I will read *Faustus*. I know the stories and still remember how disturbed I was [...]. For some reason, I find it alien and uncanny that this was supposedly penned by a man who ate and digested like other people, and who sat down to work at a desk . . .

[...] The people around us have a right to recognize themselves in our books. Jesus Christ, look at me indulging in theory and abstractions. I really am a simple soul, a child of this world, with my feet very much on the ground.

---

166 Fyodor Vasilyevich Gladkov (1883–1958): considered a classic writer of Soviet socialist-realist literature.

167 Yuri Nikolayevich Libedinski (1898–1959): Soviet writer, whose first novel, *Nedelya* [One Week, 1922], about communists caught up in a peasant rebellion in a remote town in the Urals, was one of the first significant works of Soviet literature and made Libedinski an instant star. B.R. refers to the German translation of the novel: *Eine Woche* (1961).

MAY 1961

Hoy., 10.5.

Today is our wedding day again. We gave each other pralines and expensive cigarettes, and in the morning, we played Wolf and Tiger, making a terrible din. It's wonderful to live with Daniel. We are hard at work, C. has sent back D.'s stories with a few tiny corrections—things are getting serious; the 'Net'[168] has to be finished by Whitsun, then the book will be published this year. [. . .] I am so happy that Daniel is finally going to be published.

The day before yesterday, I had an ear-splitting argument with Jon, whose bulldozer-driver story I didn't like in places. He works too superficially, barely lifting a finger—pish-posh!, as he likes saying [. . .]. Sometimes he is revoltingly conceited, and he hates it when something is expected of him: after all, in the past, people were always 'expecting something of him', and he always disappointed them. I was very angry, we shouted at each other for a whole hour [. . .].

Hoy., 15.5.

Back at work again on *Brothers and Sisters*. Finally, finally! I am moving closer to Lutz; I am, of course, writing him, not some anonymous Uli, and sometimes the pain brings tears to my eyes. Yesterday, when I described his small brown hands . . . it was terrible.

Daniel is going half-insane. His deadline is looming. [. . .] A good sign is that, despite fatigue and overwork, we never quarrel or flare up at each other. [. . .]

I have made up with Jon; I can't be angry at that big charming kid. [. . .] Today we were at the plant together, and on the way back, we drove to a new opencast mine and watched the huge bucket-wheel excavator. A yellow desert of sand, and felled trees

---

168 'Das Netz', a short story in S.P.'s short story collection *Wunderliche Verlobung eines Karrenmannes* [The Strange Betrothal of a Barrow Man], 1961.

next to the path; the leaves were still bright green and a little wilted. [. . .]

I definitely have to write about the Central Committee discussion tomorrow. Oh and for a quarter of a year, I've forgotten to mention that I met the Günter, my first husband, on my last visit to Burg. We went for a walk together, and afterwards sat in a little pub—the same one we sat in on the night of our first-ever rendezvous. It wasn't sentimental at all—in novels, these kinds of encounters always seem different—and I only became careful when I realized that Günter still loves me. Afterwards he even said so. [. . .] He has built himself a little patch of provincial happiness, complete with garden and rabbits, and he doesn't drink any more. He's learning a trade, and I wish it wasn't just to earn more money when he's finished. [. . .] Inconceivable to think that we once lived together. He's still very good-looking, one of the finest men I've ever seen. When we said goodbye, he embraced me on the street. I was shocked and glad that Uli turned up—a wonderfully carefree, loud-mouthed, good-humoured roughneck. That was all. I don't understand why I didn't write about it straight away.

Hoy., 21.5.61

Whitsun. Sunday. Rain, rain, rain, cold.

A terrible week behind us: On Monday, Daniel had renal bleeding; the next day he couldn't stand the pain any longer and went to the hospital, but left again when they wanted to keep him there. He still had to write the last ten pages of his story, as the deadline had already passed. But that put an end to work, and in the evening, I went to the writers' circle, and when I returned—after just an hour—my poor love had a high fever, was gibbering all sorts of foolish stuff, and in my panic, I ran back to the circle for help. Jon stayed with Daniel while Siggi drove me to the hospital. At night the doctor came, and he gave us a few days' grace after we had wailed about Daniel's book.

At times, when Daniel didn't recognize me, I wept with fear. [. . .]

It's wonderful to have such reliable friends [. . .]. Jon especially showed his best side; if he likes someone, he makes all kinds of sacrifices. [. . .] He's really fond of Daniel. He visited every day, and while Daniel lay very weak and exhausted in bed, he reworked the manuscripts with me, mostly until one o'clock at night. I transcribed and we actually managed it—all for those last ten pages.

Daniel got up for the first time today and is sitting at his desk again. [. . .] He should actually be in hospital under medical supervision. We're playing fast and loose with our health, and there is no end of work. Oh, for a few hours' rest, a volume of Goethe, Heine, Tacitus—dreams that we will probably have to save until we're old enough to retire. I am completely done in and worn out [. . .].

Yesterday I went with Jon to Berlin to deliver the manuscripts to Caspar. We ordered a car at the FDGB, and they promised in many friendly words that they would do what they could . . . But there was no car, and Jon found out that our lovely FDGB patrons with the big mouths had said, referring to the car, that we 'shouldn't even entertain the idea'. Very nice to hear.

We always have to jump when we're told to jump; we never turn anything down—but [. . .] for half a year K. has not managed to draw up our new contract, which should have been ready on 1.1. Perhaps we should complain to Warnke, but knowing us, we won't say anything: decency can also degenerate into stupidity. Oh well.

So, we went by train, which was totally overcrowded, and on the way, we shocked people with reports about our criminal records and the difficulty of getting a passport for stateless persons. I love play-acting like this, and Jon plays a fantastic supporting role. At the publishing house I immediately set to work on the manuscripts with C. [. . .]. This time it has to work out; this time, no stupid accident or stroke of fate can crush Daniel's chances. He's had so much bad luck in life, especially for one who's so gifted [. . .].

C. tyrannized me again. [. . .] We sat in the Press Club—Jon was also there, of course—and we were both commissioned to write a story for the Almanac, C's latest project—by the 15th August. J. is to write the blurb and advertising texts for Daniel's book. The lad is moving up in the world. He's even been invited to the congress. He must have made a deep impression on our treasured secretaries—driving a bulldozer is seen as an attractive job.

We frittered away our time in discussion; by the time we started arguing about what kind of relationship the Party has with intellectuals, we'd missed our train. C. accused me of left-wing radicalism [. . .]. He's probably right; but I prefer such people a thousand times more to spineless intellectuals and writers who shy away from portraying a positive hero, and think we're primitive because we've gone to the grass roots and have this comical idea of writing for our work mates. In Berlin they prefer to be part of the sophisticated elite, far removed from the uneducated masses.

We took the midnight train. At Ostbahnhof, I was gripped by terrible heart pains, and thought I was going to die. Jon dragged me to the nearest bench and I ripped open my blouse, otherwise I would have suffocated. A proper little breakdown, which took me a quarter of an hour to recover from. Jon was beside himself with worry. He ran to the first-aid post and fetched heart drops, and a whole crowd of idiots stood around staring at me. They would probably have stared the same way if I'd died right there on my bench. The train was freezing cold, and I lay on Jon's lap and froze, although he'd wrapped me up in his coat. Jon doesn't make a good impression on most people; [. . .] but he is one of the very few who make me feel absolutely safe and secure.

If I'm ever seriously ill ... Good God, I have nothing in reserve! I'm wafer thin, not even 98 pounds. And still I have so much I want to write!

Berlin, 26.5., early in the morning

I'm sitting in my guesthouse; Daniel hasn't arrived yet. Now he has to finish his short-story collection whatever it takes. [...] At lunch, I talked for a long time to M. W. Schulz (the man I used to call 'Joe'). Sch. had read Daniel's story, and, like Herbert Nachbar recently, found echoes of Thomas Wolfe. But Daniel has never read a line of Wolfe, and he shouldn't either for now. I can remember all too well the havoc Wolfe (who for me is still one of the greatest writers of our century) can wreak on young writers' brains—Sch. has only changed on the surface—I could still see the rest: his calmness, his enigmatic smile, his kind, wise eyes. At that time, I was too young; had I been more mature, I'd have known how to keep such an invaluable, precious friend. At first I was a bit confused and very shy. Sch. says I seem much younger and even more girlish than back then (I was 22, I think). I really must introduce him to Daniel today. Sch. has finished his novel *Dust in the Wind* [169] at last (brave to give yourself such a long time to mature!); he is a lecturer at the Literary Institute in Leipzig. As soon as they offer [...] one-year courses, I'd like to go there—with Daniel, of course.

I saw all sorts of interesting people I knew from the past, or whom I first met here. Lewin introduced me to Alexander Abusch,[170] and I acted really awkwardly out of embarrassment. He gave me a letter from a Soviet composer who wanted to write a score to the *Woman in the Pillory* for an opera. Unfortunately, I can't read the letter ... A. was very gracious, said I was even

---

169 Max Walter Schulz, *Wir sind nichts als Staub im Wind* (1962).

170 Alexander Abusch (1902–82): writer, journalist, politician, who served as GDR Minister of Culture at the time.

younger than he'd imagined. Well, that kind of asset soon gets used up, frankly. In her speech, Eva Strittmatter named me as one of the new strong talents. That's better than just being an attractive woman.

Yesterday at 10 o'clock, the glamorous opening took place. The heroes of our literary scene strode into the committee room to thunderous applause: the beautiful Anna Seghers, Strittmatter, Arnold Zweig, hunched over and nearly blind (later he gave a weird speech with numerous friendly provocations). The foreign guests were welcomed and when the name of the Cuban guest was announced, everyone clapped as if deranged; it was a show of solidarity with the Republic of Cuba. How many great names have died since the last congress! Thomas Mann, Bert Brecht, F. C. Weiskopf, Johannes R. Becher, Lion Feuchtwanger . . . The old men in the committee were afraid, you could feel it in Zweig's words; they believe that when they go, German literature will die. They don't expect anything from young writers, and they don't even want to admit that some are talented. Only Anna Seghers seemed confident; frankly, though, her appeal to the old guard to help young writers will probably fall on deaf ears. A.S. delivered the main speech at the congress, about the depth and breadth of our literature. I listened more to her fascinating, gravelly voice and the language of her lecture (an irrepressible formalist!) than to the content, which we can read in print anyway in our own good time. For the first time, I heard a speech written in an author's distinctive literary style. Each line was undeniably Anna Seghers. When I see her (and I hardly dare look at her), I feel like a child in church . . . I think I'd sink into the floor if she actually ever spoke to me.

[. . .]

In and among all this, the infamous private talks, usually more interesting, outside the conference proper. Reiner Kunze, Sakowski, Nachbar, Panitz: in short, the entire young vanguard. We all know and like one another (despite occasional malice between colleagues), which seems to me to be a good sign of a changed socialist consciousness.

In the evening I went with Jon to the guesthouse; suddenly, I was seized by the ambition to give a speech. But in the end, I lost my nerve [...].

Hoy., 29.5.

Was just writing a few lines of *Brothers and Sisters*; suddenly—neurasthenic—mad heart palpitations, I had to stop.

The congress, and everything that happened during it, completely confused me. I first have to sort myself out. [...] And I have to check my political position. The congress had too much of a right-wing spin for my liking; perhaps I have to adjust my views. I've been leaning too far to the left recently. People repeatedly emphasized the value of creative solitude, the most important task of the writer: to write [...]. True, Strittmatter cited Daniel and me as a good example of writers connected to real life, to workers, and said that since we've been at the plant, our work has matured artistically. Now I wonder whether we've already soaked up enough—for the time being at least—to be allowed to concentrate on our work again. We also have a right to self-imposed solitude now and again—as long as we get books written, mind you. Still, I feel guilty if I neglect things here at the plant. Where does it end—being obliged to put all your energy into supporting others? [...]

The second day of the congress was dedicated to young writers. Noll spoke and thanked the Party. Nachbar, impulsive and stuttering slightly, talked about our freedom ('we are not free to pass on our ignorance'). Stefan Hermlin (who appeared on the bulletin board under the headline 'Cock of the Walk') polemicized unfairly against Strittmatter. Permanent conflict between our writers and the West German Günter Grass—we can't find a common language any more, despite well-meaning attempts, and I'm afraid that not even the common task of peacekeeping can unite us any more. We've become too hectoring because we're using Marxism to say that only *we* lay claim to the highest level of knowledge [. . .] and the West Germans think we're primitive because all the wisdom and freedom and aesthetics of the Western world is stored in their heads alone, and because they don't understand our clear diction, our straight-forward, sometimes plain, language.

In the evening the State Council and the Central Committee gave a reception at the Rotes Rathaus. The road in front of the city hall was sealed off. There was a huge staircase, laid out with a red carpet; there were enormous rooms, marble and columns—it was oppressive. [. . .]. At the door, like a guard of honour of young maidens, stood all sorts of prominent figures, among whom I, half-paralysed with self-consciousness, only recognized Kurella and Abusch. I was overwhelmed because they all knew me and greeted me so nicely and called me 'squirrel', because I look like Samoilova.[171] In the great hall, we hid in a corner with Martin Viertel, who is also very shy. I like Viertel with his beautiful grey hair; he radiates peace and calm; he was also the soberest person afterwards [. . .].

Kurella made a toast, and the literary crowd pounced on the buffet and ate [. . .]. It was impossible to hear Noll's toast because of everyone chomping. I only ate a bowl of radishes and then of ice cream much later and, besides that, stuck to white wine (the only bottle of vodka was on the presidential table and was later seized by Caspar).

I'd been desperately waiting for Daniel all day long. I would have flung my arms around his neck, pulled him close and kissed him. [. . .] It wasn't until the next morning, the last day of the congress when I came sneaking through the entrance gate with a

---

171 Tatiana Samoilova (1934–2014): A Soviet actress best known for her lead role as Veronika in the film *The Cranes Are Flying* (1957), in which she has the nickname 'Belka' (Russian for 'squirrel').

hangover, that he was standing in the portico in front of the ministerial building;[172] [. . .] He'd worked all through the night. I suddenly felt very uneasy and hardly dared touch him; he seemed as fragile and transparent as glass. [. . .]

Hoy., 30.5.

I'm in a foul mood; I'd like to torture everyone around me to death. The dark, sweet mysteries of Catholicism are beguiling me again—how comforting it'd be to have faith again and be able to lay my head in the lap of the one true Church. Jon calls Catholicism the biggest show of the millennium—and I have a confused longing to kneel in a confessional box and whisper into the pale ear of a priest, liberate myself from depression and fears and be a peaceful, meek lamb under God's mantle.

[. . .] All nonsense. Of course, there's still something of my Catholic forefathers' dark faith in me. But back to earthly matters. My terrible memory for faces has put me into awkward situations hundreds of times, with people greeting and addressing me, and me not knowing who they are. I try to play it down with charm and blushes—but some people are really not worth recognizing.

[. . .] First Abusch came and chatted with me for a while, and it wasn't just because I had had a few that I was very open and in a good mood. I have no respect for men anyway (and it has nothing to do with a lack of respect for their achievements); but the next day, when Anna Seghers stood in front of me and smiled, I nearly fainted and couldn't get a word out. Abusch looked at me the way you look at desirable women, and this male look blocked out any respect for prominence and ministerial rank. I took the opportunity to report some annoying problems at the plant and he wrote everything down

172 Detlev-Rohwedder-Haus, known in the GDR as the Haus der Ministerien, built in 1935–36, was the largest office building in Europe at the time of its construction. Since 1999, it has been the headquarters of the German Federal Ministry of Finance.

and seemed amazed and outraged at our situation. Then he instructed his consultants to fix matters and promised that he would soon come and visit us at the Schwarze Pumpe. I hear the message . . . [173]

[. . .] Then there was dancing [. . .]. A young Jew with beautiful, dark Oriental eyes [. . .] chased after me like the devil after a human soul, and everyone assured me that I was clever and charming and gifted and God knows what, and finally my stern Central Committee partner, Lewin, joined me and raved about 'The Confession'. Lewin was adorable. He used to scare me because there was something robotic about him. But there he was, dancing the boogie with me and idolizing me [. . .]. We even drank to eternal friendship (without a kiss of course—otherwise a disciplinary action from the Party would have been on the cards).

At twelve the whole literary scene was drunk [. . .]. The dark-eyed Jew brought me home and said he was madly in love, and I slammed the door in his face and ran into my room. When you've been mauled by compliments and lustful glances all evening, men make you sick.

And the next morning my dear, sweet, gentle, ill Daniel was standing there, and I felt at home. [. . .]

Hoy., 31.5.

An ice-cold day to round off May. Rain and wind.

Yesterday, we had a good evening at the writers' circle. A survey on what people read; a brief—for each person individually—to read a book chosen by us and then discuss it; read part of Anna Seghers' speech; discussion—very animated, clever and passionate. Representatives of the FDGB paid us recognition for work done on the writers' circle book: 400 marks for the writers' circle, 100 marks for

---

173 An allusion to Goethe's *Faust*, I: 'Die Botschaft höre ich wohl, allein mir fehlt der Glaube' [I hear the message but I lack the faith].

K[...] (editorial work) and a weekend trip to Prague for Daniel and me.

Working passionately on *Brothers and Sisters*—and so much pain, because Lutz is always with me when I write. Not interested in anything else [...] as if my reserve of decency, self-discipline, kindness and the like are only enough for the story I'm working on at that moment. Suddenly seized by the need to push others away, make them suffer (and this too without feeling emotion). But Daniel is (still?) taboo [...]—I'm sure: when the story is finished, I'll go back to being the most gentle, good-natured person again. [...]

If the people who read my book later only knew this! At the congress, librarians approached me, wanting to be introduced and shake my hand, and then they thanked me a hundred times. I was very intimidated, even scared—there was a kind of reverence in their faces. [...] When I was talking about my new book, one said: 'We take everything that comes from Brigitte Reimann without having seen it.' Whenever someone tells me that they've read something of mine and felt joy and were moved, I'm ashamed I don't have more human kindness. [...]

A few words on the last day of the congress: there were a lot of official speeches, and at the end, the election of our executive, which was incredibly silly, bureaucratic and confused. I was sitting next to Dieter Noll, to whom I was introduced by Daniel that morning (years ago they had been friends), and we cheered at each new vote and each new complication that made Zimmering flustered, the returning officer ('Dwarf Know-It-All,'[174] as Noll called him). An entertaining election, accompanied by loud jokes and brazen heckling from Noll. Noll, the high priest ... A comedian who continually and confusingly plays the role of anything and anyone; sometimes he even plays Noll. He impressed me very much; I think

---

174 Zwerg Allwissend: a character from the radio programme *Einer gegen alle* [One Against All] with Hans Rosenthal on RIAS (Radio in the American Sector) Berlin.

his *Adventures of Werner Holt* is the best thing to have been published here in the last ten years. [. . .] He has tremendous self-confidence (or is that fake too?), a sharp tongue and a vicious, quick sense of humour—I wouldn't like to be his enemy.

I was relieved when he told me that he liked my 'Confession' very much, and thought it was far better than anything else in the 'Series'.[175]

Anna Seghers brought the congress to a close: 'We have passed the oral test—now comes the written part.'

Hoy., 2.6.

Rentzsch will be here in a minute: the new radio-play project. Maybe Daniel will take over my part—at the moment I'm obsessed with *Brothers and Sisters* and nothing else interests me.

On the evening of the third day of congress, we were invited to the Strittmatters, along with Jon and Dieter Noll. The St.s are almost the only big names in our literary firmament who treat young writers warmly. True, no real conversation took place, I was very inhibited [. . .]—we were quite exhausted from the congress (I'd hardly slept the night before), and we shy provincials were also intimidated by the presence of Minetti and his wife Münch. Noll, however, matched them with ease: he was brilliant.

Minetti was overbearing: he giggled and twittered like a homo—I've never heard a man laugh so much—and he reminded me of the young men in Koeppen's *Death in Rome*. Then, drove through the night, dead tired.

Eva Strittmatter is very fond of my book [. . .]. She spoke to Daniel about me for a long time. At first I was happy to hear what

175 Refers to the series of publications known as 'The Series' by Aufbau between 1958 and 1961 which published new authors, including Franz Fühmann, Günter Kunert, Irmtraud Morgner, Helmut Sakowski and Herbert Nachbar, among others.

she and others expect from me; but now I'm more afraid—there's nothing worse than failing people's high expectations.

Hoy., 3.6.

Futile chat with Rentzsch. The radio people have cut off our money—a month earlier than our contract stipulates. We're already a bit tight for cash and living off our car savings. At last I've found a sort of storyline. [. . .]

Terrible headache in the afternoon. Then drove out to Knappensee with Jon. The rye is flowering, grass is being mown in the fields. Smell of forest and mushrooms and hay, and later, at the lake, of brackish water. Drove through quiet little villages, which reminded me of the village—the unknown village—of my *Woman in the Pillory*. Somewhere evening bells were ringing. Something forgotten or buried came back to me.

We walked along the lake. We stood among willows and listened to the mating call of two bitterns from the reeds. Peaceful countryside, peaceful silence and mood. We had been quarrelling for a few days. Then, two days ago, we were standing at Jon's window; it was dark, there was light in the windows. A bat flitted by. We asked each other why we'd quarrelled so bitterly, but we couldn't remember. We decided that we might just as well make up.

[. . .]

Hoy., 10.6.

Daniel has been under observation in hospital since Tuesday. He has a room to himself, he has peace and quiet and he's reading a lot, and I hope he will recover a little. [. . .] Today is our wedding anniversary; I brought him red roses and a Sternchen transistor radio.

[. . .]

Today we got a reminder from the television people. I am slowly starting to panic. I am at a point with *Brothers and Sisters* where I don't like it much any more. Now the sweat and toil starts, so it seems.

[. . .]

Hoy., 14.6.

Yesterday evening, when I came back from the writers' circle with Jon, there was a telegram in the letterbox: 'The executive committee of the Free German Trade Union Association has decided to award you the literary prize of the FDGB.' The telegram was addressed to both Daniel and me. I don't know for certain which of our works has been awarded the prize, but I went pretty wild [. . .]. I'm about to go to the hospital to tell my poor, dear co-writer this good news. I'm so glad that I haven't been awarded the prize alone, [. . .] Daniel [. . .] shouldn't feel he's lagging behind. On Sunday he got the doctor to give him a temporary discharge, and we wrote the treatment for Rentzsch. I had something to confess again: a new admirer [. . .]—and dear A. B. who forgot his Party morals and professed his great love for me.

That was Saturday, after the Workers' Theatre formally approved *Man at the Door* for the festival in Magdeburg, and A. came over to tell me that he loved me [. . .] and—this sounds almost blasphemous, written in the same breath—that he will vouch for me if I decide to put my name forward as a candidate for membership of the Party. [. . .] Such an unoriginal promise for someone as clever as A. [. . .]. For some reason I always feel sorry for these hopeless fools . . . Shame that after two hours at the latest I grow tired of men who chase after me; then they're no longer entertaining.

Jon is the great exception [. . .].

We are in perfect harmony, even though we don't touch each other. In the evening, we play 'blue hour': it's dark, and light from the street falls into the room, and Jon sits in the armchair and I squat on the floor and we tell each other things we wouldn't say in daylight. We've also talked about our marriages. [. . .] He was dismayed when I told him [. . .] Daniel is the best man for me in the whole world (and probably the only one I can live with, day in, day out, without rebelling) [. . .]—and for that very reason, I'll never understand why I was able to take Jon into my heart. [. . .]

[. . .] Sometimes we feel like wayward children who have escaped the wise adults and are walking, full of curiosity, singing loudly and slightly scared, through a wild unknown forest. We play Indians, smoke the pipe of peace, talk about buffalo hunting and political economy.

Hoy., 15.6.

This morning, Daniel returned from hospital, still a bit run down and with terrible back pain. Yesterday he told me that they had examined him thoroughly, and that his heart and lungs were healthy. When I woke up this morning, I was happy and relieved to think: thank God, my heart and lungs are healthy. Much later I realized that it was Daniel, not me. [. . .]

Tomorrow we are going to M. for the award ceremony. I am quite calm now, as if it were already over and the next step up the ladder already awaits us. At the ceremony itself I'll be nervous, but it's all organized already: I have my foot carefully raised, ready to climb the next rung. I might fall, of course—maybe the rung won't hold me—but it forces me to go on, that's all. Is this ambition, pride, something worse? I don't know. The things I create and achieve don't give me any pleasure, just the act of creating them and all the torment that goes with it.

Hoy., 18.6.

In Magdeburg on Friday for the literary prize ceremony. The plant allocated us a car. I didn't feel well, staggered from one heart seizure to the next (although I've long since got over winning the prize). Masses of writers, a real festive racket, good choral concert, radio interview, dozens of telegrams congratulating us warmly. Herbert Warnke presented us with the prize. I held on tightly to Daniel's hand and, because of my headache, didn't enjoy talking to the press sharks nor the whole ceremony.

Herbert Nachbar was also there. We'd already revived our friendship after the Central Committee session; on Friday all three of us sneaked away from the banquet and spent two hours in the Stadt Prag restaurant [...]. We hit it off again really well; others find him annoyingly aloof. He's still very good-looking, but he's lost that youthful lustre of the past. I think he's on Daniel's wavelength and (half-seriously, half-jokingly, kept saying) especially admires him for having put up with me for three years. When Daniel went off for a moment, Herbert sincerely congratulated me on my wonderful husband.

Hoy, 21.6.

We've been staggering from one laudation to the next, our flat has become a flower shop, and on Daniel's desk there's a pile of leather binders with official congratulations from the plant, the Party, the district council, etc. Everyone's being terribly nice and happy for us (at least I hope they are), and that makes us even gladder than the prize itself. [...]

The Writers' Union meeting was yesterday, and I've been elected to the executive. A kind of press conference followed, where I reported on the writers' congress in front of journalists. But I had no time to prepare a report, so I relied on my big mouth. The safest bet in these kinds of situations is to give a timid apology—then they let you get away with anything [. . .]

Hoy, 4.7.61

The second day of dreadful headaches, which meant that we couldn't work. Been writing a TV drama for almost a week; it's good to be working with Daniel again. [. . .]

Hoy, 11.7.

[. . .]

I forgot to report that my book *Arriving in Everyday Life* has been published. The cover is lovely; I think the illustrator is a student of Schwimmer's.[176] I'm prepared for difficult discussions; the Curt character will be a problem for some. *Junge Welt* rejected pre-printing it because of him—but the *NBI* is going to run it instead. Good fee. [. . .]

All in all, we've earned a lot of money, I realize. In August, we're getting a Wartburg, which the district council had promised us for winning the prize. At first we hesitated, but then we checked our account and were surprised to see that we wouldn't even need to get a loan. Of course, we're very much in arrears with the radio people. Rentzsch rejected our new treatment *Thorn in the Flesh*[177] as well. [. . .] He found *Brothers and Sisters* 'too political'. In any case, we're tired of it and will ask the radio people if we can pay back the advance from our contract in instalments at the beginning of the year. Oh, well, my lovely *NBI* fee . . . Just when I'm getting a taste for earning money!

[. . .]

---

176 Max Schwimmer (1895–1960): German painter, printmaker and illustrator. In 1951, he was appointed to the Dresden Academy of Fine Arts as head of the Department of Graphics, a post he kept until his death.

177 *Haken im Fleisch.*

Hoy, 14.7.

This month I've earned at least 5,000 or 6,000 marks; I'm amazed. Today I received another 2,000. The paperback print run (30,000) of *Children of Hellas* sold down to a few copies in just 3 months.

[...]

Hoy, 19.7.

Uli came to visit; he was discharged from the army a few days ago, and begins his shipyard placement on the 25th; then he's going to study at the uni in Rostock—marine electronic engineering. He's turned into a handsome lad [...]. Today he went with Daniel to Dresden, to the Gemäldegalerie. I'm glad he loves books and paintings and music; he's like Lutz in that way. But he also has similar political views, and that scares me. If he went away too . . . So many of our young people are only interested in material things, in possessions.

Uli is very enthusiastic about my book. That's a weight off my chest—I wrote it for him [...] and people like him. I'm afraid that Lutz will react by mocking it. Perhaps the last tie between us will break when he receives the book and my letter. We've drifted so far apart . . . I kept quiet for months before I replied to his horrible letter. There wasn't a single line in which I forgot that I'm his sister and still love him (my God, is that true?), and I hope he senses it. But I told him harshly and clearly that I condemn what he did, that I refuse to tolerate terms for the GDR like 'Eastern Zone'[178] , and I expect him in future never to insult the state which paid for his studies. He won't forgive me for this latest reproach (Jesus Christ,

---

178 The term B.R. uses is *Ostzone*, which initially referred to the post-1945 Soviet Occupation Zone that became the GDR in 1949. *Ostzone* remained a common name for the GDR in West Germany, which refused to acknowledge the existence of a state in East Germany until 1972.

the quarrels we had over it!). At the very least, he'll regard it as annoying communist agitation.

I don't think I'm quite all there today. The music's to blame. I'm listening to laid-back jazz, a recording by Studio 5.[179] Played like a Bach fugue, so that you feel transported to a flute concert in Sanssouci. 'Rococo Puppet' is a strange mix of modern and anachronistic music—an impertinence really. I already have a lot of wonderful records; Daniel's going to give me a record player for my birthday, having scouted the whole town with Jon for days; in the end he only managed to get it via the district council. He couldn't keep it a secret, of course, and he's already played me most of the records, and today I'm allowed to use the player on my own. But that's his usual funny way of giving birthday surprises.

We have Chopin and Tchaikovsky, and Ravel's *Bólero*, and Beethoven's Piano Concerto no. 5 (but we haven't played that yet), and synagogue songs and Thomas Mann's draught-board scene from *Krull*—a really rich assortment of music—rock 'n' roll and jazz and a few pop tunes, played by Gustav Brom and Karel Vlach. I've been listening to music all day and am in a daze. It's a barbaric mixture, and my moods swing between melancholy and giddy cheerfulness. Work is not progressing; I planned to continue with *Brothers and Sisters*, but I've lost the thread, and of course I think it's bad and amateurish.

[. . .]

Hoy, 23.7.

I'm horribly tired again; been working all afternoon on *Brothers and Sisters*. I doubt my story more and more—doesn't help lift my mood.

My birthday was very nice. The party the evening before wasn't quite as nice. We had more guests than our flat could hold [. . .].

---

179 A Prague-based jazz band in the 1950s.

At midnight, they finally let me into Daniel's room, where my birthday table was set up. Daniel showered me with gifts; I think he spent his entire Aufbau fee on me.

On my actual birthday we were both alone, and I was calm and happy, which rarely happens. We treated ourselves to a day off; we read, listened to Ravel and Debussy and Tchaikovsky, and enjoyed the books and the music thoughtfully and blissfully. I wish there were more moments like these in our hectic life [. . .].

Hoy, 29.7.

Yesterday I went to Berlin with Jon to deliver the manuscripts to Caspar. Miserable weather. We gave our stories to Caspar, who read *Brothers and Sisters* straight away and said, 'If the story carries on in this vein, it'll be good.' It was a weight off my chest. C. was very friendly, and so was his new co-worker, who read Jon's story. We're going to be included in the almanac and C. even wants to double the number of advance copies I suggested.

A number of nerve-wracking things happened: [. . .] Jon bumped into a stack of tinned meat in a butcher's shop and sent the tins flying; I tussled with a ghost telephone that kept saying 'hello, hello,' and I began to believe in mechanical dolls like in Hoffmann; to top it all, we got stuck in the lift between two floors at Aufbau Verlag, and I was scared to death because I don't trust technology, but finally we were let out.

Spent the evening with Lewerenz and his beautiful, blonde wife in Café Praha. He told me that *Arriving* was considered one of the best books of the year.

Came here in the morning dead tired. I was laden with gifts for Daniel. And then the terrible welcome: Daniel completely crushed, [. . .] he believes he'll never accomplish anything at all. He can't concentrate, has no talent for storytelling . . . I tried to comfort him,

I got angry, I cried in the end because he wanted to leave me, not burden me any longer. He feels that I'm just 'putting up' with him. He wants to find a job. But what, for Christ's sake? He's so delicate, so sickly . . .

Hoy, 5.8.

Daniel has pulled himself together again. After a few terrible days, he was ready to get back to work. He typed up *Brothers and Sisters* for me (the broadcasting people want it) and worked into the night. He says my sentences are good to read, but difficult to write: they have no harmony. 'Like a tangle of wire,' I said. 'Like your character,' he said. He's enthusiastic about the story and thinks my way of writing is getting more and more 'French.'

That Tuesday he saw Jon kissing me at the front door. He only told me a few days later, without reproach.

Lewin (cultural department of the Central Committee) wrote me a long, friendly, clever letter about *Arriving in Everyday Life*. He thinks the book is an enrichment to our young literary scene. We were very happy about his sensitive criticism. There's one point I'd like to discuss with him: the feeling of young people towards the GDR, that they 'take it for granted'. We really do, whereas Lewin sees the Republic through the eyes of a man who helped lay the foundations and suffered terribly under the Nazis (he's a Jew).

[. . .]

Terrible evening yesterday. The Berlin crisis is intensifying:[180] a law against cross-border commuters has been passed,[181] the

---

180 When the Vienna summit between US president John F. Kennedy and Soviet premier Nikita Khrushchev (3–4 June 1961) offered no solution to problems with the German peace treaty and the question of the status of Berlin, a mood of crisis loomed.

181 The word in German for people who worked in the West and lived in the East was *Grenzgänger*. On 5 August 1961, the East Berlin City Council ordered the registration of all such 'cross-border commuters', which stated: '1. All citizens of the capital of the

Western powers have been advised, and Strauss is demanding nuclear weapons and special powers to use them. I felt physically sick when I heard the commentaries. We are teetering yet again (are still—have been for years) on the brink of war. My heart stops when I hear the sound of aeroplanes. Yesterday I was so scared, I couldn't move. I looked out of the window into the night, suddenly expecting to see that alien sun in the sky, that white ball of incandescence that would show us one final artificial dawn before we disintegrate into ash. I couldn't work, it seemed so pointless all of a sudden to worry about everyday things. I asked Daniel to get sleeping pills. I don't want to have to crawl through rubble, a wailing, burning bundle. I'd rather finish myself off beforehand.

I don't understand the world any more. Later generations—if there is such a thing—will look back on our times the way we do on the era of witch-burning and cannibalism. We are living anachronisms.

Yesterday there was a briefing here on the 'Week of Young Literature'. E. used the opportunity to demand a statement in support of a peace treaty from us. I started to rage. For once and for all, these people should stop prattling and publishing hackneyed rubbish, and work their hardest. Luckily, clever Jon intercepted my over-heated attack and—for E.—made my views, which he shares, more palatable. He expresses them better. I always go over the top.

Hoy, 5.8.

I'm listening to the second movement of the Unfinished. I have nothing but tears to express my emotion, my pride . . .

GDR (democratic Berlin) who are employed in West Berlin have to register on the basis of the order of 14 January 1953 regarding statistical collection for employment [. . .]. 2. With effect from 1 August 1961, persons referred to in article 1 have to pay their rent, land lease and costs for electricity, gas, water supply and public charges in West German Marks' (in *ND*, 5 August 1961, p.3).

This time yesterday, I was lying with Jon at the edge of a ripe field of rye: the sky was blue after weeks of clouds and rain, behind us was the forest. It was very quiet, then we heard the evening bells, tinkling distantly, as in a fairy tale, from a distant village. We didn't even know where we were—we'd got lost after a wild motorbike ride over rough terrain. Oh, the heather next to my face, the chink of sky over Jon's shoulder . . . I thought: perhaps politicians should carry out international negotiations at the edge of a maize field when the sun is going down. [. . .]

Now they've gone to the cinema. I have to work. [. . .]

My God, this music! And my worthless art . . . Stupid, sloppy, not capable of stirring anyone. Just a few well-meaning sketches on current events.

Hoy., 9.8.

Later I wasn't sorry to have stayed at home after all—it wasn't until Monday that we heard there was no car going to Berlin, and, had there been, there would have been no room for me. I'd have liked to blow up the whole club committee: those apparatchiks simply make demands, and their wonderful lack of consideration, which wastes other people's time, makes me sick. [. . .] Anyway, then, from the 5th to the 6th, we worked the whole night through. Daniel came home from the cinema, sat down at his desk and was still there when I woke up the morning. He carried on working well into the day, by which time he had a 'Spitze' column ready for the *Wochenpost*, which I thought was outstanding. A poetical observation, and much more than that: the Milky Way was 'a band of light from you to the dimension of infinity . . .'. There's something about it that I would call 'cosmic thinking'. It also makes me happy because writing it helped him overcome his crisis. [. . .]

Hoy, 11.8.

Today Daniel worked himself into the ground—seven pages of the television play, one of the most important and possibly most moving scenes. Now we need to plough on with the brigade diaries.

Yesterday, I sent Jon away for three days. The evening before, everything had still been fine. He came straight over to see us after he got back from Berlin; we drank vodka and sat discussing half the night, starting with my absurd philosophy of platonic love, to which I attach more value and dignity than carnal love, and finally, via Marx and Feuerbach, we got on to Mendelian genetics and Lysenko's theories, and Georg Maurer's wonderful poem cycle *Thoughts on Love*[182] was actually to blame: it's contradictory because his 'cosmic thinking' seems too flippant and peters out with Venus in a black pantyhose. The crown of his head touches the stars, and his feet are in the bed of some curvaceous girl or woman . . . Daniel laughed at my puritanism. Maybe I'll become a bigoted, zealous old woman, hmm? After having embraced so many men . . .

Yesterday I was a monster. I wanted to go with Jon to Dresden, and suddenly his [. . .] wife intervened: she had shopping to do in Dresden. I suddenly felt like Jon's mistress—and mistresses come second. If I'd asked him, he would have done what I wanted. But I don't like asking. I was disappointed and jealous—I could kill this woman [. . .] in cold blood.

[. . .] Sometimes I feel like an anachronism. In another time, living in another place, I would have swept that woman aside long ago.

Hoy, 12.8.

Last night—I had just shut my diary—Daniel came in, triumphant: 'What did I tell you? Your Jon is here.' He [. . .] sat glowering and silent in my room. We listened to the second movement of the

182 *Gedanken der Liebe.*

Unfinished. Finally, I asked him, more in a derisive way, whether he'd already made up his mind. . . He said aggressively that he didn't need to make up his mind; he would get a divorce. [. . .]

I was shocked: I always cause havoc, and am bitterly sorry afterwards. So, knowing me, I'll use all my powers of persuasion to make him stay with his wife. [. . .] I bring men bad luck. I was desperate —and still am—because I can suddenly put myself in Mrs K[. . .]'s position. I took away her husband (not even innocently). [. . .] I think a lot of things are coming together that have intensified the K[. . .]s' marriage crisis: Jon's weeks of unemployment (in our state, with its desperate lack of workers, they can't find Jon a bulldozer!), his growing love for writing, which Mrs K[. . .] dismisses as personal pleasure [. . .] and the fact that Jon can talk to me about all the things his wife doesn't understand; in her eyes he's now the kind of husband who fritters away his time instead of bringing in the money. We did pay him, of course, but maybe that annoyed her even more.

I don't like thinking about it now (but of course I do, all the time). I forgot to emphasize that Jon has never played the misunderstood husband with me; he's not that cheap.

Did I already write that I'm no longer as terrified as I was about the political situation? In the meantime, Gherman Titov[183] has orbited the Earth seventeen times—his spaceship is a weightier argument than an arsenal of nuclear bombs. We listened to Nikita Khrushchev's speech for an hour and a half, although the transmission was very bad. There were several massive threats, but they came at the right time; even in the West, it's obvious that a Third

183 The first 'long-haul' space traveller, the Soviet cosmonaut Gherman Titov (1935–2000). B.R. is referring to Titov's *Vostok 2* mission (6 August 1961) in which he spent more time in space than any other person till then. The mission covered over 700,000 kilometres and proved that humans were capable of living and working in space. To date, Titov remains the youngest person to enter space; he was a month short of his 26th birthday at the time of the mission.

World War would be suicidal, and they are ready to negotiate—
even on the Berlin question.

Our newspapers, of course, are spreading hysteria again—
'bounty hunters' and 'human traffickers' are all the rage, and if you
believe the articles, there's a Western agent behind every GDR citizen waiting to entice them away. For Christ's sake, anyone who
doesn't like it here should leave!

Hoy, 15.8.

Today was a good day: we wrote a whole scene, I did the washing
and got through a pile of correspondence.

Yesterday was a bad day: I had a terrible hangover and it was
really difficult to rouse myself to go to my brigade in the plant. The
highlight was the sad Russian love stories that I read the whole
afternoon and evening.

Sunday was to blame. [. . .]

I was at Jon's until half past three in the morning, and we
knocked back a whole bottle of vodka and got quite pissed, lurching
from melancholy to wild hilarity and back. I have a vague memory
that we kissed passionately in the stairwell . . . What's certain is that
Daniel was standing—unnoticed by us—a few steps away and
saw and heard everything. He came back when I'd already gone to
bed. There was a terrible scene—[. . .] first he lied that he'd met a
girl . . .

I was boiling with hate (ah, and I can't begin to grasp the extent
of my injustice), I would have left him immediately—but in truth
he'd stood half the night in front of Jon's house, staring up at the lit
window. The man is an angel.

But at least I know why I felt such hatred: I blindly trust
Daniel—despite all my own sins—I swear on his virtue and loyalty;

he's still my romantic hero, my ideal man. [. . .] He doesn't have my passion, which is ice-cold in its depths, and he's not a player by nature. What he says is the truth. If I found out that he'd had an affair, my love for him would flip into destructive hatred that very second and I'd do everything to destroy him.

[. . .]

Hoy, 21.8.

We're in a desperate mood: we're tired and need a holiday, but we won't get one any time soon. Not a day goes by without us being told or asked to write statements or the like, on the elections, on the peace treaty, on—the devil only knows. We're starting to refuse. Why this endless campaign?

Hoy, 22.8.

We're happy. We would be really happy if the political situation didn't feel so oppressive: this megalomaniac sabre-rattling ever since 13 August,[184] the uproar against 'scalp hunters'. The newspapers are using a coarser, more brutal tone than they have done in a long time.

Prison sentences are hailing down. Our politics are enough to drive you crazy.

Hoy, 25.8.

Daniel is in Cottbus yet again because of our car, which first led to a dispute between Hoy and Spremberg about who's responsible. All the promises from the district council—empty words.

[. . .]

---

184 The date when the border between the FRG and GDR was sealed and the Berlin Wall started to go up.

Prague, 3.9.61

We arrived yesterday in bright sunshine; today it's raining, but music is playing again in the small garden restaurant—in among buildings and courtyards. Last night it all looked Parisian; the small island of lights down there, parasols, laughter, voices, a crystal moon high above neon advertising. And music: I think there was music playing in every house. The high street and Wenceslas Square (we are staying at the Hotel Ambassador) are bathed in coloured lights. Everywhere you look, you're reminded of Ku'damm,[185] but without the unhealthy, hectic hustle and bustle. There's a good atmosphere in Prague. We didn't meet any drunks at night.

Heydrich wreaked havoc here—70,000 people were executed after his assassination.[186] First I was scared and ashamed: I thought the Czechs would hate us. They are hospitable and amiable.

I'm now sitting on the small terrace of the hotel under sun blinds. It's cool. I'm dizzy from looking at everything, from the throng of people streaming past and the strong Turkish coffee. You can hear half a dozen foreign languages all around; there are Negroes, Indians, Americans and Russians sitting here. The proportion of German tourists seems high.

My God, the German tourists! There's none more demanding. They take it for granted that everything's better and more civilized back home. They take pictures here, there and everywhere, and no matter if they're taking photos of the gas ovens in Theresienstadt or of Prague Castle, they have the same stupid rapture on their faces.

---

185 Kurfürstendamm, a shopping high street in West Berlin.

186 From September 1941, Reinhard Heydrich (1904–42), one of the main architects of the Holocaust, was the acting Reich-Protector of Bohemia and Moravia, the Nazi protectorate formed following the German occupation of Czechoslovakia. On 27 May 1942, he was critically wounded after being ambushed by a team of Czech and Slovak agents who had been sent by the Czech government-in-exile in London to kill him; he died a week later. The SS (Nazi paramilitary) then retaliated against the village of Lidice, where the assassin had allegedly found refuge. All male inhabitants were murdered, and the women and children were deported to concentration camps.

Yesterday in Theresienstadt, I was horrified. Looking at the barracks where the incarcerated used to lie, hungry, soaking wet, lacking air—in these surroundings, people were chatting about good Czech beer (the price of beer was the first question they put to the charming old gentleman who led us around); and one woman wanted 'so much to visit the gas chambers' and people were proud of the efficient organization in the concentration camps (the German love of order is reflected even in our murder equipment), and these damned souvenir hunters—! [. . .]

Late in the evening

I'm sitting in our hotel room; Daniel went with the others to some kind of group entertainment. I don't like being around so many people, especially such loud ones. [. . .] I'd like to spend a few weeks strolling around magnificent Prague just with him, enjoying everything we're now ticking off the list at an American pace. Rushing from one work of art to the next is exasperating.

[. . .] It's madness to spend the evenings in a foreign city in your hotel room. Maybe I'll go back down to the lounge, just to be with people. If only I weren't so shy!

The journey through the gentle landscape, children waving along the road—men and women waving too, even though they saw our German bus. There must have been a death in every Czech family, and the blood was on our hands. It haunts me wherever I go here, despite everything.

The burial ground in front of Theresienstadt's city wall . . . Here, the mother of my character Recha[187] died; I wrote that scene but knew nothing of the truth. Now I've seen it: rows upon rows of gravestones. Inside I was crying the whole time. Our Czech tour guide lost two relatives in Th. He calls us 'dear friends'. A man's

---

187 The heroine in *Arriving in Everyday Life*, whose mother, a Jew, died in the Theresienstadt/Térezin concentration camp.

remark at our table: 'I'd like to be a travel guide. But I'd take people to pubs, not cemeteries.' Perhaps that swine was a soldier who helped fill the cemeteries. And now he's sprawled in an armchair, grumbling because there's cake instead of ice cream for dessert.

Last night we met the youth of Prague. We were in Café Luxor—a gathering place for young people we would call 'rowdies'. There's no alcohol and a band played Dixieland and Charleston. The atmosphere was cheerful and high-spirited, no booze-fuelled fights. Boys and girls danced wildly and stylishly; we saw acrobatic performances. They were really going for it, but never in an unattractive way.

We were sitting at the table with two young Czechs; one, a civil engineer, spoke good German. [. . .] He loves jazz—evidently jazz was still nurtured here at a time when it was regarded in our country as an aberration or even counter-revolutionary.

[. . .] We're bowled over by beauty, overwhelmed by impressions. Prague Castle—the monastery with its library, St Vitus Cathedral, Romanesque vaults, Gothic arches [. . .], the cathedral mass (altar boys ringing their little bells, the smell of incense, rays of sun falling through the stained-glass windows [. . .]. I think one day I'll turn Catholic again. Why 'again'?) [. . .]

I couldn't speak, I was always on the verge of tears and so awestruck, it was as if my reverence had turned me to stone. The architecture, the images and books [. . .], the sinister, bloody history of the city [. . .]

I didn't go with the others this afternoon. I don't know if my exhaustion was just an excuse. It was too much, more than I could take. I felt crushed by it all.

It's almost ten. I don't want to go down to the lounge any more. [. . .]

I'm thinking of Jon. [...] Jon Crook-Ear ... that's my name for him because his right ear is mangled from a motorbike accident. [...] Jon pictures us sitting together in fifty years' time. He wants me to be a clever old lady with the fascinating ugliness of a woman who was once beautiful and knew how to take advantage of it. I tell Daniel everything.

Hoy., 6.9.

We finally have our telephone line. This makes our work easier. In a fortnight we'll have a car. Wartburgs are currently not available. We're getting a Skoda. Frankly, I don't care what we get. Now we have everything or almost everything we want ... Next year we'll get a plot of land on the lake at Spremberg and a little weekend house. Sometimes I'm weighed down or scared by this standard of living or simply that we can fulfil so many of our wishes. Yes, we work hard, but I always feel guilty about those who are not as well off. The world is still an unfair place. I also realize the dangers of this standard of living—to keep it up or even increase it, perhaps I'll begin one day to write faster, with less of a conscience, just for the money.

I spent Sunday in Prague all on my own. Perhaps it was better not to see what Daniel saw: the synagogue, pitch black, with blood-stained walls and the names of 70,000 murdered Jews; the Jewish cemetery with its jumble of tombstones—every living creature that dies in the cemetery, even birds or dogs, have to be buried there and given a gravestone. [...]

The last day was draining, especially for my gentle Daniel. He ran around the city, to the broadcasting company, to the Dilia,[188] to the state bank in order to get hold of a few more koruna from our royalties, and when he finally returned to the hotel, most of the shops had already closed. We bought a few antiques and jazz records.

---

188 DILIA: a theatre, literary and audiovisual agency in Prague.

At lunch there was wine, and the entire group got on the bus in high spirits. Only a few minutes before we left, we were all still standing in the road.

Hoy., 9.9.

I wanted to say that I suddenly spotted Rainer Kunze in the throng of people and flung my arms around his neck. We greeted each other as if we'd bumped into each other in New York City, 'among spectres the only feeling breast'.[189] Rainer looks healthy and good-looking in a way that's hard to define. He's going to stay in Czechoslovakia until January 1962; he's working for the radio.

On the journey home, I was silent among the singing, boisterous crowd, which meant that our grey-haired guide didn't manage to get another word in.

[...]

Yesterday was a very melancholic day. I couldn't write a single word, couldn't even walk the few yards to the pub to drown my sorrows.

The day before yesterday: in Berlin. First at Caspar's, who likes *Brothers and Sisters* very much. [...]

The events of 13 August have cast their shadow over our small town. It looks as if we've been waging an underground civil war. Enemies and potential enemies who, if Berlin hadn't been sealed off, would have gone to the West, are leaving their marks. Slogans daubed on schools and pavements: 'Down with the Red tyranny'. Two nights ago, the telephone cables to the district leadership offices and social institutions were cut; at night, groups of workers patrol the city.

Recently a 'tribunal' was held in the Pumpe, where two engineers who had been prevented from defecting to the West on the

---

189 From Friedrich Schiller's poem 'The Diver' (1797): 'Unter Larven die einzig fühlende Brust'.

13th were given relatively mild sentences. The workers protested. [. . .] The engineers will be stripped of their academic titles but a worker would have gone to prison for ten months.

Hoy., 14.9.

Discussions for nights on end about the Soviet nuclear tests. Am fearful of the rain again, God knows what it contains. Oh, what peaceful days we had when the rain against the window still had a certain romantic quality.

Today we saved a sparrow that had fallen into the ventilation shaft.

Yesterday Daniel picked up our car, a light-grey Skoda (Oktavia Super) from Senftenberg. I wasn't able to appreciate it: I was lying in bed, unable to live or die, bringing up bile and blood. So Jon was the first to ride in our car. Daniel is thrilled by the power of the engine. Today I drove with him, but it still feels strange, not at all like it's ours. Another substantial rise in our standard of living . . . [. . .]

The *NBI* has started publishing instalments of my novel. Eva Strittmatter has written a helpful, sensitive foreword, in which she attests to my 'wisdom and bountiful talent'.

I've had a lot of very good reviews. Today, Herbert Warnke wrote me a warm letter: he had greatly enjoyed the book, the characters weren't pen-pushers, and he thought I was on the right path. I was delighted that a busy statesman had taken the time to read a book by a beginner.

Hoy., 21.9.

I'm slowly getting used to our Skoda; at first I felt like some chance passenger. We've already clocked up the first 700 kilometres; today the car needs to go in for a check. Some of our friends have changed the way they act towards us since we got the car; they obviously presume that it's changed us. [. . .]

The day before yesterday, Jon and I went to 'our' forest. The grass is still flattened in the place where we lay down in June in the blistering sun. And it's so high all around that when I crouch down I'm invisible. At first I was afraid of the animals rustling in the bushes and going on their nocturnal hunts. It was a very warm night; the moon was the colour of an orange. The grass was brown and had no fragrance. Suddenly I felt like a wild animal. I didn't know you could experience nature like that.

Hoy., 28.9.

Survived the 'Week of Young Literature' in the end. There were readings, an evening of jazz music and a large writers' circle meeting to swap experiences, where we carried out a round-table discussion. [. . .] There was a disagreement with the Cottbus working group and its silly little dogmatists, and I closed the debate with the comment: 'Dear friends, if you had been Sholokhov's editors, *And Quiet Flows the Don* would never have been published.' They wanted to tear me to shreds—it was amusing.

Yesterday was the Reader's Ball which bored me to death. Daniel drove Jon and me to the Kastanienhof bar at 10 p.m., where, despite the noise and 'Old Comrades' (!),[190] I got a second wind. I drank a bottle of bubbly with Jon and we danced. Enough tongues are already wagging, so we don't give a shit about others' indignation.

But then we got quite sentimental, and I can't hide the fact I'm still quite down. We tried to imagine how it will be when it's over between us—although we'd like to believe that it's going to last forever and nothing can make us part. But every sin is punished at

190 'Alte Kameraden', a march by Carl Teike, not played in the GDR because of its military associations. The word *Kamerad* was often used to denote Nazi soldiers, whereas *Genosse* exclusively referred to socialists.

some point, and although others say we have no moral compass, we know very well that we're committing a sin.

Jon's waiting for his wife to divorce him at last, and he's expecting a scandal. He says that some day he'll leave, maybe for Schwedt, and then he'll ask me to come with him.

[. . .] All I know is that, despite everything and everyone, I can't leave Daniel. [. . .] Sometimes I see his hands trembling, his thin hands, and [. . .] I want to protect him, I want to give him the love I'd feel for my children if I ever had any. But I won't have any children. Perhaps I'll write a good book one day.

[. . .]

Lutz wrote me a terrible letter—eight pages long, freedom and democracy,[191] and his growing hatred for a sister who's selling herself to a despicable regime. I hardly dare carry on with my *Brothers and Sisters*.

[. . .]

Hoy, 4.10.61

Came back from Berlin the day before yesterday. Meeting at the TV company, which was depressing: shooting won't start until December, and there can't be any exterior shots—nature doesn't do what it's supposed to in front of the camera. The play will lose its charm.

In the morning we met Rentzsch, whose film has fallen through. Lack of actors. Many preferred to remain in West Berlin. Everywhere people are nervous and dissatisfied. The language in the newspapers is revolting (but masquerades as 'the hard language of the working class'); people who live near the border are being

---

191 Allusion to Bertolt Brecht's poem 'The Anachronistic Train, or Freedom and Democracy' (1947).

evicted;[192] west-facing aerials are being torn from roofs and trampled; students who do not sign the FDJ statement[193] will be exmatriculated . . . It's enough to make you lose your mind, and we're bitter and unhappy. This isn't the kind of socialism we wanted to write for. We've already been deceived once; the 'greater good' has already been cited in Germany as a justification for a thousand injustices. Three days after the election, the Defence Law[194] was passed, obliging the authorities to provide essential services, but omitting recourse to due legal procedure, which damned well looks like an emergency act.

Hoy., 9.10.

At the end of last week, something abominable happened: Günter [. . .] sent me a letter seething with insults, in which he asked me 'to fulfil my duties' in the rudest tone and to compensate him. He's demanding 2,000 German marks; if I don't immediately send an advance payment, he's going to take me to court. [. . .] Of course he has no rights; we went to the District Court at midday. [. . .] Daniel's answer to G. was written with sophisticated irony. But we're afraid that this episode will have a sequel [. . .]. This is the man I used to love: a lout with a vile character.

In the afternoon we were driving back from Spremberg where we'd picked up Renoir's *Bathers*. We drove past the scene of an accident: the road was covered with blood, and all the motorcyclists were pale, moving stiffly and unusually slowly. A few hundred

192 On 20 September police had begun forcibly evicting people living in houses along the Berlin sector borders.

193 On 16 August 1961 the FDJ made an appeal: 'The Fatherland is calling! Protect the Socialist Republic!' By November nearly 30,000 youth were obliged to serve in the GDR's National People's Army.

194 On 20 September 1961 the GDR parliament (*Volkskammer*) passed a 'law on the defence of the GDR' (*Verteidigungsgesetz*). This gave the SED leadership almost unlimited emergency powers to regulate the military and civilian services for the protection of the GDR 'in peacetime as for purposes of defence'.

metres further on, a jeep stopped so abruptly in front of us that we almost drove into the back of it. Daniel swerved in time, and we went hurtling into the left lane. If there had been any oncoming traffic, we would have been crushed. Our knees only started trembling later.

Hoy., 17.10.

Daniel has given me complete freedom (even to sleep with Jon whenever I want). He won't touch me any more: we'll live like friends or colleagues. Daniel now sleeps in his room—and at night, half-awake, I miss his face, his sleepy tenderness. He knows how to punish me, and what wears me down. Our three-way relationship is heading towards an inevitable catastrophe. [. . .]

I was sick for a week and sent to bed by our doctor. Jon visited me every day, although he also had the flu, and brought me a thousand things: records and tropical fruits and chocolates, and I should have reminded him to be more economical with his money [. . .].

So I was ill, and yet again, we didn't do any work on our damned TV play, of which we're anyway sick to the back teeth. It's no longer exciting now all of our beautiful exterior scenes won't be shot [. . .]. I'd like to get back to my prose as soon as possible; I never should have started working in a genre that has nothing to do with literature anyway.

What nonsense, by the way: me encouraging others to save money. Yesterday I bought the *Kreutzer* Sonata with my last money—a wonderful French recording with David Oistrakh—and the *Woman with Blue Eyes* by Modigliani. My room already looks like a gallery, and my account is empty . . .

Daniel was in Mühlhausen on Saturday and Sunday. [. . .]

Hoy., 19.10.

Yesterday we argued over something so disgusting and terrible that I don't even want to write it down. [. . .] Jon pleaded with me for an hour, he begged—I was frozen, like a stone [. . .].

And yet the two days we spent alone at home were so happy. The first evening was awful, frankly. We had drunk a bottle of wine, then we were sitting in my room—we had *the opportunity*. Revolting feeling [. . .]. I was icy, even disgusted by Jon for the first time. You can't take advantage of opportunities. Fortunately, he had an attack of malaria. His temperature rose quickly and it helped me get through this nightmarish situation.

That night, my gentle man called from Mühlhausen. I was so happy to hear his voice . . .

[. . .]

Hoy., 21.10.

All at once everything's fallen apart. Two nights ago, Jon called, saying that he was going to Mecklenburg to look for work in agriculture. [. . .] At first I was stunned [. . .]. I didn't feel anything because I didn't understand. [. . .] He said he was unhappy when he saw me and that he has to own me completely or just run away. [. . .]

That day my gentle man confessed at last how much he's been suffering all along . . . We were very happy the whole day long. I didn't think of Jon, couldn't think of him—maybe it was a form of self-protection. But I tried to persuade myself that anything can be forgotten, that I, I, I can get over everything. And I'd sent him away, after all. I didn't regret it: it solved a problem that has been making four people unhappy for almost nine months (but that's not fair—Jon and I still had a wonderful, adventurous, sweet life despite everything . . . sometimes, often).

And today . . . We were sitting in Café Klein. Jon came in. He had missed the train yesterday, so he said, had changed all his plans and is going to stay here after all. All this was said in the tone of a petulant boy. At that moment, I almost hated him. [. . .] He has no right to play [. . .] with other people's feelings. My poor Daniel predicted this would happen.

[. . .]

Hoy., 22.10.

This morning, I confessed everything to my gentle man—even the thing I hadn't dared write in my diary: I made love to Jon. Not one more word about it. It's over, it will never happen again, never be repeated . . . [. . .] It was terrible, but now a huge weight has lifted from my heart. How will he cope with this? He's been walking around outside since noon. I'm working. What else should I do? Each shock makes me work like a madwoman, but I don't think it's a deliberate attempt to switch off my thoughts.

[. . .]

Jon came by this morning to discuss a literary work with Daniel (who knew everything by then and still faced Jon with inimitable calm and dignity). I don't know why but I broke down again: I starting crying and couldn't stop, and when Jon came into the room, I started screaming. I couldn't bear seeing him. He asked if I would go with him to Dresden that afternoon. I screamed, I was beside myself. He left the flat. Daniel hugged and comforted me . . .

I got an awful lot done. When I work, I no longer feel sorry for myself, I lose interest in my private worries. I'm now listening to the Piano Concerto no. 5. I'll never forget how Daniel cried back then.

Hoy., 24.10.

Daniel came home completely distraught. He had only grasped what I'd done to him as the day went on. Outside in the car, he roared in pain.

We both have to start all over again.

Hoy., 27.10.

Book Week. Rushing around insanely, up to three readings a day. There's not a night when we go to bed before two or three in the morning. Good that we have the car! Otherwise our schedule would be impossible to manage.

[. . .] All the readings were very well attended, there was lively conversation (I didn't think talking to children would be such a pleasure) [. . .].

At the club we were introduced to three West German students who were visiting the GDR, and we talked until after midnight [. . .]. They were charming guys, smart, not prejudiced (they don't belong to any organization over there), were healthily sceptical and charming in the way some young academics are. They didn't know any of our young writers. We could've carried on talking to them for another three days. Again, I had the impression that our newspapers grossly distort and warp the image of the West. These boys are not non-conformists in the same way as Günter Grass, but—if such a thing exists—real advocates of coexistence, who were receptive to our world view and might someday share it.

I thought of Lutz. I can't talk to my own brother any more . . . He hates us, the way renegades hate.

Burg, 12.11.

We're at home for a day; tomorrow we'll continue our journey, I have readings in Berlin and Potsdam. *Arriving in Everyday Life* is causing a sensation and is top of the list of proposals for the FDGB Literary Award.

[...] I finished the television play in a mad hurry while Daniel did some work for the *Wochenpost*. The last scenes especially have turned out best, simply because of the strong dramatic story. Dorschan stayed with us for three days; we made revisions. D. says the directors are fighting over the play.

I've had to drop umpteen readings and answer dozens of letters, and sometimes I feel like my nerves are hot wires. But I'm still holding on: I have to finish *Brothers and Sisters* whatever else happens. Next week, we—Daniel, Jon and I—will be at the writers' retreat. [...]

After all the drama, we've become close again. [...] We can't get over it: it's stronger than us. [...] A few days later, Daniel shocked us (although we really hadn't been sleeping with each other); he invited Jon for a drive and raced around at an insane speed; he wanted to drive them both into a tree.

I have to make a decision: Daniel or Jon ... Jon says he'd marry me on the spot, wanting more than anything to bind me to him, no matter how. But the price would be destroying Daniel. I said no to Jon. Now it's all like it was before: we love each other and we try to live peacefully together, the three of us. [...]

Petzow, 25.11.61

Since last Saturday, we have been at the writers' retreat—Daniel, Jon and I—and there are fewer complications than all three of us feared. The first day was strange: back at the house again, the room where Daniel and I first met, kissed for the first time, where we got married ultimately ... Daniel is staying in the same room as he did then.

We're working: Daniel on the TV drama, Jon on his accident story, me on a Christmas story (a commission from the *Wochenpost*), which was a real bother at first because I just couldn't get to grips with it. The Defa are yelling in the main hall, while the great Maetzig remains quiet, relaxed and always polite. He made an excellent impression on us all; we'd projected our childish image of a director onto him. Fortunately, no one we know is here except Gerlach [...].

Yesterday, I had a bout of flu and a fever and spent the day in a delicious semiconscious state of heat and chills, cared for by my men. [...] They waver between jealous dislike and lively sympathy for each other, and I'm trying not to influence either one.

Petzow, 11.12.

I'm looking out of my window at the lake. It rained all night long; now the sun is shining. The day before yesterday Jon left; Jens left yesterday, and last night we finally finished the TV play. It will be broadcast in January.

[...]

I had a lot of problems with Jon: he got drunk a couple of times and acted as primitively as dear old Günter; he has a strangely split personality, and alcohol washes up nasty, repellent traits and hang-ups which he otherwise carefully controls and hides. Whether I'm sober or drunk, I'm always myself; alcohol doesn't change me, I just talk faster and become quarrelsome—but I'm quarrelsome anyway.

Living together under one roof became unbearable when I saw how Daniel was suffering. Sometimes I went for a walk with Jon when it was stormy and the waves lashed up on the small jetty. The sky was very blue, and the lake had white crests of foam, and under the willows the waves ran riot through the reeds. We were very happy and almost carefree. But I saw Daniel getting paler and gaunter.

[...] Somehow, my affection started to crumble. I always knew Jon had a weak character; here—in the company of new clever people—he made me angry; his intelligence was not a sufficient counterweight. Gerlach even tried to persuade me—perhaps out of subconscious jealousy—to break off this relationship that's causing Daniel, the much better, decent one, so much pain.

[. . .] On the eve of his departure, I told him I had made up my mind to be just with Daniel again. [. . .]

On Saturday, I went with him part of the way. The sun was shining. We said goodbye at the bend in the path. Then I shed a few tears after all—he walked down the road like an old man, Jon Crook-Ear, who I loved for a whole year.

Petzow, 12.12.

I'm still blaming myself for what I did to Jon. If he does something stupid, it'll be my fault. I took away his wife, alienated his family, thrust him into the great adventure of literature, and now I've left him alone. But Daniel . . . He is the great love of my life, despite all my straying. I will fall in love a hundred more times—it's in my nature, I can't change that. I'm tempted too often.

[. . .]

Now I have to talk about Jens.

We walked past each other for almost two weeks; we thought he was arrogant. But then we got talking and from that day on, we sat, hour after hour until late at night, and talked and argued and took a great liking to each other. Jens is unusually smart and educated if you measure him against our young writers and has a great talent for observation and knowledge of human nature. He read some of my works; we read his wonderful jazz poems. We discovered —all three of us—inclinations and antipathy and doubts in common. Jens lives in Prenzlauer Berg, in a dark, dirty working-class neighbourhood, which I fear is gradually wrecking his health. Socialism has ignored this district. But he's headstrong enough to stay there, in fact, especially there. He hears our descriptions of the beautiful sunny new town as if they are tales of a better world. But I'm sure all his grey experiences won't destroy his faith (no, his knowledge), although sometimes he's afraid that he'll end up back in 1956. That's when he founded the Young Artists' Club which later turned into something like the Petőfi Circle,[195] but he got out in time.

At some point he began to declare his love for me, in his brashest Berlin accent, which still doesn't hide his Hamburg dialect. I didn't take it seriously and laughed. He always stressed that his love for me was because of my talent as a writer; as a woman, I was impossible. (On the last day he'd got to the point where he didn't care if I was the world's worst writer: he loved the crazy, fantastic woman I was . . .)

He is a bit standoffish, or at least pretends to be [. . .]. Without me consciously working on it, little by little his self-assurance fell apart and he let himself get carried away and reckless. We were still on second name terms, we flirted—as far as I'm still able. He left last Monday but wanted to come back on Tuesday. He came on Monday night—I immediately knew why. When I saw him on the stairs, I was delighted to realize that I like him very much. From that day on, he made no effort to hide his affection. He began to smoke again out of sheer excitement, although he's been strictly prohibited (he has a serious heart problem), and I gave free reign to my maternal instincts.

He neglected work on his oratorio, wrote me poems (he says he'll soon have a whole volume of poetry), and barely slept.

[. . .] I think we've behaved throughout the whole thing in a way that doesn't mean we should feel ashamed with Daniel. Of

195 Named after the revolutionary poet Sándor Petőfi (1823–49), the Petőfi Circle was a group formed in March 1956 by prominent Hungarian intellectuals. Its members discussed the political and ideological renewal of Hungarian society.

course, Daniel knows everything, I don't want to start lying again. I was very sad when Jens left. I'm not thinking about what will happen next [. . .]. I never want to get as entangled again as I did with Jon [. . .].

Petzow, 17.12.

A weight off my chest: Daniel has been sleeping with me again at night, and I lie on his shoulder and remember what home and love and security mean.

Sometimes I admit I think of Jens too [. . .]. He's coming on Friday. [. . .] I just like being adored, or even loved; I need to feel validated, that's almost all it's about. [. . .]

I have other worries now: politics give me sleepless nights. We breathed out after the 22nd Party Congress,[196] but things are much nastier than before: never was the personality cult as prominent as it is today. Our writers are not ashamed to pen songs in praise of Ulbricht, slimy and repulsive things in which they compare him to the great, truly great Lenin: there are 'Ulbricht shrines'.[197] The whole thing smacks of religious nonsense. No, it's bitterer than nonsense. It smacks of prison air and even blood. Yesterday I cried in anger and despair.

Hand in hand with the political difficulties, there are economic ones: we have to 'make sacrifices'. Familiar noises. Culture is in decline. Sometimes we are both afraid and hope that the people will rise up again. [. . .]

196 The 22nd Congress of the Communist Party of the Soviet Union was held between 17 and 31 October 1961. During this, the Berlin crisis reached its pinnacle on 27 October with US and Soviet tanks facing one another on Friedrichstraße, ready to fire if fired upon. However, after 16 hours of brinkmanship, on 28 October, Kennedy and Khrushchev agreed to defuse the tension by withdrawing the tanks, with the US tacitly agreeing that the building of a wall to divide the city was better than a full-blown war.

197 This apparently refers to the personality cult of Walter Ulbricht, first secretary of the SED at the time, whereby corners were reserved in schools for people to pay tribute to him.

Air-raid warnings have started again. Protection against nuclear bombs—it's ridiculous and criminal. There's an air-raid shelter poster showing a mother with a child in her arms under a mushroom cloud. The artist—or whoever commissioned him—should be sent to prison. Every day we find out things that are a blow to the heart and make our literary work a torture. It's systematic work that makes the separation from the other part of Germany final . . .

I've just been down to the lake: whenever there's a storm, I'm powerfully drawn to it. It's very cold, and the waves are slapping over the jetty, which is all iced over, and the blades of grass have turned into stiff, white, icy stalks.

My gentle man is in Potsdam to get our car, which was in the garage for a week and a half. Daniel had gone for a drive with Gerlach. At 120 kilometres per hour, the engine jammed, and the gearbox and clutch were wrecked. Apart from the shock, the two of them were unhurt.

Petzow, 18.12.

We still can't bear to leave the retreat. But on Wednesday morning we're finally off. This time there was no sweet run-up to Christmas. Last night we lit a fire in the hearth and listened to the Christmas Oratorio: Manfred Bieler, Georg Maurer with his boys, of whom I think Bernd Jentsch is the most talented (they read from their poems).

Jens was here for two days and comes back tomorrow night. [. . .] One afternoon we took another car trip, and I was allowed to drive for a while. The first time, I made such an idiot of myself. I was afraid of the engine—my old nightmare: technology taking over. I was so angry with myself that I tried again—and suddenly I had a wonderful feeling.

18.12.1961

He thinks I'm a virtuous woman. In truth, I have scars that scare me; the story with Jon has drained me completely.

Burg, 25.12.61

We're back home for Christmas and we celebrated Christmas Eve like we used to when we were kids: Daddy, playing Santa Claus, handed out the presents, and there was a big, festive Christmas tree and 'Silent Night, Holy Night'. Only my Lutz-brother was missing.

At home, we had already exchanged presents on Friday, late at night. In the afternoon I had a terrible heart seizure; Jon was there and I got drunk. We'd had a terrible argument that morning [. . .]. Later, he called me [. . .]. I was already pretty drunk when he arrived, and the booze washed up the memory of the night in the woods. But still, I tried to torment him the whole time. Finally my heart got in the way. I couldn't breathe, and screamed. Jon dragged me onto the couch—it must have been a scary scene; luckily, I didn't take much in as I was too busy dying.

Jon has taken on night shifts over Christmas.

We left the retreat on Wednesday. Jens had come the night before, determined to marry me on the spot and write some great poems. Oh and he's serious; he says he's ready to part with his wife and child [. . .]. I just listen to all this and keep him at bay. [. . .] Maybe, if it weren't for Daniel . . . Yes, I'm sure I'd sleep with Jens, and we'd probably get on very well, and I would even let him interfere with my work and learn from him. He wouldn't escape lightly: I criticize him harshly and sometimes he's shocked. He'd be far more shocked if I went to task on his poetry line by line. He can do more than he demonstrates in most of his work; he's set high standards with his jazz poems.

On the last evening, we sat by the fireplace and drank bubbly, and I fell asleep on Daniel's lap.

Daniel is suddenly friends with Manfred Bieler. They're like chalk and cheese: B. is unbearably energetic, a primitive bull, huge, a two-hundredweight man, a drunkard and glutton—loves all other bodily pleasures—healthy, sceptical and gifted. But Daniel, tender and sensitive, has touched some tender strings in B.—most people love Daniel and change a little in his presence.

In the morning we drove off in black ice and snow; I drove with Jens, Daniel and Bieler. Jens took me to Caspar, and I tried to explain to him why I can't finish *Brothers and Sisters*. His fears were confirmed; he knew the pendulum would swing to the right, having swung too far left. He had a lot of sensible arguments to counter my middle-class outpourings of emotion. I got terribly upset, suddenly couldn't feel my heart and I collapsed. Jens took me to the doctor's room, stammering on the way: 'I love you, I love you.'

After half an hour I stopped shaking and crying, my heart started up again and I felt as exhausted as if I had climbed a mountain. Caspar grinned uncertainly when I staggered back into the room; but later, when he talked to Daniel, he let on how shocked and worried he'd been. He would never admit it to my face; not even if I died in front of him. [. . .]

Afterwards I went to the Press Club with Jens. We met Karl Heinz Jakobs, whom I'm very fond of now for some reason. He can write and is ugly. I had to promise Jens not to smoke any more. It's pretty dire, but I'm holding out. I smoke the occasional cigar . . . At home there was a stack of mail; the next day the Defa came; they want to film *Arriving*. And all this excitement without a cigarette! It was hard. But I made a promise, and I don't want to be dead in two years, not necessarily.

Hoyerswerda, 30.12.

The wonderful, peaceful Christmas days are over, with Mum and Dad, my little brother and sister, who get cleverer and prettier every time I see them; in fact, they're already grown up, and I only realize when they tell me about their love intrigues . . .

I am getting used to Hoy and our flat again; I've also written a few more lines of *Brothers and Sisters*. But I'd like to get away again soon, most of all back to the writers' retreat, to people with whom I—we—have more in common than just personal affinity. Jens once said that he has no real friends, and he hopes to find them in us. I suddenly feel that we have no friends either; Daniel and I are completely dependent on each other, and that's usually enough for us. But sometimes we crave some other damned writers (even though we can't stand writers, at least not in a group, all at once), with whom we can chat and share our thoughts—but not only chat.

No brother to go crazy with on New Year's Eve either. We'll go to the Schömanns for an hour: we like them very much, and they are fond of us. Ilse Sch., that diligent soul, is doing a training course as a crane operator—that tiny woman wants to drive a Rapid crane . . .

[. . .]

Jon was here once. We saw each other today too. He wanders around town all the time, as restless as the Wandering Jew, with an expression that gives me a fright. Sometimes I pity him; sometimes it's as if I'm beginning to hate him. I'll probably have no choice. Maybe there's nothing left for us to say. When he was here, he couldn't talk, just sat and looked at me, and then jumped up and ran off, and I was angry and distressed and all kinds of things. In the evening he called; I answered, but only very briefly and harshly and hung up straight away. [. . .]

Oh, when I think back to Petzow I feel homesick: the afternoons when old Marchwitza came, lonely and a bit too childish, telling us stories about his childhood and youth for hours, and who liked us because we listened to him. He said that old people are a burden to the young; the others very much make him feel this way.

He felt it from Bieler and Gerlach, whom he no longer understands. He's achieved his goal in life—to live under socialism; I don't think he understands our world and its problems any more. He is gentle and nice and thinks he has met so many good people: a polite veil over his past . . . We liked sitting with him, we laughed and were shocked by his patriarchal jokes, and, smiling a little—the ironic smile of foolish young people—we heard him say: 'The world is beautiful, and people, people are so beautiful . . . ' Is he senile? Is he wise? We told him about our lives. He wanted to write a novel about the Pumpe. On one of the evenings towards the end of our stay, he said that he had shelved his novel; he didn't think he could manage it, and he wanted to tell stories about the past, the things he knew about. It seemed to be an acknowledgement and an admission that he doesn't know much or enough about the world—the Republic, the working class of 1961—or perhaps no longer understands it.

1962

—

Hoy, 1.1.62

First off: I haven't made any New Year's resolutions. My intentions and plans are not dependent on my mood at the turn of the year. I've given up smoking. An act of willpower that amazes me. I'll probably manage if I don't constantly whinge about how much I miss my 30 cigarettes a day and the torture of nicotine abstinence.

I'm working on *Brothers and Sisters* but it's a long way from literature.

New Year's Eve was pretty awful. The city was barraged by fireworks for hours. In the afternoon Daniel and I drove to the Lusatian Mountains. At first, it was quite good fun: I learnt to drive on deserted streets. Daniel is a patient teacher, but afterwards we were both drenched in sweat. I want to take my driving test soon.

Daniel was determined to show me some kind of winter wonderland. But there were no more fairy-tale forests: the snow had melted, the streets were dirty, the sky was heavy and grey, and the bare trees along the road . . . In my heart, I felt as sad and desolate as the landscape. [. . .] I became gloomier and gloomier, and in the evening, I lay in my room, overwhelmed by deep melancholy, and I also thought of Jon, I confess. I was mad with jealousy and hatred and a love I still haven't got over. Oh, what am I saying— maybe the last day of the year was to blame, a day of reflection, and therefore remorse.

In the evening we went down to the Schömanns, whose younger brother [. . .] had concocted a Hotel International–style punch, and I drank but it didn't make me tipsy, and we chatted for hours, and it was all very snug, and everything was just as it shouldn't have been. I'm not very happy.

Hoy., 4.1.

The day before yesterday, Jon called me. [. . .]

He picked me up last night and we went to the pub next door. We were horrible to each other for an hour, really hostile, and our opposing political beliefs were a good pretext to say nasty things to each other. I wanted to go, but then we became reasonable [. . .].

Deep down I'm only interested in my story. [. . .]

I'm reading André Gide, the *Counterfeiters*. An encounter with literature—there's something tremendously shocking about it. I can only feel it, not talk about it: it's a glimpse into a world of Western culture, and we have nothing to counteract it at present. I have the impression of a wonderfully refined organism; the psyche becomes comprehensible, corporeal, it can be dissected, and I can see its fibres branching. Oh and I think I can sense that it's a book by a homosexual—but it's not camp in any way.

Hoy., 14.1.

Jens has been staying with us for a week: a good housemate who has quickly fitted in with our life perhaps for the very reason that it lacks order and rhythm. We had a lot of fun and were sort of happy this week, only with bouts of melancholy in the evening, brought on by listening to Jimmy Yancey and Mahalia Jackson and Pinetop Smith.

Jens has separated from his wife. I haven't asked him about it. I [. . .] like him very much, and sometimes I even feel I'm in love with him, [. . .] we would live alongside one another, write a few good things—but my flesh does not want his. He doesn't understand, and I can't explain it to him. [. . .]

We've read many poems together, argued and listened to wonderful jazz. Jens brought me French scent, and I am as fragrant as an elegant lady. In fact, his ambition is to make a lady out of me. He wants to marry me, my God, and, if possible, live with me in Berlin . . . [. . .]

Things are absolutely dire between Daniel and me. [. . .] He wants a divorce.

Hoy., 16.1.

Terrible headaches for three days, at full moon like always. Yesterday: discussion in the plant about the FDGB prize. I'm not looking forward to anything any more. [. . .] Sometimes it feels like I don't love anyone [. . .]. They've talked about my ruthless egotism so often now that I'm starting to believe them. I'm discovering my nastiness, hard-heartedness, my quarrelsomeness, my bloated urge for emancipation. Earlier on, a child cried in the building, just a few weeks old. I have such a terrible longing for a baby. Is the work worth the sacrifice? I will never be a good writer. I often think of death these days and ask myself whether I'm scared of it.

Hoy., 20.1.

We only got back from Berlin early this morning. Poor Daniel, dead tired, drove half the night through a hurricane, a strangely unreal night with a full moon. We spent the whole evening with Caspar, who showed his loveliest, gentlest side. He read us poetry, hummed chansons, drank moderately (that, too, is commendable—I so hoped he would give up drinking—an editor of his standing should hang onto his authors), and he even spoke to us in a tone which made me feel that he takes me seriously—normally he always argues or tries to get a rise out of me, and I'm foolish enough to get upset about his teasing [. . .] C. talked about Noll and his working methods. N. threw away a few hundred pages of his second volume and is starting from scratch. That's the kind of patience I'd like to have—such diligence; it's the only way to become a writer. [. . .]

At the studio, we had the final preview; big camera run-through. The play was broadcast by some kind of private channel from Johannistal. The bosses gathered in Fehlig's room—we didn't know most of them. I like the departmental head Kohlus best; he looks like a cross between Caspar and Noll, and seems to be the only one who isn't on the verge of insanity. For some reason, I find him very attractive even though he's one of those calm, reflective, possibly ironic types who make me bicker and snap.

We were appalled by the play, of course; the whole production is nothing like we imagined. Runkehl as Katrin plays a few strong scenes. Thate as Alexei and Müller-Lankow as Heinrich are very good. But the director is useless—the man has no style. The camerawork is completely unoriginal. Still, I almost cried at the end; the closing scenes are very strong (even though I've been sick to death of it for quite some time). Thate wrote a few of his own monologues—Brecht–Baierl style—and we fell out with him on the phone (Thate: '—over my dead body') and altogether it's been very demanding. The bosses yelled at each other—no, that's not true: they cursed the production team, and only Dorschan, the dramaturge, who was under most pressure, stayed calm and friendly.

Hoy., 22.1.

Jens came over yesterday afternoon. We, or rather I, have been waiting desperately for him to come. [. . .] I'm slowly losing my shyness towards people [. . .].

In the evening we visited Burgmann and watched *The Woman in the Pillory*; the broadcast version was far better than the preview on Friday. It's strange to know that 2 million people (the actual number was significantly higher) are sitting in front of the box, watching your play at the same time; the contact to those you've worked with is more intensive and immediate.

Afterwards we went to the Kastanienhof bar; I got tipsy and danced the whole evening (or what was left of the evening) with Jens. He's the third or fourth man in my life with whom I can dance; he lets me do my belly dances, and is only a partner insofar as he doesn't spoil my fun.

[...]

Hoy., 24.1.

All these weeks I've been fighting my affection for Jon: sometimes I even managed to make myself believe that I found him repulsive. But a few times, at night, when I was thinking about him a lot, I felt like my body was on fire . . . Last night at the writers' circle, I sat next to him again. Then I had a heart seizure and Daniel took me home. True, Jon was only partly to blame for my terrible misery (I hadn't made any headway with my work, I was really upset about the new legislation making conscription compulsory—I don't know what's happening any more, God, and I want to understand. I suffer for being constantly opposed to everything) [. . .]. Wise, much-too-patient Daniel sent Jon to see me.

We talked way too much again, and I disagreed with him—not wanting to—till I felt hostile towards him. Why do I hurt and reject everyone? [. . .] At some point I'll commit suicide just to avoid myself; some day I'll find my character unbearable.

[...]

An hour later

I am completely desperate, devastated. Just reread—stupid idea!—the prologue to my novel *Ten Years after a Death*;[198] it's been in my

---

198 *Zehn Jahre nach einem Tod.*

drawer for almost four years now. I was twenty-four when I wrote it. I used to be able to write . . . I haven't made any progress whatsoever, not the tiniest step—perhaps I'm cooler, more reasonable, I know a thing or two about composition, but that's all. The prologue is real literature. What do I write these days? It's awful: I haven't achieved anything. Someone, something has strangled me. What happened for Christ's sake? And why am I praised these days, but no one wants to publish one of my novels? Our best-known critic called me a 'significant writer'. What does he know? In the past, I used to be able to tell stories—now it all lacks power and passion. I'm unhappier than if I had the worst heartache [. . .]. I want to be able to write again!

Hoy, 2.2.62

For the past two weeks, I've tortured myself with the damned art discussion in *Brothers and Sisters.* How can people get excited by these kinds of theories! Three pages of dubious claims and evidence.

Last Friday we visited the Defa people. Reception with Jochen Mückenberger and chief dramaturge Wischnewski.[199] M. looks like a young Otto Gotsche, which I'm hoping doesn't mean they're similar in spirit. [. . .]

After dinner, the press officer took us on a tour of the studios. The familiar smell of wood and greasepaint and joiner's glue and carbon arc lights. I visited the studios the last time in '56. I suddenly remembered why the glamour, and the whole frivolous arty atmosphere attracted me so much back then.

The Woman in the Pillory has been a great success as a television play and this time the audience and critics all agreed on what they thought—a rare, happy occasion.

---

199 Klaus Wischnewski (1928–2003): theatre scholar, film documentarist and chief dramaturge at the DEFA from 1960 to 1966.

I've been seeing Jon every day again. It's no good: you can't give up a person like cigarettes. I don't even feel any pangs of conscience [. . .]. Now everything's gone back to the way things were (except that we're not sleeping with each other) and the whole helplessness will start all over again, along with brooding over solutions that don't exist. But I don't care about that for now.

Hoy., 8.2.

Back to work again on *Brothers and Sisters*. I hope my Uli doesn't swing too far to the right; he screams and scolds so much that I sometimes doubt whether I can 'save' him. He behaves entirely like my—formerly—beloved brother Lutz, who writes me terrible hate letters these days.

Visit from *Junge Welt* today. Young people will defend me in face of the wicked slatings in *ND* and *Sonntag*; they're going to start a protest campaign. I was heartbroken over the boorishness in the papers, who didn't even get their facts right [. . .]. The print-run statistics aren't proof, of course: but still, around 50,000 copies sold (within 5 months) speaks in my favour.

[. . .]

Daniel—who gets more and more beautiful with his huge, almond eyes—came back very upset from the plant yesterday. He'd been told all kinds of gossip: 'people' are upset about my relationship with Jon (whereby they think I'm an innocent victim, the men at least [. . .]). Daniel defended us. For his magnanimity alone, he deserves to be loved. Idle chatter doesn't bother me.

Sometimes it's annoying to be a writer, a public figure. As soon as I set foot in a bar, people start whispering at their tables: I am recognized and observed. People expect me to lead a perfect life— just because I write books. How ludicrous! [. . .]

Hoy., 11.2.

Yesterday was our third wedding anniversary, and on that special day, of all days, Daniel's collection of short stories arrived, which we've been expecting for so long: *The Strange Betrothal of a Barrow Man*.[200] I think the dust jacket is a bit infantile. I found some favourite sentences while flicking through which I reread with pleasure. There are entire paragraphs that show his poetry (he's more a poet than a story-teller); most of all I love 'The Lost Son Moves Out'[201] and the wonderfully self-contained sketch 'Elvis Celebrates His Birthday'.[202]

[...] We went for a drive on a cold, clear, blue early-spring day, with violet shadows across the woods: the trees beautifully veiled in dew. I was allowed to drive some of the way again, more confidently than back in winter. Then we ate out and read Daniel's book, and then it was evening—an evening with a great deal of red across the turquoise-green sky, and we raced along a few streets in among the woods, and for some reason I loved Daniel more passionately than usual in those minutes with a wild ardent love.

[...] The *Sonntag* printed a page of letters that condemned Thöns,[203] and right at the top, there was a letter from Anna Seghers, who had read my book and wrote about it. And her review was so clever and warm, it made me almost grateful to Thöns: without him, the great, revered Anna Seghers wouldn't have written these lines. I was happy. She also wrote: 'B. R. is beginning to work seriously; she takes things in, she invents.' For all its restraint, this was worth more than a dozen words of the kindest hymns of praise, and my creative ambition soared to immeasurable heights that day.

---

200 *Wunderliche Verlobung eines Karrenmannes.*

201 'Auszug des verlorenen Sohnes'.

202 'Elvis feiert Geburtstag'.

203 Peter Thöns: a literary critic.

Hoy, 22.2.62

A week in Berlin behind us. Spent most of the time in bed: flu.
[...]

Boozy evening with Lewerenz. New edition of the *Woman in the Pillory*, which I definitely want to revise—against the wishes of the publisher. Spent a ton of money yesterday: on a rococo chest for myself and a Biedermeier grandfather clock for Daniel, a real abomination, beautiful and spooky. The antique shop in Marx-Allee is a honeypot for chequebook holders. Where to put all our treasures? These kinds of luxuries aren't made for Hoy. There were splendid baroque desks—sold, of course. [...]

Met Walter Püschel again after four years. He's hardly changed; maybe he's more sceptical than he used to be, more disillusioned. But aren't we all.

After a week I hate Berlin. The city wears sexier make-up—that's about the only thing that sets it apart from the backwater. Daniel sat there every evening and was appalled at the young cynics growing up among our students.

I forgot to mention the discussion at the *Sonntag*, when I met Max Walter Schulz again. Topic: the youth of today.

Hoy., 12.3.

I finally got back to work today on *Brothers and Sisters* after correcting *Woman in the Pillory* for two weeks for a new edition. I managed to get a lot done. It was an adventure: when I wrote the first line (Chapter 7), I was as excited as if stepping onto a new blank spot on the map.

Yesterday I went to the cinema with Jon. We watched a film that churned me up terribly: *Allons enfants—pour l'Algérie*, a documentary with unforgettable footage—refugee camps and hungry, sick children. I'm hardly able to put it down on paper. In the cinema

I burst into tears at the sight of men who have lost their minds from being tortured. I've never seen anything more horrendous. When the lights went up, they were playing 'Guitars of Love' behind the curtain. I don't understand why we don't help. We could send a hospital train to these camps, we could support the Algerians in their struggle in a thousand ways. I know that many of us buy solidarity stamps,[204] but I sometimes wonder if anyone here still thinks about solidarity, whether internationalism still exists among the workers. There was a time when the starving Soviet Union donated grain to starving German workers[205] . . .

We have fostered a consumer ideology here. Socialism is a standard of living: a TV, a fridge and, to top it all, a Trabant. We have to fight this lethargy [. . .]

I'm sitting here in my room, well fed and warm, listening to Beethoven's Piano Concerto no. 5—and at this very moment, people are being tortured and murdered. Unbearable thought! Sometimes I feel like the enormous burden of the world's misery weighs on my shoulders, and I'm just a coward, suffocated by impotent pity, wanting to escape it all and do myself in.

Jon tried me to make it clear that our work, wherever we are, contributes a little towards the liberation of others. I know that too, but what good is the prospect of future socialism to those who are starving? [. . .] Why am I so middle class that I didn't manage to get up after the film and collect money?

204 In the GDR, certain political causes that were perceived as anti-imperialist (e.g. the decolonization of Africa, especially the anti-apartheid struggle in South Africa) were financially supported by the sale of solidarity stamps.

205 In October 1918 Lenin ordered grain supplies to be reserved for German workers, and on 11 November the first two trains transporting grain arrived in Germany. They were stopped at Orscha, a border station, by a German soldier's council and sent back because no instructions had been received from Berlin. The trains were attacked and robbed by the German volunteer troops (see Annemarie Lange, *Berlin in der Weimar Republic*. Berlin: Dietz Verlag, 1987).

Certainly, the state does what it can for other struggling nations. But personal sacrifices, donations from me and my neighbour, would be more important and valuable. I must do something, I have to, otherwise I'll have no peace; I can barely swallow my food and I'm having terrible dreams. Today Daniel is going to watch the film. If he agrees with me, we'll write an open letter and start a solidarity campaign.

[...]

Hoy., 16.3.

I have started a private campaign for Algeria by having my outstanding fees sent to the Algerian account. I'll keep it that way in the future. We're also going to write an open letter—'Help for Aida'.

Hoy., 17.3.

Last night, Jon came over. Daniel had gone to Dresden—to research Lukas Silbermann[206]—but I'm sure he left [...] because he wanted to give me a few hours alone. He didn't even ask any questions this morning, because I'd already cried all yesterday afternoon with anticipated remorse and shame [...]. Only once this morning— he led me to the mirror and, silently smiling, pointed to the bite mark on my shoulder.

What drives me into Jon's arms again and again? [...] Once, in a wild outburst of hatred between kissing and embracing, I choked him and bit him till he bled. He's destroying my life, a curse. [...]

'Tu, solo tu'—a Mexican song. Here are the lyrics:

You, only you, are the cause of my drinking, you have filled my life with sorrow and you are the cause of my despair, your shadow follows me everywhere, and drives me into hopelessness and drinking.

---

206 The protagonist in S.P.'s novella *Im Wartesaal* [In the Waiting Room], 1968.

MARCH 1962

Hoy., 23.3.

The night before last, Jon was with me. We pulled back the curtains—there was a full moon, the most beautiful moon I'd ever seen and it saw us.

Hoy., 28.3.

Back from the writers' conference in Halle. Met some old friends: M. W. Schulz, Deike, Nachbar, Noll. Discussion with Lewin. The magnificent Anna Seghers: her entrance during the solemn quiet of the first half hour of the lecture, when her inimitably husky voice with its charming Mainz accent rang out: 'Good morning.' She was holding a coffee cup. The room cheered and applauded her for several minutes. I felt dizzy as she passed me, beautiful, with her snow-white hair and dark eyebrows.

An intelligent contribution by Eva Strittmatter on four books: Jakobs, Reimann, Nachbar, Seeger. Bentzin spoke, Selbmann bellowed, Kurella gabbed. As always, it was livelier and more interesting in the breaks than in the main hall. TV interview with Hauser, Strittmatter, Seeger and me. They praised my wonderful naturalness—in truth, I was half-drunk.

Yesterday, a few hours with Jon . . . Afternoon: frantic meeting with the union and Party leadership. Our 'relationship' is threatening to become a scandal. [. . .] Burgmann was as clever and understanding as ever—I have real faith in him—K[. . .] just caught the whiff of a scandal and played the wild guy—he, of all people, who has already been expelled once because of his grubby womanizing. [. . .] At least people believe it's true love between us . . . There has already been an official meeting[207] because of us. Some people have

---

207 In these early years, the Party often attempted to impose what it saw as a moral code on its members; so it was not unusual that a meeting had been held to discuss the 'Reimann case'.

wanted to wage moral campaigns against us, but the Party ensured they were suppressed. [...]

The lies and slanderous remarks that have been made about us! True, we are 'public figures', and society demands that we live decent lives (is love not decent?), but however rationally and thoughtfully I look at it, I can't decide whether society has a right to tear us apart.

[...]

In the evening I got drunk. What else could I do? I was standing at the window. I thought: one leap and everything would be solved. Cowardice. Afterwards I lay in bed and cried, first for Jon, then for Daniel. [...]

Petzow, 7 April

We have been at the writers' retreat for a week now.

Two days before we left, there was a cultural conference at the plant. I gave my first public speech—a splendid speech (but I'd written it down beforehand)—about the great pleasure of thinking and the joyful landscape of art (I hope it was understood as an attack on the militant 'storming of the heights of culture').[208] Listened to eight hours of speeches ... Dreßler and I secretly drank brandy from coffee cups so that we wouldn't fall asleep; we were sitting at the top table.

The weeks before had been a mad rush, and when we arrived, we were totally shattered, pale and sick, and I cried the whole day. The night before, I'd been with Jon again. Two days ago, Daniel wrote me a letter saying he'd come home early, and had heard me moaning ... He'd turned around again and left. That night, he took

---

208 Reference to a speech by Ulbricht in the Fifth Party Conference of the SED, 1958: 'In Staat und Wirtschaft ist die Arbeiterklasse der DDR bereits Herr. Jetzt muss sie auch die Höhen der Kultur stürmen und von ihnen Besitz ergreifen' [In the state and in economy, the working class of the GDR is already in control. Now it must also storm the heights of culture and take possession of them].

his pillow and went to bed in his room. He must have suffered horribly.

[...]

Jens was eagerly awaiting us. [...] A nice, uncomplicated good soul, who's writing his first book here [...]. I've devoured a crime novel every day; we've been sitting in front of the TV every evening, as always, I've been reading my beloved Stendhal in the evenings— his diaries. He's an incredible egoist, and I feel very close to him: his vanity, his self-deception, his megalomania. He's amoral—Julien Sorel in every line. I've made a note of the sentence: 'A talent that doesn't grow fades.'

Sometimes it seems as if I'm just drifting along, everything is provisional. I've even forgotten my ambition. I'm too often tired. Here they think I'm a bit crazy [...]—I act naturally, just say what I think, and do what I say. It's so normal that others find it abnormal.

Petzow, 10.4.

Jon phoned earlier and said that's he's coming at Easter, and that the moon is shining (the same one as back then), and we planned to go outside at the same time and say hello to it. But when I went into the garden, the Petzow moon was hidden by clouds.

On Sunday, there was a very good play on TV by Aškenazy, *The Guest*. Everyday life, a pub, ordinary people, the present day. I keep trying to work out the magic of the play, and where the tension arose, which had us riveted from the very first lines. Those theories about a more attractive past no longer hold water.—This evening, a charming comedy by Turgenev, *The Provincial Lady*.

Yesterday: with Daniel in Leipzig, university clinic. They'll operate on me in May.[209] I'm afraid of being alone, then banished to bed for four weeks. I'm an impatient patient.

---

209 B.R. went to hospital to have breast-reduction surgery.

We drove at 130 kmph. This evening I'm scared of driving with Daniel. We both seem broken. This morning, senseless with rage, I tried to jump out of the car. I hated Daniel, I wished he would hit a tree. Afterwards he came and brought me a bunch of flowers. [...] He really wants a divorce. [...] I can't imagine a future without him.

[...]

Petzow, 13.4.

I'm listening to Jimmy Yancey: 'Death Letter Blues'. Music that moves me to tears. When I listen to beautiful music, I always want to write something beautiful and good . . .

I'm trying to find my way back into *Brothers and Sisters*. It's hard. Jon calls every other evening. Today we're meeting at half past seven for the Unfinished. Jon has staked everything on me.

I feel much closer to Daniel. He doesn't touch me any more; I think he feels I'm 'unclean'. Maybe he's making a mistake.

Yesterday, we talked until late into the night: Kahlau, who looks like Baal, and Lewerenz, Brennecke, Pitschmann and Jochen, with whom I quarrel loudly every day. He's religious, has the naivety of a nineteen-year-old and is unrealistically optimistic. He was a pupil of Bloch's. I like him, because he can laugh uproariously—about everything, like a nineteen-year-old.

Petzow, 18.4.

Today was the first warm day in a long time. Back to work on *Brothers and Sisters* again. But I'm not going to make the deadline. The Defa was here; first discussion about *Arriving*. It'll be the young director E[...]'s debut film.

Today we took Jochen to the station. [...] For the last few days, we have been hanging around together all the time, drinking too much vodka and having incredibly loud discussions. We're both stubborn quarrellers. The rest of the time we played billiards. Too bad. We had so much fun together; we're both somehow arrested in our development and the others watch us with benign expressions, the way people watch children playing. Sometimes I thought about the fact that I couldn't be young at the right time: the post-war years, my illness,[210] then a drunk for a husband . . . Now it's almost too late to catch up.

Jon is coming. [. . .] I'm suddenly afraid of meeting him again. There was more terrible trouble because of him: he won't be allowed to stay in the main building (it's just a pretext that the house is full, it's not even true); talk of our affair has spread around the Writers' Union [. . .]. It's all pretty revolting. [. . .]

Petzow, 27.4.

I just put on the Kučera record that Jon brought for me. It's stupid: I should know that it brings me down every time—not so much the songs, but the memories tied to them, which all end up back with Jon. I've broken up with him yet again, but I don't quite believe it myself. The whole time here together was a mess. We'd written crazy letters to each other, but when he was standing in the doorway, he was not the man I'd had in mind when I wrote them. Or I wasn't the same . . . [. . .]

Petzow, 8.5.

Reading Nikolayeva's *A Battle on the Way*.[211] A book that gives me courage: to write, to fight. The love story is driving me insane. Why does this happen to Tina? I think there's something in it that we bitterly deny exists: tragedy in a socialist society.

I am listening to that damned 'Tu, solo tu' again.

210 B.R. had polio as a child.

211 *Schlacht Unterwegs* (1962) by Galina Nikolayeva.

Petzow, 23.5.

My story is becoming more and more problematic; I have the grim feeling it won't get published. This boosts my work ethic enormously, of course. But I'm still writing it the way I planned.

[...]

Hoy., 30.5.

Nasty fight with Daniel today because of his TV contract. He's supposed to be writing stories instead of slogging away for months on a play that's just a rehash of *A Battle on the Way*. He can't relate to the topic at all. But he has great material for a novella. If need be, I would even take over his television contract.

Work with the Defa. Just had a call from the TV: *Arriving* is going to be reworked for a series.

Hoy., 7.6.

Terrible drinking binge over the past few weeks. On Sunday, we left our beautiful writers' retreat. [...]

I didn't see Jon again until we were in court: I was a witness in his divorce proceedings. Even though the jurors didn't know me, they were hostile. Only the strict, young, female judge was amenable. It was quite ugly to talk about our love, and then I got very malicious because everyone expected me to be ashamed (but I'm not ashamed at all) and harped on about their stuffy socialist decrees, and in the end, we had a loud argument that veered into theory—from Nikolayeva, all the way to my idea of abolishing marriage under communism, which shocked the jury. I noticed that the nice young court stenographer changed the term 'adulterous relationship'—as dictated by the judge—into 'love relationship' on her own initiative.

[...] Jon showed cold indifference. [...] I think he expects me to get a divorce now [...]. But I'm back with Daniel. Last week I was still hoping I was pregnant. Initially I was alarmed, because of my contracts, then I started to feel happy and picture a thousand beautiful things for the child. But in the end I was disappointed . . .

[...]

Hoy., 17.6.

A week ago today, I received the FDGB Literature Prize at the Erfurter Hof hotel. Grand ceremony, followed by dinner, all a bit too exclusive for my idea of a workers' festival. Before that, I was sent a lot of congratulatory letters and telegrams, from readers and businesses too.

Working on *Brothers and Sisters*. The factory episode is nearly finished. Yesterday, we filmed in the plant for TV, in the roaring heat, me all alone in front of the camera with a microphone in my hand. By the fourth take, I was so exhausted I could only stammer.

I'm at Jon's more often now: I already love his room. He lives on the seventh floor of a high-rise without a lift (which, with my fear of technology, I wouldn't use anyway). It took a long time before we got used to each other again. [...] He's divorced, the wording of the sentence is striking: it was a loveless marriage.

Hoy, 3.7.62

Yesterday: in Berlin for the Bentzien award; a prize in the competition for young adult literature. A few more people to look at me disapprovingly. Sometimes I'm so depressed because colleagues resent me for winning a second FDGB prize, and neighbours envy my car (in the works, there's a saying going around: 'arriving in everyday life, driving off in a Skoda', and if it wasn't so witty, I'd resent it) and there are rumours the plant is building us a luxury villa so we will stay. Someone ratted on us again to the Stasi: it went via Berlin to the district, where Jochen H. was able to intercept it. Some remark about Otto Gotsche, [...] maliciously distorted and reported to the security services as an incitement to boycott. But, as H. reported, they dealt with the case tactfully and honourably, making enquiries about us. So much malice made us despair. Don't these people see any other way to eliminate the young 'competition' and ensure that they, the mediocre ones, can keep their snouts in the trough?

Yesterday we sat together with Lewerenz and a very smart, sympathetic journalist from the *Nationalzeitung*,[212] who wanted a brief interview from me. But it turned into three hours; he had just come from Karlovy Vary and told us about the film festival and the strange behaviour of our citizens, whose know-it-all arguments are gently countered by our socialist neighbours: 'All right, we know that you are the largest GDR in the world.' [...]

Hoy., 10.7.

Today I found my first grey hair. In two weeks I'll be 29. I was shocked, which is perhaps ridiculous. Daniel laughed too; he's looking forward to my grey wisps. I don't think it's funny for women. *Brothers and Sisters* is to blame.

I'm working on the last chapter, terribly excited and already drained. Sometimes I vomit in the evening, that's how exhausted I am. What's worse is that I'm hardly interested in anything else around me.

Hoy., 16.7.

Daniel has gone to Burg (it was Mum's birthday yesterday).

This morning the sky was still grey; I woke up because the old Biedermeier clock in Daniel's room was striking wildly and

212 The *National-Zeitung* [National Newspaper] was published in the Soviet Occupation Zone of the GDR from 1948 to 1990.

frantically, irregularly, as if forced by a ghastly hand. It has never chimed—we unhooked the striking mechanism—and rationally, I must have been dreaming: but I swear I was awake when I heard that uncanny sound. I was half-dead with terror.

In the morning I sneaked into Daniel's room; that ghostly clock has always given me the creeps, and I kept it firmly in sight while I watered the plants. As if I don't know it was my conscience haunting me, the cries of the rooster at Peter's betrayal . . . I completely forget myself when Jon embraces me.

It was the first time in an infinitely long time. [. . .]

I'm working on the last pages of *Brothers and Sisters*. Today I got a letter from Dorli. My little sister is getting smart and sensible. She also wrote about our Hamburg family, from whom she feels increasingly alienated; she can't bear their condescending arrogance and superficiality, their constant 'one does not wear that' and 'you in the Eastern zone'. [. . .]

I was so happy about her letter; it's given me courage to write my story: my brothers and sisters will understand me, and with them, thousands of young people, who like Dorli 'are happy and satisfied even without the beautiful, film-star world'.

Hoy., 18.7.

Two hot days. During the day, working on the last chapter of *Brothers and Sisters*, in the evening and at night, debates with Jon about the cyclical nature of crises, about Freud, and Lenin on Freud: our heated discussions ended up in long, wild embraces. The sun was already coming up when J. left. We haven't slept for two nights; I'm just a living bundle of nerves, desire always whipping me up again. The first man I've fought with, bitterly, to the point of hatred.

Hoy., 23.7.

Daniel came for my 29th birthday: he brought Father and Uli [...].
I ran down the stairs shrieking. Later I thought: you adulteress,
where does this pure joy come from? The day before I had written
THE END under *Brothers and Sisters*. I had been drinking very
heavily (but I've been doing that every day lately—alcohol calms
me down, and I never really get drunk) [...].

They showered me with presents and roses and carnations, and
at first, I was happy, but then we had to write up the last pages [...],
and something in my head came loose again, and I couldn't muster
a kind word (and now I'm bitterly sorry!), and there was a huge
family row because I've written about Lutz and quoted from his
letters. True, Uli was on my side: he read the story eagerly and
enthusiastically. He thinks it will cause enough of an argument
among young people as it is.

No, at any rate, I acted like a pig and Daniel accused me of
becoming a real robot, loving nothing except my work, and maybe
he's not far off the mark. I made some other terrible discoveries
(apart from the fact that I have a malicious character): I live a fake
life, and I don't know when I'm really being myself—at my desk or
otherwise (Jens says I pretend to be someone else when I write); I
have no capacity for love. I wonder whether the people I create on
paper sap all my strength and courage, or whether I have no
strength or courage in the first place and that's exactly why I
give them to my characters: lovely, fine qualities that I don't have.
[...]

But when they drove off on Sunday afternoon, and Jon came
over, things swung in the other direction, and I aimed my disgust
at him. We went to the Freundschaft and drank wine and felt
morose and waited for our long overdue crisis (we had been getting
on wonderfully for a whole week)—and then it finally came when
Jon made a derogatory remark about Daniel, something minor,

sure, but it was the last straw. [. . .] I abruptly stood up and he took me home. We didn't speak a word to each other on the way.

[. . .]

Today I started a film treatment (Mehnert came last week, and we came to an agreement). I really can't live a day without work.

Hoy., 26.7.

Oppressively muggy, murderer's weather. There's going to be a thunderstorm.

Jon came back two days ago and apologized. We took a stroll at night, stood on the river embankment and kissed. [. . .]

How can I look Daniel in the eye? [. . .] At some point I shall just break down and tell him everything, out of selfishness just to shift my own desperation onto someone else. Maybe it will help if I write a book; then I can use the characters to express everything. And now I would like to get drunk again, my God.

[. . .]

Hoy., 3.8.

From Saturday to Sunday, I stayed with Jon. We woke up in a new embrace. We showered and had breakfast together, and I had that terrible feeling I sometimes used to have when I woke up next to a man who was a stranger to me.

[. . .]

On Friday we were in Berlin and I bought a few dozen Polish jazz records (a beautiful recording of the 'Saint Louis Blues'). Otto Braun, First Secretary of the Writers' Union, picked us up in the Lukullus restaurant. He wanted to persuade me to contribute to a commemorative book in praise of Ulbricht (a volume of eulogies will be published for U.'s 70th birthday), but I refused. No reasonable person can blather on about U. being a supporter of the fine arts.

B. then persuaded me to come to a reception: a Burmese guest was due. (I have to add: B. wanted to introduce me to Ulbricht, adding, 'But it's better if Lotte isn't there.' I wanted to spit in his face.) Only English was spoken at the reception, but I was able to follow fairly well. B. took the opportunity to boast excessively about me in front of the guest. What the hell? [. . .]

I had a terrible afternoon. Before the Burmese guest came, the German hosts indulged in derogatory, even contemptuous remarks about him, but when he arrived, their expressions changed: they raised their hands in a Buddhist gesture of peace and bent over backwards with friendliness. The guest didn't understand a word of German. After an hour the Germans started talking with shame-less openness across the table about how they could get rid of him as quickly as possible. At least one other person at the table was as mortified as I was: the very young interpreter sitting next to me, with whom I exchanged the occasional quiet word. He had studied in Moscow but he knew all my works. Why didn't it interest this damned bunch of snobs (they are all Party members) to hear what the Burmese comrade and fellow writer had to say about his country? [. . .]

Daniel came back early on Monday, having driven through the night. He immediately sensed what had happened. Since then we've talked. We don't want to separate yet. [. . .] Of course he doesn't want to touch me any more. Sometimes, when we drive, I'm afraid he might crash into a tree to put an end to this torture. But I still have to write, at least my novel, whose characters are beginning to form in my head.

In the morning in bed, when he's still asleep, I put his head on my shoulder and kiss him and tell him all the tender things I can't say during the day.

Hoy., 14.8.

If I collapse any time soon, I'll have a complete breakdown—but I'm determined not to, especially not now, because Daniel needs me more urgently than ever. He's been sick for a week and I've mercilessly exploited his weakness to talk him out of his TV play, and now he's prepared, thank God, to start on his novel. [. . .] Sometimes I feel like a machine that just works and works because it's been set in motion, and I'm so sick of mustering the energy for two, and still having to urge on a third party, of being a wife and lover and writer and laundry-washer and a hundred other things. Oh, of course I'm not tired, that's maudlin drivel, and even I can't take it seriously. But I don't have the resources for three; in fact, I'm worn out, running on reserve. I could do with a few weeks' rest (and on the third day at the latest, I would die of impatience). [. . .]

Hoy., 24.8.

Now it's hit me [. . .]. The worst of my hangover is almost over [. . .], and I'm down, but probably because my work rhythm got interrupted. The treatment is finished: Mehnert was here and we got drunk to celebrate the occasion, and, in the evening, I slapped Jon and flung schnapps glasses at the wall (not out of joy). And then I was hoping for a few exquisite days' holiday—but, no, shit: correspondence, laundry, a report for the Central Committee about our experiences,[213] a visit from the TV people, terrible furore because of *Brothers and Sisters*. The scripts came back with the edits: the Stasi scene deleted, the art discussion deleted; anything involving emotions or—horrible to say!—which smacked of sex was deleted, and now my lovely story can be safely studied at any Catholic boarding school for girls. Well . . . on Monday, the editor is coming: he's going to be happy. If the publisher won't budge, I'll find another. No more complaining, now's it's time for fists.

213 B.R., like other writers, was invited by the SED Party's Central Committee to write reports on her experiences.

Yesterday I wrote three pages of preliminary notes for my Franziska[214] novel, which for now is called 'Singing in the Rain'—I don't even know why.

Today we found out from the planning engineers that a nuclear bunker is being built nearby—for the Stasi. I don't feel resentment. Who will they snoop on when they climb out of their bunker onto the wasted planet? Maybe they'll eat each other later, and that's the smartest thing they can do, having forgotten to take any farmers and workers into their shelter.

Something I often think about is how we've become used to living with the atomic bomb, Mr Atom, the next-door neighbour . . . We tell Radio Yerevan[215] jokes ('proceed at a dignified pace to the cemetery so as not to cause panic'); jargon about the radius of complete destruction is bandied about—and we collect books and beautiful furniture and suffer from lovesickness. Isn't that the age-old superstition of 'it won't happen to me'? Maybe we're ripe for the next war.

Daniel will get his own flat in the next few months. [. . .] We're being affectionate and friendly to each other (apart from occasional, jittery outbreaks of malice); in the evening we go our own ways [. . .]. He no longer asks me to be accountable. He knows that I spend every evening with Jon . . . It's so horribly brutal [. . .]. To make matters worse, we get a lot of erotic pleasure from each other: we embrace every night, and every night is different, more beautiful, more relaxed . . . I just have to think about the silhouette of his shoulders over me. . . Enough.

[. . .]

Jon [. . .] has gone to visit his parents for a week. On the first night without him, I sat all alone in my room in the dark, listening

214 *Franziska Linkerhand*, B.R.'s unfinished novel, published posthumously in 1974 by Neues Leben.

215 Radio Yerevan jokes, or Armenian Radio jokes, were very popular in the Soviet Union and Eastern bloc countries from the second half of the twentieth century.

to blues and getting methodically drunk. These blues . . . you can understand why a wise government doesn't want this destructive Negro music. When Daniel came home, I was as drunk as a thousand men [. . .]. Now I can mock my sentimental mood, but that evening I was wretched, and there was a smell of gas in the air.

[. . .]

Hoy., 14.9.

Trouble with the Defa again: my treatment is going to be turned completely inside out; some artistic advisory board is meddling with my work. I'm fed up. I cancelled the sports car I wanted to buy; the price—a job that I do not desire or love—is too high for me.

We've also abandoned the plan for a summer home; our standard of living can't be cranked up any higher. I'm making plans, but for my own flat. I'm looking forward to being alone, yet I'm terrified at the same time. Always coming home to an empty flat . . . But living together is unbearable. [. . .] Sometimes I lie in bed until noon and read or doze, the days drift on . . . a terrible state. (But I'm incapable of work, although I'm not physically suffering. Yesterday I went to the doctor for a general check-up—I was also examined for cancer. As I lay on the white bed, I made a discovery: I have an attractive, flat, brown-skinned belly and the hips of a seventeen-year-old boy.) I realized that I'm one of those women who check themselves in front of the mirror every day. [. . .]

Last week we drove to Burg in a mad rush. My little Dorli-sister had written a panicked letter: she's going to have a baby and, in a knee-jerk reaction, she's handed in her college resignation and is desperately afraid. She was sure our parents would kick her out. I was very upset (Jon said I should behave as if I were about to have my first grandchild). I wanted to visit the vice chancellor in Rostock and, above all, appease my parents. We raced to Burg and met Mum and Dad—all blissful and broody at the idea of taking care of the baby for a few years. Not even a thought that I might take it, as I had imagined. Dorli had to retract her hasty withdrawal from her seminar group, and will continue to study. How little I know my own parents! I was very proud of them again.

I've finished my report for the Central Committee. I've probably committed heresy again. It took me a whole week. *Brothers and Sisters* has been approved by the publisher, including the Stasi scene: now the ministry must decide.[216] I still don't have a contract. Is this a way for them to cover their backs? I'm a bit worried.

Hoy., 17.9.

Yesterday I broke up with Jon ('again', Daniel would say, and I think 'yet again' myself, with a hint of irony—if it wasn't for that, and hope, I would probably be drunk again now it's evening). [. . .] I was already in despair over the mudslide of gossip and rumours that was drowning me—not only the rumours about my 'sordid affair' but also my fees (90 thousand for a screenplay), our car, my over-long hair and too-elegant dresses, my arrogance, and the fact that we no longer take money from the plant [. . .]. These rumours are probably invented and systematically spread from a particular place, by certain individuals.

We had a terrible showdown. Jon accused me of playing a double game and demanded that I get a divorce at last. He knocked back a lot of booze and became more and more insulting [. . .]. He was no longer the man with whom I have shared a bed [. . .]. I don't know how I got home. I walked through the rain, through the puddles; I cried all the way, and at home, I threw myself into Daniel's arms—I wanted to die. [. . .] Daniel cradled me on his chest and comforted me, then he gave me a sleeping pill and vodka and sat by my bed until I fell asleep.

[. . .] God, and I know, I know that every evening, I'll be waiting for the phone to ring with a pounding heart and that I'll

216 The Ministry of Culture gave the permission to print.

start drinking every night. If I'd gone for his throat yesterday, I think I would have cut his jugular. I'm addicted to that pig. Good to know that now he'll be sitting in his room, [. . .] full of remorse, and he'll start walking up and down in front of my window today for sure.

Hoy., 20.9.

Today the sun shone again for the first time in a while. The sky was a bit hazy, with gentle melancholic colours. I'm very unhappy. Sometimes it attacks me like claws stabbing at my heart. But I'm determined not to take the smallest step. I'm so fatalistic [. . .]; I always wait for decisions to be forced on me until I can no longer avoid them.

Hoy., 26.9.

On Thursday, Jon phoned to enquire after my health. I was so shocked just by the sound of his voice [. . .] that I collapsed afterwards, so awkwardly that I sprained my right hand.

[. . .] It's terrible without Jon. It's terrible with him. Yesterday I ran away from him again, because he was tyrannizing me with his bad temper. But I accept the reason for his mood. He's outraged by the nepotism in the plant, all these greedy money-grabbers and contract experts, to whom our new friends unfortunately belong. H. is a shrewd and clever schemer. He does everything for his friends to the point of self-sacrifice. But he finishes off his enemies coldly and systematically, carrying out ingenious plans that he calculates years in advance. I also think he's connected to the Stasi.

[. . .] We were very disappointed when we heard that H. has managed to procure his friend a contract at the plant [. . .] (they live together and are what they call 'intimate friends': H. is even accused of homosexuality. But it seems to be an intellectual friendship). You can be sure that it's well paid. I learnt that there is an article in the Party rules forbidding such cosy arrangements.

Hoy., 29.9.

Wednesday: literary ball. We sat for a while with people from a youth brigade. There are stories to be found here; we want to get to know them. We've already invited one of them: a concrete-builder, 27 years old, no professional training (he's doing it at the moment), because he had to work for his nine brothers and sisters; he has a powerful, open, worker's face—but his smile . . . My God! [. . .] He looks like a man of the future (and hopefully we haven't made a bitter mistake again). The brigade leader is an expelled student.

Petzow, 6.10.62

I'm back at the writers' retreat, this time without Daniel. I was very sad when he left [. . .]—the big day has come: he has started his novel and we're both terribly excited. [. . .] I wanted to cajole him into staying another day here. The vine leaves on the walls are crimson, the trees in front of the window are ablaze and the sky is white-blue and a little hazy—but there was no stopping him: he went back to his notes and his desk.

The work with the Defa people is still postponed. It makes me sick, I'm going crazy for some real work [. . .]. But I can't just scribble something down if I'm waiting for new feedback, new suggestions for improvement. Günter Mehnert, my dramaturge, has already visited me, and tomorrow Mischa E [. . .], the director, and I will draw up a new schedule.

Dorli wrote to me today. She has turned out to be such a lovely, decent girl. Mrs H[. . .] . . . it felt very strange to write the address—until recently she was still 'my little sister'. Now the baby is tickling her belly [. . .]. I could weep. I'm not going to know how that feels any more, now that this damned job—or my insane ambition—is eating up all my reserves of strength and love. One day I'll stand there, a mediocre talent, with a few books quickly forgotten, and then I'll remember that I'm a woman, and then it'll be too late for a child. I've already overcome my worst broodiness. For a while I was crazy for those little hands and the whole atmosphere of softness, smells and cooing.

[...]

Jon is over at the composers' retreat. Yesterday, I visited him [...]. I want to sleep with him again. But in an unfamiliar house ... He took me back to the writers' retreat, and on the way, we were terribly silly and bombarded each other with snowberries, and it wasn't until we reached the door that I saw he had my lipstick on his chin. We had talked to the housekeeper at his home earlier on, and I had assumed a chaste and discreet expression all the time so she would think I'm a decent woman, and Jon—all the time with my lipstick on his face—had talked in a serious way. But the weather was so nice, and we tramped through a carpet of yellow leaves, and because of all this we didn't feel worried. Soon we were dying of laughter, and I had to drink schnapps because everything hurt from laughing.

[...]

Petzow, 15.10.

Since [...] Michel left, I've been sitting here, weeping and drinking. I won't see him for another three days. I'm listening to the 'Storyville Blues'—my God, all day long, as if Michel were there [...].

E[...] stayed here at the retreat for three days. We were working together on the treatment. He was very strict with me; in the evening I fell into bed, dead tired. And my affection for him grew more every day. I liked his eyes from the beginning: blue eyes with black eyelashes and slanted eyelids, and his rather Jewish nose, and his boyish leanness, his calmness and gentleness and inflexibility and thoroughness [...]

In the afternoon I had a heart seizure with that horrible feeling of panic: I was so scared I started crying. My heart was thumping— but I already know that feeling when you think you're going to die. He sat down with me, wiped my tears away and held my hand, and at that moment, I clutched him—the nearest living person [. . .].

He stayed at the retreat on Sunday. We lay on the floor, he put his head onto my lap, we worked on the treatment, and in between we kissed [. . .] and drank a lot and listened to jazz all night. [. . .]

Daniel came on Saturday. I told him. What else should I do? He understands everything, everything. [. . .] I can't live without this euphoric rush of a new love with all its stages, with its pain, betrayal and self-deception. And only the other day on the phone, I had laughed when Daniel, laughing too, asked if I had already fallen in love with E[. . .].

Petzow, 17.10.

I can see from my handwriting that I was pretty drunk. Over the last two days I have made a great discovery: I love Daniel. Everyone else fades into the background compared to him. I have thought everything through carefully. I'm not in any kind of euphoric mood, [. . .] and yesterday I did not act like a good wife, which I'll never be. I'll cheat on him another hundred times, because I will fall in love with other men a hundred times—if I have that much time left—and yet, and yet . . . [. . .]

Yesterday, feeling madly in love with Michel, I seduced Jon. He noticed immediately what was going on, was morose and tried to be cold. I won in the end. It was an erotic and tactical stroke of genius. [. . .] As always, he was confused and bewildered [. . .], my smarter, superior, Jon, and I didn't feel bad at any point, even though with one man, I systematically cheated on all three. [. . .]

Petzow, 21.10.

I'm not drinking any more; today I worked on the balcony the whole time and I am brown and smooth-skinned again. We're having wonderful autumn weather. From my window I can see the sun battling through the haze above the lake, which is pearl-grey then dove-blue. This morning there was frost on the grass. I go for walks alone, the frozen leaves crackling under my feet. At such moments I am at peace with myself.

[...]

Jon left yesterday. [...] He's afraid that I'm already far away from him.

Petzow, 22.10.

Yesterday Michel came; he slept in his room, no. 8. He was really down because he hadn't managed to finish his screenplay, and then he stayed up half the night in my room, typing, and in between we listened to the New Orleans Stompers and drank Zubrowka vodka—quite a lot, I think. I lay on my bed, thinking about and working on my book, which is changing more and more and has nothing to do with the original story. Franziska is now an expelled student and a loving, degenerate person, and her Jon (will he stay Jon?) is a young worker and is—the longer I think about it—that broad-faced blonde boy I met all too fleetingly at the literary ball. As soon as I'm back in Hoy, I'll have to take a look around his construction brigade.

After midnight, Michel only wrote idiotic nonsense, and we sat down together in an armchair and told stories from the old days; about his grandmother's aniseed biscuits and Advent visits to her kitchen. [...] His face is always cool and as softly downy as the face of my Lutz-brother.

Petzow, 24.10.

Two days ago, I behaved outrageously. I was hysterical, God knows why, and at midnight, I threw Michel's treatment in his face and cursed him. (And I really believed that I couldn't work with this man. His assured poise drove me insane.) He quietly picked up the book and left. I wept in rage and wept for Daniel, and then I walked for half an hour through the cold night, and then I went to Michel and apologized. In the morning we sat stiffly and self-consciously at the breakfast table. And this afternoon he came by again and brought me a Yiddish recording; songs from the ghetto (how does he know my taste? I'd never told him about it)—a gesture reminiscent of Daniel. Michel also asks for forgiveness for the injustice done to him by offering a present. Earlier on when I was standing in front of the mirror, I thought about it, and suddenly discovered a sneaky grin on my face, which I didn't like at all.

[...]

Petzow, 29.10

Daniel was here again for three days. He looks very pale and thin— it's time I came home. It was as harmonious again as it had been last week [...]. We drove to Burg for a day, and had a gentle, lazy afternoon with Mum and Dad. What must it be like for parents to have had four lively children for twenty years, and now be alone? My heart grew heavy when I saw them standing at the garden gate, waving after us.

On Friday we went to a jazz concert with the Manfred Ludwig sextet. I've never seen jazz musicians having so much fun.

Last night I had a long talk with Dr Hajek from Prague and Walter Öhme on the economic situation of the GDR. The elections have been postponed because they can't be risked at the moment. The 'mood' (is it called a mood?) is very bad. Workers are earning less; meat and butter are rationed; there's a lack of industrial goods;

our industry is shrinking; our aircraft construction has gone wrong and cost us many millions. Unemployment is back, not only among the intelligentsia (I already knew that we had enough engineers in various branches of industry). The culprit is automation, the change brought about by the RGW[217] and, in part, probably the Wall. Since no one has been allowed to leave, the shortage of workers has been resolved.

On top of everything, we're making one psychological mistake after another. How can this continue? Walter Oehme (he's a historian) said that if we were to start evaluating the work quotas now, we would have a second 17 June.[218] But in the government, there have been no changes. A cult of personality has never existed; we have laid the foundations for socialism (Ulbricht). Voices are getting louder, finally speaking out and saying that the move towards collectivization took place too early and was rushed. Thanks to our propaganda ('We will overtake West Germany'), socialism is now seen by many as a question of living standards.

Petzow, 31.10.

I have started another little romance [. . .]. On Monday, Michel wanted to come, but then he had to go to Berlin. I was beside myself with anger. I had finished my work for the day, had a long evening ahead of me, and thought I would suffocate. I went down to see the Zeisbergs and drank a few with them and tried to be in a good mood, the whole time I was wondering whether I could call someone, to at least hear the voice of a friend. Then Grü and Arndt came:

217 RGW (Rat für gegenseitige Wirtschaftshilfe): Council for Mutual Economic Assistance (CMEA), founded in 1949 by the Eastern European states of Albania, Bulgaria, Poland, Romania, USSR, Hungary and Czechoslovakia as well as the Mongolian People's Republic as a counterpart to the OECD. Later, the GDR, Cuba, North Korea (as observers) and Vietnam joined. The CMEA was dissolved in 1991.

218 On 17 June 1953, there was a People's Uprising against the GDR government involving around one million protestors in more than 700 different locations. It was suppressed by Soviet forces using tanks; there were around 55 fatalities.

they'd heard I had jazz records, and we went to my room and listened to jazz. By then, I wasn't drinking because I was angry but because I was enjoying it, and in the end, the three of us finished off three bottles of vodka [. . .]. I danced a couple of times with Arndt [. . .]. He's six years older than me. I know a lot about him: at our age you talk an awful lot, and our generation has the same problems. A. studied medicine. He was sentenced to eight years in prison and served four. Everyone knows how these sentences came about at the time (Oehme, a resistance fighter, spent ten years in Bautzen[219]—convicted by his own people).

[. . .] For the first time I have noticed that because of my name, some people expect [. . .] erudite conversation from me. I already have a name—that's an amusing concept. I always forget the audience because I enjoy writing, and as soon as I walk away from my desk, I'm just a normal young woman who likes to laugh and drink and wants ordinary people around her—but in truth they all treat me as Reimann the writer. There's too much talk about literature here altogether—mostly about self-evident things.

[. . .] At some point after midnight I went outside for a walk with Arndt, [. . .] and everything was lovely and enjoyable and not a bit sentimental and not as dreadfully complicated as with my dear, stupid Michel. The next day I had a desperate hangover and lazed around all day, and at noon I went for a walk with A. [. . .]. He's not pushy. I'm lucky that I always fish out the smartest, most interesting people. A. is sometimes arrogant—in protest against certain idiots. He also has a tendency towards sadism, or so it seemed to me: he told me a grisly murder story in detail, although I was almost crying in fear. The description of a graveyard at midnight still poisons my dreams, as it used to when I was little and read

219 In 1946, journalist Walter Oehme (1892–1969) was arrested by the Soviet occupying forces who confused him with a Nazi named Walter Öhme. He was sentenced to 25 years in prison and spent 10 years in the Bautzen penal institution before being released and rehabilitated in 1957.

E. T. A. Hoffmann and screamed out at night. At the same time, like many cowards and people who see ghosts, I listened spellbound, avid and half-dead with horror. Well, I know that. Perhaps I'm only afraid of my imagination, which carries on spinning a half-finished tale—and is far more terrible than anything the narrator can imagine.

Petzow, 1.11.

Yesterday Michel was here from noon to evening. [. . .] We had a big day of confessions: Michel told me the story of his marriage. [. . .]

Michel paced around the room and talked and talked and asked what he should do, although he knew exactly what to do. [. . .] He was shocked when I suddenly burst out: everyone always comes to me to pour their hearts out—why me of all people? I've heard so many intimate stories lately, I could write volumes. Michel said that people considered me a person who understands and sympathizes with others. Why? I'm still very immature, I can only listen—but maybe people with a talent for listening are rare.

I've now finally learnt why our relationship has been so strangely ambivalent since that evening when he wanted to sleep with me. He took my response as a sign of my wisdom. I knew, as he did, that our story would only end in a fiasco. He's afraid of me, feels inferior to me: I'm so tremendously alive and crazy and much stronger than he is [. . .].

Petzow, 3.11.62

The day before yesterday I went to Templin with Caspar; we had two readings [. . .]. He told me the dangers I'd be facing in my future work (dangers that stem from talent). For the first time I found out that he likes *Brothers and Sisters*. He's waiting for my next book.

Although he doesn't know what it is yet (I don't know either), he's assuming I will give it to him. [. . .] C. said the writers were queuing up; they can now choose, and the numerous dilettantes that we've been propping up don't stand a chance any more. [. . .]

The illustrations for *Brothers and Sisters* have been messed up— Grapentin has resigned. [. . .]

I was back at the home at 4 a.m. Arndt was sitting in the hall; he'd been waiting for me all night. I think I was very happy about it, I think I like him. Today, the whole seminar left, and only Arndt stayed behind. He can't leave. [. . .] This afternoon we walked again for hours, the sun still warming us, and the sky postcard blue, and on the paths, the wilted chestnut leaves covering our feet. We trudged through people's gardens. I didn't know how beautiful autumn was. Or have I just forgotten since last year? In the reeds there were a thousand birds, and our swans, the ones we fed in the spring, now have a young cygnet.

[. . .]

Petzow, 4.11.

At midday I walked with Arndt to the bus. It was sunny and very warm. We didn't talk on the way, just glanced sidelong at each other and smiled awkwardly, and at the bus stop, in a sudden fit of fear, as if we could still catch up, we kissed and kissed. I think I like his voice most of all, his dialect, reminiscent of the Baltic Sea and fishing villages. Sometimes I closed my eyes just to hear his voice. [. . .] When I walked back through the gardens in the sun with my coat open, I had that complex, very physical pain in my chest which I'm familiar with and is part of being happy. But that wasn't part of the plan.

Sometimes I think about how many times I've loved, how many times I've been loved: I have a beautiful life, I have no regrets.

I once bumped into my childhood sweetheart Klaus, who, in our school days, had been a slender, beautiful boy, with blond curls and a head full of plans and bold ideas for later on. He now has a paunch and only a sparse wreath of hair. He's a teacher, without ambition, married, not happy, not unhappy, [...] he demands no more of life. I suddenly sensed how young I am compared with him, how exciting my life is: new people, new passions, always ambition, work which doesn't allow me to become complacent—a wonderful life full of discoveries. I'm never going to get old. My former school friends, even the girls, have docked in the harbour—wide, portly ships—whereas I sail out to sea every day. I'm a happy person.

Daniel called me, very excited: I wrote an analysis for the Central Committee weeks ago, about working at grass-roots level. I had made a few sharp attacks and set out my half-baked ideas. The analysis was discussed at a Central Committee meeting, as Daniel found out, and is now with Ulbricht, and will be handed to the press at the 6th Party Congress. Is it still so difficult to be brave in our country? What are the other writers afraid of?

Petzow, 6.11.

Yesterday I went with Michel to see Günter Mehnert. We were going to discuss the FDJ scene, which we are all sick to death of, but then there were so many stumbling blocks we just drank wine and complained a bit, and then I went home with Michel, who was tired and haggard as usual. [...] Early this morning as he was leaving, he kissed me on the forehead and said: 'Goodbye, mahogany girl,' and I was in a buoyant mood all day. [...]

At noon I walked around the lake again.

For two days I had stumbled along the shore like a small, tired hooded crow. Today I sang loudly (God, it must sound awful, but I only sing for myself). It was very stormy. I love storms and I love the lake when the waves surge over the banks; and sometimes a swell of water doubles over and breaks, out where the water is grey or steely blue, and it looks like a leaping giant fish with a snow-white crest.

I have lost the key to my rococo chest. Too bad. A beautiful, old one—and now I can't even get to my diaries and love letters.

Petzow, 11.11.

The days drift by, I work. [. . .]

I call Daniel every day. He's tirelessly working on his book and sometimes reads a few sentences to me. I love his voice on the phone! But what will happen when we're living together again, day in, day out? And how will things with Jon continue? [. . .] I'm worried about him.

Petzow, 14.11.

Daniel arrived yesterday morning. He'd heard I had terrible toothache and set off in the night to come here. I was still half-drunk in the morning—I'd had a lot of vodka to numb the pain. It actually helped. [. . .] The night before Michel had been here. The treatment is finished: now we have to wait for it to be approved.

[. . .] I have to try to take care of Daniel in every way I can so that he can fully apply himself to his work. I've decided to separate from Jon. [. . .] If it gets too bad, I'll move out and hole myself up for a few weeks, somewhere far away from this godforsaken town.

[. . .]

I'm longing, again—again at last—to write something—a story, it doesn't matter what.

This afternoon my dear Daniel left. I sat with him in the carriage for a while; I was very sad as I watched him leave. Sometimes

I don't know how I'm able to fall in love so often with other men
[. . .].

Yesterday, while Daniel was asleep on my bed, I wrote some
notes for my novel. God, what rewarding work! I wish I could
start writing instead of working my backside off on these other
obligations.

Franziska Carmesin is starting to take shape. Maybe—a kind
of coming-of-age novel?

Petzow, 20.11.

I'm homesick [. . .]—today I almost packed and left on the spur of
the moment.

Petzow, 27.11.

There's been snow on the ground for the past two days, half a foot
high, and the sight of the white park brings back memories of
Christmas joy.

Daniel is back here with me (he's asleep on my bed now), and
I won't let him leave until tomorrow. [. . .] Two days ago we were
in Berlin after a long, difficult journey on the icy motorway (we saw
seven smashed-up cars on the way), first at the Central Committee
in the cultural centre in Friedrichhagen, and then in the evening at
Caspar's. Bartsch was there and showed me the illustrations for
Brothers and Sisters; we'd rejected the showy drawings, and I chose
a mezzotint—he'd captured the spirit of the story and created his
own design, although we weren't sure whether he would see it
through. He'd chosen the most attractive scene (in West Berlin)
for his experiment: the face of the girl in a chaos of skyscrapers,
advertising signs, and border symbols (was it barbed wire? I don't
know; I had the impression of a BORDER—and that's what
matters.) [. . .] The discussion at the Central Committee wasn't

helped by the presence of Otto Gotsche (as long as the triumvirate Gotsche, Kurella and Rodenberg are ruling the roost, the others will be frightened off). I don't know whether he misunderstood us or just pretended not to understand. At times he seemed almost hostile towards a generation of people he's not connected to in any way and who aren't willing to be manipulated by him. We respect his achievements in the past; but now he has little to say—I think he's simply lost touch: his views are wrong—wrong for these times—and damaging. He trotted out a few monstrosities, which proved his astonishing ignorance, didn't let anyone finish and was maliciously intent on misinterpreting younger people's opinions. He said stupid things about Noll ('he hasn't yet moved on to contemporary literature, and I doubt that he'll manage in the next ten years,'—and that, despite *Werner Holt* [...]); he urged us to write about current topics—in other words, about today, *for* today—for the newspaper (but to do so exclusively) and seemed to think that we, like him, are able to write a novel in six weeks. I have made a note of the silly discussion about epaulettes on FDJ shirts for my novel.

It was gratifying to see him coming under fire from the young writers—Wiens, Hauptmann, Beierl—who stood up for us. Rücker said some clever things about ten years of wrong thinking; there were a few casually veiled attacks on the official position that there isn't a cult of personality in our country, and the older generation was reproached for lacking guts. Hauser spoke very loudly and feistily about the long overdue need to replace rigid discipline—which had been necessary during the period of illegality—with a conscious sense of responsibility and independent thinking, even against the collective. (I will also try to explore this idea in my book.)

[...]

Petzow, 28.11.

Today is Jon's birthday, and I didn't even write to him: not chivalrous of me.

The treatment has been approved and even praised by the production team, but that's not very important to me now: I'm reading Rousseau's *Confessions* . . . Had a nice evening yesterday: Reiner Kunze came over with a few young poets. Yesterday in the lounge he read Czech poems that won't be published (here, mind you). I'm glad that Reiner now appreciates me, as I always looked up to him in a way—after he quarrelled with me in the writers' group for many years and criticized me harshly, not wrongly, as I now know. But back then, he was a different man too: a strict, dogmatic comrade, cold and dry (when in actual fact, he's such a passionate man, a blaze of fire in that fragile vessel of a sick body). He was transformed after the terrible things he went through (which must have been in 1957 or '58) when he was falsely denounced, sentenced, driven out of university when he was about to take his doctorate, literally thrown out on the street. He was a truck driver for a while. Today he writes beautiful poems with breath-taking honesty—he says things about our catastrophic past which need saying; and his collection of poetry is still banned, of course. He read to me from it today. The oppressive 'The Bringers of Beethoven'[220]—like Orwell's *1984*. No, different, because it's seen from the perspective of a different, of a good, clever comrade.

We often visit each other across the balcony (his room is next to mine) and talk, always finding things in common. We're the same age. We hate the Republic's militarism, the inexorable Prussian spirit and its militant language ('the battle for grain', 'the potato front'—it's beyond a joke, my God), and I felt understood when I heard him criticize certain things as being 'fascist': jazz = nigger music; the German worker = the best worker in the world; the

220 'die bringer Beethovens' (1962) by Reiner Kunze, published in *sensible wege* [sensitive paths] (1969).

language of our press—see LTI;[221] racial fanaticism has been replaced by class fanaticism (there are examples, I'm not just generalizing); modernist painting = degenerate art. Nothing has changed.

People say that Alfred Kurella (whom I've rechristened Kuratella) said in a small circle that we're the only ones practising the right kind of cultural politics. Which really means the others are revisionists or on the path to revisionism; which also explains why they fearfully keep us away from the culture of other—even socialist—countries.

You only have to listen to our foreign guests at the writers' retreat. I'm ashamed. Hemingway? Yeah, some American, barely worth taking note of, in any case harmful, whom we read 'very critically' (this was said in front of the Cuban guest who then exploded). Louis Aragon? We don't take any notice of his speech in Prague—others publish it: worse, we couldn't prevent it, because we're called to police and protect the purity of the doctrine. The watchdog of Europe—as usual. In Moscow they call us 'the Western Chinese'.

Petzow, 2.12.

I'm still reading Rousseau's *Confessions*. For the first few days I walked around as if I'd gone mad or was under a spell, and I can't yet explain the effect of this book on me: it's not his crushing honesty, which reflects how big and how small R. is; it's not his passion and naivety, his deep connection with nature (I don't think I've ever read such enthralling descriptions of landscapes). I don't know: but I have a deep empathy and insatiability for his work and it's reawakened my desire for Flaubert's *Sentimental Education*,

---

221 A reference to Victor Klemperer's book *LTI—Lingua Tertii Imperii: Notizbuch eines Philologen* (1947), published in English translation as *The Language of the Third Reich* (2000).

which I finally know how to appreciate; and for Stendhal and Tolstoy (I've also discovered Turgenev here). Why have I only come across all this at the age of 29? God, what I've missed out on! It's reinforced my views on great, simple storytelling of past centuries. Why do we always go back to it with a sigh of relief? Although in painting I'm always in favour of new forms and expression, I'm quite conservative in literature. The frantic or primitive language of our new books, understatement in Hemingway, dissolution and decay in Grass, wild chains of associations—all this is occasionally interesting, can be discussed, and pretends to be, or is, modern. But in the end, all that remains is the wonderful, relaxed prose of the great Russian and French writers.

[. . .] Reiner Kunze was here for a few days; he left yesterday. We didn't even have time to talk about the briefing with Ulbricht.[222]

Daniel came to see me on Thursday to say that I've been invited to meet the Central Committee the next day: by invitation of Walter Ulbricht, who wanted to have a discussion with people in the cultural sector. We were quite excited—what were we actually expecting? Tolerance, sincerity—God knows what. All the great and good were sitting in the assembly room: Seghers, Hermlin, Strittmatter, Weigel, Cremer, Dessau, Langhoff, etc. I probably owe the honour of the invitation to my letter, which Ulbricht quoted and praised (Cremer carped: 'Reimann should write novels, not letters')—and it's exactly his praise I find odd. After everything I observed that day, I'm suspicious of anything that U. refers to as 'clever and excellent'. The letter isn't critical or clever enough,

222 It can be concluded from B.R.'s description that Ulbricht gave the same speech at this briefing as on 9 December 1962 at the district delegates' conference in Leipzig. He returned to her letter several times: 'I would like to express my gratitude to this non-Party writer for speaking so openly about these issues, talking about how people are changing, how the writer's work is changing, and how, in the struggle for the solution of the great tasks of production, the change of the material and cultural living conditions and the thinking of the people takes place [. . .]. It seems to me that she has made a significant contribution to the preparation of the congress' (PMA, NY 4182/681, sheet 21ff.).

otherwise it would have made U. indignant. As always, it will be published in *ND*, and there's nothing I can do about it.

I was sitting next to Hermlin and saw how much he was suffering. In fact, to the ears of a man as cosmopolitan as H., with all his ideas about literature, U.'s opening speech must have been torture: the novel should replace economics textbooks, there are conflicts everywhere, you just have to visit a plant; a machine is constructed, not built, engineers dispute, and then produce them anyway (this is just one of the banal recipes)—'and then all it comes down to is artistic expertise.'

A whole group of artists spoke, including Seghers (about 'constriction'), Weigel and Womacka, who was viciously attacked by Cremer ('you're so smooth and compliant, of course you don't have any problems'). C. was very bitter; he's still in trouble because of the academy exhibition.[223] Wiens was rudely interrupted the whole time by U.—in a very opinionated and nasty way. That and his persistent 'What's the problem?' in his vile eunuch's voice. The man is power-obsessed and doesn't permit any opinion except his own to be expressed. He's a demagogue with false, misguided arguments and takes with the left hand what he gives with the right. He has a wary aversion to Soviet art, which was noticeable when he replied to Conny Wolf's question about why *A Battle on the Way* had taken so long to be published: U. (who later referred to himself as a 'mind reader') claimed that the Central Committee hadn't known about it. On the topic of Yevgeny Yevtushenko's poems: 'Why publish them? Whoever wants to can read them aloud on Marx–Engels Square, and I'll let the security services know so that they can protect him from the people.'

It's hopeless to expect the situation of our writers to improve for as long as this Philistine with his small-minded views presumes

223 Renowned sculptor Fritz Cremer (1906–93) had organized an exhibition called *Junge Künstler* [Young Artists] at the Deutsche Kunstakademie, which was attacked on the opening day (15 September 1961) by Alfred Kurella and other members of the Central Committee. A press campaign was initiated and there were several debates with the people and artists responsible.

to be a critic. Angry dispute over modern white or grey vases, on which Beierl wrote a poem that was not published. 'Designers want to make the lives of the working people grey, while the bourgeoisie in West Germany surround themselves with colour. Our people's lives should be colourful too. An apprentice could make such vases if he just took a piece of stovepipe as a model . . . ' And so on. C. exploded, but U. cut him short. Either he's misinformed or doesn't want to hear the truth. The closing speech was appalling; finally, I burst into tears of rage and hatred for this man, for the way he lays into artists in such a vulgar way, and Daniel was scared I'd create a scene. U. stubbornly maintained that a number of writers had only read the first part of *A Battle on the Way* and used it as anti-Soviet propaganda, and he scolds us as if we are a bunch of stupid or naughty children; and at that moment, if not before, there was nearly a riot: Hauser, Party secretary of the Writers' Union, jumped up and defended himself against this allegation; even Braun (known as 'General Twit') defended writers, and Weigel disagreed . . . I don't want to write down all the vitriol and slander that was aimed at writers—enough to say it left a terrible impression and I was very demoralized.

He can't stand us—maybe he thinks we have failed as propagandists. He doesn't know that in our country, there's no need to discuss the fundamental questions any more—we have moved on. Now it's a question of artistic issues, which he knows nothing about. I will never forget that 'briefing', nor his high-pitched voice, nor his evil distortions, nor how he cut his staff short, nor his smug grin, nor the expressions of our artists [. . .]. But he must have felt the blast of iciness, because in the end, he softened a bit after he'd reprimanded Wolf, who had asked about Soviet films. (On *When the Trees Were Tall*: 'We don't need films about drunks, we don't need extremes.')[224]

---

224 *Kogda derevya byli bolshimi*, a Soviet film directed by Lev Kulidzhanov in 1961, shown in the GDR in 1968.

Later we talked to Uhse and Hauser, who looked at me pity-
ingly. I was beside myself. They were also glum but seemed used to
such performances and took it in their stride, Hauser even with a
touch of humour. Uhse asked us to call him; we want to talk again
at last. He's older and smaller than I remember [...].

During the break, Rodenberg, suspiciously friendly, joined us.
His damned striptease eyes! He tried to talk me out of working with
Michel [...] whom he apparently doesn't like [...]. Finally, R.
asked me to send him the treatment—he wanted to write back to
me personally—personally; and the way he emphasized 'personally'
... well, I saw Daniel's face. It must be easy for a woman to 'make
it to the top'.

It was a day that reduced me to a wreck; first I have to digest it
all. I should no longer talk or listen to speeches, just keep writing.

Petzow, 7.12.

Daniel has been here for two days. First, he has to recover from the
stresses and strain of Hoy; then he will return to his work on 'Jonas'.

On Tuesday Günter Mehnert and I were at the management
meeting. Professor Wilkening spoke with both barrels blazing but
Mückenberger became quite friendly after I threatened to go on
strike. Wischnewsky[225] is the cleverest of the lot: whatever he says
has substance. We're supposed to rework the end of the film, I don't
know why, but Günter obviously got it, and that's the main thing.

Things only took a bad turn when talk turned to the choice of
director. They want to boot Michel out; I've realized that for a long
time. All sorts of evasions [...]. Günter and I fought like lions, but
in vain, I'm afraid. I feel terribly sorry for Michel, whose self-
confidence has already taken a battering [...].

---

225 Klaus Wischnewski (see note 199).

In the evening we met up with Michel in the Kino Café. There we bumped into Tetzlaff, a young director with Populo,[226] and Rolf Losanski, who's also working with Günter and is now dubbing his first children's film. One of his projects had also just fallen through and we were all angry and started drinking Cuban rum. I only got to know L. briefly and we took a shine to each other straight away. He's small, dark-haired (at the writers' retreat, they thought he was my brother), funny and sassy, and thinks he's a romantic. And since he recently heard on the radio that all romantics die early, he's obsessed with the thought that he'll only make it to 39. He's now 30. In the meantime, I've also watched him dubbing and seen the way he deals with his young actors; he is a skilled teacher and has a wonderfully wicked tongue. He is ambitious and determined to become a great director, and that's what I like about him in particular.

We were no longer quite sober when Michel came, so we had the courage to tell him about the bad outcome of the meeting. He took it quite calmly; I think he's so down that nothing can shock him any more. He soon had to leave, and I sat with him for a while in his car […].

Then I went back into the cafe and we knocked back litres of rum, and probably didn't behave very well: I can remember a number of smashed cups and glasses and noise and cursing the lousy Defa, and then I drank with L., and he gave me a kiss and made fun of my big nose. I can't remember when we left in the end. Tetzlaff and L. stole a lot of glasses and spoons, and later I also found a couple of glasses in my fur coat, which I know for certain I didn't steal.

L. came back to the writers' retreat. He was getting the hots for me—despite my big nose. We listened to jazz records and drank vodka, and at around half past twelve, the taxi I ordered arrived, and L. sent the driver away again. All right, we kissed too. At some point during the night I made coffee—and when we were halfway

226 The Leningrad Popular Science Film Studios, a Soviet film-production company.

sober, I had to play the confessor again. [. . .] The young people of our generation have a great desire to pour out their hearts to one another, [. . .] mostly I like the trust and wonderful solidarity between us. [. . .]

At half past two, L. finally drove back to Potsdam. The next day he called me and asked if I would come and visit him at the dubbing studio, and yesterday I actually went. I watched closely and met a lot of people, and by the evening I was simply shattered: my empathy for everything I come across exhausts me more than hard work.

Petzow, 8.12.

We watched *It Happened One Summer* in the studio.[227] Krug was fantastic again, Grit was miscast. Günter Mehnert, who's allergic to any stories about married couples, blew up, and of course it's unfair not to give the third man (the husband, to be precise) a chance— not to even show him. Modern love, which seems to take place solely in bed, is totally unrealistic.

Afterwards we went to a restaurant with Losansky. He's even got used to my nose now. In the evening there was a scandal at the retreat: Creutz and Andrießen, who are writing a screenplay here, got horribly drunk and raised the roof. Daniel sat with them until 3 a.m. and then came to me (I had already gone to bed) [. . .]. At four o'clock in the morning, I heard Creutz sobbing loudly in the room next door, weeping over the terrible state of Germany. In the morning, he was still so drunk that he was wandering around the place in his pyjamas. He came into Daniel's room too, sat on the edge of the bed and started railing against the Germans (a feeling we share—to an extent): he was drinking in desperation, he said; the state was ruining him, and he'd prefer not to wake up at all the next morning... We were even inclined to take him seriously, since

227 *Beschreibung eines Sommers* (1963), DEFA film based on the novel by Karl-Heinz Jakobs, directed by Ralf Kirsten.

we know and understand this—and the legitimacy of some of his complaints—from other artists and intellectuals, although we refuse to give in to grim desperation and work instead.

Last night, the same palaver, boozing on the same pretext; but this time, we thought C. was just dreadful. People like him spend all day writing articles and essays, fully aware—at night they bemoan their lost freedom.

Petzow, 13.12.

I thought I had so much to say, but now everything's mixed up, and I only have scraps of memories: a few evenings with Creutz and Andrießen (we're now prepared to like each other) [. . .]; one day the lake was frozen over, and Daniel and I played exciting games breaking the ice, hurling sticks and frozen apples across the lake, and Daniel really enjoyed it and lost himself in the game, like a child.

Over the last few days, I raced from one meeting to another; mostly I was in the studio, which ended up with a few bottles of wine (and of course, Losansky was always to blame). Yesterday was very bad: Günter Mehnert and I were already wrecked by lunchtime, and more and more people collected in his room, and more and more bottles of red wine collected too, and in the evening, already quite drunk, we went to Café Linden with L., a young actor and the unit manager, then later Stahnke (who's now finished filming the television play *Fetzer's Flight*[228] with Kunert) came; he still knew me from the *Junge Welt*. [. . .] I don't think Daniel liked the rude tone of these people, and there was a bit too much talk of sleeping together for my liking, and I can't stand more than half a dozen filthy jokes. But it's all so alive and loud and interesting too; I like listening to it for a few evenings. Well—the serious

---

228 *Fetzers Flucht*, a television play, written by Günter Kunert and directed by Günter Stahnke, which premiered in the GDR on 13 December 1962.

atmosphere of publishing is simply better, and in the end, nothing beats writing books.

All of a sudden Michel turned up again, and we chatted away for half the evening. He's quite down, already starting to despair, and in fact I haven't been able to get a decision from management about the director yet. Tomorrow's going to be another tough day: 8 o'clock meeting in the studio with Wischnewsky; 11 o'clock newspaper interview; 2 o'clock Party Activists' Convention, to which W. invited me (sensations are expected); meeting Michel in the evening.

Hoyerswerda, 17.12.

We're surrounded by mess. I've taken quarter of an hour to write a few more lines, but I can already tell I won't have time to vent properly about *Fetzer's Flight*, the television play by Kunert and Schwaen with Stahnke as director. The painter is here . . .

This morning I dragged nearly 2,000 books from mine to Daniel's room, and Daniel ran around in the city 'organizing' from dusk till dawn. On Saturday my new furniture will arrive and then I can send the other things to Dorli. I now realize that I'm exhausted, but the sofa is covered in newspapers, and there are hundreds of books stacked on Daniel's couch. Well, it's not important. I haven't been to see Jon yet, and I'd rather not go, out of cowardice, as I well know. (Incidentally, as soon as I returned, I was confronted with gossip—a vile city where everyone feels obliged to stick their dirty noses in other people's private lives; even my occasional cigar smoking is sneered at. A woman who smokes cigars also sets fire to houses and rapes small children.)

We stayed in Petzow two days longer than intended. We spent the last few evenings with Creutz and Andrießen, both of whom are unusually unsociable and shy, despite their sharp tongues and quick, vicious wit. [. . .] Together we read dozens of back copies of the *Weltbühne*.[229] How similar the picture is ... (Ossietzki's essay on the KPD in 1928). How little we know of recent history; how come we're only just starting to understand how Hitler happened? Our picture of history is distorted, superficial, wrong. The Party Activists' Convention at the Defa was very interesting; Rodenberg yakked on, Knietzsch was rabble-rousing ('we have no skeletons in our closet'), the young directors, Carow, Gerhard Klein, Conny Wolf, were aggressive [...].

But even saying this fills me with hope. Geschonnek (a party member since 1928): 'I'll talk until I get a reply or until someone punches me in the mouth.'

[...]

My letter is causing a stir. Ulbricht spoke in Leipzig about this 'lesson from a non-Party member for the comrades' and recommended that all party groups should study my letter, and more and more friends and colleagues are congratulating me on my courage (but why 'courage', since I've just reported a few everyday concerns?). Today Böttcher from the district council was here and I'm supposed to speak publicly and participate in a forum of artists in our district. Why didn't they realize earlier what's going on here?

---

229 *Die Weltbühne. Wochenschrift für Politik, Kunst, Wirtschaft* [The World Stage: Weekly Journal for Politics, Art and Economics], founded in 1905 by Siegfried Jakobsohn. Managed by Carl von Ossietzky from 1926 to 1933.

1963

Hoy, 13.1.63

For a week now we've been back at the retreat. We've been slogging away really hard recently. My room is finished at last and is exactly how I imagined it, with bookshelves up to the ceiling, a proper desk, grandfather's enormous 'Kaiser's chair' (because the 99-day Kaiser sat in it) and a new daybed (we're sleeping in separate beds at the moment and for the time being, it's still very romantic). Daniel has also let me have the beautiful old clock which used to stand on the glass cabinet at my grandparents' and which now means childhood and family tradition to me. I hang up new pictures every now and then: Chagall, *The Drowned Woman*, which everyone except me finds hideous, and Henri Rousseau's wonderful self-portrait, *Le Douanier* [. . .].

We spent Christmas at home. We couldn't set off until 6 p.m. on Christmas Eve. There was snow, then we were alone on the motorway for hours, and when we passed through villages, we saw the lights in the windows and felt very festive, in the mood for singing Christmas carols. We didn't arrive home until well into the night and of course Mum and Dorli were tearful with fear.

We had a few nice peaceful days at home. Peaceful . . .

We are a horribly raucous family. [. . .] Dorli looks gorgeous with her baby belly. [. . .] Sometimes when we were sitting at the table, bawling canons with silly, invented lyrics, I looked at Dorli and still couldn't grasp that she is having a baby, since she herself is still so childlike.

[...]

We celebrated New Year's Eve at Jochen Haufe's place. Meanwhile, I was very angry with H [...], who had insisted I lend her *Kin Ping Me*,[230] noticing too late that Jon had written a— harmless—dedication in the book (which that little bitch thinks is pornography). Well, after having devoured the book she gossiped about it, lent it to her friend, and spread rumours in the club committee about the dedication. I wrote her a letter, which I hope mortally offended her, and demanded the book back. It was delivered the next day. That lousy little whore who jumps into bed with all kinds of married men (good luck to her) is full of indignation about my relationship with Jon, and I'm stupid enough to fret every time over malicious gossip like this.

I visited Jon a couple of times. I tried very hard to be cold ... [...] I hate the man, I can't get rid of him, damn it.

Petzow, 14.1.63

Today we're driving to Berlin to attend the 6th Party Congress; the Politburo invited us as guests. My letter has caused a great stir: one institution and newspaper after another has approached me (suddenly they all want stories by me too). I get a lot of letters from strangers who thank me for my encouraging and courageous article ... There's huge trouble at the works: my brigade feels as if its toes have been stepped on, and poor Järkel (whom I mentioned as the 'young blacksmith from the district administration') has been threatened by the Party secretary—he had to justify himself because he had revealed 'internal Party' information. I'm now going to write

---

230 *Kin Ping Meh: oder die abenteurliche Geschichte con Hsi Men und seinen sechs Frauen* [Chin P'ing Mei: The Adventurous History of Hsi Men and His Six Wives] (original Chinese text, 1610: German translation, 1930).

a second article for *Forum*: about the consequences of a letter.
[. . .]

Creutz and Andrießen are here again, and we sit together for a
couple of hours every day. [. . .] Daniel has suggested that we—
Creutz and I—write a television play together based on *Brothers
and Sisters*. I have the proofs here now, and C. has read them, and
is singing my praises to everyone [. . .] I'm very glad of course that
a harsh critic like him appreciates my story. Now Professor
Kamnitzer and the director Dr Köhlert are interested in adapting
it as a screenplay. I will agree to a co-production as long as he agrees
not to booze while we work.

Every day I pore over the screenplay with Michel—godawful,
hair-splitting work.

Petzow, 18.1.63

Back from the 6th Party Congress. Where to start? A lot of strong
impressions, some good, some bad. What expectations did we
have? Away with Kurella, away with Rodenberg—pah. Cultural policy is more rigid than ever (and personally: Rodenberg is busy
wrecking my film despite all the sweet words he says to me in the
corridor: 'You are the kind of woman one can be honest with', etc.—
that revolting 'from-one-person-to-another' number).

Thunder erupted over the writers' heads. Oh and only the innocent sat on the side stage: Nachbar, Wolf, Seghers, Wiens (no, he's
not innocent, the devil, and Kurella referred to his and others' past
behaviour with Ulbricht—who in fact didn't let anyone speak—as
'uncouth and brazen'), Neutsch, Pitschmann and—the only one
who was praised—Reimann, and God knows how I felt as a key
witness against others who are precious to me. Some of our colleagues, especially that snob Kunert, have laid a few modernist
cuckoos' eggs in our socialist-realist nest.

Modern . . . Jesus Christ—just tarted-up old hat, along with experiments that were already running thin in the Twenties. As always, almost every speaker felt compelled to accuse 'the writers' of some kind of misrepresentation, and in the stalls (where the delegates were sitting) they grumbled and pooh-poohed, and Bredel stirred the mood even more by telling his story about the Academy—some inconsequential gossip as it turned out. And then in a manner that reeked of denunciation (but was apparently intended to whitewash his own reputation), he got onto the Huchel case, the discrepancies of the journal *Sinn und Form*, the fights with Huchel and his highly paid contract which apparently can't be terminated (fierce muttering from the stalls).

And to cap it all, he quoted Western newspapers: 'enclave of liberalism' and 'intellectual island'. Years of work by vermin, Bredel said—and B. should know, being the president of the academy, and former Party secretary. The looks, shooting daggers at us from the stalls, gradually turned to scowls—the artistic elite sitting there as if served up on a tray. Sorry, are you clapping in the right places? Sorry, we throw huge sums of money at you and you don't turn out art for the people? If any one of us had got up to defend writers, we would have been booed and ripped to shreds. We felt uneasy to put it mildly . . . [. . .] We can't even afford to write an inner monologue for the next two years. But I understand my comrades' anger when I hear someone like Hacks saying that he couldn't find any heroes in our books.

[. . .] I may have a simple notion of heroism, over which Hacks can ride roughshod with a single quip; but he should begin by clarifying the notion of the 'hero' in literature without resorting to antiquated positive heroes from dogmatic literary theory (which, incidentally, Aragon attacked in the most recent, most strongly condemned edition of *Sinn und Form*). And what are these 'experiments' that he talks of in almost conspiratorial stage whispers? In *Fetzer's Flight* in any case, the experimental form seemed to serve only as a mask for the dryness and inanity of the story, and even that failed.

Still, I don't like all the yelling, and this pogrom mood fills me with horror: I see schematism and its poisonous flowers blossoming again, and it's ridiculous and cynical to proclaim from on high that our writers have all the freedom and opportunity for full creative expression.

Petzow, 20.1.

Conversation with Georg Maurer all morning. He told me (constantly shifting between awe and aloof amusement, his head in the clouds, child and sage) how he wrote the poems for his *Three-Verse Calendar*:[231] when the grasses and flowers were in him and he ran towards the trees to touch them, and when he understood 'water' for the first time, by the stinking River Pleiße, and when he thought he could understand the bark of the trees . . .

He is one of the greats whose poems will be understood by a wiser, more sensitive humanity—and one who sometimes desperately needs the 100 marks we feeble beginners effortlessly earn.

Daniel came back from the Party Congress last night, half frozen. At 12 midnight, it's already minus 25°C at Alex. A terrible winter, temperatures we haven't experienced for ten years or more, every night minus 27–30 degrees. The economy is in serious trouble, electricity is intermittent, the coal can't be dug out, it's iced over; in the Pumpe, the briquette factory is struggling on half power because the coal bunkers are nearly empty. Sometimes I think of Jon working alongside thousands of others in the freezing wind outside on the diggers. Sorry, and we don't have any heroes?

On the last day there were a number of people who took up cudgels on behalf of writers. Kuba talked about those who are 'too

231 *Dreistrophen-Kalendar* (1961).

cool' and no matter what you think of Kuba, he's right to reproach young writers for shying away from beautiful pathos—even despising it—and considering anything that isn't delivered 'subtly' as old-fashioned. Ulbricht was also mild and friendly, and this time I was praised again in his closing speech; even the Politburo spoke of me as a hero . . . Pathetic hero: I don't feel brave and valiant, I veer between optimism and depression. Maybe I'm just stubborn?

Petzow, 22.1.63

The writers at the retreat are all outraged or even desperate. The mood yesterday hit rock bottom. We watched the TV broadcast of the Party Congress on cultural issues, and the room erupted: everything malicious and harmful to writers and belittling towards the academy (always with the undertone: 'enemies') had been selected and edited together. The academy's splendid president sat on the Central Committee podium and grinned. Kurella has grown huge and has announced staff changes. And comrades who keep straying from the Party line (he said it with more refinement, meaning Hermlin, among others) would have to go.

Finally: Ulbricht—praise for B.R., of course, which I'm sick to death of hearing, I can't stand it any more. I'm not a witness, because saying that separates my personal life and work, muddling everything. I'm sure most of my colleagues will look at me disparagingly, even angrily, and God knows, I can't do anything about it; like a dozen others, I just wrote the mandatory analysis. Perhaps the others (meaning those cheerful, blithe windbags, and that pleasant, tall lad and professional grant-hustler, Wohlgemuth [. . .]), perhaps they just waffled away and sang the praises of the grass roots.

Every day there have been heated debates at mealtimes and in the lounge; even laid-back Eddy Klein has been a bit depressed. I like talking to Professor Kamnitzer best, who, with his Jewish wisdom, tries to be fair to both sides and calmly weighs it all up. Yesterday evening things took a bad turn. On the last day in Berlin (we were all sitting in front of the television), in came the Pioneer delegation—marching steps, march music (here, Kamnitzer disappeared), then the order: Halt! At ease! (that's when Dr Köhlert left), Pioneer announcement, chop-chop, the little Prussians, the strident voice of the one making the announcement . . .

I fled, I felt sick, I saw my own inglorious past—marching, kerchief, strident instructions. I knocked back a schnapps. Kamnitzer and Köhlert were sitting in the lounge. We were shaken, terrified: What was it all about? Why these little eight-year-old officers [. . .]? Will they be goose-stepping to their meetings by the age of 16? Jesus, yes, our generation is scarred; we can't bear this kind of thing any more, damn it. We've learnt to understand why a socialist state needs an army—but we don't understand why children need to drum, blow fanfares and yell 'Halt!'

All this sounds grumpy and crabby, and I'm sounding off about writers for pages on end . . . But in fact, the Party Congress made a deep impression on me; I heard a lot of clever things, encouraging plans and thorough analyses. What I liked most was what was said about the economy [. . .]. Leuschner talked about the Council for Mutual Economic Assistance—which was great indeed: far-ranging plans (until 1980), cooperation with the socialist states, coordination. Here was a glimpse of the world of tomorrow, a united, peaceful world [. . .] truly capable of utilizing its resources, [. . .] irrigating deserts, and turning the North Pole into fertile land.

I also felt how it stirred and moved people when the representatives of the fraternal parties were welcomed. Seventy countries and their delegates came to us, and the world sat watching, the world that will clearly become communist some day.

Then: Nikita's speech, his humour, his wonderful calm (and why shouldn't he be calm since the Soviet Union was speaking through him), his confidence—and suddenly that moment of deadly silence in the hall when he spoke of the hundred-million-person bomb,[232] which Soviet scientists have developed and can't even test because to do so would destroy Europe itself. His forceful warning of another war—without any embellishment or trivialization, as is common here: there is no escape, no protection (but weren't we told to cover ourselves with newspaper, our feet placed towards the centre of the explosion?); the first nuclear strike would kill 800 million people and destroy all the capital cities of the world. Warnings not only to the West, but to Albania and China too, who have begun uttering loud war cries and want bloody revolutions [. . .].

Incidentally, the Chinese delegate (Albania was not represented) never stood up, never stirred to applaud, made a speech like a robot on the fourth day, saying: we did not attack India, we have been attacked,[233] Tito is a bloodhound and a slave of imperialism, and we hold the banner of Marxism high . . . Scandal, Verner held a protest speech, but the Chinese delegate wouldn't allow himself to be interrupted. The room exploded . . . Please God, never let these people get their hands on the atom bomb!

The most elegant man at the top table was Gomulka,[234] who was also the most disciplined, and didn't leave his seat once during the speech. He was the only one who did not clap when writers were attacked; he was the only one who smiled when they accused us of misrepresentation and decadence. Always these extremes! The discipline was admirable (we are used to the cheerful sloppiness of writers), and the organization exemplary. There were no glitches, and not a minute's delay [. . .].

232 'Our scientists have developed a 100-megaton bomb. But a 100-megaton bomb cannot [. . .] be detonated over Europe: [. . .] The detonation would [. . .] affect both your country [the GDR] and several other countries.'—Speech by Nikita Khrushchev, (N. S. Chruschtschow, *Die Zukunft Deutschlands wird in der DDR geschmiedet*, [The Future of Germany Is Forged in the GDR]. Berlin: SED Verlag, 1963, p. 40).

233 Reference to the Sino-Indian War (20 October–20 November 1962).

234 Władysław Gomułka (1905–80): First secretary of the Polish United Workers' Party from 1956 to 1970.

Congress venue: Seelenbinder-Halle. We stayed at the Berliner Bär hotel. We were taken to lunch with the other writers at the Haus Berlin.

Did I already mention that I exchanged a few words with Anna Seghers, that I saw her, my heroine, and was allowed to help her into her coat? Heart beating fit to explode. Once she bumped into me (she's a bit clumsy or pretends to be)—I was ecstatic. A beautiful woman—and a real woman.

Hoy, 23.1.63

Tonight I'm working for the first time with Dr Köhlert; we're writing the outline for a film based on *Brothers and Sisters*. He wants to film the story. We had actually wanted to work with Creutz, but I was so shocked by his boozing and his cynicism (which he flaunted heavily) and, most of all, because he has fallen in love with me [. . .]. Yesterday Köhlert came over (his name is Lutz, my God, and when I lie in bed and think of 'Lutz', he's back with me, the brother I idolize, and my childhood returns, and that day in Sacrow when I walked around, suffocated by nervousness— and around the same time, someone shot his eye out). We talked about Creutz, and I hinted at the reason—I don't like getting mixed up with colleagues. K. said: 'And how do you know that it's not just because I like you so much that I want to work with you?' [. . .]

But he has very good, clever ideas for the film: we want to try to put the inserted texts—the memories, the feelings of the siblings—into images and use little dialogue.

Petzow, 24.1.

Yesterday, I wrote the roadmap with K. for *Brothers and Sisters*. Long debate about sibling love. [. . .]

Petzow, 26.1.

Now the worst has happened: I've also fallen in love with him and was madly happy for a whole day, and Lutz, who usually walks around the house with such modest restraint, is strutting about singing loudly, [...] and my heart is hammering wildly the whole time. We worked together for a day and wrote the film outline. Lutz sets a sharp pace, and I have to keep up, my mind focused [...]. There is no larking about or hours of chatting like with Michel and Günter. [...]

Petzow, 28.1.

Yesterday we were home; it was Mum's birthday. She turned 58, but she still looks like she's in her late forties. She's a pretty woman—or are we the only ones who think so? In any case, she's the kindest, most self-sacrificing mother ever. Now she's already fighting to get Dorli's littl'un.

'Little Sis' was there too. My D-sister is already in her 7th month but still quite slim. She's proud because the doctor has told her that her child is doing splendidly. Suddenly, what I heard about my old friend, Peter, the nuclear physicist, came to mind: his child was born without eyes; P suffers from radiation sickness.

Uli gave me a photo of himself—great honour. He looks the way our painters depict young graduate engineers: a clever, interesting, rebellious boy and incredibly sceptical. They are both proud of me, their faculty is waiting for *Brothers and Sisters*, and I have already received their invitation to a discussion. The issue of Dorli's room has been clarified [...].

It was wonderful and boisterous as always—just like home should be.

Petzow, 3.2.63

We're spending a lot of time with Walter Kaufmann, whom we both like very much. Some of his stories remind me of Jack London and there are parallels between their lives as well. Now it's Sunday and his pretty wife is here, Angela Brunner, a former painter, now an actress; she's gracious and clever, and we've immediately transferred all our Kaufmann affection to her.

Tomorrow night my Daniel is leaving, and I'm already crying at the thought that I won't see him for four weeks. He's starting his course of treatment on Wednesday. We can't even spend our last day together: I'll be picked up tomorrow morning for a meeting of the Presidium of the National Council,[235] where I am also supposed to give a speech. [...]

There's trouble again with the Defa: Michel's contract as a consultant hasn't been signed. He, of course, has retreated into a corner, sulking, as he always does when difficulties like these crop up, and Günter and I are fighting. I wrote a letter of protest to Mückenberger. I'm sick of the whole thing; Günter and I are also determined to give Michel a good kick up the arse soon. He's a sissy, he runs around with a reproachful expression while we keep going out on a limb for him.

[...]

Today there was a disgraceful article on Ehrenburg's memoirs in *ND*. The book hasn't been published here yet, and perhaps the squabbling in advance should prepare us for the fact that these kinds of books (which have been available in West Germany and many other countries for ages) are never going to be published here at all. Erwin Bekier told us this morning that he spoke to Ehrenburg two years ago. Ehrenburg said to him: 'I'm an old man, I can no longer afford to lie. I'm going to write the truth now.'

---

235 Nationale Front der DDR [National Front of the GDR]: an alliance of political parties and mass organisations in the GDR from 1949 to 1973, controlled by the SED.

Who in our country is interested in keeping the truth from us? Why, why?

Petzow, 6.2.

Late in the evening on Monday, a few hours after I'd come back from Berlin, Daniel left. [. . .] He sent a telegram that night, because he knew that I was terrified for him: the streets are slippery with ice and snow, and I know how my dear Daniel drives. But he arrived safely at 3 in the morning and on the way, he towed another Wartburg that had got stuck in a snowdrift. [. . .]

Meanwhile I'm being set upon from every direction: people want me to write articles and do readings and lead discussions— and I'm so tired. [. . .] What a job! I'm not my own person any more; sometimes it's as if I'm completely at the mercy of others, as if I had unintentionally leant over a grinder, and my hair's caught in the cogs and is relentlessly pulling me in. I no longer feel that naive sort of happiness I used to. [. . .]

Petzow, 9.2.

My life is in complete chaos yet again, there's a terrible agitation gnawing at me. I've been drinking every night, I can't cope any more. Sometimes I feel so depressed I want to crawl into a corner like a sick cat, and then a silly mood comes over me again . . . Günter Felkel has been here since Monday with his dramaturge Buerschaper. We've become friends and, in the evening, they come up to my room, we drink a few bottles of wine and talk nonsense and laugh—the way I haven't laughed since my school days (and I was sometimes kicked out of class because I couldn't stop, the tears streaming down my face). It's probably the cleverest thing I can do now: drink wine and laugh and laugh . . . When I'm in my room alone I get the doldrums.

[...] Kaufmann tried to seduce me (God, that makes it sound as if I'm a shocked seventeen-year-old kid). OK, he wanted to sleep with me. [...] He tried it on and, what the hell, has something going for him—a man if ever there was one. Now he sits there, shaking his head, looks at me and doesn't understand what's going on. Oh and neither do I. It would have definitely been nice and it felt good to hear his endearments, and I returned his kisses, but I can't go any further. There's always a point when I turn ice-cold, and I don't know if it's just because of Daniel. [...] Perhaps my upbringing is to blame and my deep scepticism, which sometimes borders on contempt, and this absurd feeling that it's all animalistic. An aroused man brings on a physical aversion, something close to disgust; I'm turned on, yes, but repelled at the same time, and in a flash I'm sober and very clear-sighted, and then I lash out, and they stand there, troubled and disappointed, and think I'm abnormal and say that I'm not a real woman. The path to these affections that I open up—not always innocently—is only ever through a meeting of minds, work, conversation, never just physical attraction. Maybe that's why this sudden change outrages me every time: a man who has just treated me like a colleague on an equal footing, talking to me like he would another man, who respects my work, suddenly discovers my breasts and hips: the writer suddenly becomes a woman he wants to possess. That's it: being possessed by someone else, letting him see my weakness—I hate that. I'm a person just like they are, as clever and hardworking and gifted as them, but I'm not an object of their desires.

I don't know why I'm going on about this. I've just realized that this is the second page of me scribbling down trivial things and I have more important stuff to think about.

I feel increasingly pulled into the 'old versus young' discussion and we've been talking about it for hours. Recently, Kaufmann took me to see Eduard Claudius (he accepted me into the union back then, '56, and he was a grim dictator—now he's an old man, but his tone is still pretty crude). C. owns a huge house on the outskirts of Potsdam; his study looks just like someone from the outback would imagine the studio of a successful writer to look: bookcases and studio couches, gorgeous carpets, an Oriental table and valuable statuettes (C. was a diplomat for a long time in Damascus and Vietnam), beautiful old furniture and a long row of plant-filled windows; and above it all, a homely, roof-like ceiling divided into coloured sections by beams.

And there this man sits, surrounded by comfort and beauty; he has money, demands high fees, but he sits there and grumbles. I am a polite person; I listened to him for a while. Then I got angry [. . .]. He doesn't read any of our books, doesn't watch films or television plays—it's all rubbish and boring. But his story, 'The Girl Gentle Cloud'[236] is the best, most beautiful thing that's been published in recent years (he says). *A Battle on the Way* is 500 pages too long and has no effect (he says). The young write for the sake of money, their dissatisfaction has to do with economics, they just want to make more money, own more than just a car and a villa (we already have both, he says). And then: when we were your age, we fought, we went hungry, you can't imagine, you don't know what unemployment is, you're spoilt, you were born with silver spoons in your mouths . . . and so on.

In the end I quarrelled with him bitterly (and when I want to, I can use crude expressions like an old working-class writer). We couldn't agree [. . .] True, he has preferred not to write a word about our lives for five years; he's into exoticism, and of course 'Gentle Cloud' is more attractive than Tina or Grit or Recha. He couldn't or didn't want to realize that we also have our disappointments and suffering and fights—as if fighting can only be done with guns, and bitterness only felt over a shortage of bread. He was astonished to hear that I live in a rented flat with two rooms.

---

236 'Das Mädchen, Sanfte Wolke' (1962) by Eduard Claudius.

He envies us our easier life—but then what did he fight for? He accuses us of being lucky—but what is his goal? [. . .] True, I am sometimes surprised at my envy for my younger siblings' generation, and I reproach them for their petty problems and trivial concerns over fashion: we had a hard time back then, had to wear wooden sandals and worked for the FDJ, and there was no fashion, no new clothes and anyway—you're all spoilt and ungrateful. The same as it ever was and it wouldn't be disturbing if it weren't for the political consequences today, which we can only speculate on at the moment. People start (who? often the West and its radio stations, quite openly) to exaggerate and exploit differences, to play off young hotheads against old comrades, and of course there might even be a serious conflict at some point. [. . .]

Now I have to deal with Michel again (to whom Günter Mehnert and I gave a severe talking-to, yelling so loudly that K. thought there was a fight going on in my room) and work on the material that the Defa has castrated so successfully that I can barely recognize the story's meaning.

Petzow, 10.2.

Operated in vain yesterday on the raw script with Michel. In the afternoon, Felkel and Buerschaper joined us, and we talked for hours about the beatniks, and in the end, we gave up trying to work: I spent the evening with the pair of them again; they watch each other like hawks, and everything's really funny and a bit edgy; in any case, we get along well with each other.

At night, a terrible nightmare again, ending with skeletons on motorcycles driving down a corridor. I woke up soaked in sweat.

I still have to write about the meeting of the Presidium of the National Council. I was asked—no, pressured—to give a speech, and my turn as speaker came up third. I had no manuscript, no notes—and that in front of a forum of professors, former officers, politicians . . . Well, I said straightaway that I was dreadfully nervous, and everybody laughed, and then it wasn't so bad. I talked about our writers and their disappointment because they had been treated so badly at the Party Congress—and of course about the 'young ones' (but where does this start to become a myth?). Then I talked about our town, its dreariness, the lives of young people who have no cinema, no dance hall, and the workers who are on the road for 12 hours a day, and then question the meaning of life: what do their lives consist of except for work and sleep?

There was 'a ripple' and 'hilarity' in the hall, as they say, and in his speech afterwards, Manfred Gerlach said that he wished for more outspoken and frank contributions like these (I'm writing this down because I'm vain: so, I can do speeches if I have to, and maybe I won't be quite as terrified in the future).

But, in fact, most of the presentations were extremely boring: they just regurgitated what we'd heard at the Party Congress a dozen times before. I was the only one who brought up concerns and gave examples, and Dr Korfes was pleased that, for once, the meeting wasn't as boring as usual (he said this loudly because he's hard of hearing and very uninhibited).

I also attacked the FDJ several times, whose damned zealotry for organization kills every initiative and restricts young people's desire for adventure. Afterwards, Müller from the Central Council spoke, and I thought it might have woken him up a bit—but far from it: he just babbled on. 'We need to educate young people, we need to have debates with young people . . . ' Our youth are heroes and a high-output shift is for them the best day of their lives . . . This man only knows the reports, not the reality.

Dr Dieckmann stood up after me and confirmed what I had said about Hoy and announced that the town will have an Aeros circus tent this year so that at least films can be shown. Later he gave me a letter from Abusch, who's been dealing with this problem too.

A few more words about Korfes (and I notice I'm trying to delay having to report on my interview with Professor Norden).[237] I travelled to Berlin with K. He was a general at Stalingrad. He knows my books because his six daughters have read them. (He says: 'The desire to produce a son fathers many daughters'—and he is proud of them. The youngest was introduced to Khrushchev—she was a delegate at the congress—and Krus. said: 'This is history, comrades.' He has a Frederician mouth and echoes of the military in his tone and is, of course, a proper gentleman, who courted me in the most gracious manner. He spoke a great deal about his time as a soldier—and how strange these reports of a professional officer seem to us and his views on the honour of being a soldier. It was OK to send hundreds of thousands of soldiers to their deaths in Stalingrad—but prisoners of war cannot be shot (at least not in the presence of generals); that was a violation of convention. You go into captivity with honour, with a car and in full war paint, while the infantry perishes in the snow. That's just as it should be. It sounded as if he was telling me about an interesting game of chess.

Petzow, 12.2.

A letter from Daniel at last: he's homesick, [. . .] has a guilty conscience because he can't get down to work; he always feels a duty towards his capable wife, but all she wants is for him to be healthy again.

We—Michel and I—are over the worst hurdle. Yesterday afternoon I suddenly found the thread and spooled it in, then slept for ten hours [. . .].

[. . .] Thousands of questions: passion and passionate art in our literature—stifled by convention and regulations and moral

237 Albert Norden (1904–1982): from 1954, member of the Presidium of the National Front of the GDR, member and secretary of the Central Committee and member of the Politburo of the Central Committee of the SED (1958–1981).

laws. I have discovered a conflicting morality: the consequences for my heroes are my consequences. I'm not capable of making their decisions; in my stories, I lead the life I should be leading—vicarious adventure, a sham life, how does all that fit together? As if I had two lives—

Petzow, 13.2.

Dr Korfes is picking me up in an hour.

I've wanted to write about Annemarie Auer for a long time, who's been here for the past two weeks, but haven't got round to it. I like her a lot, she is much cleverer than me, [. . .] we exchange smiles or looks when we're talking to men, and there's no need for explanations. She knows a lot about me. She's ten, maybe fifteen years older than me (she's very good-looking) and has probably been through a few things, and in any case, understands others' experiences [. . .]—a real woman. She's now reading my *Brothers and Sisters* and has made a lot of astute comments; I didn't know how much a book exposes the character of the author. She's discovered all my weaknesses: my ease in writing (which has nothing to do with how hard I work)—and I remember that Caspar once called me a 'workaday talent'; impossible to create female characters except the one I know so well.

Petzow, 15.2.

An insane night . . . In the evening I watched *On Tangled Paths*.[238] Damn old Fontane! I rushed straight out of the TV lounge and into my room. My heart was broken—I cried and cried and couldn't pull myself together (but I know it wasn't just Fontane—a few hours earlier I had said goodbye to Lutz Köhlert). Afterwards I took two sleeping pills, and Buerschaper sat by my bed to watch over me.

238 *Irrungen, Wirrungen,* film based on the eponymous novel by Theodor Fontane, broadcast on TV on 15 February 1963.

And then I drifted away and surfaced and heard him saying over and over again: 'I love you, I love you,' and it was like that time when I had that wonderful morphine delirium: I was disembodied, it felt like a summer's day, like floating in water, almost sinking, and only hearing the small ripples in my ear and just wanting to glide downwards. For a while I must have talked to B., but then Andersen's fairy tales came to me (and wasn't it *The Little Mermaid* back then?), and then came black dogs and graves under snowdrifts, and I sat up with a start, and my patient boy stroked me and calmed me down and said something. At three in the morning I woke up and he was still kneeling in front of my bed. [. . .] He had sat there all night looking at me, nothing else [. . .].

In the morning I was woozy from the pills, and I had a sore throat the whole day long, and now I'm tempted to take that sweet poison again tonight.

The atmosphere here has been heated over the past few days, but that can't be avoided in places like these with everyone living on top of each other. Annemarie lay in bed yesterday with heart seizures, Walter was extremely on edge because he couldn't make any headway with his work, and I crept around like a shadow, tired of playing the charming clown and cheerful innocent [. . .]. It's all a big show and I can't stand it for long. I have to get out of here. I can't bear it (and after two weeks at the latest, Hoy will bore me and kill me).

Jon called today. That's the next stress ahead of me (but don't I long for him too? I don't want to, but I sometimes lie with him at night. I feel hot when I remember it all, our embraces—) [. . .].

Yes, and Lutz was here. Why does his name still drive me insane? Bloody sentimentality. He's not my brother any more, the time with him has been buried—God, and I loved him so much. Anyway, Lutz came—the other Lutz, it's nice to write that name— [. . .] and he stood there and laughed and was happy and looked like a pirate with his bent nose. What did we actually agree on? We want to work together, of course. He thinks I'm clever and we make a good team. We trudged around outside for a while. It wasn't cold. The snow is at least a foot deep. We threw snowballs at lamp posts, and were very silly, and the colours glowed between the sky and snowy ground: the pine-clad room, the red roof of the gazebo, a yellow silk scarf, Lutz's face . . .

When we got back to my room—I'd been dreading it the whole time—he kissed me like no man has ever done before. I would die if he embraced me. I fought back like a savage. My nice artificial shield—if there's one crack, everything's lost; a wall collapses that's been protecting me the whole time. I felt so safe from temptation [. . .] God, I'm hopelessly Catholic, I'll never be rid of it. [. . .]

B. says I screamed out in fear, *They will find you*! From what depths does this horror rise?

Petzow, 17.2.

Yesterday we had a wild night; we celebrated our farewell with a lot of vodka (and this morning everyone was so drunk and hungover, the departure had to be delayed). [. . .]

Poor Annemarie is back in bed and very poorly. I'm spending more time with her and she's telling me about her life: her years of illness, when she was still 'very poor, small and shabby', about her war service in a steel mill where she had to live with whores, and disgustingly fat SA bigwigs who chased after her and promised her meat ration tokens. After the war she studied and earned a living. Then there was the PhD thesis, which caused her breakdown. Her husband is similar to Daniel: an angel of goodness, but [. . .] she has to carry all the household burdens. [. . .]

Petzow, 18.2.

If only I had been friendlier to Burschaper yesterday! I sent him out of the room so curtly. But I felt really awful, just one heart seizure after another, and in the evening, we watched Miller's *Death of a Salesman*, and it completely shattered us. But still.

Last night the doctor had to be called for Annemarie. She came to my door and knocked, but I didn't hear her. I only wake up from my deep, baby sleep with Daniel: if he comes home late or moves about his room, I react like a mother. I visited A. again just now. I found out in passing that she's almost 50. I thought she was ten years younger.

Received an invitation to the Central Committee today. They want me to collaborate with them on the new working group for literature. I'm scared to death. Where's that supposed to lead? Am I who they think I am? Or do they know me and that's the reason they want me? I've never tried to hide my reservations or hold back criticism.

So, last week I visited the Korfes. His wife is very sweet and has the bearing of Mrs General Korfe. The daughters are nice, capable, very modern girls—one an assistant film director, the other a forester. Korfes told endless stories about the two wars: about the handsome, cowardly Captain F., how he prevented Jews being shot (and I know for sure that he's not fabricating anything)—but when his division went a further 300 miles, those rescued were taken away by the SS, the fanatical Hitler Youth who were such good soldiers . . . His daughters had heard it all before and looked a bit bored. For me, it was fascinating.

Later, we drank vodka, and Korfes got a bit tipsy, and then it all got quite Prussian: with Casino cigars and gambling partners and upper-class daughters (and the young girls one also visited) and etiquette and Colonel X, and I found myself sitting in the midst of old Fontane's Berlin, and Kellermann was there and Baron

Börries von Münchhausen. Korfes courted me, and his daughters laughed at their father a little mockingly, tenderly—two worlds. [. . .]

At night

I'm dead tired, 20 pages of screenplay done. But I have to put the business with Prof. Norden behind me, and my tiredness forces me to be brief. [. . .] First he came to me to tell me how my description of Hoy reminded him of the cities in the American Midwest, where he'd lived during his years of exile: the main street, dead straight roads to the left and right, each building the same as the next, brand new and boring.

And then: the writers. I'd given a speech in my defence, and then he explained to me why they'd brought this discussion to the congress: many of the old comrades have lost their way, there's desperation and resignation, and now the comrades from the Politburo (he always referred to them as the 'PB', and I didn't even know what he was talking about) are being put on training courses, because they, too, are barely able to grasp the new problems. (I'm putting this into my own stupid, dry words)

After the conference, we sat down and talked again and—no, I still can't write it down, everything's muddled up. I told him how awful and depressing it had been with Walter Ulbricht, and Norden said: the comrades had asked him to not get so involved in literary matters any more, and to concentrate on economic problems instead. This was all said with a look that removed any doubts about whether I had understood correctly. Walter Ulbricht was overstrained . . . This too meant something else.

He asked me about my new book, and of course I brought up the question of what people are even allowed to write about these days. 'Anything, as long as the proportions are right.' Well, OK. All at once he started telling me about his friends who were murdered—some by Hitler, the others by Stalin. And his speech after Hungary: on White and Red Terror, and the reprimand he got for it from the Central Committee. And then all kinds of other things—worse things that I don't even want to write down in my diary, and all the time 'my dearest Brigitte' in a tone that first filled me with anxiety, then fear: what kind of adventure have I got myself into? A glimpse into the world of string-pullers which I don't understand and don't want to understand. I'm a writer, I'm a naive person, perhaps even stupid—I want to stay on my turf. I want to turn a blind eye to his sort, but I can't any more: I'm spellbound, watching a drama unfolding in a foreign language. Are they cynical? Have they hardened because the times demand it, or the politics (Christ, what are 'upper-level politics' anyway?) or because they've gone through terrible experiences. What is 'power'? Are the powerful wise? Are they corrupt? Are they always the hard-working ones?

Now I'm getting upset again, left with my hundred questions and my fear and a burning curiosity to get to know these *people*.

Yes, and then: my success. 'You have publicity now,' said Norden, 'make use of it in any way you can.' And now I have to put it into my own stupid, dry words again, because I can't repeat what that clever fiend said (some call him a Jesuit): I found out how they 'make' people. They've helped me along, they certainly know who to pick, and today, it's me. I have publicity because the Politburo gave me it—but tomorrow? Just one false move . . . I've never felt so exposed, so close to a precipice. I'm powerless. They can blow me away like a speck of dust. 'Dearest Brigitte, make use of it . . . ' For how much longer?

I'm seeing ghosts. I'm going crazy. I don't want to think about it any more. I feel wretched. I'm going to bed now. I want to work and write good, honest books, damn it. But they are *comrades*. Oh, and I'm such an ass, the most foolish of fools with my sentimental socialism: 'Bread grows on earth for everyone . . . .' That's it. 'And roses and myrtle and sugarplums.'[239] That's it. Exactly that. putting

239 From Heinrich Heine's satirical epic poem *Germany: A Winter's Tale* (1844).

shoes on human feet. This is the most immediate, first thing; that's why I write. I won't let them make me afraid of myself.

Petzow, 21.2.

Why do I always have such far-fetched worries? Everything went well, of course, and it was all fine at the Central Committee (what a labyrinthine building, such a mass of marble and several thousand rooms). Willi Lewin was charming (that man is worthy of a novel himself), and the finest representatives of young literature were there (a few intruders among them: that eager, devoted German Görlich and 'Dwarf Know-It-All' alias Zimmering). Dieter Noll said a lot of wise and honest things, and Lilly Becher praised me for the excerpt from *Brothers and Sisters* in the *NDL*, and they were all nice to me (I'm just mentioning this to prop up my feeble self-confidence) and the whole writer-group literature can be a useful thing, even though I'm averse to all that theorizing and think it would be better just to write books.

[. . .]

Hoy., 23.2.

In the afternoon we arrived back in town: each building the same as the next. Noise, bleakness . . . And I, a socialist writer, suddenly felt a savage hatred for everything crawling about on the streets, all those stupid, gossipy, loud people. In our building: radios blaring, children blubbering, no Daniel, the chaos of half-unpacked suitcases. I knocked back a couple of vodkas, I was so ill and tired. And then I lay down in my new room, which I first have to make my own, and wished that Jon would come.

Then he called. Straight away, he asked: Will you come over? I asked if he would come to my place instead. Jon: No, I'm not entering that strange house. (Strange . . . But didn't we discover the moon in this place, at this window, right here?) All right, then don't, I said cold, icy, disillusioned. Jon: Could we tomorrow, by any chance—? Me: We can't ever, by any chance—. I slammed down the phone.

I was in an indescribable state. I cried half the night, tossed about, couldn't sleep. My heart was racing, I carried on drinking, the heat drove me crazy, I tore off my pyjamas—in the morning I was shattered. But by morning, I'd also made a decision: it has to end now, immediately. I wrote to him because I can no longer stand his incredible selfishness, because he couldn't empathize with how miserable I was. (Daniel and little B. both sensed it. They called me, said something must have happened, they felt so anxious all of a sudden [...]) And while I was writing it, my heart felt like it was being torn bit by bit from my chest [...]. At these moments, why do we always remember the good, lovely times? [...]

Then the letter lay there, and the key that has been mine for so long, and I couldn't even cross the street. Then Rolf Järkel came, good old faithful J., a blacksmith who is now Party secretary in his workplace. He wanted to win me back over to working with the brigade. The brigade has reconciled itself to my article. I asked him to join me (he knows my story, I felt I could trust him). We took the letter and keys over, I put them in the letterbox. We rang Jon's door-bell and told him, and we heard—really heard—how it took his breath away. We left quickly and I felt like death. We sat in a bar and drank quite a lot of vodka. [...] And then Jon came into the bar. He left immediately when he saw me with J. Järkel took me home and up to my flat. And then the phone rang, and it was Jon who asked if I was just being impulsive, and I cried out in horror; I couldn't bear to hear his voice any more, and J. took the receiver out of my hand and hung up. I cried and cried for hours, and good, patient J. sat there and held my hand and comforted me, and then I drank half a bottle of vodka, but it didn't help, nothing helped. I had a wild, ridiculous longing for the Jon of the past [...]

Today I went to the conference in Cottbus. Suddenly the door to the club room opened, and a blow struck my heart: Jon strode in, long-legged and slim-hipped. He sat down next to me; I never even glanced at him. Later, during the smoking break, I was standing outside talking to the worker writers. Suddenly I started to shake uncontrollably. It's happened before; I tried to go back in, took one step, then everything went black in front of my eyes. I toppled over and found myself in the arms of some stranger. Huge uproar, I screamed and sobbed, and they took me inside, but then everything went foggy. My heart pounded through my entire my body. Wild panic: you're going to die, now you're going to die. But no one dies—not from a panic attack or an unhappy love affair. Jochen brought me to the club. We were alone in the big room and I clung to him: these turns make me ravenous for the nearest living thing. I remember that Jon came into the room, brought some kind of drops. I still have that nasty sound in my ears when my teeth bit the edge of the cup, and the wonderful sound of Jon's familiar, tender, fearful voice: 'Shall I stay with you?' I felt his hand on my face, and I said 'No, no,' but I wanted to cry out 'Yes, yes.' After an hour I managed to [. . .] get up again.

When we went to dinner later, Jon ran after me. He led me across the street by my elbow, he talked to me, I saw his face again. But I acted as if I were made of ice. Self-defence, what else? I have to bear it, I have to. [. . .] I left early. [. . .]. Now it's dark outside. The nights are awful. Today I took a sleeping pill. To forget everything for a few hours. Tomorrow I'm working, and that's good.

Hoy., 24.2.

Daniel called me this morning because he was so worried about me, and of course I pretended to be as cheerful as always. I rippled my champion boxer's shoulders, and asked modestly what he thought about babies and love, and my gentle man said enthusiastically: of course, on the spot, I'd be overjoyed—and he's never said that to me before. I was pretty happy again—and then my beloved monsieur called and talked me to death about some sensational poems by someone or other, then asked if I was eating, and I said no, because I'm not eating, just living off mango juice, and then his soft heart broke, and he wanted to drag me off to dinner. Why didn't I hang up right away? So maybe I'll have dinner with him tonight— and I hope to God he doesn't cause me any upset. I'm very ill. I don't want to completely ruin my health. Let him go to hell! So I'm going to go out with him, stupid idiot that I am, and all the time I'm try to convince myself that I'm cool and calm.

Suddenly I had a terrible suspicion: What if I made a heroic decision out of ambition? Not out of morality, not out of my love for Daniel—but out of the desire to be a person with integrity, who can represent her cause, and criticize, because she has a spotless reputation [. . .]. Sometimes I'm afraid of my job: as a writer you don't belong to yourself any more, you have such a huge responsi-bility—or does it only happen here, in this dreadful, narrow-minded place where the gossip and mean, sordid talk can hound you to death? [. . .]

The title of my new novel . . . I was in the car with an old driver from the Defa. We were driving to Senftenberg; I had frozen into a block of ice, because the whole time the man had ogled me so indis-creetly (or maybe I'm doing him an injustice, right?, and he just meant it nicely), until he said, 'Now we're entering the zone of black snow.' He spoke very emphatically, slightly pompously. Suddenly something clicked in my head. I was excited: maybe that's the title. 'Singing in the Rain' is beautiful, but nonsense, because it doesn't relate to anything.

But: BLACK SNOW.

[. . .] and suddenly I can see many more details in my book: the city, the people, the tristesse, the heroism (or what we *call* heroism), soot in snow, the makeshift life I talked about to Kurella recently, the feeling of sitting on packed suitcases: this is where a factory will be, this is where a new city is being built, and in fifty years' time if that, this here will be lakes, and our grandchildren will laugh: lignite coal? How old-fashioned! Long live nuclear power!

Hoy., 27.2.

'Black Snow' is nonsense as well. Jon just laughed at me. And there's already 'Red Snow' by Hofé. So, rather 'Ants in my Pants' or 'Bugs in my Bed' after all. A book about restless people. Idiot that I am, I told Daniel that I had dinner with Jon of course [. . .]. He immediately said that I shouldn't fool myself—it'll start all over again. [. . .] No, there's no cure for it. What on earth holds me to this vile man? He's ugly and rancorous and arrogant, he doesn't spoil me like other men, he doesn't respect me like other men, he disagrees with me in every discussion we have and scolds me in a lazy, self-satisfied way . . . He did it again yesterday afternoon when he came over [. . .]. We were pacing up and down the room and over to the window, and I wanted to show him the beautiful icicle, over a metre long, which has been hanging outside my window all the time, but the icicle had already fallen off, and suddenly Jon kissed me. That's how it was [. . .], and now it really is starting all over again. I can't stand this man, but I think I love him.

[. . .] Now we'll start lying. We'll see each other less often (but can we fool all these bloodhounds in the long run?). To live in this terrible town, you have to be a hypocrite, but I can't live as a hypocrite. Everything's gone haywire again—and yet: for the first time since that terrible evening, I've been able to work again, like a wild thing, filled with stamina.

Hoy, 2.3.63

Three days with lots going on—and today I'm fit to drop, even though it's only afternoon. In the morning my two lunatics left after ransacking the flat for two days.

On Wednesday evening, Järkel picked me up [...]. We went
to J.'s flat—and Hanke and the half-rooster Günter were there too.
They showed me their new brigade programme; I'm supposed to
sign a contract and become an honorary member of the brigade.
They've done a lot in the meantime, both economically and politically, and their programme is very interesting: they've contacted
scientists whose research they want to be the first to put into practice. The dear SED district leadership announced to the district that
the programme was their impressive achievement—even though
they didn't know what was in it and not one of them had once
visited the brigade. After J. pushed hard for a long time, he was
summoned to an audience; but he couldn't go because he had a
repair shift. I promised to call the district leadership the next
day; I said: I bet you anything they go for it ... We had discussed
beforehand how far we should take advantage of our favour with
the Politburo. Well, what do you know: I called them, told the
comrades they should damned well make the effort to work at
grass-roots level themselves—and the next morning, half of the
economics department marched in to visit Hanke. [...]

The day before yesterday at the crack of dawn, the phone rang:
Buerschaper had spent the night at the station hotel. He was in
despair because he hadn't met up with me the evening before. [...]
So, he rushed over to my place. He brought a beautiful old record
by the jazz trumpeter Jonah Jones. At midday he was due to leave
again. He stayed for two days. [...]

In the morning Michel and Günter Mehnert came over, and we
fell into each other's arms and embraced and kissed and were
delighted, then spent two tumultuous days together. I hadn't eaten
for days, because nothing tastes good when I'm on my own, so we
dug into my provisions and polished them off. We also guzzled back
two bottles of vodka in the course of the day.

We were tipsy and worked furiously the whole time, and now
and again we sang and told jokes, and Günter lay about on the floor,

and even my serious Michel went wild. I was in the middle of the rape scene,[240] and then we raped each other, and for the sake of detail, the three of them acted out every part, rolling on the carpet, kissing each other (and sometimes it was a bit weird because it seemed so real). Everyone was shouting and I was sitting behind my typewriter and couldn't write for laughing . . . We didn't get a lot done, but we had a great time.

In the evening we went to the Kastanienhof bar to 'scout for locations'. Michel drove despite a dozen glasses of vodka. We drank bubbly all night, we danced and flirted in all possible ways, and at night we took a bottle of bubbly and carried on drinking at my place and made a racket. Then Günter felt tired and we sat on the carpet. He laid his head on my chest and fell asleep, and then Michel flew into a jealous fury and there was almost a scene.

The next morning we were quite fuzzy-headed and sent Michel out shopping; we were about to die of thirst. And my dearest B. turned up again. We forced ourselves to write another scene, and then we drove to the plant. The men were obviously delighted with Hanke (and that old comedian pulled out all the stops) and were thrilled with the place. We visited the locations for our scenes, and Erwin showed us the new bay. Our old bay has changed a lot; everything has been rebuilt and is much too cramped, and Erwin has a tiny foreman's office. But it did feel like a kind of home: the warehouse, the people who shook our hands as if we'd only been away for three days; the clouds of smoke over the briquette factory . . . [. . .] We drove back along an incredibly new road (the F97 has been dug up). It was already dark. [. . .] We worked that evening till eleven, and when we'd finished the scenes for the opening credits, we lay around like perishing winter flies and Michel fell sleep— but it was beautiful [. . .] and now the first draft of the script is finished. I still have to write it up today and tomorrow. I was very

240 Curt tries to rape Recha in *Arriving in Everyday Life*.

sad when the pair of them drove off, [. . .] and I fell into bed but couldn't sleep for exhaustion.

Daniel has written me a long letter—about us, about our marriage. And: 'Your life will always be like that: a constant turmoil of work, a constant turmoil of people, a constant turmoil of positions and honours, a constant turmoil of admirers. And the cause lies in you: you are a source of restlessness, agitation and unpredictability, and no doubt this is the source of your talent. You will never find peace, no matter how much you yearn for it your whole life long, not even with me—only sometimes when your mood is gentle, briefly leaning on my shoulder, a brief intake of breath . . . '

And—this from my gentle, dearest man: 'Maybe I will start to . . . become more selfish about my work. But this means: "Can't talk right now—have to work"—when you come knocking, and of course I will open the door and put away my things, and I'll listen to your complaints and woes about work—thinking, writing and meetings—and all the other little things besides, even K[. . .], and I'll try to comfort you. That's the way life is, that's the way it is with you, that's the way I chose it. And, in the end, that's the way I love it, despite everything.'

Hoy., 3.3.

Last night I was with Jon. I already knew how it would be when I went to him. It felt like a homecoming and I was at home in his room. He bought me red slippers and a soft woollen blanket in case I want to lie down for a while or sleep. We embraced each other until after midnight. We are made for each other. We understand each other wordlessly, we only need a hint of a gesture. I have never felt desire the way I do with him [. . .].

Hoy., 5.3.

Hours of discussions with Namokel and Winkler from the district SED. The 'hero'—all right, and work chores and the economy as *the* literary topics. Sometimes I envy these people and their self-assurance in overlooking problems. Soul—whassat? We have the party statute, why do we need souls?

Hoy., 9.3.

I have just finished my article for the *Forum*. Urgent commission. I could have done with three heads and six hands over the past few days.

My Daniel is back—his nerves in shreds, he says, but the plant is already gnawing at those shreds. We weren't shy at the beginning like we usually are, and I was happy to have him back, each day all over again. On his very first night back we saw a brutal fight in the stairwell: those three aggressive brothers again. The next day, we went to an ideology conference. I had a heart seizure and Daniel had to take me to the polyclinic. It's not easy for him with me, poor thing, and I don't feel as protected or in such good hands anywhere or with anyone else, not even with Jon.

[...]

Hoy., 17.3.

What are we doing actually? Days drift by, we're tired all the time (and early spring makes us even more so) and grumpy, haven't got anything done at all. Today is Sunday. Daniel went to Leipzig with Nellessen. I'm sitting around waiting for the water to be connected again so I can take a shower. In this town of co-ordinated botch-ups, such things are a daily occurrence.

I've been reading a lot of interesting stories in *Soviet Literature*.[241] I like Rekemchuk's 'Dshegor is a Young City'[242] very much. It's a

---

241 A literary journal published by the Union of Soviet Writers in several languages from 1946 to 1991.

reflection of my concerns, set in the far north. We were very impressed by Vladimov's *The Great Ore*. I want to be able to write a story like that too. The hero Proniakin dies and life goes on without pathos, without a trace of sentimentality, and everything is as beautiful and bitter and mundane as real life. He's a very simple person—not happy, not unhappy. He doesn't have it easy, despite socialism; in fact the ore mine actually kills him, and there's not a word about the bliss of socialist society, yet the story can only be set in the Soviet Union, in a socialist ore mine.

But a story that ends in death in our country?[243] Impossible. I have said goodbye to my heroes battling for 16 hours on the Eastern Front. But who is the new hero? In the meantime, I've replaced 'hero' with 'person' and am determined not to get mired in theoretical discussions any more, but write instead. My article for the *Forum* was my last attempt—and I'm sure I'll get a thrashing because I attacked the 'propagandists of the only true, back-to-grass-roots method.' I'm caught in the crossfire again. For weeks I've been hearing the rumours about the excerpt from *Brothers and Sisters* published in the *NDL*; I opened fire at the Circle of Active Artists. And surprise, surprise: the club committee is angry with me, the district leadership is angry with me and held a meeting on the matter and Alfred Burgmann is livid, which affected me the deepest, because he recognized himself as my book's character, Party Secretary Bergemann. I don't understand anything any more. It's bad enough bumping into your anti-hero in the street, but when your positive hero is angry with you too . . . Jon explained it to me: Bergemann has human traits—weaknesses even—which make him sympathetic to the reader, but a dubious figure in the eyes of the

242 This issue of the magazine was in German and the original title of the story was 'Dshegor ist eine junge Stadt'.

243 A tragic ending of a conflict in socialist times contradicted the idea of socialist realism in literature. For this reason, books whose protagonists died at the end (e.g. *Ole Bienkopp* [1963] by Erwin Strittmatter or *The Quest for Christa T.* [1968] by Christa Wolf) came under fire from dogmatic literary critics.

narrow-minded district leadership. At the meeting, we had a raging argument. Or rather, I flew into a rage when I heard the stupid, superficial gossip: it's obscene to destroy poor Siegrist on moral grounds (they called him S., not my character's name Heiner), rather [. . .] than educating him via the story [. . .]; I haven't depicted things the way they really are in the factory (how could I not add statistics or write a textbook on economics, unpardonable!)—and then the red carpet in the Party office, the large desk—defamation of the Party, etc.

[. . .] Then I got down to the nitty gritty, and told them how the story would have been if I'd stuck to plain reality: I said it wasn't the comrades from the district leadership who helped us, but Comrade Strittmatter; and that I wouldn't be in the works today but in prison if things had turned out for me like for poor S., and if no one had lifted a finger for us because they 'didn't dare make a decision on such a delicate matter'. At this, everyone suddenly was sheepish and very quiet. I had to listen to a few more reproaches because I hadn't submitted my Central Committee letter to the district leadership (which I'm not obliged to, damn it), and then J. [. . .], who is sometimes incredibly tactless, wanted to change the subject to Kin Ping Meh, but no one took the bait. They all have guilty consciences. Confidence in the Party? [. . .] In any case, I have no confidence in our comrades here, and I won't stop fighting them and at some point this place will go to pieces—unless they find a way to finish me off beforehand. I know what's going on in the brigade. The district leadership stinks. It's been throwing accusations at me for a year now because I left my brigade—and now I hear it doesn't like me being a brigade member with equal rights. They are afraid of me because I'm not corruptible, and they'll never forgive me for the fact that Ulbricht said I had educated the functionaries—although I'm not a Party member and therefore only half a person.

Hoy., 18.3.

Yesterday Daniel was in Leipzig, today he's in Berlin. I can greet him with smiles and love, and my conscience remains clear. Not the merest whisper of guilt—nothing. I'm happy in the arms of my lover, and eventually it will all be over, but I don't like thinking about it (and deep down, I don't believe it either).

[...]

Hoy, 30.3.63

A sensational new twist: I'm insanely in love with Jon. I can't sleep with Daniel any more. We're living like brother and sister. [...] I can't even talk about my work any more with Daniel, and that's not an accusation. I can't even cope with myself. How should anyone else be able to? Daniel can't stand my constant spoiling for a fight, or the way I'm always getting mixed up in things that don't concern me. But they do concern me. I [...] feel responsible for people and all the injustice going on around here and what they're doing to me works me up. I hate the sheer stupidity of our officials, and when I have to talk to them about art, I feel physical pain. They may mean well, but for God's sake, they ought to keep their mouths shut about things they don't understand. I'll never forget the way Creutz said, 'Stupidity hangs over this country.' Sometimes I understand why the man gets drunk every night—every time I leave the club committee, I want to drink a bottle of vodka to erase the memory of these ignoramuses and their prattle. I hate being told off, and at some point, I'll probably just kill myself because I can't stand it. Yesterday, I was quite devastated [...]. I just wanted Daniel to drive us into a tree ...

Maybe when I can drive myself, I'll do it when I'm alone in the car. Sometimes I don't think I can write any more and *Brothers and Sisters* should be my last book. [...]

Huge uproar because of the poetry evening in Hoy. Haufe had prepared it all by himself, as usual. He never puts his cards on the table. And now a number of people in the district are affronted by some poems (Volker Braun's 'Cycle for Youth'[244] was considered offensive and, of course, Yevgeny Yevtushenko), and now H. is trying to pass the buck onto the talented Bergner, because some scapegoat has to be found and that scheming H. doesn't want it to be him. B.'s poems were the best by far—now they are being dismissed as decadent and nihilistic, and B. has to be the sacrificial lamb that everyone blames while they slink off into the background. H. has gone as far as to threaten Gozell with withdrawal of his support (G. is a Party candidate) if G. doesn't distance himself from Bergner. Vile stories. Jon is enraged. He's determined to bust H. and expose his schemes (which are not only aimed at B. but at a dozen others too). These people, comrades in name only, are just clinging to their posts. They're terrified they'll lose their positions and have to go back to the factory floor, and they attack and slur everyone around. The spectacle makes me feel sick. Pathetic provincial schemers who use lies and blackmail to climb the ladder.

Hoy., 31.3.

On the 25th and 26th, the cultural conference at the Central Committee took place. Lewin visited us beforehand: we were supposed to hold a discussion. We already knew that the dissenters would be brought to reckoning, and I was really nervous. We expected something of the kind back with Walter Ulbricht. At the entrance to the hall (the meeting took place in the Congress Hall of the Central Committee) I found out that I was to sit at the top table. The top-table people gathered in a back room. I felt pretty uneasy among the big names, although most of them know me—God knows how—and welcomed me. And then the big moment

244 'Zyklus für die Jugend', poem.

I've been waiting for fifteen years (since I read *The Seventh Cross*[245] in 1945 or '46, published by rororo[246] on the shoddiest of newsprint): Anna Seghers spoke to me. She tugged my hair and asked in her deep, husky Mainz voice: 'Who are you, girl with the ponytail? I've noticed you before.' I stammered my name. She said, 'I've written about you.' I saw her as if through a mist, her white, casually combed hair, her high, black eyebrows . . . [. . .] Her eyes seem very dark, but as I know from photos, they are somewhere between blue and grey. She looks a bit scruffy—a brilliant, beautiful kind of scruffiness—and her manner is as unforced as I've ever seen: at the top table, she always turned around to us and laughed, and then she chatted to tiny, frail Arnold Zweig next to her and Helene Weigel.[247] Weigel, very small and thin, was dressed in a dreadful sack-like dress and carried a shabby leather bag over her shoulder that looked like a prop from *Mother Courage*, and there's nothing more astonishing than hearing Weigel's voice, a great organ, coming from her delicate chest.

I was sitting between H.-E. Meyer and Maxim Vallentin, who was lively, and jiggled about almost indecently, lurching around in his chair, grinning, sticking his fingers in his ears and making amusing asides. The talk, held by Professor Hager, was clever and balanced, and with the expected harsh words towards Hermlin, Kunert, Hauser, Hacks and Kurt Stern.

Hoy, 2.4.63

I write an awful lot of nonsense. I just leafed through my diary and I'm blushing with shame. I must be pretty confused—politically confused, I mean—and probably couldn't cope with my all-too-sudden publicity. Sometimes I am so rude to people who are not

---

245 *Das siebte Kreuz* (1942) by Anna Seghers.

246 The paperback imprint of Rowohlt publishing house, founded in 1950.

247 Helene Weigel (1900–71): distinguished German actress and artistic director and second wife of Bertolt Brecht.

pleasant to me. Did I used to be this coarse? No, not coarse: rather, coldly polite, but perhaps that's even worse? Is this the first sign of presumptuousness?

[...]

The cultural conference: Wohlgemuth was the first speaker in the debate. His lovely uninhibitedness is gradually turning into dangerous stupidity: he spouted a lot of platitudes about the sharp weapons of literature ('we have only changed the type of weapon'), all sorts of militant stuff about discipline, and brashness about poetry ('we aren't writing odes to the immortality of cockchafers'). His 'freshness' can no longer hide his silly shallowness.

Maaßen gabbled and was slow-handclapped off; Baumert dithered around because Kunert spoke for a long time about his (Baumert's) talent, was laughed at and had to step down from the lectern; Kaul let off rhetorical fireworks, spoke without a single written note, put in a plea for Hacks, quoted the previous speaker with phenomenal accuracy and told—this was the most memorable bit— an anecdote: he had talked to the federal prosecutor in Karlsruhe, who said, 'It is not yet certain, Mr Kaul, which of us will die a natural death,' to which Kaul replied, 'If someone put a rope around your neck and pulled, it would be the most natural thing in the world.'

Felsenstein made a clever speech in polished language: about quality, about the readiness to apply the distinction of 'mastery'; Sandberg talked about his rather complicated concept of modernity ... and then the sackcloth and ashes started to rain down. Langhoff made a display of self-criticism about his production of Hacks' *Worries and Power*:[248] he had been dazzled by Hacks' talent. It was pretty embarrassing. Anyway, he's a great actor; I remember with pleasure his privy councillor in Hauptmann's *Before Sunset*.[249] And there was demonstrative applause when he stepped up to the

248 *Die Sorgen und die Macht* (1962) by Peter Hacks.
249 *Vor Sonnenuntergang* (1931) by Gerhart Hauptmann.

podium. There was much stirring in general and an excited mood in the room; there was laughter and loud murmuring, there were interjections, and it seemed to me (as far as I could judge from the top table) that most sympathies were with the critics. There were moments which were later described in the foyer as a 'witch-hunt': when members of the Politburo or Walter Ulbricht himself interrupted those justifying themselves with questions or accusations, or said, 'You don't even believe that yourself', or: 'That's not true, you're just trying to trivialize', and when there was suddenly talk about forming groups. But the witch-hunt atmosphere disappeared during the course of the conference, perhaps out of insight, perhaps due to the reaction in the room—those silent, ambiguous changes in mood that are nevertheless hard to ignore.

Everyone agreed on the subject of Kunert. 'Mass-produced people' cut no ice here. Old hat and not even attractive. Stern's offence seemed pardonable to me: a sentence on form and content, about how only content, but not form, can be dangerous. One can argue about this, as far as possible among professionals, but it should not be construed as political misconduct. Harald Hauser had 'uncertainties about the personality cult'. He asked too many questions, some perhaps provocative. He was sharply reprimanded and interrupted several times by W.U. when he spoke of his own behaviour. He must have gone through a terrible time: his hair is white and I was shocked when I saw him. I know too little about the debate in the Berlin union to [. . .] judge whether the sharp rebuke was justified [. . .] However, I know [?] to be a good, experienced comrade, and I don't think that people like Stern and Hermlin—who have decades of war and emigration and concentration camps behind them—would spread reckless or wilfully wrong ideas.

We spent the first night with Wolfgang Schreyer and Jens at the Press Club. Later Caspar joined us [. . .].

I was glad to have my old Wolfgang to myself again for a few hours. I don't know where our mutual affection springs from, our shy connection; we are so fundamentally different. Wolfgang is what you would call an experienced man, but in my company, he behaves like a schoolboy. [...] I was nineteen when we met, and he took care of me like a real friend, and I haven't forgotten any of it.

Lodging in the Christian hospice . . . On the bedside table a little book with daily sayings. The saying for the 26th (2nd day of the conference) was something like: 'I cry out to you, Lord, and you bow down to me in your mercy.' And that's how it was too.

Hoy., 6.4.

The cultural conference is receding more and more in my mind. My memories are fading. We admired Hermlin: he showed dignity and poise, spoke in a measured way (how we would have loved to mock him, every inch his lordship), defended himself cleverly and reservedly, did not distance himself as was apparently expected by Biermann and Kunert, and said he had made mistakes but did not consider himself immune to these mistakes in the future, and therefore asked not to be given any more responsibility [...]

Rodenberg talked his hackneyed utter rubbish—along with cinema rubbish—and kept taking pot-shots at young people, including me and my film. At lunch he'd showed fake innocence when I told him that my film was going to be cancelled. When I was talking to Kolus (the TV wants to do *Arriving*), Wischnewski stopped by and patted me on the shoulder and said: 'We'll come through all right.' Got to know the small, lively Mäde. Dieter Noll looks awful—yellow and grey, and his face twitches all the time.

Walter Ulbricht held the closing speech. Before that, I was trembling. I remembered all too well that meeting with him before Christmas. But this time he was very different, and my wariness

relaxed until, in the end, I even laughed: he made a few clever jokes
(I remember that he compared our 1st Union Secretary Braun—
whom we call 'General Twit'—to a traffic warden whose only function is to manage the different directions taken in the union.) He
spoke full of understanding and in a reconciliatory way, winding
up with the demand that the old stories should be left in peace and
we should look to the future: less talking, more writing. And for all
its rigid principles, it was encouraging for the artists, and I no
longer believe in a 'hard phase'.

He also gratified me by citing a few sentences by comrade
writer Reimann, from my article in the *Forum*. Afterwards, I found
out from Nahke that the article had caused trouble, and they weren't
going to print it because it was too critical and raised too many neg-
ative topics. N. was triumphant: the very next morning he wanted
to call the relevant department in the Central Committee, since HE
had approved the article. That's how simple cultural policy is . . .

[. . .]

My *Brothers and Sisters* still hasn't arrived. What do I do all
day? I don't know. I'm constantly writing letters, answering surveys,
attending meetings—it's enough to drive you crazy, and I'm as off
kilter and dissatisfied as it gets. Sometimes I don't think I can write
any more . . . [. . .] Richter and Langer from the district leadership
visited us recently: lots of preaching about morals, demands from
society. I swore the oath I have agreed upon with Jon: no intimate
relations. They pestered me with ghastly accusations about his
change of direction. When they suggested organizing a discussion
in the Circle of Active Artists on the sorry matter, I gladly agreed:
on the condition that I'd be allowed to point my finger at each and
every one of those sitting in judgement and be allowed to talk about
their love affairs . . .

My superiors chose not to go ahead with this sensational session. They know too much about each other and worry that I know

too much as well—although the others are better at hiding their affairs.

[...]

Hoy, Good Friday, 18.4.

Working on the damned survey.

[...]

Union conference on Wednesday. Put my foot in it again in every possible way: business contracts, the quality of my colleagues' work, who complained about publishers always sending back their manuscripts. Fierce debates about the poetry evening: I attacked Jochen, who showed off as a 'representative of the working class' and accused us of adopting the wrong ideological point of view (because of Bergner's poem). The word 'platform' was bandied about again [...].[250] Lewin sat next to me and smiled, then asked me later on if I wanted to join the Party. The poetry discussion will continue in the AJA[251] next week. [...] In the morning, I got the review copies of *Brothers and Sisters*. The illustrations by Bartsch have turned out well. He wrote in the *Forum* how difficult the work was. At night I read my book. I was happy: there wasn't any part I felt ashamed of.

Hoy, 23.4.63

And more sessions and meetings, and yet another bitter dispute in the union about the poetry evening. This time I was supported by Jon and Siggi Bauer, who forgot his chronic fear of poverty for once and courageously attacked his employers, and Jochen wriggled like an eel and tried to slip through the net, spitting indiscriminately at everyone. Finally, Lewin intervened; he had been sitting there

250 The word platform in this context referred to a subgroup within the Party.
251 AJA (Arbeitsgemeinschaft Junger Autoren): Working Group of Young Writers.

calmly, looking sleepy as usual (his 'Chinese presence', as Schreyer calls it). He then took down Comrade Jochen quietly and decisively, and even the 'Creature', his intimate friend Klaus, had an opinion this time. (At some point I'm going to write a story about the Creature).

Otherwise: hideous crisis, depression and gloomy despair. My brigade is making demands and I already know I'll have to disappoint them: they want me to write the story of the brigade. Not even clever Järkel understands that the things which seem tremendously important to the brigade probably won't interest others; and consideration and friendships will stand in my way, and their demands will probably end up in organized provincialism. [. . .] The story of the comrade and the Catholic girl now appeals to me more and more. Yesterday I received a letter from Bodo Uhse urging me to write an essay for *Sinn und Form*. Perhaps, I hope, his request will spur me on to work in a rational, meaningful way again at last. I can't stand this unproductive phase any more.

[. . .]

I bailed out of dear old Defa. We had an executive meeting on Tuesday and people demanded changes that I didn't want to make nor had the skill. I refused and suggested they find an experienced scriptwriter. Surprise, shock, and in the end, grudging consent. I left the room a free man. But they still want to work with me in the future. They even paid me the completion bonus. I'm still in credit—or have I become the sort of personality whose name guarantees success? Hard to imagine. I'm supposed to meet my new director in two weeks. Michel has been booted out—his children's film was bad. [. . .]

I've been waiting nervously since last week for news of baby's (or Pirino's) arrival. It was due to come striding into the world last Monday when we were at home, but no message from Burg. I'm worried about my little D-sister. She's suddenly all adult, bouncing around with her big baby belly and mothering me, her old, infertile sister. My U-brother is in a 'steady relationship'. I've met her: an intellectual girl with glasses and an energetic face, a medical student. She's definitely going to hang on to my unruly, hot-tempered brother.

Hoy., 28 4.

Susanne was born on the 22nd April. My little sister went through a terrible ordeal [. . .]. We're going home in two weeks so I can have a go at carrying around the baby and giving her a bath.

Party meeting in my brigade on Wednesday. I'm gradually starting to understand the fights between section leadership and brigade. The area secretary just talked, talked, talked: 'our people, the perspective, we orient ourselves on . . .'. The whole dictionary of jargon. But we heckled him to death and his catchphrases burst like soap bubbles. I still don't understand what drives these people— comrades—to sabotage the efforts of a brigade.—Next week I'm going to be trained in welding. I'll be an apprentice to Järkel. We have to weld pipes, which even my clumsy mitts can't ruin completely.

Yesterday, poor Daniel got a telegram from Rentzsch about the first half of his radio play: it was too literary, the language too decorative . . . I came home just at the right time to find Daniel sitting in the car, about to speed away to work off his rage and distress. How can a book be 'too literary'? [. . .] Does it only seem that way, or am I luckier with work and have fewer difficulties than he does? Something always gets in his way. Maybe I've just forgotten my misery; they say mothers quickly forget the pain of childbirth.

I admit that I'm starting to whine about my new story. No, not another line about my confusion and helplessness. The whole thing is making my physically ill. Yesterday, at Jon's, I had a dreadful heart seizure and starting crying. Bloody literature. I was at his place: first we sunbathed, played on the carpet and tussled . . . [. . .] We seduce each other over and over again, it's like our first time over and over again, the fall of man over and over again—and we're happy and amazed that it's like this after such a long time. Two and a half years, in which time most marriages go stale. But we don't get used to each other [. . .] we're even shy in front of each other despite all our passion and abandon.

3.5.

Just written the first three lines for *Farewell to the Lily*[252]—the same three lines for the dozenth time. Call from the ministry yesterday: I was asked to write a contribution for the book to commemorate Ulbricht's 70th birthday. I can't, I just can't. A thousand invitations. Completely shattered. People only have to talk to me and I burst into tears. I don't know anything any more, there's only deep dissatisfaction and excruciating unease.

Petzow, 13.5.

Just arrived, sitting on the terrace, the sun's shining, the wind's blowing and the lake is choppy.

Three days in Burg to admire little sister's baby. This morning I cried a bit because I don't have a baby. Susanne is adorably sweet of course, three weeks old and good as gold. She has long, black hair and the tiniest little fingers imaginable, and her little finger nail is the size of a pin head. I was allowed to wake her up each time [. . .], and the way the little babe wakes up is the most charming and touching thing of all—with stretching and clenched fists and lots of yawning and her tongue sticking out and the most wonderful grimaces. A miracle: the whole little creature is just a miracle. I was allowed to change and bathe her and was terrified because she was

252 *Abschied von der Lilie.*

so fidgety and wet and slippery. And those sweet rolls of fat on her neck, arms and legs . . .

Oh, it's all worth much more than a book and more than the acknowledgement that one has moved up to the front row of new literature. I'm being showered with compliments. Ebert wrote a page in the *Forum* about 'betrayed feelings'; Uhse writes in his 'Diary' (in the *Sonntag*) about my story, and he has written me a beautiful letter which I'm very proud of. He's one of the few to have recognized and named the sweet-uncanny nature of this sibling love. But bitterness always shines through, the unease—and more than unease—of an era which takes the pleasure of writing away from the writer; it's still an 'ill-fated passion'.

What's been going on all these weeks? I don't know; a lot of meetings, I think, dozens of books which I read, despairing at my inability to write. At night, walks with Jon when I forgot everything, including the day and my age, and we kissed on dark paths, and we seesawed and choked with laughter on children's playgrounds, and Jon spun me around on a children's roundabout until some disapproving people stared out of the windows, and we fled giggling into the bushes. Daniel was horrified: new national literature on a roundabout . . . That evening I was very cheerful and happy.

The ministry and Aufbau have both rung me a dozen times, harassing me for the article in honour of Walter Ulbricht. But I'm on strike, even if I end up on their blacklist for all eternity. We so *do* have a cult of personality!

Petzow, 20.5.

Today a letter from Jon has to come at long last. I'm dying of impatience and anxiety. We're just too stupid; neither of us notices how much we love each other! [. . .]

It's raining. It's a cold May; we've only had a few days of sunshine. I'm lying outside and gradually turning darkish brown. I'm always thinking of little Susanne and her tiny head that fits right into my hand.

I'm not working—I'm not even thinking about work except when I'm forced to: Dorschan came for the long-awaited radio play; Günter sometimes comes (still nothing's happening with our film); a journalist interviewed me; Kuhntz from the Kubu[253] came to recruit me as a member of the Presidential Council, but I refused. Every day I read another ode to *Brothers and Sisters* in a different newspaper but it's more likely to put a strain on me: how will my new book turn out? I'm considered to be among the vanguard of our national writers, and I'm afraid I won't live up to these expectations in the future.

Petzow, 28.5.

Three days' writers' conference in insane heat. The discussion was not up to the usual standard; for the first time, the meeting ended sooner than planned because there were no more contributions to the discussion. None of the 'vanguard' spoke up except Neutsch. As Caspar said, Dr Koch's presentation was very clever and very boring. K. has been elected first secretary, and that's the cleverest idea the Writers' Union has had for a long time. Lewin is literary secretary, Anna Seghers is the chair again. We also elected a new board (elected—well, we confirmed the list drawn up by the secretariat in a top-secret ballot); I'm on it. There was much talk about *Brothers and Sisters*; Uhse told me that if it'd been published two weeks earlier, he would have fought for it to win the Heinrich Mann Prize. Bad luck. Anna Seghers tried to tell me something about it but I couldn't understand her despite Bodo's help, and she apologized the whole time for being such a clumsy critic, but I always have the feeling she can see through to the furthest corner

---

253 Deutscher Kulturbund: German Cultural Association, founded in 1945 as the Cultural Association for the Democratic Renewal of Germany.

of my brain, the 'snake pit' of ambition and egocentricity. In any case, we understood each other enough to know that men don't take literature seriously and set more store by a woman's smile than her books. She also said something about Sappho, and I just stood there, helpless and stupid, staring at her and unable to say a word. She has a charming smile and looks as if she were three feet outside reality and what's going on around her.

Abusch took me aside and praised me, and I grinned stupidly again. How come I can write a clever book but once I get up from my desk, I turn into an incredibly stupid nitwit? (My friends even say I just pretend when I'm writing.) Abusch said I hadn't just written a beautiful and clever, patriotic book, but above all an enchanting one, and that reading it had given him a pleasure he hadn't felt in years with any of our new literature: it was charming, he said. And Ilberg: 'I'm not going to write about your book, that would be too sissy of me.'

On the first night, we were invited to Uhse's place. He lives with Mrs Werzlau, whom he divorced his Alma for. Caspar told us he normally protects his new lady from any visitors. But we met her. She's already doing that narrow-minded wives' thing of putting down her husband in front of other people by being indiscreet—without intending to, of course.

Hours of conversation in which we tried to work out the secret of provincialism—in vain as it turns out. We forgot to include talent, and we're not even blessed with talent.

Spent the next evening with Günter Caspar in the Press Club, and the third at his place. He had a good West German recording of the *Threepenny Opera*. [. . .]

Jon is hungry (but he doesn't complain). I've sent him some money. He was so weak that he couldn't do his shift. His job on the dumper truck is backbreaking. We've been speaking more often on the phone. I told him he should go to my flat and call me from there. The radio company he's writing a play for has refused to pay the retainer because he hasn't got a name yet. He told Buerschaper that the radio people should ask people with names to write their plays if that's the case. [. . .]

Hoy., 5.6.

[. . .] The first news: Bergner plagiarized his poems from a Polish poet. The circumstances are kind of amusing, but I find the whole thing criminal. So, no young genius from Cottbus after all.

The last beautiful days in Petzow . . . midsummer heat. Jens came on Monday and spent the whole day fishing tirelessly on the jetty, kitted out in a jacket and flat cap. Once we'd played and messed around for long enough, we sat in the lounge or up in his room and had wonderful conversations. Later Arnold Zweig came, tiny and frail, hanging onto his wife's arm; he's almost blind. Everyone stopped talking as soon as he entered the room. I wonder what it feels like to have achieved everything worth aspiring to in life? I remember a few pages from Zola's diary.

The sweet, dark movement from the *New World* Symphony.

Jens was sad when we left. And then this town swallowed us up again with its meticulous rows of houses, its gossip and irritating, bumbling officials. And worst of all, you gradually find yourself sinking to their level. When did I start enjoying vulgar gossip? When did I start arguing seriously with numbskulls? When did I start taking my afternoon walk past the architectural monstrosities here, like I did last Sunday, past drunks sitting in front of the restaurants who harass me?

Jon and I were reunited. I visited him every day [. . .]. In the mornings I wake up with a start from dreams and want to go to him. At the same time, there is so much about him that bothers me [. . .].

Yesterday, I got a long letter from Prof. Kurella.

Hoy., 17.6.

I've long since made up with him, failings and all. We walked around town and argued, and then sat by the roadside in the white moonlight, and what else could I do but kiss this ugly fellow K[. . .]? He's now over the worst; he received a few marks from Aufbau [. . .].

Last week we went to Dresden together, while Daniel went to Berlin to see his parents at last—it's been almost five years. They came from Hanover for a day. They had a nice time, but Daniel came home that night very unhappy: he felt the ill-fated border between him and them. It must have been terrible to say goodbye at Friedrichstraße station: people trying to watch their parents or children leave were driven back by our policemen's rifle butts.

Jon and I rode in a bus trailer in oppressive heat, being bumped around terribly and I almost cried with exhaustion. I don't want to be poor again. I don't want to be crammed into a bus again with sweaty, stinking people after having a car. Jon was angry: I'm selfish and unfair—the others would also prefer to go by car—and of course he's right [. . .].

This time, though, my money didn't help: the shops were in a shabby state and the department stores were full of ugly flags made of the cheapest fabric. Brocade evening gowns and Jacques Hein dresses were on display in—empty—Exquisit shops for ludicrous prices: clothes no working woman can wear. Prosperity is marching, prices are soaring; a pair of Synthetex trousers, which you could buy eight weeks ago for 53 marks, costs 100 today. [. . .] We sat for a while in the Zwinger palace courtyard, and when the wind changed direction, the fountain sprayed us with a veil of mist. Next to us sat a group of Soviet soldiers with shaved heads. They didn't behave like museum visitors.

I don't know what's happened to me. I'm in love. I feel as if my heart will shatter when I think of Jon—and when don't I think about him? [. . .] The earth moves when he moves. I've discovered a blissful joy in love which used to seem frivolous or even amoral. We're not shy any more about trying to beat each other in the highest level of desire and pleasure. [. . .] I shake when he kisses me in the middle of the conversation. He looks at me in the middle of a fight and says: Take off your clothes. [. . .] When I'm tired, he covers me in a blanket and holds my hand, tells me stories or sings outrageous songs to make me laugh.

Today I have sentenced myself to not seeing him. I'm dying of desire.

Hoy., 18.6.

This morning at 9.00 we were supposed to take the Vindobona[254] to Prague. We were so looking forward to it, had the travel bug, were dreaming of Prague; Wolfgang Schreyer had given me 1,000 korunas from his private account (he sometimes makes these touching gestures like a faithful old friend), and dear Prof. Kurella had written: 'Travel! You have to see the big wide world, and even if you can't make it to Florence or Madrid for the time being, the whole East is open to you . . . .' Yes, shit! Two days before leaving we received a telegram, and yesterday the letter with the reason: 'the situation among Czech writers is very complicated, as was proven once again at their last writers' congress; in addition, our literature does not find the recognition we would like in the ČSSR' . . . In short, the Writers' Union prefers not to send its underage sheep into a cave of ideologically untrustworthy wolves. We appreciate Mr Görlich's concern.[255] These Slavs even read Kafka apparently! Although we didn't find out what horrors happened at the congress

254 Express train from Berlin to Vienna via Budapest.

255 Günter Görlich (1928–2010): the secretary of the Writers' Union; wrote to B.R. and S.P. on 14 June 1963: 'We fear that our Czech colleagues are hardly able to take care of you at the moment.'

('information is objectivism'), we at least heard on RIAS that writers were the 'conscience of the nation' who supported the posthumous rehabilitation of suspected agents murdered during the Stalin era. But the GDR, playing the guard dog of Europe once again, practises the only correct arts policy and, gradually, one taboo country after another is added to the list: Poland, Czechoslovakia, Hungary . . . Today the plenary session in the Soviet Union begins;[256] Ilyichov, whom we reprinted so diligently in the past, will make a speech, and God forbid a repeated pendulum swing to the left.

We feel angry and sad. What a country! The doctrine of purity—'for Germans only'. To hell with these repulsive, stubborn, boneheaded zealots and proselytizers. I'm ashamed to belong to these people; I'm ashamed that idiotic 'blueshirts'[257] like Görlich are my colleagues. They're still the soldiers and schoolmasters they've always been.

Discussion last week about *Brothers and Sisters* in the factory plant. [. . .]

Jon and I suffered. Not a kind word about my poor *Brothers and Sisters*, just jargon regurgitated by robots whose switch had been flipped to 'literary discussion'. And then, 'sentimentalism', scandalous in this context. I still remember it. Back then people said 'human sentimentalism'.

Hoy, 24.6.

We made it through the workers' festival.[258] Willi Lewin visited us on Thursday. He has Daniel's cast-iron charm when he tries to say

256 A special Ideological Commission of the Central Committee (of the Communist Party of the Soviet Union) was held on 18 June 1963. The commission, set up in 1962 by Khrushchev under Leonid Ilyichov, a member of the Party Secretariat, operated an extremely repressive policy towards the arts. (See Rosalind J. Marsh, *Soviet Fiction Since Stalin: Science, Politics and Literature*. New Jersey: Barnes and Noble, 1986.)

257 A reference to FDJ zealots.

258 Fifth Workers' Festival in Cottbus, 21–23 June 1963.

nice things to me. He's so nicely schizophrenic [...]. L. offered me his support if I wanted to join the Party. But I don't want to. I have too many doubts and I couldn't keep my mouth shut or say yes for the Party's sake.

[...]

Book bazaar in Cottbus on Saturday. Dieter Noll was there. All of the Central Committee's elite was strolling about. Chatted to Abusch for a while, who had visited Hoy. The district minions were standing nearby and trembling. I imagine they probably pulled themselves together before the higher authorities arrived. Got a gentle rebuke from A., because I didn't collaborate on the Ulbricht book. But he took it back right away: the deadline had been very tight. I want to know what he really thinks about this kind of cultish homage.—Spent the evening with Noll.

Hoy., 1.7.

I've long since made up with Jon again, of course; we had a huge scene with tears and hitting and wild accusations and counter allegations, without quite knowing why. Sometimes I dread the thought that I might become sexually dependent on him, or he on me. I've always been scornful of sexual dependency and at the same time, it seems sweetly dangerous. Now I've tasted the other side of that sweetness. [...] I want to scream, tear him apart and cry with happiness at the same time, I want to be flesh of his flesh. His shoulders are covered with bite wounds, and afterwards I kiss the bloody marks, and he lies beside me and looks at me with his fingertips. It's torture to walk across the street without being allowed to stop, kiss, touch each other's hips.

Hoy., 3.7.

Bodo Uhse is dead. When I first heard the news, I thought: suicide. I still see his furrowed boy's face that evening when we were with him. He was bitter and sad. He drank a lot, and there are those kinds of suicides. We couldn't believe it at first and it still hasn't sunk in. We really loved him. He was just on his way to becoming a great writer: the essay on Venturelli, the Rivera story. I envied him his deep understanding of art and his beautiful relationship to it; his literary replication of the process of painting reminded me of Thomas Mann. His kinship with music. And he was chivalrous— but not in the modern way of being fair or gentlemanlike—and these qualities alone made him remarkable in a country where the men are as unchivalrous as in ours.

He was only 59. We feel sad. It's hard to grasp that we won't see him again. It's unfair. I can remember with intense clarity our first meeting in Petzow, every turn of his head, his gesture of defeat when he pointed to the scattered pages—notes for his essays in the volume *Figures and Problems*[259]—and I hear his voice again when he said to us, 'You'll finish what I can no longer do.'

[. . .]

Hoy, 9.7.

I've been wanting to write for a week about the reception at the State Council—Ulbricht's birthday—but I was suddenly seized by such an urgency to work that I wrote down the treatment of the planned TV film in a few days, surprising even myself. [. . .]

Read Alexei Ignaticv's *Fifty Years in the Ranks* and—great discovery—the *French Notebooks* by Ilya Ehrenburg, which moved me intensely. On every page, I find agreement, which makes me feel triumphant and happy, and clearly formulated ideas that were only blurred sketches in my head. A hundred lines of his essay on Stendhal relate directly to me. It's encouraging too: I can't be a fool after all because I've come to the same conclusions as the intellectual

259 *Gestalten und Probleme* (1959).

Ehrenburg. I find his essays more interesting than his novels; he's a wonderful expert in French literature, which attracts me more and more, year after year. I'm encouraged by all he has to say about realism—and what diverges from our official cultural policy. And this too: the French writers' love of painting and architecture. So is it a coincidence that I am also attracted to these related arts?

Tomorrow I'm going to Berlin to visit Professor Henselmann,[260] who will show me his construction site, the design for a wall frieze, the plan for a dome construction—he wants, so he writes, to put me to use. I'm afraid I won't pass the test . . .

So, the reception . . . Dynamo Sports Arena, a red carpet which the Holy Trinity strode across in unison, a standing banquet (with bananas!), bubbly, a lot of interesting and then just loud conversations with Prof. Koch, Sindermann, a thousand people I don't know, with Erik Neutsch, who tried to recruit me for the Halle district. The best impression: the three workers from the plant who guided me everywhere, covered in medals—clever, capable, tactful and very self-confident people, who moved around the banquet as if they were having lunch at home.

Hoy, 14.7.

Back from Berlin. I'll write about Henselmann when I have more time—we, Daniel and I, fell madly in love with him and his whole family.

An evening with Caspar. He's now giving Daniel a grant so he can feel independent of me at last. Visited Jens briefly. Didn't like it—he was too much the poet.

---

260 Hermann Henselmann (1905–95): influential architect. Appointed head architect of the city of Berlin in 1953, he designed flagship buildings for East Berlin such as the Haus des Lehrers and Congress Hall in Alexanderplatz and the housing complex of Leninplatz.

Yesterday a letter came from Jon and in the afternoon he called me, having just come from the train station. Being stubborn I hadn't given him a sign of life all that time: I wanted to know how I would bear up without him—I didn't want to feel so damned reliant on him. In the evening I went over; he looks better [...]. We were shy and happy [...] and suddenly I had to cry: it's nice that we're back together. He brought me black lingerie (we laughed with embarrassment) and of course jelly babies and liquorice ...

Today I've been lying on the couch all day reading Zola's *Lourdes* and feeling very ill among so many cripples.

Hoy., 18.7.

Monday in Berlin again. University Clinic. Operation expected next week.[261] [...] In the evening at the Press Club [...]. A few noisy people in the club were pretending to be bohemian, but they weren't worldly wise, just another breed of provincial. In the afternoon I sat alone in the press cafe for a while, which was teeming with suspicious-looking girls and Levantines ('camel-drivers', as they say in Berlin)—beautiful Orientals who study here or in the West and diligently hustle on the side. Two female students at my table: one was 'in a tight spot again'—and as I was busy 'reading', craftily turning the pages unread, they talked about the next urgent abortion, the address for which Anita from the 'Sofia' would get them. Prices were signposted across the table. They were smoking HBs that Americans had thrown to them from their cars. The girl in the tight spot gazed around from under her blue eyeshadow and described her philosophy on life: it divided people into men with and without a car, the latter hardly belonging to the human race. All around, amateur whores, perhaps sent to study by their bosses. Well, Berlin is a stupid, rather unappetizing sort of Babel. But the lime trees at Friedrichstraße train station smelt so sweet [...].

261 A breast-reduction operation.

I still haven't written about Henselmann, perhaps fearing I might go into rhapsodies [. . .] I'd balked at his invitation for a long time because I know that I get dumbstruck by my awkward shyness. But my fear vanished as soon as we arrived his house (Uhse's former house in Niederschönhausen) when he came walking towards us. True, I was quieter than usual, overwhelmed by impressions: the whole family gathered with a real banquet in our honour, and all his children are personalities—natural and self-confident, quick-witted and clever—and there was a trusting tone between the parents and the children which revealed their beautiful friendship. Henselmann drank huge amounts of wine in his enthusiasm; he was immediately on first-name terms with us (but not in that over-familiar way—we were taken into the fold like brothers and sisters). He embraced and kissed us effusively: he's so alive, boundless, impulsive and sensitive, he's kind, he's an artist, he's bursting with vitality—a wonderful person. He's full of anecdotes, knows all the prominent figures, was a friend of Brecht's. He gets overheated, loud and enthusiastic, cunning and melancholic, goes back to laughing—the man is one big firework, a volcano of ideas and passions [. . .]. He loves *Brothers and Sisters*, the whole family cried when they read it and—I'm not kidding—they started crying at the table again when they told me about it: it was adorable, I was happy. H. thinks I'm going to be a great writer. He was so boundless in his praise that it made me deeply, awkwardly embarrassed. I die of fear when I'm praised: What if I disappoint him with the next book?

The next morning he came to the hotel for breakfast. One more thing that makes him so adorable: he is a glorious egoist, overflowing with feeling and tells me about himself, his family and very intimate details with an openness that alienated me at first: it was as if we'd know each other for years, had laughed cried together a hundred times . . . We then visited the construction sites in the morning, and he showed us his culture centre[262] which is modern

262 Haus des Lehrers, Alexanderstraße.

and generous in its design—and for which he was criticized that same evening. He was terribly depressed, then he laughed again slyly: 'I'm going to have regrets. I'm going to keep building.' We visited Womacka's[263] studio; W. is working on a two-storey-high frieze for the house. What I don't like about his oil paintings is resolved here in the best possible way: the frieze is colourful and bubbling over cheerfully with gold and silver and vivid colours.

We went out for lunch and talked all afternoon. [...] In the meantime he's written to us: he was very harshly criticized in front of a silent plenary,[264] [...] He's been through a terrible few days. [...]

Hoy., 22.7.

The day before yesterday I saw Jon again at last . . . We were so shy, so excited and happy that we couldn't even make love; we lay looking up the sky, smelling the summer evening scents, whispering and kissing. Jon said, 'With you I can walk the streets and argue like you were a pal of mine, and I can make love to you like with a wild cat, and sometimes, in between, you lie there like a real woman.'

We've just said goodbye. Tomorrow I have to go to Berlin, to hospital. I'm terrified. Early this morning I cried. It's so good that Daniel is here, my beloved big brother and tender friend.

---

263 Walter Womacka (1925–2010): artist who designed the Mexican-style mural on the exterior of the Haus des Lehrers, the headquarters of the Berlin Teachers' Association at Alexanderplatz.

264 At the Seventh Plenary Meeting of the German Bauakademie [Academy of Architecture] on 12 July 1963, where ideological issues in architecture were discussed, Henselmann was accused in particular by the academy's vice chairman Prof. Edmund Collein of not promoting industrialization or using prefabricated parts in mass construction. He was also accused of being dissatisfied of what had been achieved to date in GDR building industry, and of passing on his dissatisfaction to younger architects. (See *Deutsche Architektur*, Issue 11, 1963).

An insane summer with drought and tropical heat; no rain for weeks, not even a thunderstorm. Out in the woods, where I sometimes sit in the evenings with Jon, there's an intoxicating smell of corn. The birches are already yellowing.

Yesterday was my 30th birthday. Daniel gave me a tape recorder. He had taped himself reading his story of Lukas Silbermann, as I'd asked him. There are passages in it I consider great literature. [. . .]

In the evening Jon and Buerschaper came over. B. had jazz recordings for me: Charlie Parker, Armstrong, Errol Gardner. Got a huge package from the best family of all.

Berlin, 25.7.

In the Charité hospital since yesterday. I have a single room. The friendly young ward doctor told me that Goebbels and Adele Sandrock had already lain in my bed.

I can wave to Daniel from the balcony when he leaves. Everything is a bit old-fashioned here. 'Venerable' might be the best description for the building. Day and night, the dogs in the research lab opposite bark themselves hoarse—big German shepherds that give the impression they've been vaccinated with flu bugs.

It's so lucky that Daniel is close by today! Henselmann brought me here early in the morning; I stayed at his house the night before. He looked after me in the most touching way, gave me plenty of good advice for dealing with nurses and doctors, and introduced me to everyone here in a way that stunned them into respectful astonishment. He is endearingly vain, and clever enough to show it with irony. When he left, and I was standing alone in my room, I had to cry, and a little later, when I was registering and getting shouted at by an outrageous administrator because some information was missing in my papers, I lost my composure completely. I called Daniel at the hotel. He came immediately, I threw myself in his arms and was comforted. [. . .] Despite my passion for Jon, I only feel secure with Daniel [. . .].

We met Henselmann for lunch on our first day in Berlin. He was badly affected by the bitter, angry criticism he'd received from the Association of German Architects,[265] the Party group and the academy, although he tried to gloss over it by joking. He spoke of the 'dictatorship of the untalented'. He was accused of ambiguities on the issue of industrialization. I can't yet say the extent to which the allegations are justified, but it seems to me that H. is right in saying that we all need those average kinds of architects who build clean, good, functional buildings, but none of that should be considered fine architecture. I can find many parallels with our concerns over literature.

They also claim that he seduces the young. This is true. He seduced us, and we are over the moon about it. But the claim that 'young people' have turned away from him in disappointment, as Ullmann says, doesn't seem credible to me. We always meet young people at his place [. . .]. Strange, by the way, how often intelligence goes hand in hand with good looks in this generation. Or has my notion of beauty changed so much? H. thinks I'm pretty too, even if I would describe my face as ugly, almost coarse. I have none of that clear-skinned fineness or daintiness that I admire in some girls. Well, that's just by the by.

In the afternoon we met Ullmann, the Party Secretary of the VEB Berlin project, who had asked me for an appointment. The Party group is worried about me, because I've fallen into the hands of the professor, a demagogue. [. . .] It's all pretty touching, but also annoying and it was only my interest in twisted people that made me to promise to speak more often and in more detail to U. about all my problems. He sees H. as a kind of attractive devil (he even compared him to Klaus Mann's *Mephisto*), thinks he's politically

---

265 Bund deutscher Architekten, founded in 1903.

dangerous, professionally uninteresting—a 'dazzling soap bubble', as he called him. He expresses the kind of loathing for him one can only feel for a former idol.

Of course the conversation revolved around industrialization again—construction using prefabricated parts—and of course U. is right: we must build as quickly and as cheaply as possible. Although he asserted that it isn't a question of generation, there was a constant insinuation that the 'old generation' couldn't be trusted because they haven't grasped the necessity of industrial construction, or have even sabotaged it. But it seems to me that these standard buildings don't represent the face of socialist architecture, even if their facades have a variety of designs.

I suspect that modern architecture is similar in the East and West. What if architecture is not too closely tied to class; what if it were the expression of a modern attitude of mind that we share— many aspects of it at least—with the West? I have to think it over; it's probably not Marxist. But Marxism, too, must be revised; it has to be brought up to date with the latest state of science, which lies in the nature of the matter. The Chinese letter was a warning shot,[266] and things that still sound heretical today (why have we taken on that expression from the Inquisition, even if only for unofficial use?) will be taken for granted tomorrow. Who would have guessed three years ago that the VVB[267] would work along the principle of corporations—that the directors would be called 'corporate

266 The Chinese letter: 'On the Open Letter of the Central Committee of the Communist Party of the Soviet Union' (in *ND*, 20 July 1963). The resolution was a response to a letter from the Central Committee of the Communist Party of China dated 14 June 1963 to its Soviet counterpart. The SED leadership accused the Chinese communist leaders of dogmatism and a lack of social democracy.

267 VVB (Verein Volkseigener Betriebe): Association of State-Owned Businesses, the economic governing body of companies and plants in GDR industry. With the introduction of the 'New Economic System of Planning and Management', which had been adopted by the Economic Conference of the Central Committee of the SED and the Council of Ministers (24–25 June 1963), the VVB was granted greater independence.

owners'? The economy is being overhauled and turned around; but only recently, people were barred from the Central Committee and even punished for hinting at ideas practised today. And besides, we are all victims of Stalinism.

Speaking of Stalin: the part of the conversation with U. that got on my nerves most was about Stalinallee,[268] now renamed Karl-Marx-Allee, and later, people joke, it will be called Mao-Tse-Tung-Allee. U., indignant and embittered, accuses H. of building in 'wedding-cake style'.

Berlin, 26.7.

Yesterday interrupted, very pleasantly, by Daniel and my old Walter Lewerenz, whom he had dragged along. The publisher sent me red roses. We drove together into the city, to the ritzy Ganymede wine bar, where they serve an excellent plum brandy. W. talked about the ridiculous and vile insider intrigues at Neues Leben, to which the 'clochard' Sellin and our Bruno Peterson have fallen victim. H. once told us that P. was one of the bravest comrades in the resistance movement. He didn't reveal any information, although he was beaten half to death by the Nazis before the Reichstag fire trial.

[...]

I'm making notes on Sartre's *What Is Literature?* (not his most meaningful sentences, but the ones that refer to my thoughts on language and style): '[...] One is not a writer for having chosen to say certain things, but for having chosen to say them in a certain way. And, to be sure, style makes the value of the prose. But it

---

268 Stalinallee, as it was called between 1949 and 1961, was a major thoroughfare in East Berlin redesigned by Henselmann and a group of other GDR architects. In the wake of de-Stalinization following Stalin's death in 1953, it was renamed Karl-Marx-Allee in 1961 and has kept this name to the present day. The buildings are designed in 'wedding-cake style' (in German *Zückerbäckerstil*), i.e. with distinct tiers, each set back from the one below and with ornamental tiling. In the Soviet Union, this style was associated with Stalinist architecture; hence the criticism of Henselmann.

should pass unnoticed. [. . .] Subjects suggest the style; but they do not order it. There are no styles ranged *a priori* outside of the literary art. [. . .] In short, it is a matter of knowing what one wants to write about [. . .]. And when one knows, then it remains to decide how one will write about it. Often the two choices are only one, but among good writers, the second choice never precedes the first [. . .]. If one considers subjects as problems which are always open, as solicitations, as expectations, it will be easily understood that art loses nothing in engagement. On the contrary, just as physics submits to mathematicians new problems which require them to produce a new symbolism, in like manner the always new requirements of the social and the metaphysical engage the artist in finding a new language and new techniques. If we no longer write as they did in the eighteenth century,. it is because the language of Racine and Saint-Evremond does not lend itself to talking about locomotives or the proletariat. After that, the purists may forbid us to write about locomotives. But art has never been on the side of purists."[269]

Noon.

Just spent an hour in the photo lab. I talked to the photographer (he studied pedagogy) about psychoanalysis and hormones and found out abominable things about hybrids and hermaphrodites. Crazy material for a book: you can artificially breed homosexuals through hormone injections, you can split personalities, change their psyches, the build of their bodies. He showed me pictures of men who had received hormone injections for prostate diseases, after which they grew breasts like women. Things are getting interesting here in this institute. This morning, I had a debate with the professor: he abhors Rilke and won't accept anything written after Goethe. The young doctor stood next to him and smiled. He

---

269 Jean-Paul Sartre, *What Is Literature?* (Bernard Frechtman trans.) (London: Routledge Classics, 1993), pp. 16–17.

seems—if I can venture the word—more progressive than many of his colleagues, who still distrust and loathe the state.

To counter the professor's claim that literature had no effect, he gave the example of the USSR and their mass readership.

Tonight, for the first time in weeks, a long thunderstorm. It was high time: the trees had started shedding their leaves. Yesterday temperatures reached 40°.

[...]

Berlin, 27.7.

Henselmann has just been here, with a Polish black-haired doll, which he presented to me as a 'portrait of a grandmother'. We chatted for an hour, about eroticism among other things, and of course about architecture. The criticism in Karl-Marx-Stadt was not as harsh as it was in Berlin, and the Party, which still loves its artists (perhaps the way one loves badly behaved but inventive children), has commissioned him to build the German Embassy in Bucharest. I'm going to see him this afternoon. He has been reading *Brothers and Sisters* again [...]. H. said that there are only three or four writers in Germany who are as talented as I am.

Yesterday, I was in town again with my Daniel-husband. He bought me a consolation dress—simple elegance, the way he likes it (I'm more of a peacock)—and for the occasion we even managed to get hold of a nylon anorak, or a 'swallow', as they call them in Berlin. Then we went to the club to eat, I didn't want to call anyone, I wanted to be alone with my guardian angel. Afterwards, back in my room, I felt like crying. [...]

How nice that everyone is so sweet to me. I suffer terribly when people are unfriendly. [...]

Back to Ullmann. He calls H. irresponsible because he built Stalinallee and, in doing so, put back development by ten years:

a brick, cement, a beer,[270] and everything was aimed towards steel and concrete, he says.

Anyone who has a general idea about our economy can disprove this argument: we didn't have steel or concrete at the time. Ullmann continued: all these decorative elements, the whole style— no, H. should have refused. We objected that there were Party orders, or suchlike—which at the time were far stricter than they are today. U. didn't accept this; basically, he reproached H. and the other architects in the same way that we reproach the generation that managed to survive fascism partly undamaged: 'You should have defended yourselves.' I suddenly realized how much more tolerant we are (although we're only a few years younger than U.); those who don't know the background information shouldn't insult the intelligence of those who complied with Stalinism—whether just appearing to, or with conviction.

But now we know that H. really did receive a Party commission at the time, which he refused (and we all know how such refusals were treated). He wanted to leave the Republic and was only held back by Bertolt Brecht, who, himself under suspicion, struggled a whole night long for his soul. That night, they became friends. [. . .]

Berlin, 29.7.

Saturday was another loud, cheerful afternoon and evening with Henselmann [. . .]. In the evening we drank bubbly; it was a kind of farewell party, because today H. is also going to hospital for a general check-up. The excitement of the last few weeks has taken its toll on him. His hands have been trembling wretchedly. [. . .]

Spent the whole day with Jon yesterday. We sat [. . .] in the Trichter with Mieze Frahm and argued about architecture, which

270 An allusion to a bricklayers' song during the GDR called 'Ein Stein, ein Kalk, ein Bier' [a Brick, Cement, a Beer].

nearly turned into a serious row. Jon raged and railed against 'those scoundrels, those pigs who put you in a yoke to carry out their ends, who wrap you in their charms'—he's jealous of H. and what might happen between us. With all the screaming about architecture, we misheard each other again, but what are conversations, after all? Little more than sketches, a great deal of waste; the spaces filled with thoughts, or notions sloppily prepared by the speaker remain empty for the listener or he fills them in according to his own ideas. Later, at the Press Club, we made up, drank a bottle of wine, tried to gossip (but there's not much going on in Hoyerswerda), and then we got on to literature [. . .].

In the evening we strolled through Berlin for a while. The horizon was still apple green, the moon already out. There was a gap between newly plastered facades and leftover ruins, a few benches in the bushes; we sat on a bench in front of an old house with a lit-up balcony, where young people, maybe students, were kissing, and in the room, there was noise and wild dance music, and the occasional, bittersweet tearjerker. And we tried to find it all kitschy. Then it got dark, and we stayed there, watching the moon, listening to the music and cheerfully raucous voices, and we kissed and trembled, and kissed, and it was like a bad film, enough to make you cry.

Then Jon took me back to the Charité.

This morning, in the X-ray institute, I sat opposite a boy with amputated legs.

Berlin, 6.8.

I'm gradually getting back on my feet again. Horrible week, bloody and dirty and hot, full of fever and pain. My Daniel came; once when he called and heard me crying on the phone, he drove here straight from Hoyerswerda. No one compares to him.

Henselmann calls me every day. I got a letter from him today; he has been reading Stendhal's *Diaries* and loves them as much as I do.

Outside August is insanely hot, suffocating and lovely. I'm dying of impatience. I want to get out of here. Reading a lot: Sieburg, Thornton Wilder, Musil (for whom I feel nothing but respect), Jorge Amado's *Gabriela* [. . .].

Berlin, 11.8.

I'm allowed to go home tomorrow. The last days were ugly; blackish blood trickled non-stop from one of my sutures. My breasts look terrible, as if hacked by sabres, but the doctor says that the scars will fade to almost nothing over time.

[. . .]

Hoy., 16.8.

I have bouts of panic about money, and unnecessary expenses make me nervous. There's no reason for serious concern yet—I have a small amount put by, which we can live off for a year. But the worry still remains. I've ditched so many drafts that I'm terrified to death I can't write any more.

Jon has been caring for me tenderly the whole time. He comes every day, buys and cooks lunch for us, and between frying pan and pot he quarrels with me about Sartre, architecture (this, of course, is always aimed at my adored professor) and the socialist attitude to life. Every hour with him means intellectual tension. While I have moved on to something else (something 'concrete', i.e. practical), he stops eating and gives me a lengthy lecture, and although he tires me out, even irritates me, I love him for it: his thoroughness, his abandonment to thought. I'm reading Simone de Beauvoir, *The Second Sex*, and in her analysis, I recognize with dismay many things that happen to us every day—Mrs R. with husband K.—and realize what connects and separates us.

Yesterday, I was at his place again for the first time. When he saw me in the bathroom, he laughed at me: he said he has many more scars. [. . .] I really look quite passable again, the wounds have healed quickly and neatly, and I'm no longer in pain.

[. . .]

Hoy., 20.8.

Daniel is back. We stayed all Sunday in bed, wonderful slobs, drank too much coffee, smoked too many cigarettes and talked, talked, talked . . . We talked about our divorce too. We were amazed to realize that it wouldn't change anything about our relationship: [. . .] we would live together like brother and sister, work together, cook, travel. Some registry office stamp is just an external thing, a concession to our surroundings. We were as united as in our best times together.

[. . .]

Hoy., 27.8.

For two days, Daniel and I have been talking about our divorce. Daniel will file the lawsuit. No, not lawsuit: Monsieur K. should not be mentioned. [. . .]

Over the past three years, I don't think I realized how terribly Daniel suffered. Yesterday he told me that he'd lost his capacity to love me, that he no longer had any love for me—and that despite everything he was clinging to me with a painful affection.

And I, full of self-disgust, felt my vindictiveness rise during our conversation, a vicious, quarrelsome, petty vindictiveness towards him for wanting to put an end to a terrible state . . . [. . .] What am I carping on about? Why can't I find the decency in myself to accept the situation? My energy, praised by all my friends, the brutality that Daniel has started to attribute to me, are only qualities I acquired to save myself from going under. But I sometimes wish, only to myself, that I didn't always need this level of energy, always close to hysteria.

But well, why speculate? Daniel [...] made one last proposal for a mediation: I should send K. away forever, without any face-saving compromise; then we could try to start over from scratch. But can we really do that? [...] And another thing that I can't talk to him about, of course: I have discovered my body and the bliss of physical love with Jon, I am eager for his caresses [...]. Yesterday I walked around as if in a daze. All at once a question hung over everything: what for? [...] I have no one left to care for, no one left to hope for. Jon does not need my care or my hope. But perhaps all my strength and emotion will be invested in my work. Jesus, if it wasn't for my job ...

[...]

Last week, two days with J. in Halle. Discussion about *Divided Heaven*[271] (influenced by an article by that renegade Zehm in *Die Welt*) and *Brothers and Sisters*. [...]

The discovery of journalism once again: After months of hesitation, the *Lausitzer Rundschau* has printed an article about the shortcomings of the new town. An amazing response: I spoke from the residents' heart. Wherever we go, people thank me for my openness in dealing with the problems simmering in this town. I foresee trouble: Hoy is officially considered the model of a beautiful socialist town. But it's a dreary hive of workers.

Met Christa Wolf in Halle. I was pleasantly surprised at how much she's changed; her face has become more feminine, more relaxed, even more delicate since she's been writing; the traces of hardness have disappeared. And—she doesn't dare start a new book

---

271 *Der geteilte Himmel* (1963) by Christa Wolf, published in English translation as *Dvided Heaven* (1976) and *They Divided the Sky* (2013).

and has struck upon a fortunate solution: a biography of Anna Seghers.

Hoy., 13.9.

Criticism is spreading across town. I've stirred up a wasp's nest. A few counterattacks [...]. On the other hand: official endorsements from companies or sections, and the sympathy of my many known—and anonymous—associates. Recently, the government has been making an effort, and the SED district administration has quickly become involved, and is devising plans for a clubhouse—makeshift of course.

[...]

And Jon? The love of my life. New discoveries. He bathes me, and I lie in the green water under mountains of foam (K.'s own formula) and am happy with my body, and Jon crouches beside me and likes it too, and after bathing he wraps me in a big towel and carries me to his bed and, behold, these are new, stirring adventures too.

Ahrenshoop, probably 17. 9.

Only a few minutes break: I'm reading Ehrenburg's *People, Years, Life,*[272] a West German edition; the book won't be published here. I love E's essays more than his novels and the memoir deeply moves me. He knew Modigliani . . . A contemporary of mine yet separated by an endlessly long time, or seeming separate, very close and very far away.

Wolfgang [Schreyer] drove his brother and his terrible sister-in-law to Stralsund today. I'm housesitting. Outside it's foggy; even in the house, everything is damp and cold. From my window I can see the sea in the haze and hear the monotonous—reassuringly

---

272 *Mensch, Jahren, Leben: Memoiren 1960–1965* (1972) by Ilya Ehrenburg; first published uncensored in the GDR in 1978.

monotonous—sound of the waves. Until yesterday we had glorious autumn sunshine and lay on the beach all day. Straight away on the first day—Saturday—I went swimming with Wolfgang at night. It was very chilly, the sea was choppy and we swam out to the sand bank in the dark.

[...]

The house is very nice and spacious under its grey thatched roof. It's a few metres' walk through hard beach grass and across the dunes to the beach. How I love the sea! Wolfgang is a sweet, attentive host. When he left today he said I should go and have breakfast at the table ... He had put a bottle of vodka and a box of chocolates there for me. Sometime in the winter we want to live here on our own for a while. We still have that same shy tenderness for each other. We lie for hours in the sand and talk to each other, in no hurry—there's time here. W. says that I've turned out to be an original personality. Sometimes I find myself strange because of my severity and almost religious resolve.

Hoyerswerda, 2 October 63

Daniel [...] doesn't love me the way he used to—and how could he?—and his gentle, distanced respect makes me feel like I have to fight for him again, win him back—but for what? That's possessiveness, addiction to female triumph.

[...]

On Sunday, I'm flying to Moscow as a delegate of the Writers' Union for German Book Week. First I resisted, and I'm still scared but I'm starting to look forward to it.

Ahrenshoop is a faraway dream. Just the sea, sun, inertia, the heat on my skin, the happy evenings playing Mikado and listening to tapes of American pop music that makes you so wonderfully gaga. Can't even picture it any more. Here there's noise, bustle, phones ringing, aggravation, sometimes a quick pleasure, and haste, haste.

One visit is worth writing about: on Saturday the dean of the Law Faculty at Oxford came over (as a guest of the National Council). An Englishman, if ever there was one—but he's Swabian. [...] He accomplished the feat of liberating me within five minutes of the stupid shyness that comes over me in the presence of strangers. He is one of the most charming men I have ever met, and breath-takingly polite. He didn't sit down until I did, and got up as soon as I left the room, and before he came, he'd read *Brothers and Sisters*, which he said was excellent. He brought something of the 'scent of the big wide world' with him. He has the right to sit at the Queen's table, has eaten with Kennedy and Truman, knows Nikita and is a friend of Agatha Christie and her husband, an archaeologist, (Ch. is apparently similar to the old lady from the *Ladykillers*); he speaks, if I've counted correctly, nine languages, studied art history, Egyptology and law, fell in love with Samarkand because of a poem, visited it and raved about it: as beautiful as in a fairy tale, the Orient that we know from *A Thousand and One Nights*—but without the hunger.

Daube[273] said he was a reactionary to the core, and it seemed to me that he was playing with it; but he doesn't provoke. He argued against the admission of women into the Oxford Debating Society but for the abolition of Paragraph 175[274] which says nothing about his own inclinations: he is an *homme de la femme*. We argued, of course. Whenever people get onto the subject of equality, I hit the warpath. I only need to hear the words 'the dignity of women' ... this way of putting women on a pedestal is just a subtler way to devalue them and brush them aside. But whatever: he is refined. He

---

273 David Daube (1909–99): dean of the Law Faculty at Oxford and pre-eminent scholar of ancient law.

274 Paragraph 175 of the German Penal Code criminalized homosexual acts among men (1871–1994).

knows the strangest poems by forgotten poets. He tells fairy tales like Scheherazade. I was enchanted, and I wrote down the fairy tale of the Persian architect, who grew wings for the sake of the love of his life. The kiss that was so passionate that it left a burn mark . . .

[. . .]

Last night I stayed overnight with Jon. On the way to see him, my heart was pounding in my throat, as if everyone was watching where I was going. We embraced, lay exhausted, embraced again, slept entwined, and when I half awoke, his strong hand lay in my lap. Still half-asleep, he pulled the cover more tightly over me. Towards the morning I heard the shift buses passing by. Jon brought me breakfast in bed. I said to him, happy and with a terrible sense of betrayal: 'Good morning, dear husband.' I shouldn't do it, I shouldn't do it, but why, for God's sake, is it so delightful?

Hoy., 4.10.

Yesterday I wrote to Annemarie Auer and suddenly noticed how affectionate I feel towards her and how much I care about her affection. It was a real 'woman's letter': I think I'm starting to become a woman after all, with all sorts of strange women's worries.

[. . .]

Waiting for Turba, the head of the youth commission at the Politburo, and Nahke from the *Forum*. Terribly nervous: the telegram just said 'urgent matter'. What could it be? Collaboration on something, a new task—in any case, something that will successfully stop me from finally, finally concentrating on my book.

At lunchtime, a Party visit from the Pumpe. In the evening, readers' forum in the secondary school. It's about my article in the *Lausitzer Rundschau*. The chief architect of Hoy is furious with me. They are even trying to get the Academy of Architecture to come tonight. It'll be good for my book.

Moscow, 8.10.63

In Moscow since last night. Difficult to grasp after two and a half hours' flying time with two hours' time difference—and Daniel had definitely not even arrived in Rheinsberg by the time I arrived at the airport, among forests, dark blue evening sky, lights, a confusion of languages, the IL18 plane very white against the sky and forest.

On Sunday I broke down in tears in front of Jon and told him I was afraid, that I wanted to call it off and say I was sick, and would be too, from fear—a terrible fuss. He gave me good advice for my flight and stay, taught me a few words: thanks, please, an ice cream—and *morozhenoye*[275] tastes wonderful in a country where cream still flows. I've forgotten all my school Russian, but I'm sure I'll soon pick it up again here.

Daniel brought me to the airport on Monday in Berlin, and I was as excited as a country bumpkin boarding a train for the first time. I can laugh about it now and I'm already looking forward to the return flight (because I'll be homebound and I'm already homesick), but at the time, I felt more like crying. My passport, passport control, the flight booklet, the transit room—all new experiences and a great adventure [. . .]. But Christa Wolf is a good travelling companion: friendly and relaxed and experienced and much more adult than me.

In the aeroplane, my curiosity was stronger than my fear of flying; I only knew it from films: no smoking, putting on seatbelts, the droning noise, the drive to the runway, the flickering grey circle of the propellers. Anxiety at take-off, ringing in my ears, slight nausea, but all that is pardonable. We were sitting in the first row and all we could see were the wings and blue sky the whole time, and a few clouds lit up red by the sun. Just once, after we'd already passed Vitebsk, we got a glimpse of brownish countryside when the plane tilted, a meander in the river, a patch of forest. I made a note:

---

275 'Ice cream' in Russian.

6,000 m altitude, 650 km/h, outside temperature −28 °. Sometimes, when the plane climbed or fell, it felt like sitting in a monstrous lift [. . .].

A German embassy car drove us into Moscow. A friend of Christa, the secretary of the union, welcomed us and had dinner with us—Russian titbits: partridge, salads, a carafe of vodka, lots of ice cream. The Hotel Kievskaya (at Kiev railway station) is pretty primitive by our standards, the *dushevaya* or shower is in the basement, the lady's room dire—and so on, but it doesn't matter, the people are nice.

At night on Lenin Hills, on the bridge over the Moskva, row upon row of lights on the opposite shore, the river dark; when we turned around, we could see the brightly lit Lomonosov University. You can go everywhere by taxi—they are ridiculously cheap. The people are very simply dressed—rustic, I even dare say; no comparison to the fashionable crowds in Berlin.

Now and then, you see young people with modern haircuts, tight trousers; I haven't spotted a girl in trousers yet. [. . .] From the ceiling in the hotel foyer hang fabulous crystal chandeliers, and some metro stations look like Greek temples.

This morning at the embassy we were given our schedule and our 100 roubles. That's a lot of money considering the prices in kopecks on the menus. [. . .] Our Prussian punctuality is funny; here's there's a lot of time and casualness, we first have to get used to the Moscow pace. At the union and in editorial offices, work begins at around 11 o'clock, and not even that is certain. The Union is housed in a beautiful building, a former Russian palace, one-floor high, with driveways and white columns and semicircular outbuildings—it's the home of the Rostovs described in Tolstoy. In the club there is a charming dining room, a little staircase carved out of wood and galleries and lodges and lathed wooden columns, and it all looks like a backdrop to the fairy tale of *The Beautiful Vassilisa*.

The most astonishing thing about Moscow is that it's Russian in a way that fits exactly to the impression from films and books. On Wenceslas Square in Prague, I never had the feeling of being abroad and foreign like I do here. A stunning sight: Red Square, the Kremlin walls [. . .], endless hills of towers and onion domes, and all this, Byzantium and old Russia, all so fine and incredibly distant, far away in the past like a fairy tale. A city of contrasts: wooden houses with porches, high-rise buildings, wide-span bridges, shabby little shops, broad boulevards and bumpy, adventurous winding lanes, and all this close together, no transition, strange and attractive. And then the aristocratic palaces, low, painted yellow or pink and with rows of white columns, and you wouldn't be surprised to meet Anna Karenina at the wrought-iron gate.

[. . .]

Moscow, 10.10.

I've already shopped on my own in the GUM,[276] with 'это и это'[277] and it was quite funny. GUM is a monstrosity with a great deal of marble, staircases and galleries and mirrors on the ceiling ('only foreigners and provincials shop there,' says our guardian angel St.) I've got to cart home souvenirs—babushkas and dolls and the like, and a bottle of brandy for Jon. If you hear what people earn (a skilled worker up to 120 roubles), prices suddenly don't seem that low. But I still have no feeling for the money because, in spite of myself, I keep thinking kopecks and pfennigs are worth the same.

Moscow, 10 in the evening

Just come back, a bit tipsy, from our hotel restaurant. I just wanted to have a coffee, but you don't get five minutes to yourself here. The people at my table, correspondents from Murmansk and the

---

276 GUM: a Russian department-store chain dating back to 1893 with a large branch on Red Square.

277 'That and that' in Russian: she was pointing at different things.

Caucasus, began to chat with me straight away: a bit of German, a bit of Russian, and we communicated brilliantly with scraps of words and gestures. They are called Sasha and Aljoscha, and we said *nasdorovye*[278] quite often, then of course I had to drink vodka with them (at every meal, there's a decanter of vodka on the table), and we were in a very good mood. The stiff, reserved attitude of our country, where everyone wants to sit alone at their own table, doesn't exist here. The people all around us were high-spirited (this is a kind of transit hotel for people from Belorussia, from the Don and the Dnieper), and they danced the *Topoк* in a circle to modern dance music, and hooked arms, stomping and clapping and laughing like in films. Maybe it's very good to stay in this hotel where we are the only foreigners. You meet the most interesting types—many farmers, the men in fur hats, the women in big head-scarves. We are slightly despised by the waitresses because we eat so little. Monstrous quantities are eaten and drunk here. [. . .]

Alyosha and Sasha know most of the writers in the GDR. People read even on the stairs of the metro. The taxi driver reads while he's waiting for customers. In front of shops there are prams (the children are wrapped as if it's deep winter)—among the pillows lies a book.

Last night we saw a shopping queue on Gorki Street—we expected a sensation; people were queuing for books in front of a book stall set up in the street. The theatres are sold out.

Moscow, 11.10.

At night, Sasha called my room to let me know that he 'love me' and Christa and I laughed until we had cheered up again [. . .]. And then at night, in the dark, in a strange city—you tell others things that you would not tell them during the day, and Christa is the kind of person you can tell everything, and you know it's safe with her. She teases me, but in a very friendly way: I'm schizophrenic and a

278 'Cheers!' in Russian.

terrible person in general. I think we get along well now (according to my childish categories she's one of the 'good people') and I like her very much.

Next door someone sings arias from *Rigoletto* until late at night—and he starts again early in the morning. Here in general, everyone moves about very freely, loudly and happily, the radio is always blaring, and we've got used to it now.

The day before yesterday, we met Yuri Moskolenko, a cameraman at Mosfilm. He dragged us through Moscow by taxi that night [...] and he was irrepressibly proud of his city. Again and again, he asked: '*Kharasho*?' And we answered again and again with conviction: '*Ochin kharasho*.'[279] So the communication worked brilliantly. He said he was glad that Stalin had been interred in the Kremlin wall; but Khrushchev, he said, would end up in the mausoleum. Yuri immediately attracted our attention because of his thick grey hair, and we exchanged our knowing opinions about him; his face is still youthful, a Stefan Hermlin type. Afterwards, we heard that his hair had turned grey when he was being held in prison by the Nazis and going to be shot as a spy.

[...]

Went to the Molodaja publishing house today, which is publishing *Arriving*. The galley proofs are already done. The translator is a nervous young man with a sympathetic clown's face. [...] I invited him too—and, of course, my guardian angel Stedshensky. Tomorrow there will be a huge banquet, because I received my fee cash in hand at the publishing house; I didn't know what to do with it all. I'm going to bring it to the bank tomorrow: the trip to Samarkand is fixed.

Moscow, 12.10.

Our money has been paid: 850 roubles. That's quite a lot of money, I think. I have kept back 50 roubles for wining and dining.

---

279 'Good?'—'Very good!' in Russian.

Now I'm sitting alone in Restaurant Dnepr [. . .]; I can't write up in the room anyway, it's freezing cold. The Moscow winter is making its presence felt after a radiant autumn, of which we caught a few sunny days—and the hotel doesn't have central heating although it's already dropped below zero at night. And there's only cold water. We're freezing, I've caught a cold. This is clearly a *gostinitsa*[280] for toughened Don Cossacks.

Last night Sasha called again: 'I to love . . . '. He wanted to go for a walk, but I had already undressed for bed. He'd learnt a sentence by heart: 'Sleep well, dear Brigitta.' [. . .]

This morning we were at the German Embassy, but the conversation—in a much too official setting—did not quite get off the ground; it was all diplomatic restraint. These formal conversations just aren't productive, and the private meetings are far more interesting. We then visited a bookstore where many GDR books are sold. Even at this early hour for Moscow—eleven o'clock—the buyers were already crowding around our stand. The books are two-thirds cheaper than back home.

Then: the Moscow traffic. It's simply incredible. I have never seen so many cars in my life (at least every second one is a taxi). The traffic rules are hard to work out, there aren't any crossroads and no one seems to stick to the speed limit (60 km). Side by side in six or eight lanes, the cars whiz by in dense lines, taking crazy corners and using adventurous driving techniques; in fact it's a miracle that there aren't cars rammed into each other every 100 metres.

I've nearly been run over by these mad drivers at least three times, and on the first few days, the streets were a shock. But a mysterious higher power stops the cars at the last second, all brake-slamming and gear-crunching, and you can probably throw all these Volgas on the scrap heap after a year. This careless attitude is everywhere; even new houses look shabby, and there are only small sums available for building care and maintenance.

---

280 'Hotel' in Russian.

Yesterday morning we drove through the new Cheryomushki district, which was a real disappointment to me. After reading our architecture magazines, a brilliant image had evolved in my mind. Of course, plenty is being built, and quickly (in the centre there are constant diversions due to the many building sites) but it looks sloppy—much gloomier than Hoyerswerda. Even the brand-new shops look old-fashioned; the facades of the houses are much more monotone than ours, and most things are painted a dirty green, along with the light brown of the bricks cladding the buildings. At first we thought the buildings were made of brick, but it's all panelling, and the ugly additional cladding is necessary because the plaster can't withstand the heavy frosts. The paint on the window frames has already flaked off, and the impression of sadness is heightened by the fact that there are no curtains in the windows like back home; you only see the grey and white net curtains everywhere covering the lower half of the window.

The market building is interesting, its dome covered with a kind of steel mesh. Here the kolkhoz farmers sell their vegetables, fruits and meat. There's no price control, and the farmers' prices are higher than those in the city. The modern market has the character of an Oriental bazaar, despite the red scales and tiled stalls. Enterprising Armenians come here by plane, sell grapes and 'kuma' (hazelnut-shaped fruits with pulp as sweet as candy floss) and do their utmost to cheat, while they make beautiful eyes at women. We bought pomegranates from a Georgian with a pitch-black moustache, big red fruits that only resembled pomegranates on the outside and were filled with a red berry that looks like our blackcurrants.

[...] There's no more spitting on the street; buckets are put out for rubbish on every corner—extremely bizarre-looking containers in the shape of vases and amphoras, mostly silvery bronze and unspeakably kitschy.

Kitsch is a real plague—but, of course, there have been more pressing problems over the years than striving for civilized

European taste. The Stalin era adds to the mix, and some houses resemble pure butter-icing cakes. Of course, in some places this pageantry constitutes a style with a certain atmosphere, and then it's downright adorable. We were in a bar that simply glittered with gold and bronze and crystal, and at the windows, which were illuminated in pink and light green, there were lace curtains like in old films. But it was cosy [. . .]: a ballroom in which Vronsky might have danced with Anna.

The metro stations are subterranean marble palaces, with heavy chandeliers, reliefs and historical paintings, and I'm never sure whether to laugh or be touched, and in any case, you understand the Muscovites' pride—if you don't judge everything by standards back home—and that's the dumbest thing you can do in a foreign country. The escalators in the metro shocked me; I couldn't be persuaded to use them a second time. Infinitely long, steep descending shafts. [. . .] I found it nightmarish, but everyone else thought it was funny, and Muscovites even read on them while they glide up or down.

I've just been interrupted; everyone is always talking to you here. This time it was someone dying of curiosity because I'm always writing—and the second person, incidentally, who thought that my handwriting was Arabic. True, it's hardly decipherable as Latin, and there was a lingering suspicion as to whether I was really German. 'All Germans are blond,' one of them told me, who thought I was Georgian. [. . .] I'm recalling more and more Russian phrases and words, [. . .] and I convey the rest with facial expressions and gestures. I'm starting to gain a little confidence now, feel more secure and can give all the information they want: how old, where from, whether married, how many children, which profession, how long in Moscow—and that Moscow is *ochin kharasho*. [. . .]

Moscow, 13.10.

Georgi, the beautiful Georgian, black and slim, has won my heart. He's from Tbilisi and works as an engineer at an institute of electrical engineering. He's one of the few elegant men I've seen, with skin-tight trousers, a casual sweater, and a nylon jacket, which he got from an Italian in exchange for a gold watch. [. . .] He speaks as much German as I speak Russian, and yet knows Heine off by heart ('I don't know what it means'), knows a few words of English, and over an hour we held a lesson of sorts, making astonishing progress, in which we described and repeated all the objects to be found in the restaurant in both languages until the words sank in.

[. . .] When he said I was twenty years old, I first thought it was just one of those oriental compliments, but then it occurred to me that Christa said how women age prematurely here. It's also striking how few attractive or pretty women there are, by our definition (in comparison, we're both almost beauties.) Then, as we walked through the streets, I noticed the marks of fatigue on many faces, a weariness that veils people's features. Life is much more difficult here than back home: still a housing shortage (even people like St. lived with the whole family in one room for years), a lack of industrial goods and all sorts of comforts and amenities; the shops are so overcrowded in the evenings when people come home from work that the stores in Hoy seem empty in comparison. There are still too many economic difficulties, and this year the harvest has been bad, and the Soviet Union had to buy thousands of tons of wheat from America. [. . .]

In Cheryomushki, right next to the new houses, I saw dilapidated huts such as the most imaginative draughtsman couldn't have dreamt up: gloomy cottages, just heaps of wooden planks, patched up everywhere and slanting, with tiny, dirty windows—images like the slums of big American cities. Christa says the cottages in most of the villages are no better than these miserable sties, and when you see this, you understand the admirable achievement a new district represents. In circumstances like these, aestheticism is an unaffordable luxury.

The Lomonosov University is oppressively magnificent. But the new Pioneer Palace is beautiful, functional, completely modern with huge glass frontage, sweeping staircases, tastefully painted walls and a tropical hall with a pond and climbing plants under domed skylights. There are hundreds of rooms for all kinds of social circles [. . .], a ballroom, two theatres with state-of-the-art technical equipment, an astronaut room with a pressure chamber [. . .]. When the building (which is actually a cleverly linked chain of houses) was put up, there was a huge discussion about formalism, which it took Khrushchev to stop. I have not seen a better, brighter place in any Western architectural magazine—and it offers space for 7,000 children [. . .].

Last night, all our friends were here [. . .]. A lavish spread with caviar and chicken and sturgeon on a skewer and salads and—and . . . well, a Russian meal. And a lot of vodka, goes without saying. [. . .]

At around 9 o'clock I had to go to my room because I had registered a call to Rheinsberg (my plane doesn't leave until tomorrow evening). Kostya came after me. He told me when we were alone that he had been sentenced to death under Stalin, then pardoned to a sentence of 25 years. He served five years in a gulag, where so many of the best writers were killed—and the nervous disease that makes his hands shake, or sometimes even his whole face, is due to this. I remember with horror the moment when he said he had very little time [. . .].

Moscow, 14.10.

I'm sitting in the restaurant and having palpitations: later I'm meeting the beautiful Giorgi again. That evening when the others had left our room (we drank another bottle of cognac together), I bumped into G. in the corridor; he had been patrolling up and down the whole time.

We then sat for another hour in the 'lounge,'—actually just a spacious niche in the corridor, with a small table and two leather armchairs.

Last night we went out for dinner together: caviar and chocolate and a lot of five-star brandy. I had bought a German–Russian dictionary, and we went on expeditions into foreign languages. [. . .] The man is a volcano [. . .]. Hard to resist those eyes and long, black fluttering eyelashes [. . .].

At night, we went for a walk in the area around Kiev station. On this occasion I made some other discoveries: G. only speaks broken Russian; the Georgians despise the Russians; not all 'Soviet people' are perfect socialists by any means [. . .].

Tonight I fly back to Berlin, and—a miracle: I'm already homesick for Moscow, and it is difficult for me to leave this city.

Hoyerswerda, 16.10.

True: homesick for Moscow, and longing a little for the handsome Giorgi.

The last afternoon we spent together: 'You must laugh,' he said, 'you are so beautiful when you laugh,' and I laughed, and there were always reasons to do so—the grotesque misunderstandings, the weird twists in conversation (once, when I wanted to order a mocha, I asked for a 'muscular coffee'), and Giorgi kissed the two small moles over my right breast and said, 'my beautiful spots,' because we could not agree on the translation of 'beauty spots'. [. . .] Christa, half-amused and half-worried, warned me to behave, but I was determined to anyway, despite stammered words in musical Georgian, [. . .] despite a bended knee and moving descriptions of having to endure sleepless nights [. . .]. And despite his flowery art of seduction: only three know about it—Giorgi, Brigitta and God. But maybe God has something against it? No, no, he's a young god, he looks away and smiles.

Hoyerswerda, 17.10.

Yes, God looks away, and Giorgi is far away, and three days' romance and passion. Of course I resisted. Always the same. Boring. And yet I can't stand prudish women.

Christa stayed for two more days. I hugged her, unexpectedly even for me, as we said goodbye. I think I've grown fond of her. [...]

Another afternoon with Kostja. A splendid collection of letters and pictures of great men—Pasternak, Mayakovsky and Lilya Brik, Ehrenburg. [...] I suddenly realized who Pasternak was when I saw his photos. It was like a blow to the heart, the face of an Indian, the most beautiful and defiant face I have ever seen. I would have loved him, from the first moment.

Kostya showed me a book of P.'s Shakespeare translations, which P. had sent K. in Vorkuta with a dedication for which anyone else would have been forced into exile: ' . . . with a hot kiss and heartfelt hug . . . ' and: 'Kostya, they can say whatever they want— I know you're a fine man.' I've already mentioned that Stalin had a weakness for P. and felt a kind of mystical connection to him. There's a strange story (it is shortened, the letter still exists): when Stalin's wife died, it was officially called suicide. Muscovites swear he killed her—the Writers' Union wrote a letter of condolence and 30 writers signed it. P. refused, writing a letter to Stalin himself: 'Yesterday (the date of Stalin's wife's death) I thought of you for the first time as an artist . . . I was there and saw everything.'

I met many people who had been in prison for ten years or more during the Stalin era. Kostya told horror stories about Vorkuta. The Georgians still love Stalin. I didn't believe it and asked

Giorgi. He said, 'Stalin is a Georgian.' We even agreed that Stalin was a criminal, that he decimated the cream of the Russian intelligentsia—and Giorgi finished the conversation, very proudly, with: 'But he is Georgian.'

The farewell to Moscow: it was raining, it was cold, it was dark, but the walls of the houses were decorated with small lights.

A young employee from the embassy picked me up and Giorgi was fuming with envy.

So the itinerary for my big trip has been extended: Tbilisi. For God's sake, a whole city full of such insane specimens of men . . . He walked me to the car, and we hugged and kissed each other on both cheeks, Russian style (and the young discreet diplomat did not hear what we were whispering). Radiant Moscow was left behind, and then came the huge airport and all the formalities were concluded in five minutes. Back home in Schönefeld, they took half an hour, with sharp questions and the penetrating gaze of men wearing uniform caps.

So I boarded the plane alone, as confident and calm as a globetrotter, and next to me sat a trader in female slaves from Beirut, incredibly fat and clever, who supplied me with Lucky Strikes and sympathized because I didn't like the take-off. Afterwards I got so used to my adventure that I even slept for a while and dreamt all sorts of pleasant things about Giorgi. Daniel picked me up in Schönefeld, and the amazing experiences made for a report as long as the drive home. Daniel was amused by my handsome Georgian but demanded with gentle vindictiveness that I tell Jon about him. [. . .]

Hoy., 18.10.

Hoy has claimed me back, hair and hide. To say nothing of the mountains of letters, an invitation to the Academy of Arts; [. . .] readings—well, and so on.

[...]

On Tuesday, just when I wanted to go over to Jon's [...], a car stopped at the door and Prof. Henselmann took me in his arms [...]. We drank a coffee at my place and chatted, and H. seemed cheerful and confident as he was showing me the material from the 7th plenary session of the German Academy of Architecture: in it he is criticized with a sharpness that far exceeds anything that has ever happened to writers when exposed. It gets close to denouncing H. as an enemy of the state, who knowingly sabotages our development in the building industry.

Of course, his comment on the 'dictatorship of the untalented' has created a lot of enemies (including that building gangster Paulick, who ruined the main road). But H. can't fool me any more; I saw, too, how pitiably his hands were trembling.

Before we went over to Glück auf, he kissed me, and all at once, I felt that any moment his professed paternal feelings would be swept aside. The man is a lover right down to his fingertips—and love, I think, is something all-encompassing in his life, as with most artists, enveloping women and flowers, work and art alike, that eroticism and sensual pleasure that colours every gesture, every thought, every action of certain types of artist like us. 'You are flesh of my flesh,' said H., and perhaps I love him for this siblinghood, his vanity and self-love, and his play-acting in which I rediscover myself. That's why H. considers *Brothers and Sisters* to be one of the best books in Germany—we're on the same wavelength. [...]

Over in Glück auf, we ordered wine and then bubbly, and then wine and bubbly again and we had a big feast; a companion joined us, the driver, a graduate engineer; H. was a firework display, becoming more and more exuberant, and in the end, my head was spinning too although I'm pretty resilient (in Kiyevskaya I drank the Georgians under the table). Sometime in the evening H. invited Elisabeth, whom I had long recognized by her voice, to our table. She can bellow fantastically. We have often heard her cursing at night, her husky metallic voice penetrates metre-thick concrete walls.

She is a very small, skinny person with a big, restless face, unsteady eyes, twitching features. [. . .] We suspect that she has suffered a terrible shock, psychologically and mentally, and that seems to be confirmed. She has no inhibitions, and when she drinks (and she drinks every day) she becomes dreadful. I have never heard more obscene things from a woman's mouth.

But H., in his drunken mood, invited her over and she came and her hackles rose immediately. She even talked the eloquent H. into a corner [. . .]. But H. did not let himself be intimidated; he can also be incredibly vulgar, albeit in a charming way, and likes to play up his working-class background. In the end, he managed to make Elisabeth shed a few tears, and that was when I lost professional interest in this peculiar case, and saw his intellectual addiction to analysing fellow humans as an insult to the girl and felt only pity for her. I said, 'Would you like to pay me a visit tomorrow?' She looked at me suspiciously, then said yes. (The next day, of course, I was a little afraid.)

[. . .]

Hoy., 20.10.

Finally alone with Jon, I was unable to make love with him, despite passionate desire. Moscow was still too close [. . .].

I stayed with Jon overnight, startling myself out of a deep sleep a few times, where I dreamt about a high-speed drive alongside towering walls, out of a Moorish waiting room, and from the walls all around, eyes looked back at me with long, black, trembling eyelashes.

The next evening, Elisabeth came in a pretty blouse, all demure. At the door she took off her shoes. She brought two packets of Karo with her, because she had heard me complaining the night before that there were no more of my favourite cigarettes. She was quite starchy when she came into my room and saw my piles of books. 'Can you live here?' She has a room in a high-rise, but it isn't furnished because she drinks away all her money. Maybe a lot of people just need someone to listen to them. Sometimes I think I'm a very nice person ('not conceited at all,' says E.), because so many people tell me their most intimate stories. [. . .] Elisabeth [. . .] tells stories very vividly, visually—and she didn't use any obscene expressions the whole evening—in her raspy voice, which doesn't go with her slim body at all [. . .].

She grew up in poverty, one of six siblings.

Her father lost a leg in the war. For a while she had to share her bed with a mysterious uncle [. . .]. But despite all the poverty and restrictions, it must have been a loving family—that's what her siblings' funny, tender nicknames revealed. She also worked in the forestry, and she talked enthusiastically about planting trees, and so precisely that you could learn how to do it by listening. But she was too weak for to work. As a seventeen-year-old, she had a nervous breakdown [. . .], she sat around at home for two years in the corner and cried all the time. She never got over the shock. Then she started at the factory; those were the bleak beginnings, when they lived in barracks, and that's where she learnt to drink. Her whole family went over to the West. She's very lonely. When she comes home from work, she goes to the pub and gets plastered. From what I hear, she doesn't let men get close to her. She's also very honest and has a strong moral code. [. . .]

We talked until about midnight. Then Jon came, and Elisabeth immediately changed; [. . .] she said a few things that embarrassed Jon and me. When we said our goodbyes, she said very happily, 'At last, an evening when I'm not going home tipsy.' I gave her my books, and when I saw her standing at the door, so small, with her very plain, twitchy face, I asked her to come back again soon.

Another piece of news that may soon have serious consequences: Turba was waiting for me at the airport to ask if I would
like to work in the Politburo's Youth Commission.[281] I agreed.
Meanwhile, I have learnt of the bitter resistance (in the Politburo)
to the youth communiqué.[282] Turba had spoken to Ulbricht, who
said I had too much to do here. But the work interests me; there
are stories to be unearthed.

[...]

Evening

Went to vote at noon, a very simple affair. And all that preparatory
work!

[...]

Hoy., 28.10.

Call from Turba: invitation to the first meeting of the Youth
Commission and to the Central Committee meeting, at which I am
supposed to give a speech. I tried to refuse, but T. persisted. On
Sunday I chatted with four FDJ secretaries who told me some interesting stories. Now I've scribbled away at the speech for two days
but feel that it's pointless in the end. Heads will roll again. I still

---

281 In the reform phase at that time, Ulbricht sought to modernize the system through
targeted systemic reforms. In youth policy, there were internal disputes with Erich
Honecker, particularly concerning the work, the structure and scope of the FDJ.
Ulbricht suggested creating a youth commission at the Politburo, where certain issues
could be dealt with across departments, and resolutions prepared and controlled for
the Central Committee. Therefore, the commission should not only consist of representatives of the Central Committee departments and the state apparatus, but also
involve active artists. In 1963, Kurt Turba and his deputy Heinz Nahke, gave the student
magazine *Forum* a new profile, based on the awareness of problems and shared responsibility of readers. It was an enormous success, and Ulbricht appointed him as a director
of the new youth commission at the beginning of July 1963. He was immediately asked
to draft the 'youth communiqué', on the basis of which youth work should be changed.

282 The youth communiqué, which was published in the *ND* on 21 September 1963,
went far beyond issues concerning young people in the GDR—it spoke of fundamental
questions of the intellectual climate.

think back with a kind of hatred to the forum where none of the officials shook hands with us, and where I had to listen to so many nasty insinuations and accusations.

On Friday, first session of the new executive committee of the Writers' Union. The whole thing was a bad joke. Lewin rattled off his report, then there was supposed to be a discussion, but no one spoke. We have nothing to say to one another. And for what? The secretaries do the thinking for us. Afterwards I spoke to Prof. Koch. After he told me too that our people are not ready for certain books from the Soviet Union, I gave up, but not without expressing my astonishment at how 99.5% of this immature population voted for their socialist government.

In the morning, a nice conversation with Lewerenz. He's a smart young man, and I feel like going back to Neues Leben because of him. Topic: the generation problem that doesn't officially exist.

Berlin, 30.10

4th plenary session of the Central Committee. Norden is talking just now, a keynote speech. Yesterday, our first Youth Commission meeting. 17 members. Turba looked terribly exhausted. He was completely done in afterwards.

Hoyerswerda, 4.11.

Discussions for three days with two young architects, a Greek and a German, who are conducting detailed sociological investigations in our city. They are actually working in opposition to their superiors. They've compiled a questionnaire and distributed it in schools—a kind of opinion poll that won't meet with approval at the Academy of Architecture.

Yesterday, they were very depressed when the first sheets came back; most people had filled them out wrongly or didn't respond with the exact figures required for the evaluation. Sure, the questionnaire has its issues—but at least it's a first brave attempt. They hope that the results get published, and it certainly won't be down to chief editor Flirl (another awkward young man I met here in Hoy when he met us before going to the *Forum*). It's terrible to see how many detours we're taking, how much strength is untapped, how mistakes fossilize into dogma.

The blueprints are unimaginative, sometimes just unreal. On paper it looks good if there are three stadiums planned for the city, but we don't have the materials in reality. We talked about what a socialist city should look like, the extent to which socialist life is dependent on spaces where people meet. [. . .] The Greek [. . .] speaks excellent German and has a very sharp mind [. . .]. He's also spent some time in Paris. How come people are marked so unmistakably when they've spent time in big foreign cities? I thought 'Paris' the moment he entered my room and made some remarks about my pictures and Chagall.

So, the questions: Division into housing estates—how big should these estates be? Do they need a club, a centre (actually a precursor of the city centre)? Are spaces for the residential communities enough? How do people look for contact with others? Do they look for it at all? [. . .] What should the centre look in order to provide a neutral space to meet? [. . .]

Plans for dormitory towns with centres just for social life. How far do green spaces replace individual gardens? I'm making very haphazard notes: I'll examine them more closely to have solid material for my book.

I have a thousand other questions: How does the mentality of a population affect the development of socialist life? Are we even looking for social interaction? And what does it mean: living standards? Why does a person change, and how do they change? On a number of levels, all this concurs with the problems we face in the Youth Commission! Our first session was short. Everyone talked about their ideas. A one-way process, without any real information or assessment of the situation—Horst Schumann. Turba had expected this and told me beforehand that I should give Sch. some real counter-arguments. Turba has bitter experiences; there is enough resistance to the youth communiqué, also in the Politburo. He told me how difficult it was for Ulbricht to assert his ideas—if it'd been possible, people say he, U., would have been excluded from the Party.

Hoy., 10.11.

Nahke was here, telling scandalous stories about universities and companies. He's terribly nervous. Some idiot might have denounced us for our conversation. Sometimes we're overwhelmed by so much inadequacy, but we won't give up, especially not now. 'Because we have it bad, we support it,' says the headline of a review in *Die Welt*.[283] A campaign is being waged based on the youth communiqué—I can't hear that word any more. The surest way to strangle good deeds.

Heard today—unofficially—that I didn't win the Blechen Prize, for which I was nominated, because of my criticism of the socialist residential town. I also know that they hate me and would 'shoot me down' if I weren't protected. Now even I'm saying 'them'—and feel it too. What, no Kafkaesque world here any more?

Hoy., 12.11.

Terrible headaches again crippling me for days. Yesterday we broke open the rococo chest, where my diaries and a bundle of love letters were lying. I'd lost the key. Afterwards I read and read, and the past and the present merged into one. I lost all sense of time.

283 A broadsheet German daily which was bought by the West German journalist and publisher Axel Springer in 1953. In the late 1960s, Springer was attacked by the German student movement for the political opinions through the tabloid *Bild* and the other Springer media, and became a target of protest marches and direct actions.

Hamburger, the chief architect, visited me. He was lovely, ready to talk and help me with my book, nobler in spirit than these officials, who hate me. H. is a tired, old man [...]. He says he imagined he would build a beautiful city and later, when he was old, pay the occasional visit from Dresden, walk down the streets of his town and drink coffee.

The funds for the central buildings have been rigorously cut. While talking to him, I re-drafted my book (and how many times will I do that?): Franziska is not a heroine like in *Battle on the Way*; she comes, full of brilliant plans, to a city that demands nothing except sober calculations, and quick, cheap construction. No space for personal ambition—an anonymous person in a collective and her heroism consists in saving three inches worth of building materials to make the corridor wall after much fiddling with the plans. Sometimes I have fantasies about a book like Goncharov's *A Common Story*. In the end, where are the passionate dreams of youth? You don't turn the world upside down. And, a terrible thought: Where's flaming love? Smothered in a conventional marriage, in the common bathroom, in washing clothes, watching television and 'what shall we eat tomorrow?'

[...] Berlin, an evening with Henselmann. He'd invited his entire working group, gifted young people, who have been sent to project planning offices where the work gives them no satisfaction. H.'s fault? He gave them the dream of great architecture—and they get to draw doors. [...] Henselmann's enthusiastic lectures on the friendship between architects and writers ... [...] Insight hasn't distanced us, that's a big thing. I also love what people call his errors or weaknesses.

Saturday with Jon in Glück auf. We sat with Elisabeth, who was quite drunk, but nice to me and pitiable despite everything [...]. Later he brought her home because she was being insulted by drunks [...]. A young locksmith kept me company until J. returned. They kept bringing schnapps to our table [...]. At first

I was offended, but then the waitress and the locksmith said: 'It's fine, accept it. You're so well-known here—people like you because you stood up for them.' Another moment that made me love my profession above all else.

[...]

Hoy., 23.11.

Today I started my 'Franziska' book.

Hoy., 27.11.

Threw away the first two pages and started over and over again. The style I have in mind—the way Zola writes—is something I can't do: it's probably down to the material.

[...] Lack of interest in fellow human beings. The first days in a miserable mood, so the usual. [...]

Threw away a pile of old photos and love letters—as if you could burn the past. In comparison to the past, I'm almost a paragon of virtue now.

Hoy., 28.11.

Drank out of anger yesterday, too many phone calls, too many visitors. Two journalists from the West German magazine *Revue* had announced a visit at lunchtime: they came only in the afternoon. [...] They were researching Christmas preparations in the GDR, they interrogated and photographed me, two very passable young boys that let you imagine the coexistence of the two Germanys. A GDR journalist was also present whose function was not quite clear [...]. After the moody Christmas shots, I finally managed to walk over to Jon's with my present, but he was very upset because he'd had to wait so long. It was already evening. He had imagined so many beautiful things for his birthday, and then we sat around, utterly miserable ... In the evening I had a date with the journalists again, because I thought J. was on night shift, but he had just cancelled the night shift—in short, everything went wrong, as usually happens with planned parties. [...] In the end, we went to my place, [...] and the journalists came over with a bottle of whisky. We chatted and at least agreed on jazz and architecture. One of them seemed to be a decent person, the other one was too clever for me. He railed against Marlene Dietrich for her 'leftist tours' back in the day, and I don't think he even understands why we were outraged. Anti-fascist work seems to be a kind of betrayal of the Fatherland to him. For a few minutes, the tone of our conversation was sharp. I didn't like his expressions either (we have distanced ourselves from each other in language), words that are no longer used here. He has no associations with the word 'gassing'.[284]

A topic that never fails to amaze: rent prices. The reporter pays 520 DM for a four-room flat.

[...]

Hoy., 29.11.

A young French writer visited (not yet professional; he's an employee at a textile factory), a member of the French Communist Party, and his supervisor, a clever young Bulgarian, who is studying at our film school. He's written a script that nobody will film here:

---

284 In the original here, it says: 'von "jemanden verladen", was aus dem Rotwelsch kommt, bis zur Scheußlichkeiten wie "bis zur Vergasung". Er hat keine Assoziation bei diesem Wort "Vergasung".' Presumably, the phrase *jemanden verladen* ('to dupe someone', but without the pronoun 'someone', meaning 'to load' as in cargo) had Nazi associations possibly connected to the 'loading' of people onto trains like cargo to take them to concentration camps. The phrase *bis zur Vergasung* (literally, 'until gassed') became widespread in connection with poison-gas missions in the First World War; however, in the consciousness of many people it is related to the mass extermination of the Jews with gas under National Socialism. The use of the phrase is therefore considered inhuman today (source: https://goo.gl/NyoZ9L; last accessed on 2 July 2018).

very lyrical, full of visions and symbolism. Not to my taste either;
I like films with strong stories.

In the evening we met again [. . .]. A pleasant evening. Politics
at the dinner table, as usual. Although I claimed not to understand
a word of French, I got an ear for the language so quickly (my Latin
helped me) that I was sometimes able to follow without translation.
In the end, Pavlov told horror stories from Bulgaria, stories of trans-
migrating souls and experiences in a mental institution where he
once filmed, and I was afraid to be so alone in the flat. [. . .]

Two letters from the Soviet Union: a fiery love letter from Giorgi,
who says that without me he is 'always in a bad mood' [. . .].

A letter from Kostja with sarcastic remarks about his colleagues
and especially about the stupidity of other Rilke translators [. . .].

Kennedy has been murdered.

Hoy., 12.12.

All the time I've been working on my story. Sometimes I write
quickly and suspiciously easily; now it's getting tedious. Thirteen
pages. The other day, Caspar was here, like a spring breeze as usual
(even after a bottle of vodka). He thought Daniel's manuscripts
were excellent, mine exciting. Well, he's curious, and that's something. Yesterday the first crisis: I found the story irrelevant, all love
stories, not just socialist ones.

In the meantime, separated from Jon for three days. My fault,
as usual; he never quarrels. He had given my slippers to a girl who
was at his place with her boyfriend. My beloved red slippers . . . I
realized too late it was a declaration of love to me: he had lent them
to her out of gratitude because she loved my *Brothers and Sisters*
and spoke so sweetly of me. I hurled the slippers away from me in
rage. I went crazy ('looking daggers,' Jon said) and ran away. For
three days I almost died of heartbreak, couldn't eat, and when we
saw each other again, I wept for an hour. [. . .]

Hoy., 22.12.

Three days in Halle for the Union meeting, came back with the flu. Yesterday up again. [...] lecture by Koch, a brilliant analysis of Strittmatter's *Bienkopp*. We listened in raptures for three or four hours. Presentation by Sindermann—demagogic nonsense when it came to 'high politics'; smart and lively when reporting on his district.

In the evening, authors' reading [...]. Industrial literature with accidents, just heard 'catalyst' the whole time. Much of the time together with Lewin; always with the oldies in the evening. I felt like I was with a bunch of mummies (Gotsche, Wangenheim, Tschesno-Hell), they start every second sentence with: 'In the Weimar Republic, we ... ', 'When we had our toy soldiers ... ' Consternation at the poems of the young. As so often, I liked Kurt Stern best: he's wise, restrained and gracious.

[...]

Hoy., 30.12.

[...]

Christmas at home was beautiful, incredibly noisy and there was uproarious silliness as usual. [...]

Pa played a snowman this year for a change because he couldn't find his Santa Claus outfit; he came in with a laundry basket full of presents. During the four days there was only one quiet afternoon when the whole family sat together around the table. Uli was quite the doctor, the only calm, quiet person among us [...]. For the first time we didn't miss Lutz; we're all angry with him for writing such ugly things about *Brothers and Sisters* and everyone in the family felt insulted [...].